CHRISTIAN MINISTERIAL PRIESTHOOD

A SEARCH FOR ITS BEGINNINGS IN THE PRIMARY DOCUMENTS OF THE APOSTOLIC FATHERS

CHRISTIAN MINISTERIAL PRIESTHOOD

A SEARCH FOR ITS BEGINNINGS IN THE PRIMARY DOCUMENTS OF THE APOSTOLIC FATHERS

RAY ROBERT NOLL

CATHOLIC SCHOLARS PRESS

SAN FRANCISCO • LONDON

ii

Library of Congress Cataloging-in-Publication Data

Noll, Ray Robert, 1934-
    Christian ministerial priesthood : a search for its beginnings in the primary
documents of the Apostolic Fathers / Ray Robert Noll.
      p. cm.
    Includes bibliographical references and index
    1. Pastoral theology--History of doctrines--Early church, ca. 30-400. I. Title.
BR195.P36N65 1993
262'.1'09015--dc20
                                              93-6444
                                                 CIP

I wish to rededicate this research to my father, who died in 1974,
and to my mother, who lives with us in California,
and to dedicate this new publication to my wife, Jean,
and to our children:
Jerry, Veronica and Christopher.

TABLE OF CONTENTS

FOREWORD

Dr. Noll's book: *Christian Ministerial Priesthood: A Search for Its Beginnings in the Primary Documents of the Apostolic Fathers,* is a valuable contribution to the current historical reevaluation of the development of priesthood within the Christian community. In both recent and not too recent times, a number of generalized statements have been made by Church leadership, both theological and ecclesiastical, which have attributed positions on priesthood to Clement of Rome, Ignatius of Antioch, Polycarp, Barnabas, Hermas, and the author(s) of the Didache. Such statements have, at times, drawn from these apostolic writers conclusions which neither the texts nor the contexts allow. Such statements were and are still made, however, to maintain theological positions of a "dogmatic" or a presupposed nature. One found such statements rather widespread in various manuals of theology, but one continues even today to find such interpretations in other ecclesiastical writings, even those which come from very high positions of Church leadership. The best of contemporary scholarship, however, finds many of these kinds of statements and positions totally unacceptable, and their continued appearance is an embarrassment to Catholic teaching. Dr. Noll's study, though first published in a modest form in 1970, remains of great assistance to writers of this present decade, since Noll has already indicated and documented several positions on these apostolic writings which do not render a faithful reading of the key Christian authors of this important second century. The newly-written opening chapters by Dr. Noll help one move from his earlier presentation of the Apostolic Fathers to the scholarly insights on these same chapters which writers of the present decade have developed.

The Apostolic Fathers, writing in the late first and early second centuries, speak of various forms and names of ministry, which do not

x

correspond with any exactitude to the "bishop, ... priest," and "deacon" of theTridentine-to-post-Vatican-II Church. What came to be seen as "standard" for an understanding of bishop, priest and deacon during the last five hundred years is seen to be, in the light of history, but one of the ways in which ministry in the Catholic Christian community has been formed and developed. Although a rethinking of ministerial priesthood has been and remains a sensitive issue in the Roman Catholic Communion, nonetheless, the Catholic Church today, at all its levels, must face the historical data on priestly ministry in its fullness and correctness and be willing to make all necessary theological adaptations.

Kenan B. Osborne, O.F.M.
Franciscan School of Theology
Berkeley, California

Given the growing shortage of priests in the Catholic church in this country as elsewhere, the discussion about the nature and origin of the ministerial priesthood is going to become more important as the years go by. Anything that can throw light on this question is going to be very welcome as a resource for the intelligent discussion of this issue.

Dr. Ray Noll's book can very well be such a resource. Its focus on the Apostolic Fathers and the very early years of the development of priesthood is an area that will be crucial in the discussion and about which we have not a great deal published in English. His work is careful and scholarly. It should be a very valuable and timely contribution to this important discussion.

William V. Dych, S.J.
Fordham University
New York

PREFACE

My interest in the historical evolution of ministerial priesthood began back in 1967 at the World Council of Churches' Graduate School of Ecumenical Studies in Bossey, Switzerland. Visiting professor Yves Congar, O.P., speaking to the 80 participants that year from more than a dozen countries and 24 different Christian communions, noted that after more than 30 years in ecumenical work, he was convinced that **the major ecumenical problem** centered on Christian ministry. He maintained that the difficulties surrounding ministry and priesthood were the key ones that would have to be solved if the ecumenical movement was ever to make any genuine progress in the future. During the course of the discussion, addressing himself to the Roman Catholics present, he remarked how little had been done by Catholic scholars of our day on the historico-theological foundations of priesthood. This, he urged, was a crucial question and one genuinely worthy of all the painstaking study it demanded. At that discussion, I decided to do my doctoral work on some aspect of the origins of ministerial priesthood.

In autumn of that year, while doing a semester at the University of Tübingen, I enrolled in a seminar conducted by Hans Küng entitled "Die Wandlung des Priesterbildes." I chose to do my seminar paper on a search for Christian priesthood in the Apostolic Fathers, the first group of authentic Christian writings after the New Testament. It was fascinating to read these ancient documents comparatively in the Greek with German and English translations at hand. Although I did not find any leader of a Christian community called a priest (*hiereus*), I did find here and there a mention of the Jewish priesthood and also on occasion some use of sacral-cultic language touching on Christian worship. Later Professor Küng in a conversation pointed out that there was still a great deal to be done on the relationship between the sacral-cultic language and the various forms of ministry in the Apostolic Fathers, and suggested that it would make a good subject for a dissertation.

The following spring, when I was back in Amsterdam preparing for the licentiate exam in theology, Professor Pieter Smulders, S.J., introduced me to the work of Abbé Jean Colson on ministry and priesthood in the Apostolic Fathers. He had reviewed Colson's *Ministre de Jésus Christ ou le sacerdoce de l'Évangile* (Paris, 1966) for the Dutch theological review *Bijdragen* (28/2, 1967, p. 217), and felt that Colson had not completely succeeded in answering with respect to the Apostolic Fathers the central question at issue, namely "how the Old Testament and pagan nomenclature for the priestly class found its way into the Church, and along with it the sacral-cultic conception of priesthood and of Christianity." When I mentioned that I was thinking of taking this issue as a dissertation topic, he immediately volunteered to help me as much as possible. Later that year, I prepared a licentiate paper on the ministry and sacral-cultic terminology in *1 Clement* (here included after several re-writings as Chapter III) and the project was under way.

That same year Professor Smulders introduced me to an extraordinary patristic scholar and respected colleague, Professor André Benoît, Director of the Institut patristique at the University of Strasbourg. Professor Benoît, also a personal friend of Père Yves Congar and an ecumenist in his own right, was especially interested in second-century ministerial issues and agreed to take me on as a doctoral candidate. Two and a half years later, after research sessions in Strasbourg, at the Maison Études in Paris and at the library of the Catholic Theological Institute (KTHA) in Amsterdam, I defended my doctoral thesis "Recherches sur les origines du sacerdoce ministériel chez les pères apostoliques" at the University of Strasbourg before a jury made up of Professors Benoît, Prigent, Trocmé and invited guest Pieter Smulders, S.J., from Amsterdam. After slightly more than three hours, the jury ruled that the thesis had been defended "avec distinction" albeit with a slight American accent. Thereafter, according to the custom in the French university system, 25 copies of the thesis were distributed to the French library system to be recorded and catalogued. Officially, however, this research basically written in English with occasional quotes in French and German (à la mode alsacienne, if you will) has never been published in an English-speaking country.

Recently Dr. Robert West, editor-in-chief of the newly established

Catholic Scholars Press, San Francisco, saw this doctoral work and invited me to update it with a new bibliography and newly written chapters that would both discuss the multiple issues involved in the beginnings of Christian priesthood and assess the impact of the scholarly research of the past 20 years on my original work in the Apostolic Fathers, and then publish it as the first volume of the new Catholic Scholars Press. I am indeed grateful for this opportunity.

Acknowledgments

With this publication I want to thank again my original mentors in this project, namely Professors André Benoît of the University of Strasbourg and Pieter Smulders, S.J., of the Catholic Theological Institute, Amsterdam. My grateful appreciation goes to Dr. Robert West and his colleagues at Catholic Scholars Press, San Francisco, for this publishing opportunity, especially to Diane Spencer Hume who scanned the text and formatted the book. I wish to extend particular thanks to Dean Stanley Nel and Associate Dean Gerardo Marín of the USF College of Arts and Sciences for their encouragement and student help support, to my chairman, Fr. Dan Kendall, S.J., of the USF Department of Theology and Religious Studies for his support on many levels for this project, and to my student assistant, Bhagman Singh, who prepared the bibliography and arranged much of the scanned text. A most sincere thanks also to Kenan B. Osborne, O.F.M., William V. Dych, S.J., and my USF colleagues John H. Elliott and Hamilton Hess for reviewing sections of the text and making constructive suggestions. Finally, I would like to thank the research staffs of the USF Gleeson Library, of the GTU Flora Lamson Hewlett Library in Berkeley and Professor Stan Nelson and the research assistants at the Golden Gate Baptist Theological Seminary Library in Mill Valley (CA) for their personal kindness and assistance.

CHAPTER I

CHRISTIAN MINISTERIAL PRIESTHOOD
AND THE APOSTOLIC FATHERS

OUTLINE

A. Basic Issue: The Sacred and the Profane
B. The Era of Sacralization
C. The Apostolic Fathers
D. Methodology

A. THE SACRED AND THE PROFANE

The rise of ministerial priesthood within Christianity belongs to a broader and more fundamental issue that has been with us from the dawn of civilization – the problem of the sacred and the profane. The existence of a sacerdotal group, be it of an ancient pagan culture, or of the Levitical family of Israel, or that which grew up within Christianity, represents an answer that has already been given to the problem of the sacred and the profane. That answer (and it is perhaps the only common denominator among the various forms of priesthood) is that there are certain persons, places and things which are or ought to be set apart from ordinary life for the primary reason that they possess in themselves or have been endowed with a certain sacredness. In turn, either expressed or implied is the understanding that those persons, places or things which do not possess this sacredness belong to the domain of the profane.

The priestly tradition in ancient Israel, for example, bears eloquent testimony to the answer to the issue of the sacred and the profane in Israel. The cult, the instruments of cult, as well as those who performed it were set apart as sacred, and laws of ritual purity were prescribed for all those who in any way participated in the official worship. Ultimately the Temple priesthood took control of most of Israel's worship life, and with that came the continually recurring tendency on the part of the priestly authorities throughout Israel's history to formalize and ritualize not only the official cultic worship but every aspect of religious life. It was against this tendency and the abuses associated with it that the prophets spoke out loudly and clearly. Haranguing against religious formalism and denouncing mightily those who fostered it, they called the people back to a worship of the Lord that proceeded from the heart and was first and foremost spiritual.

It is in this context and within this prophetic tradition that we find Jesus of Nazareth and his message, for as Père Congar has pointed out:

> Jesus has taken up and accomplished the program of the prophets. ...
> The prophets never ceased to criticize the formalism of the cult, never ceased to say that the true cult was that of the heart, that the true sacrifice is the offering of one's life in loving obedience to God;... Moreover they announced the end of the separation, indeed the distinction between the sacred and the profane. It is the life of a person as it unfolds itself in the world that is the material of his cult.
> Jesus completes this step. He surmounts, one must even say he abolishes the ancient frontier between the sacred and the profane. There is but one sacred reality, His body, at the same time temple, sacrifice and priest. For the Christian, all is sacred except that which he profanes by sin, but this sacred is not so by way of being set apart.[1]

The late Anglican Bishop John A. T. Robinson at the 9th Downside Symposium on "The Christian Priesthood" echoed similar sentiments:

> The crucial thing that Christianity did was to end the distinction on which late Judaism rested between the holy and the common. This end was symbolized by the rending of the Temple veil from top to bottom at Jesus' death (*Mark* 15:38). Henceforth nothing could be common or unclean (*Acts* 10:14-15) — or therefore unpriestly. Christianity celebrated as one of its distinctive marks the *koinonia hagion* — the making holy of the common and the communialization of the holy. And with the communalization of the holy went the communalization of the priesthood. For this was its sphere of operation. There is

for the New Testament no longer any separated space or holy time, no sacred realm or hieratic caste, no particular order of ministry that is priestly - for the whole is.[2]

And yet the truth of the matter is that relatively early in the history of the Church a development took place which produced a separate, sacred group, as well as a sacral-cultic interpretation of Christianity, thereby effectively re-introducing the Levitical answer to the problem of the sacred and the profane. As one Catholic theologian from Strasbourg put it:

It is undeniable that the Christian tradition little by little "recouped" the sacerdotal connotations that the first centuries had set aside. Moreover the ministers of the Church began to conceive their task as a mediatory and sacrificial action; they returned progressively to the levitical idea of the priest, functionary of the sacred. The Christian "priests" were becoming the ones in charge of the local sanctuaries, men "separated", members of a clergy, invested with particular powers over sacred things.[3]

B. THE ERA OF SACRALIZATION

The period during which this sacralization of the Christian ministry took place can be fairly well established. We know that nowhere in the New Testament is the Christian minister considered to be a priest (*hiereús*). Nor is the minister in the Christian community associated with a sacral terminology such as *hieráteuma, hierateía, hierôsúnê* (terms that designate "priesthood") or *hierateúein* (meaning either "to be a priest, to function as a priest" or "to offer the sacrifices").[4] The first step in this development, the one that occupies us here, appears to have been the emergence of a single bishop (*monepískopos*) at various places in the Mediterranean world supplanting the earlier charismatic and then committee forms of church order along with a parallel development of sacral-cultic language and attitudes whereby the people gradually begin to see their *monepískopos*, their primary liturgical officer, as a "high priest" (*archiereús*) representing Jesus Christ, the High Priest. The second step of this development, namely the emergence of the presbyter-priest is described by Dom Gregory Dix in his classic essay on "The Ministry in the Early Church:"

We begin to meet the 'parish priest" - the presbyter who teaches and ministers the sacraments to a detached congregation only occasionally visited by its bishop, though the latter still nominally remains its 'high-priest' as in pre-Nicene times. The old episcopal title of 'priest' begins to be used of individual presbyters early in the second half of the fourth century - at first with qualifications - *sacerdos secundi ordinis, hiereús* (not *archiereús*) to avoid infringing the bishop's prerogative as '*high*-priest,' the sense of which was still strong. But by the end of the century it is used of presbyters without hesitation.[5]

Thus roughly between the completion of the New Testament corpus and the year 400 C.E. a development takes place in the early Church which makes a high-priest first of the local bishop and then later a priest of each individual in his college of advisors, the presbyters.

What we must say, unhesitatingly and unambiguously, is that our 'priestly' phraseology, though very old, is still not primitive. It has undergone a development; it has a history. The history, especially, is of the utmost importance for our present situation and some of our present difficulties.[6]

Precisely then the problem is this:

How did the Old Testament and pagan nomenclature for the priestly class find its way into the Church, and along with it the sacral-cultic conception of priesthood and of Christianity.[7]

Probably the most effective way to trace out this sacralization process would be to study all the Christian documents of that three hundred year period that in any way employ priestly terminology. That would make an ideal project for an ecumenical team of patristic scholars, although it would no doubt take years to cover all the material thoroughly. There is, however, an ancient Chinese proverb which says that "a long journey begins with the first step." And a first step, it seems to me, would be the first collection of authentic Christian documents after the New Testament corpus, namely those writings that have come to be called *the Apostolic Fathers*.

C. THE APOSTOLIC FATHERS

This corpus of authentic Christian documents dating roughly from the latter part of the first century down to about the middle of the second century, is a relatively small collection compared to the New Testament corpus before it and the massive literature of the Great Church that follows it. In many ways the literature of the Apostolic Fathers compared to the other Christian literature of the Early Church is like the narrowest part of an hourglass.

Generally considered by patristic scholars as the primary documents of the Apostolic Fathers, i.e. the most substantial ones historically and theologically, are: *I Clement*, the *Letters of Ignatius*, the *Letter of Polycarp*, the *Shepherd of Hermas*, the *Epistle of Barnabas* (or *Pseudo-Barnabas*, as it is sometimes called) and the *Didache* (or *The Teaching of the Twelve Apostles*). Also included in some collections of the Apostolic Fathers are a number of less important documents from roughly that same period, namely an anonymous homily called *II Clement*, the *Martyrdom of Polycarp*, a collection of fragments both from *Papias* and from *Quadratus* and the *Letter to Diognetus* (which is sometimes listed with the works of the Apologists).[8] These latter documents, while not unimportant in the collection of the Apostolic Fathers, do not deal in any direct way with material relevant to our search. Consequently, on the advice of my mentors in this study, I have confined my investigation to the first-mentioned primary documents of the Apostolic Fathers.

D. METHODOLOGY

The methodology I have employed here is to treat each document (or collection thereof in the case of Ignatius) according to a two-step pattern. First, an attempt has been made to situate the document(s) in its historico-theological context. In general this has called for a discussion of origin, dating, authorship, literary genre(s), basic contents and kind of Christianity represented — a discussion sometimes longer, sometimes shorter depending upon the particular problems posed in each case. Secondly, within the specific historico-theological context of each document, I have tried to analyze what is said about Christian ministry and what is said in sacral-cultic language that might tell us something about the beginnings of Christian priesthood.

An exception to this methodology is the chapter on the *Didache* (the last one in this study). Its historico-theological context has so eluded scholars ever since its discovery by Bryennios in 1873 that even today we can not even point to a few of the major critical problems upon which there is a genuine consensus of scholars. Thus I have (1) discussed the *Didache* in general, i.e. its discovery, form, style, content, (2) analyzed its ministerial structures and sacral-cultic language, and (3) merely presented the major unsolved problems of higher criticism and indicated the direction of my own thinking on these problems after having read much of the research. Unfortunately the dating and origin of the *Didache* (or the various parts thereof) even after more than a hundred years of research still remain an open question.

NOTES

1   Y. Congar, O.P. "Le sacerdoce du Nouveau Testament," in *Vatican II - Les Prêtres (Unam Sanctam, 68)*. Paris: Éditions du Cerf; 1968: pp. 252-253.

2   J.A.T. Robinson."Christianity's 'No' to Priesthood." *The Christian Priesthood* (9th Downside Symposium, edited by Nicholas Lash and Joseph Rhymer). London: Darton, Longman & Todd; 1970: p. 13.

3   C. Wackenheim. "Le fondement théologique du sacerdoce ministériel." *Mémorial du Cinquantenaire, 1919-1969: Faculté de Théologie Catholique*, Palais Universitaire, Strasbourg; 1969: p. 422.

4   Cf. P. Fransen. "Priestertum" in *Handbuch für Theol. Grundbegriffe*, p. 340; J. Schmid. "Priester" in *LThK*, pp.743-744; J. Colson. *Les fonctions ecclésiales aux deux premiers siècles*, Paris, 1956, p. 165; the only example that might be considered as an exception is found in Romans 15:16 where St. Paul calls himself *"leitourgón Christoû Iêsou"* ... *"hierourgoûnta tó euaggélion toû theoû."* On this passage *The Jerome Biblical Commentary*, "Romans", Jos. A. Fitzmyer, S.J. (Englewood Cliffs, N.J., 1968) states:*"To be a minister of Christ Jesus to the Gentiles:* Paul describes his role in liturgical language, using not *diakonos* ("servant," as in 2 Cor 3:6; Eph 3:7; Col 1:23), nor *oikonomos* ("steward," as in 1 Cor 4:1), but *leitourgos* (cultic minister). In his mission to the Gentiles he sees himself as a priest functioning in God's sanctuary. For if all Christian life is to be regarded as worship paid to God (Rom 13:1ff.), the spreading of Christ's gospel is easily compared to the role of sacred minister in that cult. Paul insinuates that the preaching of the word of God is a liturgical act in itself. If Clement of Rome (*Ad Cor.* 8:1) could look on the OT prophets as the cultic ministers of God's grace, then this applies even more to the "apostles and prophets" of the NT (Eph 2:20; 3:5). Cf. Rom. 11:13; 2 Cor 3:3; Phil 2:17. *the offering of the Gentiles:* Obj. genitive; it is the evangelized Gentiles who are consecrated and offered to God as an acceptable sacrifice. Since the end of all sacrifice was to bring about in some way the return of sinful man to God, Paul looks upon his work among the Gentiles as a form of sacrifice, for their conversion has achieved that very purpose. The Apostle offers to God not slaughtered animals, but repentant man. He thus achieves in reality what was symbolized in the sacrifice - the return of men to God."

5   Dom G. Dix. "The Ministry in the Early Church - A.D. 90-410". *The Apostolic Ministry*. Dir. of. K. E. Kirk. London: Hodder & Stoughton; 1946: pp. 281-282. He also notes that the term *sacerdos secundi ordinis* was "used first in the West by Optatus, *Adv. Donat.* (A.D. 369). *Hiereus* is found on the gravestones of presbyters in Asia Minor c. A.D. 360. It is to be noted that this attaching of the eucharistic 'priesthood' to one order destroyed the old relation of the celebrant to the congregation. The bishop was the 'high-priest' in the midst of the whole 'priestly' people of God, not by way of distinction from the presbyters. The 'presbyter-priest,' who fulfilled the bishop's '*high*-priestly' liturgy by celebrating, really set up a false distinction between himself and the people by taking the lower title of 'priest' instead of 'high-priest'."(p. 282, note 1)

6   J.-P. Audet. *Structures of Christian Priesthood*. London: Sheed & Ward; 1967: p. 127.

[7] P. Smulders, reviewing J. Colson's *Ministre de Jésus-Christ ou le sacerdoce de l'Évangile* in *Bijdragen*, deel 28, aflevering 2; 1967: p. 217.

[8] Ref. K. Bihlmeyer. *Die Apostolischen Väter*. Tübingen: J.C.B. Mohr (Paul Siebeck); 1956: pp. vii-ix; R. M. Grant. *The Apostolic Fathers: An Introduction.*, New York: Thomas Nelson & Sons; 1964: pp. 1-12 *passim*.

Chapter II

A Survey of Recent Literature

Outline

A. *Clement's Letter to the Corinthians (1 Clement)*
B. *Ignatius'* and *Polycarp's Letters*
C. The *Epistle of Barnabas*
D. The *Shepherd of Hermas*
E. The *Didache*
F. Christian Priesthood and the History of Ministry

Since the six chapters which follow are presented here as they were first written and defended some years ago, I would like to devote this chapter to a survey of the considerable research that has been done in the Apostolic Fathers over the past several decades, with an eye toward discussions of language or structures that could have facilitated the rise of Christian priesthood. I will add to this a brief survey of the burgeoning literature on Christian priesthood and the history of ministry that has been published since Vatican II.

A. Studies in *1 Clement*

Since 1970 major works on *1 Clement* have been published by Barbara Ellen Bowe, Gerbert Brunner, Harold B. Bumpus, Edmund W. Fisher, John Fuellenbach and James J. Jeffers.[1] Also during this period more than a score of research articles either on a particular dimension of *1 Clement* or on ministerial structures or sacral-cultic language in *1 Clement* have appeared.[2]

Among the major works, particularly impressive is John Fuellenbach's 533-page dissertation written under Johannes Quasten in 1977 at The

Catholic University of America and published in 1980 as *Ecclesiastical Office and the Primacy of Rome: An Evaluation of Recent Theological Discussion of First Clement.* He not only summarizes all of the recent studies of *1 Clement* on the issues of dating, author, occasion, purpose, structure, literary form, sources and background (mostly German texts), but also analyzes the recent work on church structure in *1 Clement* by 16 major Protestant scholars (all writing in German) and about 20 Catholic scholars (more than half in German). His 113 pages of meticulous notes and 18-page bibliography make it a very valuable, indeed an encyclopedic instrument.

Although Fuellenbach's primary interest is to compare the best recent Protestant and Catholic scholarship on the issue of Roman primacy and church office in Clement, he can hardly avoid the issue of priesthood. In his "Critical Evaluation and Conclusion," Fuellenbach notes that most scholars today agree that Clement makes only an analogous connection in 40-41 between the orderliness of religious practice in Israel under the Levitical cult and the orderliness that should exist in Christian religious practice at Corinth. This is also my position here in Chapter 3. He writes that

> No one who studies *1 Clement* can overlook the reference made to the Old Testament cult. Most scholars are convinced that this reference does not mean that Clement is transferring the Old Testament cult into the New Testament. One can only speak in an analogous way of a transfer from one testament to the other.[3]

Fuellenbach points out that there has been a noticeable change over the years on the part of Catholic scholars as to whether *1 Clement* contains any claim for a Roman primacy. What he sees as new to the Catholic understanding is the number of scholars who argue that the Roman Church in the time of *1 Clement* was ruled by a college of presbyter-bishops and that this seems to have become a common opinion in contrast to the views offered by older scholars.[4] Thus, according to Fuellenbach,

> The certainty with which earlier times had judged and seen a primacy claim in *1 Clement* is gone. What is surprising is the ease with which the traditional arguments of outstanding patrologists are put aside and positions taken which Protestant authors have held since Harnack. On the whole, it seems safe to say that the question of a primacy claim in *1 Clement* is no longer raised.[5]

In attempting to summarize the host of opinions with regard to the permanency and exclusiveness of Clement's office theory, he notes that

> For most of the Protestant authors the arguments are based on 'foreign elements', i.e., on the world order idea or on Old Testament cult and Judiastic ideas of ordination and succession...In both cases, the claim to permanency and exclusiveness cannot be substantiated from the original kerygma and, consequently, cannot be regarded as legitimate...
>
> The majority of Catholic authors (and Anglican as well) regard the episcopal model which appears in the office theory of *1 Clement* as a more refined stage than that disclosed in the New Testament, as apostolic in the sense that the permanency and exclusiveness of this model rest on a decision made in apostolic times as part of the event of revelation. ...
>
> A change can be observed in the sense that a growing number of Catholic authors challenge the exclusiveness of the episcopal model by regarding the other models of the New Testament as being as valid dogmatically as the episcopal one.[6]

Barbara Ellen Bowe in her *Church In Crisis: Ecclesiology and Paranesis in Clement of Rome* sees a real danger in studying *1 Clement* of missing the main purpose of the letter and focusing on the issue of some deposed presbyters. She states that

> *stásis* [discord] and the restoration of communal harmony, not the maintenance of ecclesiastical office, is the primary concern of *1 Clement*. The letter states this clearly in 63.2 where it defines itself as an "entreaty for peace and concord."[7]

Her positions on Clement's chapters 40 and 41 concur with mine here in Chapter 3. She states that

> Clement begins his discussion in chapter 40 by referring to the analogy with the appointed order of services in the Old Testament. Ideas of order, appointment and rank figure prominently. However Clement offers here not a paradigm but an *analogy*. An exact correspondence, on the basis of this text, between the High Priest, Priests, Levites, and Jesus as High Priest, presbyter/bishops, deacons is unwarranted.[8]

And she adds that

> The function of the analogy, however, is to demonstrate not so
> much a priestly hierarchy to be replicated in the Christian
> offices (Clement no where does this), but to illustrate the
> value of an ordered system and the necessity of faithfulness to
> "what God has appointed."[9]

While I agree that, given Clement's manner of expression, it is not
possible to establish from these paragraphs any clear data with respect to a
Christian priesthood, we do appear to disagree on the overall tenor of
Chapter 44. I say 'appear to' because like her I do not believe that the
Corinthian office bearers are seen primarily as cultic officials, but rather as
those involved in a much broader ministry. Nor would I disagree with her
(and Lightfoot) that the *prosphérein tà dôra* are not limited exclusively to
the Eucharistic gifts of bread and wine, but I would say, in disagreement
with her, that Clement's use in 44 of *prosphérein* and four times of
leitourgía for the work of the office holders, both terms of which are also
used by Clement elsewhere within this letter to describe aspects of the
Levitical cult, show that *1 Clement* is beginning to suggest a subtle transfer
of priesthood **terminology** to the broader work of the Christian overseers.
This reveals, I believe, what Jean Colson has called a certain *mentalité
lévitique*[10], granted that it may be driven by a desire for order, peace,
concord and perhaps fear of gnostics and other internal troublemakers, but
in any case a mentality that would not be disappointed to see the Christian
ministry "develop in the direction of a spiritualized version of the Levitical
order."[11] If Clement had spoken somewhere in his letter of the 'priestly
community' of the faithful as in *1 Peter*, or, if in the three instances where
he speaks of Jesus Christ as High Priest, he would have mentioned 'according
to the order of Melchisedek' that occurs so often in *Hebrews*, I would think
differently.[12] Though I agree with virtually every aspect of Bowe's analysis,
I would add that with all the sacral-cultic language that is used in the letter,
even though there is clearly no transfer of the reality of priesthood from Old
to New Testament to be found, there is a justaposition of priesthood
language and an occasional use of terms that in Greek at this time meant
cultic when used of the Levitical order and generally not cultic or at most
only analogously cultic when speaking about the Christian officers. My
contention is that a kindly and admiring attitude toward the orderliness of

the Levitical priesthood already in *1 Clement*, with Clement speaking for the Church at Rome, would speak volumes in terms of possible solutions for permanency of a Christianity at once buffetted by persecution from without and division from within.

Christology and soteriology in *1 Clement* are the themes of two dissertations written respectively by Harold B. Bumpus, an American who completed his work at Tübingen, on *The Christological Awareness of Clement of Rome and Its Sources*, and Edmund W. Fisher, who wrote his dissertation, *Soteriology in First Clement*, under Hans Dieter Betz at the Claremont Graduate School (CA). Bumpus' two-part text first analyzes the Christological titles in *1 Clement* and then in part two discusses the function of Christ in Clement's understanding of salvation history. He sees Clement's Christology as emerging from

> a Jewish-Christian school of theology (also seen in the Shepherd of Hermas and the Didache) that was soon to perish, precisely because its categories of thought were mostly limited to a Jewish cultural milieu not especially congenial to the Greek majority in the new church and because it lacked in its tradition adequate prototypes for a fruitful development of Christological awareness, at least as a tool for greater insight for the Hellenistic world in which it was to grow and expand its missionary activities.[13]

Thus in focussing primarily on the sources of Clement's Christological categories and finding them to resonate most with those found in Jewish intertestamental literature,[14] Bumpus touches only very indirectly on our problematic.

Edmund Fisher, in concentrating on *Soteriology in First Clement* does mention the term *archiereús* (High Priest) as applied to Christ both in *1 Clement* and in *Hebrews*, but does not discuss this in relation to ministry or ministerial structures. He simply states, in agreement with Lightfoot, that

> Chapter thirty-six of *1 Clement* echoes both the ideas and the language of the *Epistle to the Hebrews*. The theme of Christ as the High Priest who makes offering for sin found chiefly in Hebrews chapters eight through ten is the central theological theme of the *Epistle to the Hebrews*. The term *archiereús* occurs in Hebrews 2:12, 3:1, 4:14, 15, 5:1, 5, 10, 6:20, 7:26, 27, 28, 8:1, 3, 9:7, 11, 25 10:11 and 13:11. In addition to the

present passages, *I Clement* uses the term in 40:5, 41:2, 61:3 and 64. Since the term is widely used for Christ by early Christian writers of all schools its occurrence without further support would not establish a connection between the two documents.[15]

Gerbert Brunner in his masterful work, *Die theologische Mitte des Ersten Klemensbriefs,* has concluded that chapter 44, describing the struggle *epi toû onómatos tês episkopês,* is the heart of the letter,[16] and that its literary genre is precisely that, viz. just a letter, albeit an impressive and lengthy one, to a partner church carrying no special authority or juridical clout,[17] certainly not reflecting or claiming any sort of Roman primacy.[18] But, says Brunner, the particular historical situation in Corinth was new and demanding — never before had *presbyter-episkopoi* of a church been displaced — and the way it would be solved would clearly have an impact on the whole Church and could become a paradigm case for the future.[19] According to Brunner, Clement, who reports the tradition that the Apostles did appoint overseers and deacons for some of the churches (ch. 42), and in chapter 43 adds a parallel story of the choice of Aaron's tribe when there was quarreling over which tribe God would choose for His priesthood and ministry *(eis tò hierateúein kaì leitourgeîn autô),* goes on in chapter 44 to interpret this tradition of 'appointing' as rather an apostolically given **'order'** of office. It appears to Brunner that Clement, realizing his theory goes beyond the tradition received, appends to his account that the Apostles "afterwards added the *epinomè* (Lake: "codicil"[20]; Lightfoot: "continuance"[21]; Kraft: "stipulation"[22]) that if they should fall asleep, other approved men should succeed to their ministry *(leitourgían)*." Thus, according to Brunner, Clement after reinterpreting the apostolic tradition of 'appointing' bishops and deacons into an apostolic 'order' of office, argues that to displace someone from that order who has served humbly, peacefully and modestly would be a serious sin.[23]

The question, of course, is: What right did Clement have to reinterpret the apostolic tradition in this way? Brunner would say that by this time (he holds for a 96 C.E. dating) the churches were growing, having authority problems as we have seen in Corinth and gradually becoming a Mediterranean world church. With this it was apparently becoming clear, at least as viewed from Rome, that the Christian churches of the Mediterranean needed more than the simple, *familial* structures of the past, that the Church needed to become a recognized, structured, authoritative corporate body in order to survive.[24] In Brunner's words:

Das Christentum musste eine rechtliche verfasste Körperschaft werden, wenn es nicht zerfallen wollte.[25]...
Kirche als organizierte Struktur mit institutionalizierter Autorität hat sich als Grundthematik gezeigt: Die institutionelle Sicherung der Autorität als solcher ist die theologische Mitte des Briefes.[26]

In short, he sees the bold statement of *1 Clement* 44 as a first-century preamble *(Praeambulum)* to the Apostolic Constitutions and apostolic church orders of future generations.[27] Fuellenbach, who authored the survey mentioned earlier, says in his analysis of Brunner's work that

> it might be said that, according to Brunner, *1 Clement* marks the "institutionalization of authority and structure in the Church" caused by the necessity of the historical situation. With this view, Brunner affirms the evaluation and findings of most of the Protestant scholars investigated in this [Fuellenbach's] study. The only difference between them (and it is an important one) exists in the fact that Brunner does not judge this new stage of development as a falsification or something that should be regarded as a regrettable incident, or, at least, something that led to a deprivation of the Christian faith.[28]

A final major work on *1 Clement* is that by James S. Jeffers on *Social Foundations of Early Christianity at Rome: The Congregations Behind 1 Clement and the Shepherd of Hermas*, his doctoral thesis from UC-Irvine in 1988, which he then reworked and published with Fortress Press in 1991 as *Conflict At Rome: Social Order and Hierarchy in Early Christianity*. Jeffers does with *1 Clement* and the *Shepherd of Hermas* the kind of sociological and cultural exegesis that John Elliott[29] and Bruce Malina[30] have done for New Testament studies. He states in his introduction that he will present evidence from documents, inscriptions and archaeological remains to show that Roman Christianity's unique course resulted in part from the rising authority of Christians who were enamored with the ideology of the Roman ruling classes.[31] According to Jeffers, *1 Clement* is especially imbued with the ideal of the 'father of the family.'

> Clement appears to have combined New Testament principles with the Roman upper-class ideal of the *paterfamilias* who

exerts ultimate power and authority over his household. Such a model lends itself to the main point of Clement's letter, that order and harmony must reign in the community if dire consequences are to be avoided.[32]

Jeffers maintains that the way *1 Clement* embraces this Roman ideology suggests that the letter represents not even a majority of Christians at Rome but rather the beliefs of a small group of relatively wealthy free citizens and slaves of the aristocracy who could overlook past persecutions and the non-acceptance of Christianity by the Roman elite because they believed that the government was basically benevolent.[33] He notes that

> As well-treated slaves of the aristocracy, they understood and appreciated the Roman *patria potestas* ideology of the family. They saw the father in their families as the *paterfamilias* from whom all other family members were to learn their duties. Clement treated his congregation as a single household based on this model: church leaders like the *paterfamilias*, deserved unquestioning honor and obedience, and the followers must know and remain in their proper places in the hierarchy.[34]

The closest Jeffers comes to discussing our question of the rise of Christian priesthood, however, is when he is comparing the different approaches of *I Clement* and the *Shepherd of Hermas* to authority and office in the church:

> Both affirm the need for leaders within the group, but Clement equates leaders with officeholders and sees them as an elite within the congregation. These leaders have specific responsibilities that they alone can fulfill. Although all members have their places of ministry, Clement's use of the Levite analogy shows that the officers in this group are responsible for the leadership and *sacerdotal* [my emphasis] aspects of ministry, unlike the typical sect.[35]

Dating of *1 Clement*

One of the few points of massive consensus among Christian scholars has been the 95-96 C.E. dating of *1 Clement*. The great patristic luminaries of the later 1800's, Lightfoot in England and Harnack in Germany, arrived independently at this dating for numerous good reasons. Probably about 95% of scholars from their day to our own have shared that opinion,[36] including myself when I wrote Chapter 3 that follows here.

I find it necessary, therefore, to draw attention to the fact that in recent years a growing number of scholarly voices are beginning to question this 95-96 C.E. dating in favor of a more probable 69-70 dating. Highly questioned today is the only piece of internal evidence (i.e. in 1.1: "Owing to the sudden and repeated misfortunes and calamities *[symphoràs kaì periptóseis]* which have befallen us...") which clearly convinced Lightfoot and Harnack that the letter appeared after a Roman persecution of Christians under Domitian. Although to date there does not appear to be any consensus among scholars that would overpower the opinions of Lightfoot, Harnack and many others, the movement is significant and the issue is being discussed in patristic circles. Should a consensus develop for an earlier dating, then it would certainly have a profound impact on all the analyses of *1 Clement* by Protestant and Catholic scholars down through the years, including my third chapter here (although, I believe my conclusions would still remain valid). And it would surely have an significant impact on the history of ministry and priesthood.

The issue as described by Thomas J. Herron in his 1989 *Studia Patristica* article begins in 1913 with George Edmundson's Bampton Lectures at Oxford which took up anew a statement of Lightfoot that the author of *1 Clement* was a kind of "secretary of the Roman Church" and possibly not an/the *epískopos*. Edmundson went on to propose that the letter could have been written as early as 70 A.D.[37] Ann E. Wilhelm-Hooijberg also drew this conclusion in 1975[38] as did the late Bishop John A.T. Robinson in 1976.[39] Herron and Bowe both maintain that L. L. Welborn, an American scholar, has shown convincingly that the opening lines of the letter do not refer to a persecution under Domitian as Harnack and Lightfoot had concluded.[40] And surprisingly Brunner and Jeffers, who both hold for the traditional dating, both reject the position that the letter's opening lines refer to a persecution of Christians under Domitian.[41] Bowe, in analyzing the situation, also opts for an earlier dating but "no earlier than ca. 80 CE."[42] Fuellenbach supports the later date of 93-97 but adds that the theories of Wilhelm-Hooijbergh and Bishop Robinson "are not completely improbable, but do not yield enough evidence to abandon the traditional dating."[43] Herron, who writes nine years after Fuellenbach, argues still more convincingly than either Wilhelm-Hooijbergh or Bishop Robinson, in my opinion, for a dating prior to the destruction of the Temple. After reviewing the arguments of Wilhelm-Hooijberg and Robinson and adding eight additional arguments of his own he concludes that

> in the absence of any durable connection of *1 Clement* with the reign of Domitian, on the basis of internal textual references and external theological considerations, the most probable date for the composition of *1 Clement* would seem to be 70 A.D.
>
> My remaining analysis has convinced me of this: if the received, traditional date for *1 Clement* had been 70 instead of 95, no amount of argument could induce us today to move it *from* 70 to 95. I propose, then, that we remove this massive bias, and begin to consider anew the many substantive theological consequences an earlier date for *1 Clement* would have.[44]

What would be the substantive consequences with regard to ministry and Christian priesthood of a C.E. 69-70 dating of *1 Clement*? It would (1) certainly solve the problem of Clement's speaking of the Jerusalem Temple in Chapter 41 in the present tense, as if it were still existing. It would still exist (at least until September of 70), and his analogy between the orderliness of the Jerusalem Temple cult and the orderliness that should exist in the Christian ministry would be all the more poignant. Moreover, it would render moot the point made by some commentators that Clement as a Judeo-Christian or at least as a Christian positively disposed to the Aaronic priesthood in juxtaposing these two orders is suggesting that the Christians might do well to set up a similar-type of priesthood (Why would a Judeo-Christian want to set up another cultic priesthood, if there already is a highly respected and appreciated one operative?). (2) The interchangeable use of the terms *epískopoi* and *presbýteroi* in *1 Clement* would more closely resemble the situation in the Pastoral Epistles and allow a more reasonable length of time for the development of a monepiscopacy like that of which Ignatius speaks (96 to 107-110 C.E. would be a very short development period!). (3) The earlier date would also account for Clement's apparent obliviousness to the friction between Christians and Jews that arose in the years after the fall of the Temple. On this point, Herron[45] quotes Annie Jaubert, who in her *Clément de Rome* holds to the traditional 95-96 dating, but then clearly recognizes the paradox in Clement's attitude.

Le principal argument qu'on ait invoqué contra l'origine juive de Clément, c'est l'absence dans l'epître de toute allusion aux problèmes juifs du temps. Aucune discussion sur le légalisme juif (sabat, circoncision); il ne semble pas que l'auteur ait ressenti dans sa chair le conflit des observances; le peuple juif actuel est comme inexistant. Or, par ailleurs, Clément assume hardiment l'héritage de Israël et toujours de manière positive. Il y a là un paradoxe qui n'est pas complètement éclairci, car il parait invraisemblable qu'a la fin du premier siècle de notre ère la communauté juive de Rome et la communauté n'aient pas eu de rapports difficiles.[46]

And (4) finally, perhaps of least importance, an earlier date might better explain why of the three messengers mentioned in the letter (ch. 65) as bringing it personally to Corinth, namely Valerius Vito, Claudius Ephebus and Fortunatus, no *praenomen* is given for Fortunatus, thereby suggesting that this latter person is already well known to the Corinthian church. Edmundson[47], Robinson[48] and Herron[49] all believe that given an earlier date the Fortunatus mentioned here could indeed be the Fortunatus mentioned by Paul in *1 Cor.* 16:17, and Herron notes (no. 32) that the possibility that this Fortunatus may be a contemporary of St. Paul coincides with Eusebius' belief that Clement, the author, is the same Clement mentioned in *Philippians* 4:3 (*H.E.* 4, 23,11). Should this be the case, then the ministerial structures at Corinth mentioned in the Letter — presbyter-overseers and deacons — would date back to within about five years of Paul's death.

All in all, it does not seem impossible that Clement could have written this letter as an emanuensis of the Church at Rome in 69 or 70 (or 80) and still have been the/a bishop of Rome in 96 C.E.

B. STUDIES IN THE *LETTERS OF IGNATIUS OF ANTIOCH* AND *POLYCARP OF SMYRNA*

Over the past twenty-five years, the great majority of writing on the Apostolic Fathers has focused on the *Letters of Ignatius of Antioch.* During this time, six recognized Ignatius scholars have published their research[50] and at least 85 additional research articles on Ignatius by other scholars have appeared in the journals.[51] Relatively little has been done on the *Letter of Polycarp to the Philippians* aside from a new (1985) translation and commentary by Henning Paulsen which is included in the second volume of

Die Apostolischen Väter (*Handbuch zum Neuen Testament*, 18), and a handful of research articles by other scholars.

Of the research volumes on Ignatius, three challenge the generally accepted authenticity of the Middle Recension of the Letters set out by Lightfoot and Zahn in the last century (R. Weijenbourg, J. Rius-Camps and R. Joly), two are new translations and commentaries (W. Schoedel and H. Paulsen) and two are systematic analyses (C. Trevett and H. Paulsen).

Reinoud Weijenbourg produced from Rome in 1969 an almost 500-page volume, *Les lettres d'Ignace d'Antioche*, which compares line for line Ignatius' *Letter to the Ephesians* in the Long Recension and in the Middle Recension and concludes that the Middle Recension was not the original, but rather a later fourth-century abridgement of the original Long Recension. This position, although astutely presented, has not found much favor among patristic scholars over the years. W. Schoedel, I believe, speaks for most of Weijenbourg's reviewers when he states that "the cumulative weight of the evidence is not impressive."[52]

Josep Ruis-Camps published in 1980 from the Orientalium in Rome a 413-page text, *The Four Authentic Letters of Ignatius, the Martyr*, attempting to show that Ignatius of Antioch originally wrote only four primitive letters, all from Smyrna to the Magnesians, Trallians, Ephesians and Romans. According to Ruis-Camps, the letters which in the past were generally held to have been written from Troas, i.e. those to the Philadelphians, to the Smyrnaeans and to Polycarp, were originally either parts of one of the four primitive letters or in the case of the *Letter to Polycarp* an almost total fabrication. In his lengthy appendix (pp. 345-385), he (1) reconstructs the 'primitive' Magnesians from Middle Recension Magnesians and Philadelphians, (2) reconstructs 'primitive' Ephesians from Middle Recension Ephesians and Smyrneans, (3) presents the undivided but heavily interpolated *Letter to the Trallians*, (4) counts the *Letter to Polycarp* as spurious but maintains that the second part retains several passages from the original ending of 'primitive' Ephesians, and (5) simply presents the text of the uninterpolated *Letter to the Romans*, which was unknown to the forger/interpolator who probably was, according to Rius-Camps, the young bishop of Philadelphia whose authority was being threatened and who sought to bolster his episcopal authority through a set of texts bearing the authority of the martyr Ignatius.[53]

Rius-Camps maintains that in the Middle Recension

we are faced with two distinct ecclesiologies. Ignatius' own, based on the trilogy: God as Father, Jesus the Messiah as only Mediator, the community as a gathering of the members of his Body; and the interpolator's one reducible to a binary scheme: bishop/church. ...
while Ignatius has recourse to "one submission" to Jesus the Messiah, that is, the unanimous gathering of the community members to celebrate the Eucharist, the interpolator directs this submission to the person of the bishop (and the presbytery).[54]

Thus, according to Rius-Camps

The interpolator corrects Ignatius' archaic ecclesiology with a much more developed one. To the single bishop, supervisor and coordinator of all the communities of a Roman province (Syria: Ignatius; Asia: Polycarp), he opposes the monarchical bishop, at the head of each of the important communities ... ; with the presbytery or senate of the community elders (even though never mentioned by Ignatius) he contrasts a presbytery depending on the bishop, as his spiritual crown.[55]

In short, Rius-Camps sees such 'interpolated' statements as "the bishops, established in the most distant regions, are included in the plan of Jesus Christ" (*Eph.* 3,2e) or "the bishop with the presbyters and deacons who are with him, were appointed by Jesus Christ's disposition, whom he has established and confirmed according to his own design by his Holy Spirit"(*Phld.* insc.) or that the bishop of Philadelphia does not possess the supervisory ministry "by his own initiative nor by any human agency nor for vanity, but by the love of God the Father and the Lord Jesus Christ"(*Phld.* 1,1) as arising

from the need the forger feels to prove the apostolic (allusion to the Didascalia) and, what is more, divine origin of the hierarchical trilogy.[56] ...
That the forger of the Ignatian letters was preoccupied by the *hierarchical organization* of the church becomes evident in the clauses he drew up to interrupt the sequence of the primitive letters (*Eph.* 20 and *Mg.* 13) or to head or end the new ones (*Phld.* Inscr. -1; 10-11 and *Sm.* 12).[57]

Clearly this book, to quote one reviewer — C.P. Hammond Bammel, "is a monumental piece of work"[58] and genuinely 'unconfessional' coming from a Catholic scholar. What is a bit surprising is that few, if any,[59] scholars — Catholic, Protestant, Orthodox or Anglican — in the past decade have blessed his hypotheses with anything more than hesitant scepticism. The exhaustive review of his text by Hammond Bammel, I believe, is representative of most reviewers.

> With regard to the main hypothesis of the book, it may be allowed that there is nothing particularly implausible in itself in the idea that a genuine core of Ignatian letters was expanded and interpolated by a forger. Once he has stated this theory, however, Rius-Camps has a completely free hand in identifying and eliminating what he imagines to be the work of the forger. Thus there is nothing to restrict him in raising criticisms against Ignatius' letters and then answering them by cutting out or rewriting the passage concerned. ... In a sense therefore his theory is bound to 'work', but on the other hand it cannot because of this be said to be proved correct. ... The type of argumentation he uses makes the reader sceptical from the start. ... The details of his argumentation are difficult to follow ... , but more importantly because they fail to convince... The thoroughness with which Rius-Camps goes on to work out the consequences of his rearrangement of the letters, the new picture of Ignatius himself, the motives of the forger and his procedure, ... is impressive. ... All this fails, however, to compensate for the implausibility of much of the argumentation in the initial diagnosis and proposed solution of the problems presented by the received text. The new reconstruction remains unproved and unprovable.[60]

A third and final challenge to the authenticity of the Ignatian Middle Recension, *Le dossier d'Ignace d'Antioche,* was published in 1979 by Robert Joly of the Free University of Brussels.[61] His compact text concludes that the Letters are a forgery dating from between 160 and 170 C.E. He begins by attempting to prove that the forger started by interpolating chapter 13 of Polycarp's *Letter to the Philippians* to include mention of a collection of Ignatius' letters.

> Il s'agit de lancer sous l'authorité de Polycarpe, le corpus apocryphe des Lettres d'Ignace.[62]

W. Schoedel comments that here "Joly's arguments are strong, they are not decisive."[63]

Joly's chapter on the monarchical episcopacy maintains that the three-fold office structure in the Letters is clearly an anachronism for the early second century, but he gives, as Hammond Bammel notes, "no explanation for the origin of the institution."[64]

His real strength, however, appears to lie in his philological analysis. He lists a number of terms in the Letters that, he argues, betray a state of development beyond the early part of the second century, e.g., *he katholiké ekklesía, christianismós* and the adjective *christianós*[65], *apostolikós, haíresis,* and others. He also notes the unusual and/or advanced uses the Letters make of *páthos, euaggélion* and *homilía,* to mention a few. On this point Hammond Bammel also comments that

> This phenomenon might be taken as providing an indication of Ignatius' date, if we possessed a large body of Christian literature deriving from the same milieu. As it is, we only possess a very small portion of the Christian writings which were produced in the second century, and what we do have derives from a variety of different backgrounds. ...
>
> There is nothing improbable in the supposition that Christian terminology developed more quickly at Antioch than elsewhere, indeed *Acts* xi. 26 suggests that this was the case.[66]

In short, there are certainly Christian terms used by Ignatius that can be shown to be in common usage during the second half of the second century, but that is no *ipso facto* proof that they were not in some use during the first decades of the century.

Aside from a supportive review by Charles Munier,[67] Joly's argumentation has not met with much support from the wider scholarly community. The conclusion of the lengthy review by Gilles Pelland of the Gregorian University is probably a fairly representative one.

> Malgré son érudition et son ingéniosité, il n'a pas renversé la thèse traditionnelle concernant l'authenticité et la date approximative des lettres d'Ignace. La letter de Polycarp pose problème, il est vrai, mais pas au point d'exclure toute explication satisfaisante et de rendre suspect son témoignage sur s. Ignace.[68]

It appears, then, that all three attempts in recent years to challenge
the authenticity of the Ignatian Middle Recension, namely by Weijenborg,
Rius-Camps and Joly, have failed to gain a consensus in the scholarly world,
despite the fact that, as Christine Trevett puts it,

> the *Middle Recension* does contain intriguing silences,
> inconsistencies and anomalies. Were it not so, writers would
> have had less occasion to posit the work of forgers.[69]

This means, of course, that the Lightfoot analysis of the late 1800's still
holds sway in the 1990's. It also means, ministerially speaking, that the
Ignatian Letters remain the only account of a three-fold Christian hierarchy,
i.e. of a single bishop with presbyters and deacons, that we have in the first
decade or early second decade[70] of the second century. Although none of
the 'challenging' authors take up the issue of priesthood or sacerdotal
terminology in the Letters (it is not their purpose), I believe that, with the
Lightfoot analysis still in place, the Bishop's conviction that "there is not
throughout these letters, the slightest tinge of sacerdotal language in reference
to the Christian ministry"[71] also stands, i.e. until the opposite can be shown.
In Chapter 4, I will challenge that "slightest tinge" with arguments that
Ignatius' *Letter to the Ephesians* 5:2 presents a symbolic application of
sacerdotal terminology (*entòs toû thusiasteríou*) to "the bishop and the
whole assembly."[72]

In 1985 two excellent translation/commentaries of the Middle
Recension were published: one in America by William R. Schoedel of the
University of Illinois at Urbana entitled simply *Ignatius of Antioch*
(*Hermeneia* series, Fortress Press); the other in Germany by Henning
Paulsen in the *Handbuch zum Neuen Testament* series, No. 18, *Die
Apostolischen Väter II* (J.C.B. Mohr [Paul Siebeck] in Tübingen). The
Schoedel book, 300 pages with 30 pages of introduction, is probably the
best single text on Ignatius since the work of Robert Grant in 1966. It is a
veritable goldmine from a scholar in superb command of the literature. The
brief, 126-page text by Paulsen is an excellent reworking and updating of
Walter Bauer's 1920 translation/commentary of the Middle Recension with
a new 15-page bibliography. Paulsen's text also includes the *Letter of
Polycarp to the Philippians*.

Finally two systematic studies — one from Germany, one from
America — deserve mention here. Henning Paulsen's 1978 *Studien zur*

Theologie des Ignatius von Antiochien (Vandenhoeck & Ruprecht in Göttingen) runs the gammut from the history and methodology of Ignatian research, Ignatian eschatology, paranesis, view of martyrdom, pneumatology, notion of salvation, christology, and a section on ecclesiology and Eucharist.

Christine Trevett's very recent text, *A Study of Ignatius of Antioch in Syria and Asia* (The Edwin Mellen Press, 1992), features chapters on the Ignatian enigmas, on the churches in Antioch and Asia, on the person of Ignatius and on his opponents.

Neither have much to say about sacral-cultic terminology directed toward community ministers, although Paulsen does comment briefly on the use of *thusiastérion*.

> Dies zeigt nicht nur die prägnante Rolle, die der Eucharistie von Ignatius in der Auseinandersetzung mit den Gegnern zugewiesen wird, sondern vor allem z. B. die Alternierung des Begriffs *thusiastérion*. Im Gegensatz zu einer Auslegung, die bei diesem Terminus vor allem den Opfercharakter betont wissen will, bleibt festzuhalten, das sich für Ignatius *thusiastérion* an der Gemeinde and ihrer Einheit orientiert.[73]

In general this is certainly the case, although in *Eph.* 5:2 the orientation of *thusiastérion* seems clearly to be around the prayer of the bishop **and** the "Gemeinde". Trevett recognizes in the Letters the start of a shift in authority from the charismatic leader to the office holder.

> In the writings of Ignatius we find ourselves close to the beginnings of that process which brought the transfer of esteem and authority from the charismatic to the office holder. Ultimately, indeed, *charismata* were deemed the possession of officials and the roles of priest, prophet, teacher, king and much else were embodied in the person of the bishop (*Did. Apost.* ii. 25, 7).[74]

The Letter(s) of Polycarp to the Philippians

Simon Tugwell begins a chapter on Polycarp in his recent book, *The Apostolic Fathers*, with a superb sprinkle of British understatement: "Polycarp is more interesting as a man and as a martyr than he is as a writer."[75] I would concur, with perhaps one exception (to be discussed in chapter 5), that Polycarp is singularly uncreative. Aside from the fine work of William Schoedel[76] and Henning Paulsen's translation/commentary already mentioned, very little has been done on Polycarp over the last two decades except perhaps for several articles by Boudewijn Dehandschutter from Louvain.[77] The Letter's unity, however, is still discussed, namely whether we are dealing with one or, as P. N. Harrison posited in 1936, two letters. Over against a host of scholars since Harrison, Schoedel and Paulsen both support the unity of the Letter. Their arguments are strong, but no stronger, I believe, than Harrison's two-letter hypothesis with the 120 C.E. dating for chapters 1-12 as proposed by L.W. Barnard which I support here in chapter 5. No priesthood-type language in the Letter is applied to the Christian ministers and the two instances of such terms, namely Jesus Christ as "eternal High Priest" (12:2) and the widows as the "altar of God" (4:3) are discussed in chapter 5.

C. STUDIES IN THE *EPISTLE OF BARNABAS*

Over the last twenty-five years, several critical texts[78] and roughly 20 research articles[79] have appeared on the *Epistle of Barnabas*, sometimes called the *Epistle of Pseudo-Barnabas*. The best known of these is the 1971 *Sources Chrétiennes* critical edition of the Epistle by Pierre Prigent of the University of Strasbourg using the Greek text established by Robert Kraft. There is also an Italian translation and commentary published by O. Soffritti in 1974, and a University of Bonn doctoral thesis in 1971 by Klaus Wengst entitled *Tradition und Theologie des Barnabasbriefes*.[80] Most of the research articles focus either on the relationship between the Two Ways material in *Barnabas* and in the *Didache* or on *Barnabas'* anti-Jewish polemic or on a possible Syro-Palestinian origin of the Letter. In none of this material that I have been able to consult have I found any comments on sacral-cultic language or Christian ministry that goes beyond the discussion of this in chapter 6.

D. STUDIES IN THE *SHEPHERD OF HERMAS*

Over the last two decades, this longest document of the Apostolic Fathers has been the subject of ten books,[81] nine dissertations[82] and about 85 research articles.[83]

The most recent (1991) and largest (589 pages) of these is the superb work of Norbert Brox, *Der Hirt des Hermas*, in the *Kommentar zu den Apostolischen Väter* series (KAV, 7) from Göttingen. In his discussion of church order in the *Shepherd*, Brox simply mentions that the document "zeigt kein grosses Interesse an dieser Thematik."[84] And he adds

Die dürftige Statistik ist anschaulich: An Ämter bzw. Amtsträgern erwähnt H[ermas] explizit im ganzen Buch nur je dreimal Presbyter und Bischöfe, zweimal Diakone, ausserdem wenige Male "Hirten", Lehrer und Propheten (s.u.).[85]

About bishops in the *Shepherd*, Brox says simply

Es gibt die Bishöfe im P[astor] H[ermae] nur im Plural wie auch die Presbyter. Die römische Kirche war kollegial geleitet. Der Monoepiskopat ist zur Zeit des H[ermas] in Rom noch keine Realität und keine Prätention.[86]

He also mentions that any clear profile of the office of the bishop or the relationship between the bishops and the presbyters is simply not to be found in this text.[87] Nor does he raise the issue of a sacralization of ministry.

Four of the recently published works on *The Shepherd* take a sociocultural approach to the material. Carolyn Osiek, RSCJ,[88] of the Catholic Theological Union in Chicago analyzes the *Rich and Poor in the Shepherd of Hermas*. As noted earlier, James S. Jeffers[89] of the University of California at Irvine compares the Roman social context in the congregation of Hermas with that of the congregation of Clement, arriving at a number of key insights. Harry O. Maier at the University of British Columbia writes on *The Social Setting of the Ministry as Reflected in the Writings of Hermas, Clement and Ignatius*,[90] and Martin Leutzsch's recently published dissertation from the Ruhr-Universität Bochum aims to perceive the social reality behind the text (*Die Wahrnemung sozialer Wirklichkeit in "Hirten des Hermas"*).[91]

Their discussion of ministerial structures in the church at Rome is quite tangential to their broader interest in the social milieu of these early Christians, and all see much more in the document than just the traditionally accepted purpose of introducing a second forgiveness after Baptism . Maier puts it this way:

Rather than demonstrating a concern over post-baptismal sin, the frequent references to wealth and property and their misuse by members in Hermas' community suggest that the primary concern of this author is to maintain the purity of the Christian sect through proper attitudes toward and uses of wealth. For Hermas, problems in the community have arisen because of inappropriate social attitudes. The proclamation of repentance is presented primarily to exert a form of social control on the group, in order to stem the tide which Hermas regards as divisive and destructive.[92]

With regard to ministerial structures, Osiek notes that "Hermas lists five groups of officeholders, all in the past, either Jewish or first generation Christian "[93] namely apostles, overseers, teachers, ministers(deacons) and prophets, and that

> when the author indirectly reveals information about church government structures, it is about a collegial presbyterial group: the *proēgoumenoi tēs ekklēsias* (Vis. 2.2.6); *proēgoumenoi* and *protokathedritai* (Vis. 3.9.7); *presbyteroi prohistamenoi tēs ekklēsias* (Vis. 2.4.3), all terms meaning approximately the same as Justin's term *prohestōs*, the presider at assemblies or worship. If *episkopoi* and *diakonoi* are still contemporary terms, they are presumably synomymous with this collegial leadership group.[94]

Osiek does not take up the issue of sacral-cultic language in relation to the ministers.

Jeffers' book makes the point that "Christianity in Rome in the first and early second centuries was not an organizationally and ideologically unified 'church.'"[95] He sees the congregation that produced *1 Clement* as a small group of the 'social elite' of the Roman church, and that which produced *The Shepherd of Hermas*, a group which "probably represented the larger number of Christians in Rome in that it did not have much contact with the Roman elite."[96] He sees Clement's Christian community gradually embracing the hallmarks of Roman society, namely the centrality and absolute authority of the *paterfamilias* within a very orderly, hierarchical society. Side by side is the community of Hermas, operating from a much more charismatic authority base and a strong suspicion of the very Roman society and government that made martyrs of so many of their fellow Christians in past decades. Jeffers describes the attitudinal differences between Hermas and Clement.

> Unlike Clement's, Hermas's attitudes toward office and authority in the congregation resemble those of a sect. He does not locate authority solely in the officeholders. He

places a high value on congregational involvement. Hermas
does not share Clement's uniformly high regard for church
leaders. He is told to exhort Roman Christian officeholders to
"reform their ways" in accord with his revelation (*Vis.* 2.2.6).
Hermas did not reject all leaders, however. He saw the time of
the apostles as a golden age, then one or two generations past,
when the leaders "always agreed among themselves," listened
to each other and enjoyed peace (*Vis.* 3.5.1) By contrast,
Hermas repeatedly chastises the present leadership of the
Roman churches. He warns them not to desire the "chief
seats," and to stop acting like poisoners (*Vis.* 3.9.7). They
need to correct one another and establish peace among
themselves (*Vis.* 3.9.8,10)[97]

When it comes to the issue of how authority figures get and keep their
authority in the community, Jeffers points out that

Unlike *1 Clement*, but like the classic sect, the *Shepherd* does
not legitimize proper authority figures by their appointment
to an office. Rather, it legitimizes them by their behavior and
actions. Proper leaders, according to Hermas, worked hard,
taught with pure motives, and tirelessly served those in need
(*Sim.* 9.25.2; 9.27.2-3). Hermas emphasizes not their unique
function within the group but their faithfulness to provide for
the spiritual and material needs of the congregation.[98]
      Godly bishops are identified with hospitable people who
open their homes to needy members. ... Hermas also refers to
prophets in the church. ... In light of his prophetic message
and his concern over the quality of the present bishops and
presbyters, he may have elevated prophets to a place of honor
equal to officeholders with more regular duties.[99]

As with Osiek, so also with Jeffers who throughout his analysis of the
Shepherd makes no note of any type of sacral-cultic language applied
directly or indirectly to the ministers of the church. This may have much to
do with the fact that despite the numerous officeholders mentioned, Hermas
gives no real profile of the functions of any of them, except perhaps for the
Christian prophet and the false prophet in Mandate 11.[100] Then there is also
the issue of Hermas' soteriology (which will be discussed in chapter 7) that
does not view Jesus' crucifixion as the major salvific act nor see his death
as either an atonement or a sacrifice and thus will hardly feel a need for any

'priestly' group to perform rituals that would mediate in one way or another this saving event to the Christian people.

The Dating of *The Shepherd of Hermas* is still a much discussed problem because it touches both on the author's purpose and on the social situation when it was published. The *Muratorian Canon* has Hermas writing the document when his brother Pius sat in the 'cathedra' of the church of the city of Rome.[101] But, says H.O. Maier,

> If this is correct, the *Shepherd* was composed sometime between A.D. 139 and 154, the dates of Pius' episcopate. The internal evidence, however, seems to suggest an earlier date of composition. In *Vision* 2:4.3 Hermas is instructed to send a copy of the words that the old lady tells him to Clement, who "then will send it to the cities abroad, for that is his duty...." Most scholars identify this Clement with the author of the first letter to the Corinthians, which was composed in the last decade of the first century. In addition there is no evidence in the document that monarchical episcopacy existed in Hermas' church. Hermas, indeed, seems to assume a presbyterial organization of the community ... which is consistent with an earlier date. Finally *Vis.* 3:5.1, with its reference to apostles, bishops, teachers and deacons, some of whom "have fallen asleep," but some of whom are still alive, suggests an earlier date than the mid-second century.[102]

This dilemma has, of course, given rise to theories of multiple authorship. Among recent writers, W. Coleborne[103] has posited at least six authors, S. Giet[104] three, C. Osiek[105] and A. Carlini[106] agree basically with Giet. This line of reasoning was seen earlier in the works of M. Dibelius[107] and W. Wilson[108] among others. The single authorship approach has about an equal number of adherents as that for multiple authorship. Single authorship with various periods of composition was the position of A. Harnack[109] long ago and among recent authors it is held by R. Joly,[110] J. Reiling,[111] A. Hilhorst,[112] M. Leutzsch,[113] and N. Brox.[114] In chapter 7, I will argue for a single authorship of a two-part work.

E. STUDIES IN THE *DIDACHE*

Over the past two decades, four critical editions of the *Didache* have been published — one in French,[115] two in German[116] and one in English[117]

— plus several key books on the *Didache*[118] and about 40 research articles.[119] Willy Rordorf and André Tuilier authored the *Sources Chrétiennes* edition, *La Doctrine des douze apôtres*, in 1978. Kurt Niederwimmer published his *Die Didache* as the first volume of the KAV (Kommentar zu den Apostolischen Väter) at Göttingen in 1989. Georg Schöllgen produced *Didache: Zwölf-Apostel-Lehre* for the Herder *Fontes Christiani* series in 1991. And also in 1991, Brent Walters published the *Didache* text for the *Ante-Nicene Archive* collection from San Jose, CA. Among other key texts worthy of note are: the not-so-recent work of Stanislaus Giet, *L'énigme de la Didachè*, published posthumously in 1970[120] and the recent text of Clayton N. Jefford, *The Sayings of Jesus in the Teaching of the Twelve Apostles*, a 1989 publication by E.J. Brill of his doctoral dissertation at the Claremont Graduate School.[121]

Since, as is pointed out in chapter 8, the *Didache*, more than any other of the Apostolic Fathers, possesses a combination (four sets) of sacral-cultic terms that potentially could give rise to a Christian priesthood, I will survey these more recent critical editions and research texts as to how they understand the didachist to be using these four sets of sacral-cultic terms usually associated at the beginning of our era with the Jewish (or a pagan) priesthood.

Here we are speaking about (1) the three uses of *thusía* (sacrifice) in ch. 14, (2) that the prophets "are your highpriests" (*hoi archiereîs humôn)* in 13:3, (3) that the *episkopoi* and *diakonoi* are to be chosen "for they also *minister* to you the *ministry* of the prophets and teachers" (*humîn gàr leitourgoûsi kaì autoì tèn* **leitourgían**), and (4) the use of the term "holy" *(tò hágion)* when applied not to God but to the earthly church: 9:5, 4:2 and 10:6.

(1) On the use of *thusía*, Rordorf notes that

Le rapprochment avec la première *Épître aux Corinthiens*, qui exalte le souvenir de la mort du Christ à propos du repas eucharistique, pourrait laisser croire qu'il faut accorder une signification précise au substantif *thusía* , qui apparaît à trois reprises au ch. 14 de la *Didachè* (14, 1.2.3). De fait, dans notre texte, ce substantif assimile apparemment l'eucharistie à un sacrifice, conformément aux interprétations de la tradition chrétienne la plus ancienne. [122]

To this he adds the admonition of Audet (p. 462) that it would be wrong to be too explicit in this area, probably, I suspect, because the *Didache* makes no mention of the sacrifice of the Cross nor of Jesus as Highpriest. On the *thusía* question, Niederwimmer asks

> Was ist mit *thusía*, dem beim Mahl dargebrachten Opfer gemeint? Es liegt nahe, unter *thusía* die heilige Handlung der Eucharistiefeier zu verstehen, bzw. *thusía* näherhin mit den eucharistischen Elementen zu verbinden (wie das z.B. Just. dial. 41,3 ... geschieht). Did. 14,1-3 brächte dann den ältesten expliziten Beleg für die Auffassung des Abendmahls als Opfer. Indessen ist diese Interpretation nicht sicher. Der Kontext erlaubt noch eine andere Möglichkeit, nämlich *thusía* speziell auf *eucharistêsate* zu beziehen: das Opfer, von dem hier mehrfach geredet wird, wäre dann das eucharistische Gebet, das die Gemeinde darbringt.[123]

Schöllgen gives the position of Rordorf/Tuilier and then adds that

> Andere deuten es auf die "Eucharistie"—Feier insgesamt, manche noch enger auf Brot (und Wein) als eucharistische Gaben; die Didache wäre dann der früheste Zeuge einer ansonsten erst seit Justin sicher feßbaren Tradition, die die Eucharistie als Opfer versteht. Eine eindeutige Lösung dieser Frage läßt der Text wohl nicht zu.[124]

(2) On 13:3 where the prophets are called "your highpriests", Niederwimmer states

> Die Stelle 13,3 ist wichtig für die Position des Didachisten gegenüber dem Judentum. Das alttestamentliche Kultrecht wird in freier Weise auf die neuen, auf die kirchlichen Verhältnisse übertragen und verändert. Um den Rang der Propheten herauszustreichen und um die Versorgungspflicht der Gemeinde zu sichern, parallelisiert der Didachist die christlichen Propheten seiner Zeit mit den *archiereûs* des alten Bundes und macht so die Propheten (metaphorisch!) zu "Oberpriestern" der Christen, — eine auffällige Formulierung, die in der frühchristlichen Literatur keine direkte Parallele hat.[125]

And André de Hallieux in a lengthy article on "Les ministères dans la *Didachè*" points out that

La qualification de *archiereîs*, donnée aux prophètes au v. 3, ne vise pas nécessairement une fonction liturgique. Il peut s'agir, en effet, d'une simple comparison implicite, purement formelle: de même que les prémices étaient dues aux prêtres, ainsi le même commandement de l'Ancien Testament ou, peut-être, une ordonnance évangelique (cf. I Co 9,14), demande aux chrétiens de les donner à leurs prophètes.[126]

(3) With regard to the passage in 15:1 that the *epískopoi* and *diákonoi* minister (*leitourgoûsi*) to you the ministry (*leitourgían*) of the prophets and teachers, Rordorf notes simply that "les évêques et les diacres exercent les fonctions liturgiques (*leitourgía*) des prophètes et des docteurs et le texte ne permet aucune distinction spécifique à ce sujet."[127] Niederwimmer, on the same text, notes that

> Die Sprache des Didachisten ist hier betont gewählt: *leitourgeîn leitourgían* ist Paronomasie, der Sinn des Ausdrucks im Kontext leider nicht völlig deutlich; er bezeichnet jedenfalls den heiligen Dienst, den Propheten und Lehrer ebenso wie die "Ortskleriker" an der Gemeinde tun. Die Pointe der Aussage in V. 1c ist klar: beide Grupppen sollen nebeneinander und miteinander fungieren können.[128]

As an aside, one issue that invariably arises at this point of text discussion is the strange situation of the "missing presbyters." With the recognized Judeo-Christian influence in the *Didache*, it is certainly unusual that there is no mention of *presbýteroi* anywhere in the text. Some say that we are dealing here with an earlier level of development, before the notions of overseer and elder are fused;[129] others hold that at the time of the *Didache* the terms *presbýteroi* and *epískopos* were synonymous;[130] still others hold that the whole beginning of chapter 15, the hapax mentioning the *epískopoi* and the *diákonoi*, was written in later as an interpolation.[131] By far, though, the most creative and attractive solution to the non-mention of "presbyters" in the text comes from Clayton Jefford who holds that the intended audience for at least part of the text were the presbyters themselves, i.e. it was the elder, honored ones of a particular church community who were "to appoint overseers and deacons" and that throughout chapters 7 through 15 they were being instructed on how to baptize, etc.[132]

34

(4) On the use of the term "holy" other than for God, i.e. in 4:2, 9:2 and 9:5, Rordorf mentions briefly that

> Précisions à ce sujet que l'adjectif *hágios* (sainte) revient cinq fois dans les prières eucharistiques de la *Didachè;* puisque la divinité sainte est présente lorsque la communauté locale est assemblée et puisque ses saints dons sont distribués aux fidèles à cette occasion (9,5), il faut aussi que ceux-ci soient saints, c'est-à-dire qu'ils soient dignes de la grâce de Dieu.[133]

And Jefford notes that 9:5b "Do not give anything holy (*hágion*) to the dogs" is clearly an indication of some dependence on the Matthean tradition even though the context for the *Didache's* version (those who may eat of the Eucharist) is not reflected in the Matthean account.[134]

The dating of the *Didache* still remains something of an enigma, although the major critical studies reviewed here, namely Rordorf/Tuilier, Niederwimmer, Schöllgen and Jefford all reject the notion of a later artificial construction and consider the text as appearing during the late first century or beginning of the second, and all seem to prefer Syria or the Syrian-Palestinian border area as the place of origin. [135] These are basically my positions in chapter 8, although I am inclined to agree with E. Peterson in mistrusting the Bryennios text as the "authenticum" of the *Didache* for reasons given there.

In summary, then, with regard to the *Didache's* four uses of sacral-cultic language:

(1) Rordorf, Niederwimmer and Schöllgen all recognize, on the one hand, that ch. 14 can be seen as containing the earliest Christian reference to the Eucharist as a sacrifice (*thusía*) [and sacrifice is what priests offer up!], but, on the other hand, they also note, as does Audet, that there is no clarity in the text as to precisely what is included under the term "sacrifice": the elements (bread, wine, other gifts), the thanksgiving prayer of the community, their own interior states of self-offering, all or some of the above. Moreover, the absence of any mention in the document of the "sacrifice of the Cross" or Jesus as "Highpriest" only complicates the matter.

(2) On the issue of the prophets as "your highpriests," Niederwimmer sees the didachist here drawing a metaphorical parallel and de Hallieux cautions that this simple comparison should not be seen as necessarily implying a parallel liturgical function in the prophets, but perhaps an equal right, like the Levitical priests, to a good 'first-fruits' meal for their

labors. He cites Paul in *1 Cor.* 9:14 on an apostle's right to food and drink (for himself and Barnabas).

(3) The issue of *leitourgeîn leitourgían,* however, is a different matter. This combination of terms would in a community with Jewish background normally carry cultic overtones with regard to, in Niederwimmer's terms, "den heiligen Dienst" or as Rordorf puts it: "the overseers and deacons exercise the liturgical functions of the prophets and teachers." In short, we do appear to have here the vocabulary of Levitical priestly service applied to the Christian prophets, teachers, overseers and deacons. This is discussed further in ch. 8.

(4) On the use of the term "holy", especially in *Did.* 9, Rordorf speaks of "the holy gifts that are distributed to the faithful" and Jefford shows how the text that follows the didachist's admonition "not to let anyone eat or drink of your Eucharist except those who are baptized", namely: "Do not give what is holy *(hágion)* to dogs," is clearly dependent on the Matthean tradition, i.e. that found in *Mt.* 7:6. Thus expressed, the meal elements take on a very sacral dimension, as also evidenced at an even earlier date in *1 Corinthians* 11:27-30.

F. Recent Studies on Christian Priesthood and the History of Ministry

Among the books explicitly on Christian priesthood are those authored by J.-P. Audet, R. Brown, J. Colson, J. Coppens, A. Descamps, D. Donovan, J. Elliott, A. Feuillet, J. Galot, E. Kilmartin, H. Küng, J. Lightfoot (re-printed), N. Mitchell, R. Moberly, J. Mohler, K. Osborne, D. Power, F. Ramos, T. Rausch, K. Schelkle, A. Sousa and A. Vanhoye.[136] To these works should also be added a number of specific texts, namely the Downside Symposium on *The Christian Priesthood* edited by N. Lash and J. Rhymer (1970), the research papers on Holy Orders from the Centre de Pastorale Liturgique published first in Paris (1957) and then in English by The Liturgical Press (1962), the 775-page volume on *Ministries in the Church in India* edited from New Dehli by D. Amalorpavadass in 1976 and Bernard Cooke's 677-page *Ministry to Word and Sacrament: History and Theology* (1976) which deals extensively both with Christian priesthood and with the history of ministry.

Among recent research articles exclusively on Christian priesthood are those by K. Becker, C. Blaisdell, H. Bouesse, R. Bower, R. Bradley, R.

Campiche, C. Clark, Y. Congar, J. Crehan, A. Cunningham, J. Delorme, G. Denzler, J. Dixon, B. Dupuy, B. Esquerda, P. Fink, P. Flores, D. Forrester, P. Fransen, D. Geaney, A. Greeley, D. Greeley, R. Greenwood, J. Grindel, T. Groome, P. Gy, J. Hardon, M. Harris, P. Hebblethwaite, J. Hind, J. Hotchkin, R. van Kessel, A. Kokkinakis, P. L'Huillier, W. Löser, G. Mollat, H. Montefiore, R. Murray, B. Neumann, R. Norris, D. Passi, L. Patsavos, Pope Paul VI, H.B. Porter, J.A.T. Robinson, P. Rosato, L. Sabourin, E. Sauras, H. Schmitz, E. Shelp, A. Thannikot, J. Thome, J. Tillard, H. Waldenfels, J. Webster, J. Wright, and D. Wuerl.

Among recent books on the history and/or theology of ministry in a more general sense are those by W. Bausch, P. Bernier, J. Burtchael, M. Lawler, R. McBrien, R. McCormick and G. Dyer, H. Nouwen, T. O'Meara, J. Rademacher, E. Schillebeeckx, L. Sofield and C. Juliano, J. Walsh and J. DiGiacomo, and J. and E. Whitehead.

The following have authored research articles on ministry in a broad sense from an historical and/or theological focus: G. Baum, W. Burghardt, G. Carey, Y. Congar, S. Dianich, P. Eisenkopf, P. Empie & T. A. Murphy, D. Geaney, T. Jacobs, E. Jay, E. Kilmartin, G. Konidaris, P. LeBlanc, H.-M. Legrand, G. Magnani, J. Moingt, W. Portier, E. Schillebeeckx, J. Seguy, P. Van Beneden, B. Van Iersel & R. Murphy, H. Vogt and J. Zizioulas.

From among the books and articles written explicitly on Christian priesthood, I would like, as a way to deal with this large volume of material, to present some brief excerpts representative of the common range of scholarly opinion on these matters and follow that up with a brief synthesis essay. My hope is that both the excerpts and the synthesis in attempting to present a broad overview of the issues and complexities surrounding the origin of Christian priesthood will thereby also provide a helpful introduction to the more detailed analyses of the major texts of the Apostolic Fathers in the six chapters that follow. Here then are the excerpts and my synthesis.

From the late Anglican Bishop John A. T. Robinson:

Early Christianity appears to have been marked by no anti-priestly strain, and both Jesus and Paul carefully refuse at their trials to be trapped into disrespect for the high priesthood (John 18: 22-3; Acts 23:4-5). The legalism of the scribes and Pharisees was evidently seen as a much greater menace. It should not therefore surprise us as much as perhaps it does that Acts 6:7 casually records that 'a great many of the priests were obedient to the faith.'

... Moreover, the early Church was not anti-priestly - though ... it soon found itself involved in polemic against the *necessity* of the sacrificial system, as it was also against the necessity of circumcision and ritual ablutions. But, unlike Judaism, it found a completely satisfying *replacement* for it (*a*) in the true high priesthood of Christ (this is the great theme of the Epistle to the Hebrews) and (*b*) in the true priesthood of the whole body of the Church (which interestingly enough receives no treatment in the Epistle to the Hebrews).

In support of the latter, early Christian apologetic (as we find it reflected in both I Pet. and in the Apocalypse) brought together two Old Testament texts: You shall be to me a kingdom of priests and a holy nation. (Exod. 19:6) - and - You shall be called the priests of the Lord, many shall speak of you as the ministers of our God (Isa. 61:6).[137]

From Albert Vanhoye, SJ, of the Pontifical Biblical Institute:

By its imposing volume, the priestly christology of the Epistle to the Hebrews brings out very clearly the most important point of the Christian position in regard to the priesthood: there is only one priest in the full sense of the term and this priest is Christ. Christ alone has been able to fulfill effectively the essential function of the priesthood, which is to establish a mediation between God and mankind. He is the sole mediator... A single new priest succeeds to the multitude of Old Testament priests. [138]

From Kenan Osborne, OFM, of the Franciscan School of Theology, Berkeley, CA:

In the apostolic and sub-apostolic Church the "Letter to the Hebrews" did not have a great deal of influence. In the West, Clement of Rome in his letter to the Corinthians alludes to this writing. In the middle of the second century Hermas makes a brief allusion to it as well. In the East, there was greater appreciation: Clement of Alexandria, Origen, Pantanus. The West began to accept this letter as canonical only in the latter part of the fourth century. In the first three hundred years of the Church, the letter did not play any noteworthy role in shaping the understanding of priestly ministry. From 400 onward it plays a stronger role.[139]

From the exegesis of *I Peter* by my USF colleague John H. Elliott on the key terms *basíleion hieráteuma* — so often (mis)translated as "royal priesthood":

> *Hieráteuma* means "body of priests." It does not mean "priesthood" which is rather the equivalent of *hierateía*, a more static and more abstract term in comparison with the *nomen actionis hieráteuma*. *Basíleion* does not mean "royal" in v. 9 but is an independent substantive signifying "royal residence or dwelling place." In v. 5 this substantive is interpreted as the "house(hold) of the Spirit." Both terms are corporative and have been interpreted by the author of I Peter in this sense. It is semantically inadmissable to attempt to reduce either of these words to an individual-distributive classification and thereby to suggest that each individual believer is being depicted as a "king" and a "priest." ... As the other corporate predicates, both *basíleion* and *hieráteuma* are only ascribable to the community *qua* community and only relevant in this context *qua substantiva corporativa*.
>
> Just as *basíleon* bears no implication of "royal rule, kingly freedom, or royal dignity and status," so *hieráteuma*, though it denotes a people close to God, does not imply *in se* the abolition of mediation or the conferment of "priestly rights and prerogatives." The significance of *hieráteuma* lies not in its cultic connotations, but together with *basíleion*, in its designation of the electedness and holiness of the Divine Regent's Community.[140]

From the English Jesuit Robert Murray on the earliest application of priesthood language to the Eucharist:

> The earliest explicit application of priesthood language to the eucharist (though this must not be misunderstood as though it were 'proving' a modern controversial thesis) is by referring to it the prophecy of Mal. I: 12, 'For from the rising of the sun to its setting my name is great among the gentiles, and in every place incense is offered to my name and a pure offering'. The *Didache* (which if not certainly of the first century, surely contains much material from the apostolic period) in ch. 14

applies this text to the eucharist and calls it 'your sacrifice' (thüsia).[141]

From Hervé-Marie Legrand, OP, of the Institut catholique on the presidency of the Eucharist in the pre-Nicene church:

> If we summarize the testimonies of the pre-Nicene Church, a general perspective emerges. The bond between the apostles and presidents of the Eucharist is to be found only with Clement and secondarily with Hippolytus. The perception of the president of the Eucharist as an explicitly sacerdotal figure is not attested before the beginning of the third century (Hippolytus, Tertullian, Cyprian). On the other hand, with all of the witnesses we note that it is a fact, and most often it is axiomatic (Clement, Ignatius, Justin, Tertullian, Hippolytus, Cyprian and the canonical tradition deriving from Hippolytus), that those who preside over the life of the Church preside at the Eucharist.[142]

From P.M. Gy, OP, of the theology faculty at Le Saulchoir on the early terminology of Christian priesthood:

> With Clement the comparison with Old Testament 'cultual' terminology seems as yet to have been no more than a comparison; archiereús and hiereús are still not applied to the bishop and Christian presbyter as properly pertaining to them. We can reasonably conclude from this that sacerdotal terminology, archiereús, hiereús, sacerdos, was adopted by Christians to describe their hierarchy in the second century, in the subapostolic age, and that it sprang from Old Testament typology.
>   Christians of the subapostolic period nowhere explain why they adopted a terminology with which the New Testament had wished to break, but the texts show us clearly that the idea of priesthood was developed at the same time as that of sacrifice, and in conjunction with it.[143]

From Anglican scholar Richard A. Norris, Jr., on the beginnings of Christian priesthood:

> I Clement (44) ... supports the authority of the official ministry by arguing, first, that it stands in succession to the "apostles",

who not only appointed the first elders and superintendents but also arranged for subsequent succession in their office. This ... is an argument which depends on the identification of the Twelve as "apostles" in the Pauline sense - and on the belief that people like Paul regularly *appointed* elders. Further, though, Clement (40-41) takes the crucial step of likening the ministry of the Church to the priesthood of the Old Covenant. He insists that just as God ordered the old Israel, so he imposes an order on the new *ekklēsia* of Christ.

With Clement and Ignatius, however we see that these same officers [overseers and presbyters] ... are also the leaders of the community's cult and that their cultic activity is conceived in sacerdotal terms. The *Didachē* (14) already describes the Eucharist as "your sacrifice" and speaks ... of prophets as "high priests." Ignatius (Mg. 7:2) for his part speaks of the "one altar" of the Eucharist, suggesting a sacrificial understanding of the rite. It is *I Clement*, however, which is most explicit along these lines. In this work, bishops are spoken of as persons who "have offered the sacrifices" (44:4), and the worship of the Church is described as "cult" (*leitourgein*) which involves "offering" (44. 3-4).

The custom of referring explicitly to the president or bishop as *hiereus* or *sacerdos* appears only in the third century and later. There can be no doubt, however, that from the beginning of the second century the idea was current that one dimension of the office of bishop or presbyter was a priestly and cultic one.What we call "priesthood", then, emerges in the course of the second century as an office of great complexity indeed. [144]

From J. M. R Tillard, OP, on the issue of the 'participation' of ordained ministry in the priesthood of Christ:

La question, déjà difficile à cause des incertitudes sur la validité du vocabulaire sacerdotale pour qualifier le ministère, est encore compliquée par l'emploi du mot *participation*. [Cf. Vatican II doc. *Lumen gentium*, para 10.] ...

Il nous semble donc que l'affirmation conciliaire faisant de l'épiscopat (et des autres ministères) une participation à la consécration et à la mission du Christ exige d'être équilibrée par une théologie attentive à respecter l'unicité absolue du sacerdoce et du sacrifice du Christ. Le Seigneur de la gloire ne donne pas à ses ministres une "participation" à son sacerdoce telle qu'elle impliquerait une addition à sa plénitude et à son unicité. La "participation" - s'il faut employer ce mot - est à comprendre dans une ligne *sacramentelle* et leur pouvoir porte sur la transmission des biens du salut d'une façon *sacramentelle*. L'Esprit qui a saisi Jésus à son baptême dans le Jourdain et l'a ensuite glorifié en consecrant par la Résurrection le don de lui-même sur sa Croix, donne aux ministres de l'Eglise de transmettre les biens du salut en étant "signe et instrument" du Grand Prêtre de l'Alliance Nouvelle.[145]

From Peter Fink, SJ, of the Weston Jesuit School of Theology:

The principal ministry of the ordained, by way of embodiment and mutual iconography, is to activate and thus call forth the priesthood of the church. This is in no way surrogate activity, the ordained acting *in place of* the church, for even in its most token expression all liturgy is the action of the entire church. It is not a kind of exclusive elitism, the ordained going where none can follow. It is just the opposite, an inclusive elitism, if you will, an advance journey *per modum sacramenti* into the future of the church in order to call and advance the church as a whole into that same future.

It is unfortunate that these two manifestations of the priesthood of Christ ['embodiment' and 'mutual iconography'] are frequently taken to be in opposition, as if to elevate one it were necessary to diminish the other. ...

The faithful will never know what their own priesthood is if they never see it embodied for them, nor will they be inclined to embrace and activate that priesthood if no one summons them to do so. Conversely, the ordained will never properly understand, much less fulfill their own ministerial priesthood unless they recognize it as ordered to and educated by that priesthood into which the assembled church is being formed. [146]

Synthesis:

The earliest Christians, most of whom were Jews of Jesus' time, clearly had no need for priests, because they already *had* priests — those in the Jerusalem Temple, who led worship and offered the sacrifices. Moreover, that first generation of Jewish Christians, when they were not worshipping in the Temple, also worshipped God through their union with Jesus in the memorial-type fellowship meals he had led them in. But these meals, which very much involved prayer, did not involve offering sacrifice as such.

The earliest Christians, however, were not anti-priestly. They might have been strongly opposed to the hypocricy of the Scribes and Pharisees, as was Jesus, but they were not opposed to priests [Robinson]. In fact, many of their first converts were Jewish priests. Still, as the early missionaries like Paul and Barnabas claimed more and more Gentile converts, and as the movement in Jerusalem came under challenge from Jewish authorities, they began to distance themselves from the necessity of the sacrificial system, of circumcision, of the ritual ablutions, etc., and ultimately in the generations to come found a satisfying replacement for this (a) in the one high priesthood of Christ, the great theme of the *Epistle to the Hebrews*, where a single new priest succeeds to the multitude of Old Testament priests [Vanhoye], and (b) in the true priestliness of the whole body of the Church, as reflected in *1 Peter* and the *Apocalypse*, but not in the *Epistle to the Hebrews* [Elliott].

But now the Christians, spread throughout the Mediterranean world, began to experience with Nero the start of ten off-again, on-again persecutions of their 'Way'. There were many martyrs; there was great sacrifice of life. Often they huddled in private homes throughout the Mediterranean lands to eat together, memorialize the death of the Lord and remember those among them who had sacrificed their lives as Jesus had for the growth of the Kingdom. And gradually, responding to Paul's admonitions, they began to separate the agape meal from the special thanksgiving prayers thereby creating the possibility of seeing this *eucharistia* as something qualitatively more than a togetherness meal.

Gradually also in the second century, as the New Testament canon begins to come together, Christians in the East begin to take seriously that aforementioned anonymous document called "The Epistle to the Hebrews." Clement of Alexandria and Origin see it as Scripture. But in the West it was only accepted as 'canonical' in the latter part of the fourth century [Osborne]. But then again, no wonder many Christians, especially in the West, were so sceptical. This epistle/sermon challenged them to envision Jesus, the carpenter-layman from the kingly line of David, metaphorically as their High Priest offering up to the Father the sacrifice of himself: Jesus the sole mediator, the once and for all time High Priest, and that according to a pre-Levitical priestly order of Melchizedek, the priest of (Jeru)Salem who offered gifts of bread and wine to Abraham when he arrived in the land of promise. For some it was clearly a fantastic story worthy of being dismissed. None of the other 'canonical' materials about Jesus saw him as a priest, let alone the great High Priest. But the Epistle was beautifully written and well reasoned. So while it did not have much initial impact on the Christian communities, especially in the West, it was still very much around, extant, and Clement of Rome and Polycarp of Smyrna both reflect its message of Jesus Christ as High Priest.

In conjunction with this, the faithful of that early sub-apostolic period were also challenged by *1 Peter* and by the *Apocalypse* to see themselves as a 'priestly' people. This did not imply that each one of them was a priest, but rather that the whole community was/is made up of those who are elect and holy, and to express this fact the community was described, by adopting the covenant formula of *Exodus* 19:6, as a body of priests or a priestly community [Elliott].

It appears, however, that those often persecuted, sub-apostolic Christians were only able to feel comfortable with the Christian use of Old Testament priesthood language after the Jerusalem Temple was destroyed and ceased to function and when the cultic notion of sacrifice began to be coupled in a practical way with their weekly celebration of the Eucharist.

The earliest example of this, if the *Didache* is in fact as first-century early as some claim, shows up in chapter 14 of that text where it is coupled with the prophecy of Malachi: that everywhere "a pure sacrifice" is being offered up to the Lord, and where that which the Christians bring to the Sunday eucharist is spoken of as "your sacrifice"[Murray]. Here also the Christian prophets are called "your high priests." But the "sacrifice" that is spoken of here could simply be, as many have since pointed out, the spiritual sacrifice of one's self and one's prayers of thanksgiving to the Father. To offer that up you would not need an explicitly sacerdotal figure. Nor is there any connection of this "pure sacrifice" with Jesus or the Crucifixion, nor the recognition of Jesus' death as a "sacrifice" as we find, for example, in *1 Corinthians* 5:7: "Christ, our Passover, has been sacrificed." Consequently it would take more time and communal reflection on the material gifts as part of that "sacrifice" before any sacerdotal terminology could be authentically applied to the presider at the Eucharist. In fact, the perception of the president of the Eucharist as an explicitly sacerdotal figure cannot be attested to prior to the beginning of the third century (Hippolytus, Tertullian, Cyprian), but it is clearly attested (Clement, Ignatius, Tertullian, etc.), indeed axiomatic in most cases, that those who preside over the life of the Church preside at the Eucharist [Legrand].

Sacral-cultic language continues to show up in authentic Christian writings throughout the late first and on into the second century. Clement of Rome compares the orderliness of the Temple service of the high priest, priests and Levites with the orderliness over which the presbyter-overseers should preside, they who "in a holy and blameless way have *offered up the gifts*" (ch. 40). It is true he does not apply the terms "highpriest" or "priest" to the overseers or presbyters as properly pertaining to them, but we can reasonably conclude that this sacerdotal terminology was adopted by Christians to describe their hierarchy in the second century and that it sprang from Old Testament typology. The texts also show us clearly that the idea of priesthood was developed at the same time as that of sacrifice and in conjunction with it [Gy].

Ignatius of Antioch speaks of the place where the Eucharist is celebrated as "the altar" or "the sanctuary" (*thusiastérion*). Nonetheless in the few authentic sub-apostolic, non-canonical Christian documents which we have, there are still relatively speaking few examples of priesthood-type language being used — surely a factor that makes this era so difficult to decipher and so incredibly interesting. It seems clear, however, that from the beginning of the second century the idea was current that one dimension among many of the office of overseer or presbyter was a priestly and cultic one [Norris].

Early on it became abundantly clear that, if *Hebrews* is correct and there is only one High Priest, Jesus Christ, then if one could ever imagine a ministering priesthood in Christianity, it would have to be in some way a participation in that priesthood of Christ, just as, if the faithful together form a priestly body, it too must in some way be a participation in that one priesthood of Christ.

The Second Vatican Council of the Roman Catholic Church, which recognizes a ministerial priesthood, states in its *Dogmatic Constitution on the Church* (*Lumen gentium*, no. 10) that both the common priesthood of the faithful and the ministerial priesthood, each in its own way "is a participation in the one priesthood of Christ." There is a danger here, though, that a Christian ministerial priesthood might be seen as adding something to the fullness and uniqueness of Christ's priesthood. Thus it is important to realize that it is the action of the Holy Spirit who gives to the Church's ministers in a sacramental way the capacity to convey the means of salvation by being for the community *a sign and instrument* of the one High Priest [Tillard].

Consequently the principal ministry of the ordained is to activate and call forth the priesthood of all the faithful. Whatever it is that the priest is called upon to do, he can only do it *with* the people of the Church. His act of forgiveness is at the same time a summons to the Church to join him in that forgiveness. His act of offering must be at the same time a summons to the Church to offer itself. The ordained priest stands in the midst of the community with his ministry ordered to those whose own 'Amen' is necessary to complement and complete what he does. In this sense Christ is not out there somewhere but very much among us in the sacramental ministry of the ordained, summoning us to become one with Him in His worship of the Father and in His saving work for the world. We as a community will never know what our own priesthood is unless someone embodies it for us and summons us to activate it. Nor will our minister ever properly understand, much less fulfill his ministerial priesthood, unless he recognizes it as directed toward and educated buy that priesthood into which the whole Church is being formed [Fink].

In the following six chapters, we will be investigating each of the major documents of the Apostolic Fathers and looking in greater detail for their use of sacrificial and sacerdotal language, a use that in the third century would contribute to the large scale sacerdotalizing of Mediterranean Christianity.

46

Notes

[1] Bowe, Barbara Ellen. *A Church in Crisis: Ecclesiology and Paranesis in Clement of Rome*. Minneapolis: Fortress Press (Harvard Dissertations in Religion, 23); 1988. 158 pages.

Brunner, Gerbert. *Die theologische Mitte des Ersten Klemensbriefs*. Frankfurt am Main: Josef Knecht; 1972. 177 pages.

Bumpus, Harold Bertram. *The Christological Awareness of Clement of Rome and Its Sources*. Cambridge, Mass: University Press of Cambridge; 1972. 196 pages.

Fisher, Edmund Warner. *Soteriology in First Clement*. Ann Arbor, MI: Xerox University Microfilms; 1974. [Claremont Graduate School, CA, Ph.D. Religion]

Fuellenbach, John. *An Evaluation of the Recent Theological Discussion of First Clement: The Question of the Primacy of Rome*. S.T.D. thesis, Catholic University of America; 1977. 533 pages.

Published as: *Ecclesiastical Office and the Primacy of Rome: An Evaluation of Recent Theological Discussion of First Clement*. Washington, D.C.: The Catholic University of America Press; 1980. 278 pages.

Jeffers, James Stanley. *Social Foundations of Early Christianity at Rome: The Congregations Behind I Clement and the Shepherd of Hermas*. Thesis (Ph.D. History) *University of California, Irvine; 1988. 344 pages.*

Published as: *Conflict at Rome: Social Order and Hierarchy in Early Christianity*. Minneapolis: Fortress Press; 1991. 215 pages.

[2] Cf. Bibliography: *Clement of Rome*.

[3] Feullenbach, *op. cit.*, p. 130.

[4] *Ibid.*, p. 145.

[5] *Ibid.*, p. 146.

[6] *Ibid.*, pp. 135-136.

[7] Bowe, *op. cit.*, p. 23.

[8] *Ibid.*, p. 145.

[9] *Ibid.*, p. 146.

[10] Jean Colson. *Clément de Rome*. Paris: Les éditions ouvrières; 1960: p. 20.

[11] Ray R. Noll. "The Search for a Christian Ministerial Priesthood in 1 Clement." *Studia Patristica* 13(=TU 116 [1975]): p. 252.

[12] Note the comment of Jean-Paul Audet that "Clement never used the sacral term *hiereis* to designate the presbyter-bishops. On the contrary, *hiereis* is used once for the 'priests' of the Egyptian religion (25:5) and twice for the 'priests' of the levitical order (32:2; 40:5). And *arkhiereus* is used twice for the levitical 'high priest' (40:5; 41:2), and three times for Jesus himself in his state of glory with the Father (36:1; 61:3; 64). It is also significant, on the other hand, that Jesus 'priesthood' here seems to be placed in the line of the 'order of Aaron' rather than in any prolonging of the 'order of Melchizedek' (this latter is not named; 32:2 mentions Levi with such evident favour that he appears to have priority over Judah; Clement may be further suggesting a levitical descent for Jesus;

compare Heb 7:1-28)." *Structures of Christian Priesthood*, p. 126. See also R. Murray. "Christianity's 'Yes' to Priesthood." Ed by N. Lash & J Rhymer. London: Darton, Longman & Todd; 1979: pp. 33-34.

[13] Bumpus, *op, cit.*, p. 173.

[14] *Ibid.*, pp. 62ff., 126ff.

[15] Fisher, *op. cit.*, p. 198.

[16] Brunner, *op. cit.*, p. 110 ff., 152.

[17] *Ibid.*, p. 148.

[18] *Ibid.*, p. 146, note 19.

[19] *Ibid.*, p. 58.

[20] Kirsopp Lake. *The Apostolic Fathers, I.* (Loeb Classical Library) New York: Macmillan Co.; 1912: p. 85.

[21] J.B. Lightfoot. *The Apostolic Fathers.* Grand Rapids: Baker Book House; 1967 (reprinted from the 1891 Macmillan edition): p. 32.

[22] Robert M. Grant and Holt H. Graham. *The Apostolic Fathers: A New Translation and Commentary, Volume 2, First and Second Clement.* New York: Thomas Nelson & Sons; 1965: p. 74.

[23] *Ibid.*, p. 120.

[24] *Ibid.*, p. 158.

[25] *Ibid.*, p. 158.

[26] *Ibid.*, p. 162.

[27] *Ibid.*, pp. 150-151.

[28] Fuellenbach, *op. cit.*, p. 100.

[29] E.g. John H. Elliott. *A Home for the Homeless: A Sociological Exegesis of 1 Peter, Its Situation and Strategy.* Philadelphia: Fortress Press; 1981.

[30] Bruce J. Malina. *The New Testament World: Insights from Cultural Anthropology.*

Atlanta: John Knox Press; 1981; also: *Christian Origins and Cultural Anthropology: Practical Models for Biblical Interpretation.* Atlanta: John Knox Press; 1986.

[31] Jeffers. *Conflict At Rome...*, p. 2. In addition to Jeffers work, we should mention here also two fine recent works on Christianity in ancient Rome, both of which are much wider in focus than Jeffers' analysis, but which do treat *1 Clement* and the *Shepherd* briefly among many other texts:

Peter Lampe. *Die stadtrömischen Christen in den ersten beiden Jahrhunderten.* Tübingen: J.C.B. Mohr (Paul Siebeck); 1987 [English translation forthcoming from Fortress Press] and

Michael Mullins. *Called to be Saints: Christian Living in First-Century Rome.* Dublin: Veritas Publications; 1991.

Neither of these texts, however, deal with our problematic.

[32] *Ibid.*, p. 125.

[33] *Ibid.*, p. 141-142.

[34] *Ibid.*, p. 142.

48

35 *Ibid.*, p. 178-179.
36 Thomas J. Herron. "The Most Probable Date of the First Epistle of Clement to the Corinthians." *Studia Patristica* ed by E. Livingstone; 1988; 21: 107.
37 G. Edmundson. *The Church in Rome in the First Century* (1913): p. 203ff, quoted by Herron, p. 107.
38 A.E. Wilhelm-Hooijbergh, *op. cit.*, pp. 266-288.
39 J.A.T. Robinson, *Redating the New Testament* (1976): pp. 312-335. Note that Herron agrees with the position of Raymond E. Brown (*The Churches the Apostles Left Behind*, p. 14) that Robinsons's view is too broad for the whole New Testament to be dated before 70 A.D. without, however, discounting Robinson's arguments on behalf of an earlier dating of *1 Clement* (cf. Herron, p. 120, footnote 41).
40 L.L. Welborn. "On the Date of First Clement." *Journal of the Chicago Society of Biblical Research.* XXIX (1984): p. 41.
41 Cf. Brunner, *op. cit.*, pp. 101-102; Jeffers, *op. cit.*, pp. 90-94.
42 Bowe, *op. cit.*, pp. 2-3.
43 Fuellenbach, *op. cit.*, p. 22.
44 Herron, *op. cit.*, p. 121.
45 *Ibid.*, p. 120.
46 A. Jaubert, *Clément de Rome. Épître aux Corinthiens* (SC 167). Paris: Éditions du Cerf; 1971: p. 30.
47 Edmundson, *op. cit.*, p. 199.
48 Robinson, *op. cit.*, p. 333.
49 Herron, *op. cit.*, p. 117.
50 R. Weijenbourg, O.F.M. *Les Lettres d'Ignace d'Antioche: Étude de critique littéraire et de théologie.* Leiden: E.J. Brill; 1969.
W. R. Schoedel. *Ignatius of Antioch: A Commentary on the Letters of Ignatius of Antioch.* Edited by Helmut Koester. Philadelphia: Fortress Press; 1985.
W. Bauer and H. Paulsen. *Die Briefe des Ignatius von Antiochia und der Polykarpbrief. (Handbuch zum Neuen Testament,* ed. H. Lietzmann, Ergängungs-Band, *Die Apostolischen Väter, 2)* Tübingen: J.C.B. Mohr (Paul Siebeck); 1985.
R. Joly. *Le dossier d'Ignace d'Antioche.* Bruxelles: Éditions de l'Université de Bruxelles, Université libre de Bruxelles, Faculté de philosophie et lettres; 1979.
J. Ruis-Camps. *The Four Authentic Letters of Ignatius, The Martyr.* (Orientalia Christiana Analecta, 213) Roma: Pontificium Institutum Orientalium Studiorum; 1980.
H. Paulsen. *Studien zur Theologie des Ignatius von Antiochien.* Göttingen: Vandenhoeck & Ruprecht; 1978.
C. Trevett. *A Study of Ignatius of Antioch in Syria and Asia.* (Studies in the Bible and Early Christianity, Vol. 29) Lewiston: The Edwin Mellen Press; 1992.
51 See articles after 1970 in Bibliography: *Ignatius of Antioch.*
52 Schoedel, *op. cit.*, p. 5.
53 Rius-Camps, *op. cit.*, p. 302.
54 *Ibid.*, p. 181.
55 *Ibid.*, p. 298.

[56] *Ibid.*, p. 299.

[57] *Ibid.*, p. 163.

[58] C. P. Hammond Bammel. "Ignatian Problems," *Journal of Theological Studies*, N.S., 33/1; April, 1982: p. 67.

[59] The Jesuit patrologist, Charles Kannengiesser, however, had kind words to say about his methodology. Ref., *Recherches de science religieuse*, 67/4 (1979); p. 604.

[60] Bammel, pp. 68-69.

[61] Joly, *op. cit.*

[62] *Ibid.*, p. 26.

[63] Schoedel, *op. cit.*, p. 6.

[64] Bammel, p. 79.

[65] Justin Martyr does use this term, but only in the genitive. Ref., G. Pelland, S.J., "'Le dossier des Lettres d'Ignace d'Antioche': À propos d'un livre récent," *Science et Esprit*, 32/3 (1980); p. 287-288.

[66] Bammel, pp. 73-74.

[67] See Charles Munier, "À propos d'Ignace d'Antioche," *Revue des sciences religieuses*, 54/1, Jan 1980; pp. 55-73.

[68] Pelland, *loc. cit.*, pp. 296-297.

[69] Trevett, *op. cit.*, pp. 14-15.

[70] Note that S. Davies makes a strong case for a 113 C.E. dating of the Letters in "The Predicament of Ignatius of Antioch." *Vigiliae Christianae* 30 (1976): pp. 175-180.

[71] J.B. Lightfoot. *The Apostolic Fathers*, Part 2: *S. Ignatius, S. Polycarp* London: Macmillan, 1885, 2nd ed. 1889; Vol. I: p. 381.

[72] There is really no doubt that *thusiastérion* is sacrificial language dealing with either the space or place where (Levitical) priests offer sacrifice, thus to some extent it is also sacerdotal language. The issue, of course, is what Ignatius intended when he used the term and then how can we best get at that. It is a difficult call. Corwin and others have shown us how enormously sacral-cultic the Mediterranean world of the first and second century actually was. The term in Ignatius could have carried some strong sacral-cultic overtones; he certainly seems preoccupied (at least in his letter to the Romans) with the sacrificial dimensions of his impending martyrdom. On the other hand, his use of the term could have been completely symbolic, simply metaphoric. A respected friend to me and many, the late Cyril Richardson of Union Theological in New York saw it in the latter way:

"In Ignatius there is no clear evidence that he considers the Eucharist as a sacrificial rite – indeed he never even alludes to the death of Christ as a sacrifice. ... Hence the antecedent probability is that his use of *thusiastérion* has little to do with any sacrifice of Christ. *Thusiastérion* is a Hebrew, not a Greek, word. It is not found outside the Septuagint and Jewish and Christian writers. In order to prevent a confusion of Jewish with heathen sacrifices, the Septuagint purposely never uses *bōmós*, though the words are interchangeable in Philo.

Whatever may be the truth about the connection of the practice of the sacrificial cult with the theories of its origin, it is plain that the centre of heathen and Jewish religion was sacrifice. Particularly with the Jews was the unity of this worship established around one altar, and this centralizing influence of the altar in Judaism impressed itself upon the early Church (I Clem. 41.2). It is probably in this sense that Ignatius uses the term. ... By the altar he means the visible centre of Christian worship and fellowship, as the bishop is its personal centre. Around the bishop and the one recognized place of meeting is established the unity of the Christian Church. So he sums up in Phil. 4.1, 'One loaf, one cup, one Church, one bishop.' 'Altar' is thus a metaphor for the Church... . This seems clear from Tral. 7.2 and Eph. 5.2 where it signifies a place in which the Christian worshippers assemble. If they are outside the Church they lack the bread of God (Eph. 5.2); it is perhaps noteworthy that they do not lack the flesh of Christ, which we would expect if the idea of the sacrifice of the Eucharist were uppermost in the mind of Ignatius." C.C. Richardson. *The Christianity of Ignatius of Antioch.* New York: Columbia University Press, 1935, pp. 101-102.

73 Paulsen, *op. cit.*, p. 156.

74 Trevett, *op. cit.*, p. 119.

75 Tugwell, Simon, O.P. *The Apostolic Fathers.* Harrisburg: Morehouse Publishing; 1990:p. 129.

76 Schoedel, W. R. *The Apostolic Fathers - Volume 5: Polycarp, Martyrdom of Polycarp, Fragments of Papias.* Camden: Thomas Nelson & Sons; 1967. Also: "Polycarp's Witness to Ignatius of Antioch." *Vigiliae Christianae* 41(1);1987: pp. 1-10.

77 Dehandschutter, Boudewijn. "Polycarp's Epistle to the Philippians: An Early Example of 'Reception'." *The New Testament in Early Christianity* (ed. J.-M. Sevrin). Leuven: Leuven University Press; 1989: pp. 275-291. See, also, his "Le Martyre de Polycarp et le développment de la conception du martyre au deuxieme siècle." *Studia Patristica* 17(2); 1982: pp. 659-668.

78 Prigent, Pierre. *Épitre de Barnabé.* Sources Chrétiennes, No. 172. With Greek text established and presented by Robert A. Kraft. Paris: Les Éditions du Cerf; 1971.

Soffritti, O. *La lettera di Barnaba.* Alba: Edizioni paoline; 1974. 132 pages.

Wengst, Klaus. *Tradition und Theologie des Barnabasbriefes.* Berlin: De Gruyter; 1971. Habilitationsschrift - Bonn.

79 Refer to Bibliography: *Barnabas.*

80 I have not been able to access these two latter texts.

81 Brox, Norbert. *Der Hirt des Hermas. (Kommentar zu den Apostolischen Vätern, Siebenter Band)* Göttingen: Vandenhoeck & Ruprecht; 1991. 589 pages.

Haas, C. *De Geest Bewaren: Achtergrond en functie van de pneumatologie in de paranaese van de Pastor van Hermas.* 's-Gravenshage: Boekencentrum; 1985. 361 pages. Summary in English. [title means: Keep (yourselves) in the Spirit: Background and Function of Pneumatology in the Paranesis of the Shepherd of Hermas.]

Hellholm, David. *Das Visionenbuch des Hermas als Apokalypse: Formgeschichtliche und texttheoretische Studien zu einer literarischen Gattung. Vol. I: Methodologische Vorüberlegungen und makrostrukturelle Textanalyse.* (Coniectanea Biblica: New Testament Series 13:1) Lund: CWK Gleerup; 1980. 211 pages.

Hilhorst, A. *Sémitismes et latinismes dans le Pasteur d'Hermas.* Nijmegen: Dekker & Van de Vegt; 1976. 208 pages.

Jardine, William. *The Shepherd of Hermas: The Gentle Apocalypse*. Redwood City, CA: Proteus Publishing ; 1992. 159 pages.

Jeffers, James S. *Conflict at Rome: Social Order and Hierarchy in Early Christianity*. Minneapolis: Fortress Press; 1991. 215 pages.

Leutzsch, Martin. *Die Wahrnehmung sozialer Wirklichkeit im "Hirten des Hermas"*. Göttingen: Vandenhoeck & Ruprecht; 1989. 286 pages.

Maier, Harry O. *The Social Setting of the Ministry as Reflected in the Writings of Hermas, Clement and Ignatius*. Waterloo (Ontario): Wilfrid Laurier University Press; 1991. 230 pages.

Osiek, Carolyn. *Rich and Poor in the Shepherd of Hermas*. Washington, D.C.: Catholic Biblical Quarterly Monograph Series, Vol. 15; 1983. 184 pages.

Reiling, J. *Hermas and Christian Prophecy: A Study of the Eleventh Mandate*. Supplement 37 to *Novum Testamentum*. Leiden: E.J. Brill; 1973. 197 pages.

[82] Davidson, James Edwin. *Spiritual Gifts in the Roman Church: I Clement, Hermas and Justin Martyr*. Ph.D. Thesis - University of Iowa. (On microfilm) Ann Arbor, MI: University Microfilms International; 1981. 201 pages.

Gollar, Walker Lyddane. *The Shepherd of Hermas and the Gospel of Truth of Valentinus: Two Early Christian Perspectives on Salvation*. Dayton, OH: Thesis (M.A. in Religious Studies) – University of Dayton; 1983. 82 pages.

Jeffers, James S. *Social Foundations of Early Christianity at Rome: The Congregations Behind I Clement and the Shepherd of Hermas*. Ph.D. Thesis. University of California – Irvine; 1988. 355 pages.

Moyo, Ambrose. *Angels and Christology in the Shepherd of Hermas*. Ph.D. Thesis - Harvard University; 1978. 214 pages.

Nijendijk, Lambertus Wilhelmus. *Die Christologie des Hirten des Hermas: exegetisch, religions- und dogmengeschlichlich untersucht = De Christologie van de Herder van Hermas: een exegetische, godsdienst- en dogmen-historische studie*. Utrecht: Th.D. Thesis – Rijksuniversiteit te Utrecht; 1986. 239 pages.

Smith, Martha Montague. *Feminine Images in the Shepherd of Hermas*. Ph. D. Thesis – Duke University; 1979. 229 pages.

Strock. A. Wallace. *The Shepherd of Hermas: A Study of his Anthropology as seen in the Tension between Dipsychia and Hamartia*. Ph.D. Thesis – Emory University; 1984. 289 pages.

White, John Carroll. *The Interaction of Language and World in the Shepherd of Hermas*. Ph.D. Thesis – Temple University; 1973. 241 pages.

Wilson, John Christian. *Toward a Reassessment of the Milieu of the Shepherd of Hermas: Its Date and Its Pneumatology*. Ph.D. Thesis – Duke University; 1977. 302 pages.

[83] Cf. Bibliography: *The Shepherd of Hermas* here and a still broader one in N. Brox, *Der Hirt des Hermas*, pp. 554-576.

[84] Brox, *op. cit.*, p. 533.

[85] *Ibid.*

[86] *Ibid.*, p. 535.

[87] *Ibid.*, p. 536.

52

88 In addition to this text (Washington, D.C.: The Catholic Biblical Quarterly Monograph Series, 15; 1983) see also: "The Genre and Function of the Shepherd of Hermas," *Semeia: An Experimental Journal for Biblical Criticism.* 1986; 36: 113-121; "Rich and Poor in the Shepherd of Hermas," *Harvard Theological Review.* 1978; 71: 322-323; "The Second Century Through the Eyes of Hermas: Continuity and Change," *Biblical Theology Bulletin.* Fall 1990; 20: pp. 116-122; "Wealth and Poverty in the Shepherd of Hermas," *Studia Patristica.* Ed by E Livingstone. 1982; 17(2): 725-730.

90 In addition to this text (*op. cit.*, note 81) see also: *Social Foundations of Early Christianity at Rome: The Congregations Behind I Clement and the Shepherd of Hermas.* UC-Irvine - Ph.D. thesis; 1988. 355 pages; "The Influence of the Roman Family and Social Structures on Early Christianity in Rome." *Proceedings: Society of Biblical Literature*; 1988: pp. 370-384; "Pluralism in Early Roman Christianity." *Fides et Historia*; 1990: 22: pp. 4-17.

89 See note 81 for bibliographical information.

91 See also note 81 for same.

92 Maier, *op. cit.*, p. 59. Also, Osiek: "I would maintain that the purpose of *The Shepherd of Hermas* is neither the proclamation of a second repentance nor the opportunity to perpetuate moralization in apocalyptic garb, but the translation of eschatological vision into realistic terms." in "The Genre and Function ..." *Semeia* (1986) 36: p. 119.

93 "The Second Century Through the Eyes of Hermas..." *Biblical Theology Bulletin* (1990) 20(3): p. 118.

94 *Ibid.*, p. 119.

95 Jeffers, *Conflict at Rome ...*, p. 195.

96 *Ibid.*, p. 143.

97 *Ibid.*, p. 177.

98 *Ibid.*

99 *Ibid.*, p. 178.

100 Cf. J. Reiling, *op. cit.*, chapter 3, pp. 27-57.

101 The text of the Muratorian Canon can be found in L. Duchesne, *Le Liber Pontificialis*, Paris: Cyrille Vogel; 1886-1892, 1:132. See an excellent discussion of these connections in Jeffers, *Conflict at Rome ...*, p. 107 ff.

102 Maier, *op. cit.*, p. 55. See, also, Simon Tugwell, O.P. *The Apostolic Fathers.* Harrisburg PA: Morehouse Publishing; 1990: p. 63.

103 W. Coleborne, "The Shepherd of Hermas: A Case for Multiple Authorship and Some Implications." *Studia Patristica* 10(2); 1970: pp. 65-70.

104 S. Giet. *Hermas at les Pasteurs: Les trois auteurs du Pasteur d'Hermas,* Paris: Presses Universitaires de France; 1963.

105 C. Osiek, *Rich and Poor in the Shepherd of Hermas.* Washington, D.C.: The Catholic Biblical Quarterly Monograph Series, No. 15; 1983.

106 A. Carlini, "La tradizione manoscritta del Pastor di Hermas e il problema dell'unità di composizione dell'opera," in: *Festschrift zum 100 jährigen Bestehen der Papyrussammlung der Österreichischen Nationalbibliothek.* Papyrus Rainer; Wien; 1933: pp. 29-37; also "P. Michigan 130 (Inv 44-H) e il problema dell'unicità di redazione del

Pastore di Erma." *ParPass* 38; 1983: pp. 29-37.

[107] M. Dibelius. *Der Hirt des Hermas*. Tübingen: 1923.

[108] W.J Wilson, "The Career of the Prophet Hermas," *Harvard Theological Review*. 1927; 20: pp. 21-62.

[109] A. Harnack. *Geschichte der altchristlichen Literatur bis Eusebius* I/1. Leipzig: 1893. Nachdruk 1958; pp. 49-58.

[110] R. Joly. *Hermas le Pasteur*. Paris: Éditions du Cerf; 1958.

[111] J. Reiling. *Hermas and Christian Prophecy: A Study of the Eleventh Mandate.* Leiden: E.J. Brill; 1973: p. 24.

[112] A. Hilhorst. *Sémetismes et latinismes dans le Pasteur d'Hermas.* Nijmegen: Dekker & Van de Vegt; 1976: pp. 19-31.

[113] M. Leutzsch. *Die Wahrnehmung sozialer Wirklichkeit im "Hirten des Hermas".* Göttingen: Vandenhoeck & Ruprecht; 1989: pp. 23-31.

[114] N. Brox. *Der Hirt des Hermas*. Göttingen: Vandenhoeck & Ruprecht; 1991: pp. 15-33.

[115] W. Rordorf and A. Tuilier. *La Doctrine des douze apôtres (Didache).* Sources Chrétiennes, No. 248. Paris: Éditions du Cerf; 1978. 221 pages.

[116] K. Niederwimmer. *Die Didache*. Kommentar zu den Apostolischen Väter, Erster Band. Göttingen: Vandenhoeck & Ruprecht; 1989. 329 pages.

G. Schöllgen. *Didache: Zwölf-Apostle-Lehre*. (Also: W. Geerlings. *Traditio Apostolica: Apostolische Überlieferung.*) Freiburg: Herder; 1991. 358 pages.

[117] B.S. Walters (ed.). *Didach'e - Didache ton Dodeka Apostolon: The Unknown Teaching of the Twelve Apostles*. San Jose CA: Ante-Nicene Archive; 1991. 224 pages. This text is not presently available to me.

[118] S. Giet. *L'énigme de la Didachè*. Paris: Les Éditions Ophrys; 1970. 283 pages.

C.N. Jefford. *The Sayings of Jesus in the Teaching of the Twelve Apostles.* Leiden: E.J. Brill; 1989. 185 pages.

[119] See Bibliography: *The Didache*.

[120] Professeur Giet was on the way to deliver his final lecture on "L'énigme de la Didachè" on April 2, 1968, when he had a massive heart attack and died.

[121] Jefford introduces his text with a superbly compact survey of French, German and British/American *Didache* research from the publication of the Bryennios text up to 1989.

[122] W. Rordorf & A. Tuilier, *op. cit.*, p. 70. On this treatment of *thusía* in the *Didache*, Rordorf adds (pp. 71-72):"mais, comme l'a justement noté R.R. Noll, le langage sacrificiel des Pères apostolique, et spécialment celui de la *Didachè*, devait exercer, sans le vouloir, une influence certain sur les conceptions liturgique et ministérielle de la théologie postérieure." (R.R. Noll, *On the Origins of Ministerial Priesthood: Studies in the Primary Documents of the Apostolic Fathers* [Thèse 3e cycle, Université de Strasbourg, 1970, pp. 215-272.] L'auteur présente une étude approfondie et nuancée des passages en question.").

[123] Niederwimmer, *op. cit*, p. 237.

[124] Schöllgen, *op. cit.*, p. 70.

54

[125] Niederwimmer, p. 232.

[126] A. deHallieux. "Les ministères dans la Didachè." Irenikon; 1980; 53:19.

[127] Rordorf/Tuiliers, p. 73.

[128] Niederwimmer, pp. 242-243.

[129] Schöllgen, p. 73.

[130] See, e.g., J.B. Lightfoot. The Apostolic Fathers. London: Macmillan & Co.; 1912: p. 215. Also Robert Grant. The Apostolic Fathers: An Introduction. New York: Thomas Nelson & Sons; 1964: pp. 160-173.

[131] See, among others, Aaron Milavec, "The Pastoral Genius of the Didache: An Analytical Translation and Commentary." Religious Writings and Religious Systems. Ed. by J. Neusner. 1989; 2: p. 119.

[132] See C. Jefford, op. cit., p. 127. He notes here also that "the marked change of address from the second person singular to the second person plural, which also is divided roughly along chapter divisions, might be understood as the difference between materials that were addressed to individual candidates for baptism and materials that were addressed to the presbyters as a group."Cf., also, C.N. Jefford, "Presbyters in the Community of the Didache." Studia Patristica 21; 122-128.

[133] Rordorf/Tuilier, pp. 45-46.

[134] Jefford, op. cit., p. 140.

[135] Cf. Rordorf/Tuilier,pp.96-99; Niederwimmer, pp.78-80; Schöllgen,pp.82-85; Jefford, pp. 18-19.

[136] For bibliographical information on these authors' texts and on the texts and articles which follow, consult the General bibliography: Christian Priesthood and the History of Ministry.

[137] J.A.T Robinson. "Christianity's 'No' to Priesthood." The Christian Priesthood. Ed by N. Lash and J Rhymer. London: Darton, Longman & Todd; 1970: pp. 6-7; 12.

[138] A. Vanhoye, S.J. Old Testament Priests and the New Priest : According to the New Testament. Peterham, MA: St. Bede's Publications; 1986: 312-313.

[139] K. B. Osborne, O.F.M. Priesthood: A History of Ordained Ministry in the Roman Catholic Church. New York: Paulist Press; 1988: p. 27.

[140] J.H. Elliott. The Elect and the Holy: An Exegetical Examination of I Peter 2: 4-10 and the Phrase 'Basíleion hieráteuma'. Leiden: E. J. Brill; 1966: p. 223..

[141] R. Murray, S.J. "Christianity's 'Yes' to Priesthood." The Christian Priesthood. Ed by N. Lash and J. Rhymer. London: Darton, Longman & Todd; 1970: p. 30.

[142] H.-M. Legrand. "The Presidency of the Eucharist According to the Ancient Tradition." Worship; 1979; 53: p. 427. E. Schillebeeckx also makes this point regularly throughout his book Ministry: Leadership in the Community of Jesus Christ. New York: Crossroad ; 1981.

[143] P.M. Gy, O.P. "Notes on the Early Terminology of Christian Priesthood." The Sacrament of Holy Orders. Collegeville, MN: The Liturgical Press; 1962: pp. 113-114.

[144] R. A. Norris, Jr. "The Beginnings of Christian Priesthood." Anglican Theological Review, Supplementary Series: 9; 1984: pp. 25-26.

[145] J. M. R. Tillard, O.P. "Ministère ordonné et sacerdoce du Christ" Irénikon;

1976; 49: pp. 148, 161-162. See also on this issue the thorough article by Philip Rosato, S.J., "Priesthood of the Baptized and Priesthood of the Ordained: Complementary Approaches to Their Interrelation." *Gregorianum* 68, 1-2 (1987): pp. 215-266.

[146] P. E. Fink, S.J. "The Sacrament of Orders: Some Liturgical Reflections." *Worship*; 1982; 56: pp. 492-493.

CHAPTER III

CLEMENT OF ROME

OUTLINE

A. *1 Clement:* Date, Occasion, Style, Ministerial Framework
B. Structure and Rhetorical Devices
C. The Four Analogies in Paragraphs 37-44
D. The Problem of *prosenegkóntas tà dôra* in 44:4
E. Conclusion

A. DATE, OCCASION, STYLE AND MINISTERIAL FRAMEWORK

The *First*[1] *Epistle of Clement to the Corinthians (1 Clement)* was written according to the general consensus of scholars in 95 or 96 A.D.[2] and addressed "to the Church of God which sojourns at Corinth" from "the Church of God sojourning at Rome". Although Clement's name is never mentioned in the letter, his authorship of it never seems to have been doubted in antiquity, and Eusebius and Jerome state explicitly that it came from Clement. It is, in fact, the earliest piece of Christian literature outside the New Testament for which the name of the author, place and date are historically attested.[3] Unfortunately the letter tells us nothing at all about the Church order at Rome when it was dispatched[4] and only a moderate amount about the contemporary ministerial setup at Corinth. "One or two" arrogant and impudent individuals have rebelled against the Corinthian Church leaders and deposed them. By far the greater part of the community was drawn into this "unholy and detestable schism", which was a scandal even to their pagan neighbors. That Clement's endeavor to restore order was successful seems clear from a statement made by a later bishop of Corinth, Dionysius, in a letter to Pope Soter (about 170 C.E.), that Clement's epistle, together with Soter's own letter, was being read at Church assemblies.[5]

Catholics are sometimes inclined to see in this epistle an actual proof of their belief that even at this early date the bishop of Rome was regarded as the head of the universal Church. There is, however, no explicit expression in the letter of such a primacy.[6]

Clement's theology, often cast in Stoic-Hellenistic thought patterns, has a specific Jewish thrust and reveals what J. Colson in his book *Clement de Rome* (Paris, 1960) calls a "mentalité levitique". The rather lengthy quotations from the Old Testament, which do not always tally with our standard text of the Septuagint (LXX),[7] and the comparatively few New Testament references have led some authors to the conclusion that Clement was most likely of Jewish descent.[8] Whatever the case, he was certainly familiar with the principal letters of Paul as well as the *Epistle to the Hebrews* and repeats practically verbatim from *1 Corinthians* Paul's earlier exhortations to humility (cf. para. 47), his image of the body and its members (para. 13), and his praise of charity (para. 49).[9]

Church leadership at Corinth, as given in *1 Clement,* was exercised by a college of *presbyter-epískopoi* with deacons at their side.[10] The various expressions for the Church leaders (*hēgouménoi, presbýteroi, epískopoi*) show that the terminology is still quite unfixed and that the actual boundaries of their areas of competence have been in flux.[11] Still the generally interchangeable terms *presbýteroi* and *epískopoi* are not exactly the same. The latter is here, as in general everywhere else, a term of ministry, a particular job and function, the ones who have the "supervision" *(episkopè)*. With the term *presbyter,* on the other hand, the dividing line between ministerial and patriarchal authority is rather fluid. He can be taken under the ministerial term *presbyter* (e.g. 54:4; 57:1) but he can also be seen as worthy of respect simply as *elder* (e.g. 1:3; 21:5), and the two more or less run together.[12] It seems indeed that for Clement *presbyters* are generally all those who in some way or other hold authority in the Church of Corinth (cf. 47:6; 54:2; 57:1).[13] The letter itself makes no mention of a monarchical bishop (*ho epískopos*) either at Rome or at Corinth[14], but only that of a collegial responsibility for the leadership of the service and the life of the community.[15] G. Konidaris explains clearly the reason for this. At Antioch, the center of missionary activity in the early Church, there emerged, for any number of organizational or practical reasons, a fixed leader from among the presbyterial college. He was given the title *ho epískopos.* By 100 A.D. this structure had already spread widely throughout East and West Asia Minor. In Rome and throughout the West, it was true, the presbyters were often called *epískopoi,* but the singular seems to have been carefully reserved for the Lord. "Gott allein wird *ho epískopos* genannt." Thus Clement quite humbly in his magnificent prayer of paragraph 59 speaks to the Lord as "the Creator and overseer of every spirit" (*ton pantòs pneúmatos ktísten kaì epískopon*). Consequently it is no surprise that Clement does not call himself nor anyone else at Rome *ho epískopos.* This reserve appears to have lasted in the West down to the time of Irenaeus who uses the term *presbýteros* three times for the bishops of Rome.[16]

B. STRUCTURE AND RHETORICAL DEVICES

There can be little doubt in the mind of anyone who makes even a scant reading of Clement's letter that he is very much preoccupied, enamored if you will, with the idea of order and peace in the Christian community. He has drawn on all his literary and rhetorical talents to produce a text with such a unity of style and thought that individual passages, and especially those bearing on the ministry, can hardly be understood without a clear awareness of the letter's structure as well as of the often highly embellished rhetorical devices which he employs.

We turn first to the structure of the letter. This consists roughly of an introduction (paragraphs 1-2), two main parts (3-36 and 37-61) and a recapitulation (62-65). The first main part could probably best be seen as a homily to the entire congregation on the effects that jealousy and envy have had in the history of the Old and New Covenants.

> He launches into a comprehensive survey of ancient Jewish and contemporary Christian history to show that all disturbances in the past were due to "jealousy and envy," while all blessings ever were, and always will be, attendant upon the preservation of peace and concord among men, and, above all, upon submission to authority. Order, he holds, is the expression of the will of God; disorder, the seed sown by the Prince of this world. This is the theme of Part I (3-36).[17]

The predominant rhetorical device in this part is the *example.* In fact, the whole letter up to the end of paragraph 32 consists of one long series of examples broken up by rather lengthy Old Testament quotations. As "examples from antiquity" of how jealousy and envy have wreaked their havoc in mankind, he cites the cases of: Cain and Abel, Joseph and Esau, Moses and the Pharaoh, Aaron and Miriam, Dathan and Abiron, David and Saul (4-5); "noble examples of our own generation" are for Clement the sufferings of Peter, Paul, Danaids and Dircae (5-6).[18] Another rhetorical device used in this first part is *typology*. In 12:7 the scarlet cord of Rahab is taken as a type of "the Blood of the Lord", and in 24-25 day and night, the crops and the mythical phoenix are given as types of the Christian's resurrection. Clement rounds off his collection of examples, types and Old Testament citations with a striking passage that reminds one of the writings of Martin Luther:

> Consequently, all were honored and made great, not through themselves or their own works or the holy lives they led, but through His will. So we, too, who have been called by His will in Christ Jesus, are sanctified not through ourselves, or through our wisdom or understanding or piety or any works we perform in holiness of heart, but through faith by which Almighty God has sanctified all men from the beginning of time. To Him be the glory forever and ever more. Amen. (32:3-4)

The first part then concludes with four paragraphs of paranesis and more or less general admonitions to the Christians (33-36).

The second main part (37-61) is directed towards the specific disorders at Corinth. Here the author's theme is the "rule of service" (41:1)[19] which leads to that peace and order which should exist in the Christian community. In the first eight paragraphs of this section (37-44) — where most of the material relevant to our discussion is found — Clement makes a subtle change in his use of rhetorical devices. Whereas he had previously been working with independent examples, Bible quotations and occasional typology, he now switches to four admonitory analogies. Still within the context of these analogies — and this is what complicates things considerably — he continues using examples but now as supports for and embellishments of the analogies. It is here, I believe, that most of the misinterpretations of Clement occur, namely when an example whose whole *raison d'être* is simply to develop a particular analogy is taken out of context and treated as a totally independent example.[20] That Clement up to this point has been working almost exclusively with independent examples naturally only increases the tendency to do this. A further complicating factor is that Clement's analogies are developed as admonitions and this admonitory tone permeates everything that has to do with the analogies including, of course, the examples.

Since in reading the text it is quite easy to lose sight of precisely what is being likened to what, I should like to list the analogies as clearly as possible, for within the framework of these four analogies, as we have said, lies most of what Clement wished to reveal of his own thought on the ministry.

1. We, the army of Christ, ought to be able to be likened to the imperial army. (37:1 4)
2. We, the body of Christ, ought to be able to be likened to the human body. (37:5 -38:1)
3. The orderliness in which our Christian communities should serve God ought to be able to be likened to the orderliness that existed in Israel's service of the Lord. (40 & 41)
4. The action of "our Apostles" who "also knew ... that there would be strife on account of the office of the episcopacy" to forgo such a disorder ought to be likened to the action of Moses when "the priesthood had become an object of jealousy and the tribes were quarrelling as to which of them had been honored with that glorious dignity." (43 & 44)

Paragraph 45 brings a return to Old Testament examples. Clement speaks of the kind of people who would treat unjustly "men who were serving God with holy and irreproachable steadfastness", those who, for example, would throw Daniel into the lion's den or Ananias, Azarias and Misael into the fiery furnace. Such "hateful men and scum of the earth" are first admonished with the words of Jesus about those who give scandal (46), then with the example of Paul's earlier handling of factiousness at Corinth (47), and finally with an Old Testament quotation urging observance of the Law (48), all of which he concludes on a very positive note with his own description of what a genuine Christian should be:

> Let a man be a man of faith, let him be able to utter knowledge, let him be wise in the discernment of arguments, let him be pure in conduct; surely he must think all the less of himself, the higher he apparently ranks, and seek the common good and not his personal advantage. (48:5-6)

Clement follows this up with a brief, very beautiful homily on love

(49-53), again abundantly sprinkled with Old Testament quotes, to which he immediately appends his solution for the Corinthian crisis:

> Now then, who among you is noble, who is compassionate, who is full of charity? Let him say, "If I am the cause of sedition and strife and schism, then I depart; I go wherever you wish; I do whatever the majority enjoins; only let the flock of Christ have peace with the appointed presbyters." (54:1-2)

This he supports with examples of people willing to sacrifice themselves for the common good both "from the heathens" and from the Old Testament: Judith and Esther (55). After another long Bible passage, he reiterates his solution for the crisis reinforcing it with a quote from the Book of Wisdom (57). Then follow two paragraphs of progressively stronger admonitions to "submit to the presbyters" (58—59:2). Finally he closes the letter with a long prayer for understanding, forgiveness and peace (59:3-61), parts of which were very likely derived from an earlier eucharistic prayer,[21] and three paragraphs of recapitulation (62-65).

C. THE FOUR ANALOGIES IN PARAGRAPHS 37-44

The first two of these admonitory analogies, namely that of the imperial army (37:1-4) and that of the human body (37:5 -38:1) are quite short and separated from the last two by four verses of paranesis and a paragraph (39) of excerpts from *Job* (4:16-18; 15:15; 4:19-5:5). Both of them strongly stress orderliness and subordinated action. "*Each one in his own rank (hékastos en tō idío tágmati)* carries out the orders of the emperor and the commanders" (37:3). "The smallest members of the body are necessary and valuable to the whole body, but all work together and unite in subjection (lit.: use one subjection — *hypotagē miā chrêtai*) to preserve the whole body" (37:5). The sentence joining these two analogies ("A certain organic unity binds all parts and therein lies the advantage" 37:4b .) which is itself directed to the army, seems to suggest that Clement in composing the first analogy was reminded of Paul's analogy of the body and its members in *1 Cor.* 12:12-27 and immediately included it in his letter. In a certain sense, too, this second analogy gives something of an exegesis of the first in that it sets the key idea of the *tágma,* the settled-order ("Each *one in his own settled-order...*")— also from Paul (*1 Cor.* 15:23)— in the practical context of the Christian community. The *tágma* here means that each Christian living in Christ should subject himself to the service of his neighbor according to the gifts which he possesses. "Let our whole body, then, be preserved in Christ Jesus *and let each be subject to his neighbor according to the special gift bestowed upon him* (lit.: according as he has been placed in his charism)" *kaì hypotassésthō héksatos tō plēoíon autoû, kathōs etéthē en tō charísmati autoû* (38:1).[22]

The third analogy (40-41), taken from the Old Testament, has to do with the duty of observing order in the community, especially in Church services, and the necessity for a diversity of functions in the Church. An important pre-note, one very often disregarded in trying to give an interpretation of this section, is that here Clement gives his description of the Old Testament cultic situation in the present tense "as though the temple and its services were still existing,"[23] whereas in fact they had passed out of existence more than a quarter of a century earlier. The truth of the matter is that this is not so unusual. The authors of *Barnabas* and the *Letter to Diognetus*, as well as Justin Martyr and Flavius Josephus do the same. For them, and very likely for most early Christians of Jewish descent, Clement not excluded, it still did exist "in spirit" and in the Scriptures.[24] Although Clement's unwillingness to regard the Jerusalem temple and its cultic services as definitively past is, in a sense, understandable — they had undoubtedly become for so many the concrete representation of that very Covenant which Jesus had come "not to destroy but to fulfill" — nonetheless, his bias in this matter does present a hindrance to the clear reading and understanding of the analogy in paragraphs 40 and 41. With this as well as the actual destruction of the Temple (70 A.D.) in mind, I have taken the liberty of translating Clement's present tenses in these two paragraphs as past tenses.

> Since these things were made known to all of us and we had searched into the depths of the divine knowledge, we were obliged to carry out in order (*táxei*) all the things which the Master (*ho despótēs*) had commanded us to do at appointed times. 2 He had ordered the sacrifices and services (*tàs prosphoràs kaì leitourgías*) to be carried out, and these not thoughtlessly or disorderly but at fixed times and hours. 3 Where and by whom He desired these things to be done, He Himself had fixed by His supreme will. Thus all things were done religiously, acceptable to His good pleasure, dependent on His will. 4 They, therefore, who made their offerings (*tàs*

prosphoràs) at the appointed seasons were acceptable and blessed; for since they followed the laws of the Master *(toîs nomísmois toû despótou)*, they did not sin. 5 For to the high priest special functions *(ídiai leitourgíai)* were given, and to the priests *(toîs hiereûsin)* the special office (lit.; place, *ho tópos)* had been assigned, and upon the Levites special ministration *(ídiai diakoníai)* were incumbent. The layman *(ho laïkòs ánthrōpos)* was bound by the rules for the laity (toîs laïkoîs).

Here he breaks off the analogy to insert his theme sentence (41:1):

> Let each of you, brethren, in his own settled-order *(en tō idíō tágmati)* be well pleasing to God with a good conscience, reverently taking care not to deviate from the established rule of service *(kanóna tês leitourgías)*.

Then he continues the analogy:

> 2 Not in every place, brethren, were the daily sacrifices offered *(prosphérontai thusíai)* or the free-will offerings or the sin offerings or the trespass offerings, but only at Jerusalem; and even there the offering was not made except before the sanctuary at the altar *(pròs tò thusiastérion)* where the gift to be offered *(tò prospherómenon)* was inspected for blemishes by the high priest and the aforesaid ministers *(dià toû archieréōs kaì tòn proeireménōn leitourgôn)*. 3 Moreover, those who did anything beyond that which was agreeable to His will, were punished with death. 4 You see, brethren, the greater the knowledge that was intrusted to us, so much the more were we exposed to danger.

It should be noted, first of all, that paragraphs 40 and 41 clearly form a unit, and that this unit presents an admonitory analogy in the form of a description of the divinely willed *tágma* manifest in practically every facet of Israel's life. A second point to be noted is Clement's application of this analogy to the New Testament situation in 41:1, namely that just as Israel had a divinely willed *tágma*, so do the Christians; and just as a Jew by keeping to his own settled-order could be pleasing to God with a clear conscience so long as he reverently did not deviate from the prescribed rule of *leitourgía* (which in Israel was the clear pattern described here of having sacrifices offered and attending services conducted by the special caste of sacred ministers), so also the Christian could be pleasing to God and in good conscience so long as he took care not to deviate from the established Christian rule of *leitourgía* (which Clement at this point does not elaborate any further). He had, however, already discussed the Christian *tágma* in 38:1, i.e. that "each be preserved in Christ Jesus and ... subject to his neighbor according to the special gift bestowed upon him." Nonetheless, there is still a clear overlapping of Old and New Testament terminology in Clement's use of *leitourgía* in 41:1. This term and its verb *leitourgeîn* undoubtedly present a problem if only due to the wide range of meanings and uses they have and which Clement puts them to in his letter,[25] for although he does not use the Old Testament sacerdotal nomenclature such as *hiereús*[26] and *hierateúein* when speaking of the Christian presbyter-epískopoi, he does use *leitourgeîn* and *leitourgía* in the New Testament context.[27] Nonetheless, according to J.-P. Audet

> it is important...to note that in Clement's writings, *leitourgeîn, leitourgía and leitourgós* only carry a ceremonial and sacral meaning when they refer to the levitical priesthood (32:2; 40:5; 41:2 except perhaps in 41:1). The author in fact turns to the more general sense of a 'service' of the community every time he deals with the responsibility of the presbyter-bishops towards their 'flock', or with the 'function' each has in the good ordering of the *ekklēsía* (8:1; 41:1; 44:2,3,6; compare 9:2,4; 20:10; 36:3; *hierateúein*, associated once only with *leitourgeîn*, 43:4, refers to the levitical priesthood.[28]

When Audet writes "except perhaps in 41:1", it is clear that he does not want to exclude Christian worship, especially the celebration of the Eucharist, from the content of *leitourgía* in 41:1, although he also sees in it "the more general sense of a 'service' to the community." Indeed, there is every reason to say that *leitourgía* is used here in its broadest possible sense, i.e. as a dedicated service to God and to the community, a service covering every phase of Christian community life.

That the whole of this analogy (40-41), with the exception of Clement's theme sentence (41:1): may rightfully be read in the past tense and thus as *dealing exclusively with the Old Testament cultic situation* is supported not only from the external evidence of the actual destruction of the Jerusalem temple in 70 C.E. with the consequent cessation of the Jewish sacrificial cult either immediately or shortly thereafter, but also by certain internal evidence from the letter itself. There is, first of all, Clement's use of *ho despótes*, the Master. Let us presume for the sake of discussion that these two paragraphs, 41:1 excepted, although apparently a description of Israel's cultic practice, can just as well be read as a description of the ideal well-ordered Christian cultic activity which should be taking place within the community at Corinth. Who then would *the Master* in 40:1 and 40:4 be? None other than "our Lord Jesus Christ". And in place of "the Master" we could just as well read that "we ought to do in order all things which (our Lord Jesus Christ) commanded us to do at appointed times" (40:1), and that "those who make their offerings at the appointed seasons are acceptable and blessed, for they follow the laws of (our Lord Jesus Christ) and do not sin" (40:4). The problem is that Clement uses this title of *ho despótes* 21 other times in the letter,[29] always addressing God, the Father "of our Lord Jesus Christ" "the Creator and Master of the universe." Not once does he call Jesus Christ *ho despótes*. In short, to maintain that "the Master" referred to twice in paragraph 40 means "our Lord Jesus Christ" involves a gross misuse of the internal evidence of the letter. And it is difficult to imagine where stronger evidence could be found in this case.

Another small but important piece of internal evidence lies with "the aforesaid ministers" mentioned in 41:4. It is, to say the least, extremely speculative to hold that the "priests" and/or "Levites" of 40:5 are meant to allude to or typify Christian 'priests' when these very "aforesaid ministers" are explicitly stated in 41:4 to be those who at the altar in front of the sanctuary in Jerusalem inspect for blemishes the victim(s) for the temple sacrifice.

What Clement, in fact, does want to show and show clearly — and does so quite successfully given the limited space he allots to it — is the orderliness of religious practice under the Old Covenant,[30] but "a positive image of the ancient Levitical order does not in itself imply that the author represents the pastoral office of the Church as a new 'priesthood.'"[31]

Moreover, when Clement *does* have a chance to draw a real Old Testament parallel with the Christian ministry, he does so, and quite directly, e.g. that the Old Testament knew the terminology then currently in use for the Christian ministers (42:5):

And this was no innovation, for a long time before the Scripture had spoken about *episkópōn* and *diakónōn;* for somewhere it says: 'I will establish their *episkópous* in observance of the law and their *diakónous* in fidelity'.[32]

Now if Clement goes to the trouble of pointing out a parallel between one[33] of the LXX[34] non-cultic uses for the word *epískopoi* and the same title then being used for the leaders of the Christian community — a mere question of terminology hardly as important as the existence of a Christian priesthood — would he not *a fortiori* point out a direct parallel between the Old Testament priesthood or priestly functions and that in the New Covenant, had it been possible? This is something he certainly does not do, although he would have had an ideal opportunity to immediately after 40:5.

One final point on this analogy is the question of the *ho laïkòs ánthropos* who at the end of 40:5 "is (was) bound by the rules for the laity." The adjective *laïkòs* shows up only three times in the later Greek translations of the Old Testament (*1 Samuel* 21:5-6; *Ezekiel* 48:15 and 22:16) and never coupled with *ánthrōpos*.[35] On these grounds one might question whether this reference to "the layman" could possibly refer to the Old Testament situation. First of all, it should be noted that in the text itself the verb of this sentence *dédetai* stands in the exact same tense and voice as the verbs in the previous sentence dealing with the "high priest", "priests" and "Levites", namely the present-perfect passive, and seems clearly a continuation of the thought. Secondly, the adjective *laïkòs* is equally rare in the New Testament, the Apostolic Fathers and all the orthodox Christian literature prior to the third century as it is in the later Old Testament translations. Aside from *1 Clement,* it appears three times in Clement of Alexandria and once in Origen.[36] The phrase seems actually to have come from Clement's Jewish background:

> There is more reason to think that the word (*laïkos*) has been borrowed directly from Hellenistic Judaism. The first author who uses it, Clement of Rome, was probably of Jewish descent; one finds the expression in the Pseudo-Clementines[37], the principal work of heterodox Judaic Christianity; and the context in which Clement of Rome uses it, in his letter to the Corinthians, has to do with the cult of the ancient Temple, exactly as in the Jewish translators of the second century.[38]

The last, longest and most embellished of the four analogies is found in paragraphs 43 and 44:

And is it any wonder that those in Christ who were entrusted with such a work (*érgon toioûto*)[39] have appointed those mentioned (*toùs proeirēménous*)[40]....? 2 For when jealousy arose concerning the priesthood, and the tribes were quarrelling as to which of them had been honored with that glorious dignity, Moses himself commanded the rulers of the twelve tribes to bring him rods... 4 And he said to them, 'Brethren, of whichever tribe the rod shall bud, this is the one God has chosen for is priesthood and ministry (*eis tò hierateúein kaì leitourgeîn*). 44:1 Our Apostles also knew, through our Lord Jesus Christ, that there would be strife on account of the office of the episcopacy (*epi toû onómatos tês episkopês*). 2 For this reason, equipped as they were with perfect foreknowledge, they appointed those already mentioned, and afterwards gave instructions, that when these should fall asleep, other approved men should succeed to their ministry (*tên leitourgían autôn*). 3 We consider therefore that it is not just to remove from their ministry (*apobállesthai tês leitourgías*) those who were appointed by them, or later on by other eminent men, with the consent of the whole Church, and who have served (*leitourgésantas*) the flock of Christ blamelessly, humbly, quietly and unselfishly, and have moreover, over a long period of time, earned the esteem of all. 4 For our sin is not small, if we eject from the episcopacy (*tês episkopês apobálōmen*) those who have blamelessly and piously offered the gifts (*prosenegkóntas tà dôra*). 5 Happy the presbyters who have before now completed life's journey and taken their departure in mature age and laden with fruit: for they have now no fear that anyone will dislodge them from the place which has been built for them (*apò toû hidruménon autoîs tópou*). 6 But we see that you have removed some men of excellent behavior from the ministry (*leitourgías*) which they fulfilled blamelessly.

The first question we must ask here is where precisely the analogy rests. Does it say, for example, that just as there was a coveted priesthood in Israel which led to strife among the tribes, so now in Corinth the coveting of the New Testament priesthood, the *episkope*, has led to strife and disorder. One must admit that there is undoubtedly a very strong temptation among Roman Catholics to read it this way, for we have a priestly tradition which goes back centuries upon centuries. Clearly the points of dispute are "the glorious dignity" of the Old Testament priesthood and the office (*ónoma*, lit.: name, title) of the Christian *episkopé,* but the analogates are the action of Moses in the midst of the dispute and the action of the Apostles who realized that a similar dispute could arise in the Christian communities. The issue is indeed one of religious leadership but the analogy here is clearly concerned with likening the action of the Apostles with that of Moses. That this was undoubtedly Clement's intent can be seen from the way he works the analogy so as to put the Apostles into a situation which could reasonably parallel that of Moses. This he does by equipping them with "perfect foreknowledge". It was not an easy parallel to construct, even for Clement. Whether or not the *episkopé* was meant to be seen as a priesthood, in any case, does not rest on this analogy. There are, as a matter of fact, a number of good reasons to think that Clement did not see the episcopal office as connected with priesthood at all. We see here in 43:4, for example, Clement's application of the infinitives *hierateúein* (i.e. to offer sacrifice) and *leitourgeîn* (hendyadys, most likely) to the Old Testament priests. The former term, clearly sacrificial in meaning, he never applies to the New Testament minister; the latter, however, and also *leitourgía,* both of which can or cannot have sacrificial overtones,[41] are applied four times in paragraph 44 to the Christian ministry. Worthy of note, too, is that the personal noun *leitourgós* is never used by Clement to denote the Christian leader(s), even those who preside at the Eucharist, although he had many opportunities to use it in this way. He does, nonetheless, employ it for the sacral figures of the Old Testament: the prophets in 8:1, the priests in 41:2 and the angels in 36:3 following the example of *Heb.* 1:3 (which also quotes *Ps.* 103:4).[42]

The use of *tópos* in 40:5 and 44:5 is a point worth investigating for the possibility of a Christian 'priesthood' implied in *1 Clement.* In the former, "the special *tópos* had been assigned to the priests"; in the latter, the presbyters (here synonymous with *epískopoi)* "who have before now completed life's journey" have "no fear that anyone will dislodge them from the *tópos* which has been built for them."

> The word *tópos* admits of two interpretations. Either: "these men will not be dislodged from the *place* which has been built for them," that is, heaven (cf. *Matt.* 25:34); or: "being dead, they are no longer exposed to the danger of ejection from their *office.*" For the former sense, see *Clem.* 5: 4 & 7.[43]

It seems that by the time of Clement *tópos* had taken on besides its many other meanings[44] also that of "an office"[45] and that Clement here is making a play on the word. This comes out rather clearly when we read 44:5 and 6 together. Those presbyters who have died after a long and fruitful life can certainly not be dislodged from their rightful *place* in heaven, but had they been living they would surely have run the risk of being removed from their *office*; for "we see that you have removed some men of excellent behavior from the ministry which they fulfilled blamelessly." It is one thing, however, to admit that Clement is making a play on the word *tópos*; it is another to say that at least one of the meanings of *tópos* here is *office* and that the Old Testament priests according to him "had been assigned a special office" and, therefore, *tópos* in 44:5, when it means an *office*, clearly denotes a sacerdotal office. This would be a false conclusion. Moreover, the possibility could still exist that the *presbyter-epískopoi* were given a divinely willed office, a pastoral office, which was not a priesthood.

D. THE PROBLEM OF *PROSENEGKÓNTAS TÀ DÔRA* IN **44:4**

The final problem we have to face in this last analogy, one of the most difficult in the whole letter for that matter, is the question of *prosenegkóntas tà dôra* in 44:4. The reason for this is not only that the phrase permits of several different translations, e.g. "who have offered the gifts" (Lightfoot[46]), "who have presented the offerings" (Roberts[47]), "who have offered the sacrifices" (Lake[48]), but also because this precise combination of words, i.e. the verb *prosphérō* with the plural of *tò dôron*, is found nowhere else in the letter. The words, however, do appear separately. *Prosphérō* appears six other times in the letter, four of which times it is associated with *thusía* (sacrifice).[49] Its substantive *hē prosphorá*, the offering, appears three times and in two of these cases, which we have already seen (40:2 and 40:4), it refers to the Old Testament sacrifices. The other instance (36:1) proclaims "Jesus Christ, the High Priest of our offerings" (*tòn archieréa tōn prosphorón*). Thus of the nine other uses of *prosphéro* and its substantive, six are associated with the Temple *thusíai.*[50] Consequently the more frequent combination with *prosphérō*, at least for this letter, is *thusía*.

The noun *dôron* shows up six other times in the letter: 4:2, 19:2, 23:2, 32:1, 35:1 and 35:4. The latter five talk about the "gifts of God" to man and consequently lay outside the scope of our discussion. But the first of these, a word-for-word citation from the LXX text of *Genesis* 4:4-5, brings *dôron* and *thusía* together in the description of the sacrifices of Cain and Abel:

And after some days Cain offered to God a sacrifice (*thusían*, *MINeHĀH*) from the fruits of the earth, and Abel for his part, offered of the firstborn of his flocks and of their fat. And God looked kindly on Abel and his gifts (*dôrois, MINeHĀTŌ*) but paid no attention to Cain and his sacrifices (*thusíais, MINeHĀTŌ*). (*1 Clem.* 4:1-2)

The question is whether *thusía* and *dôron* here throw some light on the meaning of *prosenegkóntas tà dôra* in 44:4. Striking about the above text is that *dôra* and *thusíai* of the LXX cited by Clement translate the thrice repeated MNHH of the Hebrew. This, then, sets the question back a step. Now we must ask if there is a fixed sacrificial meaning of MNHH which would be carried over to the *prosenegkóntas tà dôra* of 44:4.

Two points should be kept in mind in trying to answer this question: first, the Hebrew verses in question here come from the Jahwistic (J) tradition as does all of *Genesis* 4 [51]; and, secondly, in the later Priestly (P) tradition MINeHĀH takes on the specific sacrificial meaning of a cereal offering, but that prior to this tradition the word meant any type of sacrifice or sometimes simply a present, without any sacrificial overtones at all.[52] In the *Genesis* text we are considering, however, it certainly carries the meaning of sacrifice.

The overall use of *dôron* in the LXX as a translation of MINeHĀH, nonetheless, moves more in the direction of "the secular present given between men." It uses *dôron* to translate some 16 different words in the Hebrew Bible.

The word appears 163 times and in 30 instances[53] translates MINeHĀH. In 25 of the 30 cases *dôron* means "the secular present given between men", very often as the tribute freely given a king.[54] Thus although *dôron* can quite properly be the translation of MINeHĀH meaning "any kind of sacrificial gift", it nonetheless is the word consistently chosen by the LXX translators when MINeHĀH means the secular present given by one Old Testament personage to another. And this is the case in 11 of the 12 uses of *dôron* in *Genesis* (4:4 excepted) and in 25 out of 30 appearances in the whole LXX where *dôron* translates MINeHĀH.

This data shows that *dôron* pertaining to Abel's sacrifice of "the firstborn of his flocks and of their fat" is a quite permissible but rather unusual translation of MINeHĀH, especially for *Genesis*. On these grounds I believe I am justified in concluding that *dôrois* in *Gen.* 4:4 is, first and foremost, a stylistic twist on the part of the LXX translators to avoid using *thusía* three times within a verse and a half. The data shows us furthermore that, aside from 44:4, *dôron* both throughout *1 Clement* and in *Gen.* 4:4-5 (*1 Clem.* 4:1-2) has no fixed sacrificial meaning, but at times takes on one when placed in a sacrificial context, and that the prevalent meaning of the word in the LXX text of *Genesis* (92 percent of the cases) is simply that of a gift between persons. This is about as far as we can go in trying to discover the precise meaning of *prosenegkóntas tà dôra* from internal evidence.

As far as external evidence is concerned, this expression makes no further appearance in the whole corpus of the Apostolic Fathers. The only passage to shed the slightest bit of light on the problem is a single phrase from Ignatius' letter to the Smyrneans (7:1) where the Eucharist is called the "gift of God" (*tê dôreâ toû theoû*, using the noun *hê dôreá* without *prosphérō*).

In the New Testament corpus we find the combination only in its two strongest Judeo-Christian documents: *Matthew* and the *Epistle to the Hebrews*. *Mt.* 2:11 tells of the Magi who "offered him gifts". In *Mt.* 5:23-24 the man who "brings (his) gift to the altar" and remembers that his brother has something against him is admonished to return and "offer the gift" only after he has been reconciled with his brother. Finally, in *Mt.* 8:4 the only leper who returns to give thanks is told to go, show himself to the priest and "offer the gift which Moses commanded as a testimony to them." These three texts of *Matthew* do indeed evidence a fairly strong sacrificial mentality. Still it seems much more likely that Clement takes the combination from the *Epistle to the Hebrews* where it is clearly connected with an ecclesial order. *Hebrews* 5:1, 8:3 and 9:9[55] all have to do with the function of the Jewish high priest, and in each case with the verb *prosphéro* we find the fixed combination *dôra kaì thusías* (both gifts and sacrifices).[56] These three passages from *Hebrews* form part of an analogy much more developed than any we have heretofore met in *1 Clement*, namely between the Levitical high priest and Jesus Christ, also a high priest but with as his type not Aaron or the sons of Levi but Melchizedek, that mysterious figure from *Gen.* 14:18 and *Ps.* 110, an ancient Canaanite priest-king of (Jeru)Salem, one who not having been an Israelite could hardly have been a priest of the (Old) Covenant. This likeness with Melchizedek is repeated again and again in the Epistle (*Heb.* 5:6, 5:10, 6:20, 7:15, 7:17). Clement, on the other hand, although he displays an obvious familiarity with the Epistle and calls Jesus a high priest on three different occasions (36:1, 61:3, 64), never once mentions the name of Melchizedek in his letter. J.-P. Audet notes

that Jesus' 'priesthood' here (in Clement) seems to be placed
in the line of the 'order of Aaron' rather than in any prolonging
of the 'order of Melchizedek' (...32:2 mentions Levi with
such evident favor that he appears to have priority over Judah;
Clement may be further suggesting a levitical descent for
Jesus; compare *Heb.* 7:1-28).[57]

In any case, here is an instance where Clement by reiterating the connection
between Jesus and Melchizedek could have placed a positive hindrance in
the way of a sacral development along Levitical lines, but did not do so.
How purposeful this was, though, is probably something we shall never
know.

Still again something he did not do was employ the exact wording of
Hebrews: prosphérein dôra te kaì thusías. Whatever the precise function of
the *epískopoi* at the Christian assembly was, it seems clear that it did not
have to do with *thusía* (from *thúō* [comp. *thūmós*=Lat. fümus]) as it was
generally understood under the Old Covenant. There, with but a few
exceptions such as *Psalms* 49 and 50, it was used consistently for a material
offering made to God, usually on an altar and usually destroyed by burning.[58]
Clement's idea of sacrifice, on the other hand, finds its expression in the few
exceptions just mentioned, in the already highly spiritualized concept of
sacrifice in *Psalms* 49 and 50:

18:16-17 (*Ps.* 50:18-19):
For, had you wished a sacrifice, I would have offered it; but
in whole burnt offerings you take no delight. A sacrifice to
God is a contrite spirit; a contrite and humble heart God will
not despise.

35:12 (*Ps.* 49:23)-(immediately prior to 36:1: "Jesus Christ,
the High Priest of our offerings"):
A sacrifice of praise will honor me, and there is the way I will
show him the salvation of man.

52:3-4 (*Pss.* 49:14-15, 50:19):
And again he says: Sacrifice to God a sacrifice of praise, and
pay to the Most High your vows; call upon me in the day of
your affliction, and I will rescue you, and you will glorify me.
For a sacrifice to God is a crushed spirit.

Clearly genuine *thusía* for Clement was nothing other than that prayer of

praise and petition which issues from a humble and contrite heart.
Working on the supposition that this concept of *thusía* is what
Clement meant by the *dôra* in 44:4, as Harnack[59] and Kittel[60] do,
prosenegkóntas tà dôra becomes the office of those who speak out the
prayers of praise and petition in the name of the people at the Eucharistic
celebration, possibly along the lines of the models found in paragraphs 9
and 10 of the *Didache* or even 60 and 61 of this letter. Knopf takes the
same stand but adds that it means also the offering of the Eucharist
itself.[61] G.G. Blum maintains that if there is, in any case, an actual
bringing of gifts implied (i.e. not just a spiritualized conception of the
gifts), then in this context it could only mean the elements of the Eucharist
which were brought by the bishop.[62] Harnack, however, states apodictically
— and there are few who would disagree with him here — that it is
impossible to prove that already in the time of Clement the elements of the
Eucharist were called *dôra*.[63] The Migne footnote on *dôra* says simply: "it
is ambiguous whether they are the first fruits, acts of thanksgiving, alms,
etc."[64]

The Migne commentary on *1 Clement* 44:4 given by J.B. Cotelier
begins by stating: "Priests offer gifts (*dona seu munera*) to God, prayers of
the faithful, unbloody sacrifices, the holy Eucharist."[65] Taken by itself, the
statement may well be true, but in context it implies that the presbyter-
epískopoi of *1 Clement* have already been clearly established as Christian
priests' — the very point to be proved. He then gives a dozen or so patristic
texts dealing with "the gifts" and "offering the gifts", all of which (with the
exception of Ignatius' letter to the Smyrneans: 7:1) date from the third
century or later. Since we are interested in testimony most contemporaneous
with *1 Clement*, at least his two earliest references, namely from Tertullian
and Origen, bear mentioning here even though they were written more than
a hundred years after *1 Clement*.

The Tertullian reference comes from *Adversus Marcionem* 9(207-8
A.D.) where treating *Mt.* 8:4 — "Go show yourself to the priest, and *offer
the gift* which Moses prescribed." — the first of the Latin Fathers comments:

> The argument takes into account the elements, such as this law
> of the prophet, which have formed his (the leper's) thinking
> and which indicated that a man, once a sinner, who was
> suddenly healed by the word of God, ought to go to the Temple
> and offer a gift to God (*offerre munus Deo*), that is to say, a
> prayer and thanksgiving (*orationem et actionem gratiarum*)

in the Church, through Jesus Christ, the universal priest of the Father.[66]

Noteworthy indeed is the predominantly spiritual meaning he attaches to "offerre munus Deo", but it seems rather doubtful that Tertullian is referring to the Christian eucharistic celebration. And there is certainly no connection made with the function of the bishop. The Origen citation is from his *Homilia XIII, In Exodum* where the Body of Christ in the Eucharist is spoken of as the "consecrated gift" (*consecratum munus*),[67] but here too there is no tie-in made with the bishop's office nor is the phrase connected with "offerre". So much for Origen and Tertullian.

Of the five patristic Greek lexicons at my disposal[68] nowhere is to be found a reference to the use of *dôra* with *prosphérein* or separately in the Christian literature prior to Origen. This leaves a gap in the sources of more than a hundred years, ample time for considerable development in meaning to take place.

From the middle of the third century on, however, we find many references to the celebration of the Eucharist as *prosphérein tà dôra* , e.g. Eusebius,[69] the *Constitutiones Apostolorum*,[70] and Gregory Nazianzen[71] to mention only a few, as well as countless references to the Eucharistic elements as *tà dôra*.

One early third century work not mentioned in the Migne commentary on *1 Clement* 44:4 but used extensively by Dom Gregory Dix in his treatment of "The Ministry in the Early Church"[72] is Hippolytus of Rome's *Traditio Apostolica* (approx. 215 C.E.) Although only a Latin translation of the original Greek is extant, it is clear that *prosphérein tà dôra* stood in the original version of the prayer for the ordination of a bishop (paragraph 3) and that Hippolytus, just as Clement, uses it for a set function at the Christian assembly. The critical text from the *Sources Chrétiennes*[73] reads as follows (the italics are mine):

Da cordis cognitor pater super hunc servum tuum quem eligisti ad episcopatum pascere gregem sanctam tuam et primatum *sacerdotii* tibi exhibere sine repraehensione servientem noctu et die, incessanter repropitiari vultum tuum et *offerre dona* sanctae ecclesiae tuae, spiritu primatus *sacerdotii* habere potestatem dimittere peccata secundum mandatum tuum, solvere etiam omnem colligationem secundum potestatem quam dedisti apostolis, placere autem tibi in mansuetudine et

mundo corde, offerentem tibi odorem suavitatis per puerum
tuum Jesum Christum....
Qui cumque factus fuerit episcopus omnes os offerant
pacis, salutantes eum quia dignus efrectus est. Illi vero offerant
diacones oblationem quique imponens manus in eam cum omi
presbyterio dicat gratias agens: Dominus vobiscum.

Here we find a great deal more than in Clement. There is now a New
Testament 'priesthood' (*sacerdotium:* lines 3 & 5) and a bishop who "manifests
the primacy of the priesthood", although neither the bishop nor the presbyter
is ever called a priest *(sacerdos).*[79] Nonetheless, two passages in paragraph
9 which state that a presbyter "does not ordain a cleric" *(clerum non ordinat)*
and that a deacon "is not ordained in the priesthood" *(non in sacerdotio
ordinatur)* show clearly the presence of a select sacerdotal group made up of
bishops and presbyters. Since the celebration of the Eucharist is not mentioned
explicitly anywhere in the list of episcopal functions (lines 2-10), it is quite
clear that the "offerre dona", nowhere contained in the prayer for the
ordination of a presbyter (paragraph 8), was used in the time of Hippolytus for
the bishop's part at the Eucharistic assembly. Does this mean then that the
"dona" would be the Eucharistic elements? A possibility, but Hippolytus does
not say so. Strangely enough, whenever he gives a description of the actual
offering of the Eucharistic elements, he always uses the words "offerre
oblationem" instead of "offerre dona" (note line 13; see also paragraphs 4,5
and 23). Moreover, the combination "offerre dona" is also a hapax in
Hippolytus for which he, like Clement, gives no further explanation.

One could go on to list examples from the fourth, fifth and sixth
centuries where the Eucharistic elements were spoken of as *tà dôra* in
Palladius, Theodoret, Cyril of Alexandria, John Chrysostom and Gregory of
Nyssa, or the use of *prosphérein* meaning "to celebrate the Eucharist" in
Athanasius, Eusebius, and the Councils of Ancyra, Neocaesarea, Nicea,
Laodicea, Chalcedon and Carthage but all of these have the limited value of
being at least two hundred years or more removed from the writing of *1
Clement,* two hundred years which saw enormous changes and developments
in the Church.

Nonetheless, there is a value in checking the partistic sources on this
problem, even granted the gap of a century, for they help to establish rather
securely that *prosphérein tà dôra* remains associated in the Christian
tradition with the celebration of the Eucharist, and that the more this
celebration becomes fixed and systematized the more *tà dôra* takes on the

exclusive meaning of the bread and wine, either prior to the celebration or in it as the Eucharistic elements. We must honestly admit, though, that the precise function of the *presbyter-epískopoi* in *1 Clement*, i.e. exactly what they said and did when they "offered the gifts", remains a mystery. Nor would it be justified for us to conclude that when we have discovered exactly what a bishop said and did when he "offered the gifts" in the fourth or fifth century, we have discovered the actual meaning of *prosenegkóntas tà dôra* in *1 Clement*. There is undoubtedly a tremendous temptation to jump to conclusions here on grounds of the tremendous wealth of later patristic references.

E. CONCLUSION

We began with the general question of how the pagan and Old Testament nomenclature for the priestly class found its way into the Church and with it the sacral-cultic conception of priesthood and Christianity. Specifically, we asked whether such sacerdotal nomenclature or sacral-cultic conception of Christianity is to be found in *1 Clement*. First we examined the background of the letter, its style and ministerial framework. It was clear that at the time of Clement both the terminology for the ministers and the boundaries of their areas of competence were in a state of development. We discovered that Clement, just as the New Testament corpus, never applies any of the clearly sacrificial terminology of the Old Testament (*hiereús, archireús, hieráteía, hierosúne, hierateúein*) to the Christian leaders. But with this the problem was not solved. Was there perhaps the implication of a Christian 'priesthood' in his use of such terms as *leitourgía, tópos, ho laikòs ánthropos, tágma, thusía, prosphorá and prosenegkóntas tà dôra*, or generally in the whole context of the letter? In trying to answer this question, we found it necessary to make a structural analysis of the letter as well as an acquaintance with Clement's use of rhetorical devices. Our analysis showed that the letter contains at least two fairly complete sermons, many lengthy Old Testament quotations, long strings of examples, many paragraphs of paranesis, a highly embellished (possibly Eucharistic) prayer, and four intricately developed admonitory analogies (37-44).

Within these analogies was Clement's 'theology of ministry.' At paragraph 37 he made a switch of rhetorical devices from prior independent examples and Old Testament citations to these analogies which themselves were partly built with examples. We also noted that when it came to speaking of the old cultic order in paragraphs 40 and 41, Clement was unwilling, for understandable reasons, to see the Jerusalem Temple service as a definitively past historical fact. By admitting his treatment of the Temple cult in the present tense as a fairly common, pious, but unhistorical phenomenon (*Barnabas*, the *Letter to Diognetus*, Justin Martyr and Josephus do the same) and by considering points of internal evidence such as his use of *despótēs* and "the aforesaid ministers" (41:4) which show he was clearly and exclusively speaking of the Old Testament order, we opened the way for a translation of paragraphs 40 and 41 in the past time. This put his references to the "high priest," "priest," "Levites," and "the layman" in the context of history where they belong; it brought them out clearly as historical examples which support his theme of a divinely willed *tágma* or *táxis* for the Christian community, based on — as we saw in 38:1 —"the special gift bestowed upon each one;" and it reduced considerably the grounds for that ever-present tendency which some commentators on Clement seem to have of discovering types of a Christian 'priesthood' in practically every mention he makes of the Old Testament hierarchy. Moreover, his clear and well defined use of typology in the first half of the letter, e.g. paragraphs 12 (Rahab's scarlet cord) and 25:2-5 (the mythical phoenix) could not but lead one to think that had he intended the officers of the Temple cult to be types of a Christian 'priesthood' or hierarchy, he would certainly have made it more explicit. In fact, whenever he *did* have a chance to draw a real parallel between the Old Testament context and the Christian ministry, he did, and did so very clearly, e.g. the terms *epískopoi* and *diákonoi* in 42:5. In other words, to quote J.-P, Audet, we have to be aware that

> even otherwise careful historians sometimes naively let themselves be caught in the trap of anachronism. They will, for instance, explain to us, with no further qualification, that Clement of Rome used the 'ancient (i.e. aaronic) priesthood' as a figure of the 'Christian priesthood' — which does not just simplify, but actually misconstrues Clement's thought.[75]

And this can happen very easily if one does not take into account that the examples used in the four analogies of paragraphs 37-44 are not presented as independent examples like the more than a score of those in the first half of the letter, but are subordinate to and dependent upon the 'prime analogate' in each of the analogies.

This we saw was especially true for the fourth analogy. It was constructed by Clement with some difficulty to serve as a lead-in for his own solution to the Corinthian crisis. While one could hardly deny a parallel in paragraphs 43 and 44 between the Old Testament priesthood and the Christian *episkopé*, still this parallel remains quite secondary and subordinate to the actual analogy itself which compares the action of Moses in a crisis situation concerning the religious leadership of Israel with the action the Apostles took to perpetuate the episcopacy. In other words, to make his point about the action of Moses and the Apostles he had to bring in the Levitical priesthood and the Christian episcopacy. Nor should we be especially surprised that Clement sets up his solution for the Corinthian situation *via* an Old Testament crisis. The closer we get to the Apostles and their contemporaries, the more we can expect to find the firm conviction that the Christians form the New Israel. It was certainly one of the most contagious convictions of the first Jerusalem community and was to play a major role in the Apostolic teaching, especially that on the Resurrection. But to say that in paragraphs 43 and 44 Clement was trying to make the Christian *episkopé* into a priesthood, is to miss the whole point of the analogy as well as, perhaps, his solution which follows.

We saw that the use of the term *leitourgía*, which in the LXX has a clear sacral-cultic meaning, holds in Clement's New Testament context to its more general and original[76] meaning of a service to the community, with the exception of its use 41:1 where it is given as a commission to every individual member of the Christian community — "Each one of us, brethren, must ...(take care not) ... to deviate from the established rule of service" (*leitourgías*). Here the sense was that of a totally dedicated Christian service to God and to the community which certainly could not have excluded the celebration of the Eucharist but also could not have been so exclusive as to apply only to the Eucharist and that as a sacral-cultic act.

An investigation of the use of *tópos* in 40:5 and 44:5 revealed that although Clement makes a play in 44:5 on two meanings of the word, the use of the word in the letter is so commonplace that there are no grounds for concluding that one of the meanings it could have in 44:5, namely *an office*, in any way implies a sacerdotal office as it clearly seems to in 40:5.

The problem of *prosenegkóntas tà dôra* was a complex one. The letter itself did not enlarge upon it and it stands as a hapax in the Apostolic Fathers. Clement's use of *dôra* in 4:2 for the sacrifices of Abel — quoting the LXX *Genesis* 4:4-5 verbatim — also provided no conclusive evidence, for it is an exceptional stylistic use of the word by the LXX Fathers and in 11 of the 11 other uses of *dôra* in *Genesis* it means an interpersonal gift. The three uses of the combination in *Matthew* showed indeed a strong sacrificial leaning, but if the phrase does come from the canonical Christian writings, it seems more likely that it was taken over from the thrice repeated phrase for the function of the Levitical high priest (*prosphérein dôra te kaì thusías*) in *Hebrews,* which in Clement is shortened to *prosphérein tà dôra.* Nonetheless, in *Hebrews* this function is never applied to any of the *epískopoi* but only to Jesus Christ, the once for all high priest of the New Covenant. If this was his source, it is quite understandable that Clement would drop the *te kaì thusías* of *Hebrews* since we saw that for him genuine *thusía* stood more in the line of that highly spiritualized development found in *Psalms* 49 and 50. The problem would, of course, be solved if we could discover the precise meaning of "offering the gifts" for the Christians of Clement's time. Perhaps to them it was a genuine sacrificial term and the Eucharist was seen as a sacrifice; perhaps it was a phrase which they took over from Scripture and gave a completely new meaning. Reliable contemporary Christian sources which treat this question are lacking until the first decades of the third century. The exact nature of the phrase in Clement remains a mystery although Ignatius of Antioch writing a little more than a decade later speaks of the Eucharist as the *dōreá toû theoû.* Hippolytus uses the phrase in his *Traditio Apostolica* as an episcopal function at the eucharistic assembly, but does not enlarge upon it nor mention anything about the nature of the *dôra.* Among fourth and fifth century authors the phrase clearly means the celebration of the Eucharist and "the gifts" the eucharistic elements.

In short, there is no term or function in the New Testament context of *1 Clement* which we can point to as possessing an unequivocally sacral or sacrificial meaning. The strongest candidate for such a meaning would undoubtedly be *prosenegkóntas tà dôra.* Unfortunately the only clarifications of this combination come from later patristic periods when a Christian theology of sacrifice and the sacral had developed or at least become articulate. We should admit quite honestly that considering the whole context of the letter, it seems clear that Clement would not have disapproved the establishment of a spiritual type of priesthood in Christianity using the Old Testament terminology. Had he made mention of the priesthood of the faithful or Jesus Christ the high priest according to the order of Melchizedek, we might be inclined to think otherwise. Still it is unfair to make too much of Clement's neo-levitical mentality. His primary object was to restore order to the Church of Corinth. Steeped as he was in the Scriptures, he did not want the Christians to forget the rich heritage they had received from Israel. The fact that he had not completely come to grips with the *de facto* cessation of the Temple cult at Jerusalem shows he was not yet clear in his own thinking as to precisely how far the continuity with the Old Covenant should go. It must indeed have been a very difficult problem for any Christian of Jewish descent. Consequently we should not try to read into the document any further theological clarity which at the time certainly does not seem to have been present for Clement.

82

NOTES

¹ As opposed to the so-called *Second Epistle of Clement*, one of the oldest extant Christian sermons, which has little to offer our investigation aside from 17:3 where the Presbyters are named as the admonitors of the Christian community: "And let us seem to believe and pay attention now, while we are being admonished by the presbyters, but also when we have gone back to our homes, let us remember the commandment of the Lord."

² J. Colson, *Ministre de Jésus-Christ ou le sacerdoce de l'Évangile*, Paris, 1966, p. 216: "...la date la plus conmunément admise est soit la fin du règne de Domitien (95-96), soit le début du règne de Nerva (96-97)." Cf. also F.X. Funk, *Patres Apostolici*, Tübingen, 1901, t. I, pp. XXXVI-XXXIX.

³ Cf. J. Quasten, *Patrology*, Vol. 1, Utrecht, 1950, p.43.

⁴ Dom G. Dix, *op. cit.*, p. 255.

⁵ J.A. Kleist, *Ancient Christian Writers*, Vol. 1., London, 1946, p. 5.

⁶ *Ibid.*, p. 4.

⁷ *Ibid.*, p. 6.

⁸ J. Quasten, *op. cit.*, pp. 50-51; also Kleist, p. 3, and many others.

⁹ H.F von Campenhausen, *Kirchliches Amt und geistliche Vollmacht in den ersten drei Jahrhunderten*, Tübingen, 1953, p. 94.

¹⁰ G.G. Blum, "Eucharistie, Amt und Opfer in der Alten Kirche" in *Oecumenica-1966*, Gerd Mohn, 1966, p. 22.

¹¹ J. Neumann, "Der theologische Grund für das kirchliche Vorsteheramt nach dem Zeugnis der Apostolischen Väter" in *Münch, Theol. Zeit.*, Jahrg. 14, 1963, p. 256.

¹² H.F. von Campenhausen, *op. cit.*, p. 91; Dom G. Dix, *op. cit.*, p. 256, note 2, gives a third possible meaning of *presbýteros* in Clem., namely that of a predecessor (44:3), citing Hippolytus, *Tr. Ap.* 36:12, and Irenaeus, *Ep. ad Vic.*, in Eusebius, *H.E.* V, xxiv,14. He holds that in certain places Clem. may be playing on the double meaning (e.g. 1:3; 44:3).

¹³ J. Lécuyer, *Le Sacerdoce dans le Mystère du Christ*, 1957, p. 351.

¹⁴ One might try to build a case for a monarchical bishop at Corinth about the time of Paul's first Corinthian letter from the use of *andrí* in *1 Clement* 47:4, but in context it is quite clear that "a man approved by them" (Apostles), refers either to Paul or to Apollos (cf. *1 Cor.* 3 and 16:12), both of whom were itinerants.

¹⁵ Cf. G.G. Blum, *op. cit.*, p. 22; also J. Colson, *Les Fonctions Ecclésiales aux deux premiers siècles*, Paris, 1956, p. 190:" Il est remarquable, aussi, que Clement affirme qu'un presbytérium collégial exerçant l'épiscopè était la form originelle du gouvernement local de l'Église, non le système monoépiscopal déjà existant dans certaine Églises(et peut-être à Rome même) quand il écrit effectivément."

¹⁶ G.Konidaris, "Warum die Urkirche von Antiochia den `proestôta presbýteron' der Ortsgemeinde als 'ho Epískopos' bezeichnete" in *Münch. Theol. Zeit.*, Jahrg. 12, 1961, pp. 281-283. Note that Konidaris maintains (on pp. 278-279) that even before the existence of the monarchical episcopate there was in the Christian communities a *proestos* or chief presbyter who functioned when the Apostle or charismatic founder of the community was absent: "Der Proestos (Justin) und die Presbyter weideten die Ortskirche, solang ein Apostel nicht da war. Alle diese heissen östlich von Ephesus Episkopen. Aber die Stelle des "proestòs presbýteros" war eigentliche sedes apostolica. Deswegen ist es verständlich, warum die demütigen Herren, die an Stelle der Apostel im Presbyterkollegium sassen, solange diese abwesend waren oder nach ihrem Tode als Prasidenten fungierten, in *Ehrfurcht und Anonymität lebten. Die Anonymität charakterisiert die Zeit der*

sogenannten Apostolischen Väter. Das wird uns besonders im I. Clemensbrief bestätigt, wo uns die Demut der Gemeindevorsteher am deutlichsten vor Augen tritt. Es ist ein bisher unbewertetes Faktum in der Geschichte des Urchristentums, dass nämlich nur sehr wenige Namen der ersten Kirchenführer uns erhalten geblieben sind."

[17] J.A. Kleist, *op. cit.,* p. 5.

[18] Examples of people who called others to conversion are: Noe (7:6), Jonas (7:7), the prophets (*hoi leitourgoi tês cháristos toû theoû*) (8:1) and the "Master of the universe Himself" (8:2 4). As examples of obedient people Clement gives: Enoch, Noe, Abraham, Lot, (counter-example) Lot's wife, and Rahab (9-12). Further "glorious examples" proposed for imitation are: Elias, Eliseus, Ezechiel, Abraham, Job, Moses and David (17), In day and night, sun, moon, stars, seasons, seas and oceans, winds, springs, and the smallest of animals are to be seen as examples of order in the world (20). Abraham, Isaac and Jacob are given as examples of people who did what was right.

[19] G.G. Blum, "Eucharistie, Amt und Opfer...", p. 19.

[20] See, e.g., J. de Watteville, *Le Sacrifice dans les textes eucharistiques des premiers siècles,* Neuchâtel, 1966, pp. 40-44 (passim).

[21] Cf. E. Kilmartin, S.J., *The Eucharist in the Primitive Church,* Englewood Cliffs, N.J., 1965, pp.156-157.

[22] Note the resemblance with 1 Peter 4:10: "As each one has received a gift (*hékastos kathôs élaben chárisma*) employ it for one another, as good stewards of God's varied grace."

[23] J.A. Kleist, *op. cit.,* p. 112.

[24] F.X. Funk, *op. cit.,* p. 151: "E tempore praesenti non sequitur, templum Hierosolymitanum tempore auctoris adhuc stetisse. Clemens eo uti potuit templo etiam deleto. Animo enim videt cultum iudaicum adhuc vigentem, describens, ut e c. 40 apparet, quae a Deo praecepta fuerunt, non quae adhuc fiebant. Similiter loquuntur Barnabas c. 7-9, auctor epistulae ad Diognetum c. 3, Justinus Dialog. c.117, Iosephus Fl. *Antiq.* III, 7-11."

[25] For a treatment of *leitourgeîn* and *leitourgía* in the Apostolic Fathers, esp, *1 Clem.,* cf. G. Kittel (ed.), *Theol. Wörterbuch zum Neuen Test.* (TWzNT), Band 4, Stuttgart, 1942, pp. 235-6. Note esp.: "So soll nun jedes einzelne Glied der christlichen Gemeinde an seinem Platz Gott wohlgefallen und *tòn hörisménon tês 1. autoû kanóna* nicht überschreiten (41:1). Wenn nun auch hier der Begriff *leitourgía* sich die Aufgabe *aller* Glieder der christl. Gemeinde bezieht, so doch in 44:2-6 speziell auf das Bischofs-und Presbyteramt."

[26] J.-P. Audet, *op. cit.,* p. 126: "On the contrary, *hiereîs* is used once for the 'priests' of the Egyptian religion (25:5) and twice for the 'priests' of the levitical order (32:2; 40:5). And *archireús* is used twice for the levitical 'high priest' (40:5; 41:2), and three times for Jesus himself in his state of glory with the Father (36:1; 61:3; 64).

[27] Cf. P. Grelot, *Le Ministère de la nouvelle Alliance,* Paris, 1967, p. 15

[28] J.-P. Audet, *op. cit.,* p. 126.

[29] *1 Clem.* 7:5, 8:2, 9:4, 11:1, 20:8, 20:11, 24:1, 24:5, 33:2, 36:1, 48:1, 49:6, 52:1, 55:6, 56:16, 59:4, 60:3, 61:1, 61:2, 64:1.

[30] Cf. D. Rudolf Knopf, *HANDBUCH ZUM NEUEN TESTAMENT, Ergänzungs-Band: Die Apostolischen Väter,* Tübingen, 1920, p. 114: "Die drei Arten von Priesterpersonen sind wohl sicher zu Unrecht als Typen von Christus, Presbytern, Diakonen, oder von Bischof, Presbytern, Diakonen beurteilt worden. Clemens will nur von der Ordnung des alten Bundes reden, und die Opferarten in 41:2 darf man nicht auf christliche Kultübungen deuten."

[31] J.-P. Audet, *op. cit.,* p. 125.

[32] Clement's reference is to *Isaias* 60:17.

[33] Cf. *Dictionnaire de la Bible, Supplément II*, Paris, 1934, col, 1308: Le titre *epískopos* a souvent le sens de surveillant, *Num.*, IV,16; II *Paral.*, XXXIV, 12; I *Macch.*, I,51; de chef des armées, *Num.*, XXXI, 41; *IV Reg.*, XI, 15, 18; de gouverneur, *Jud.*, IX, 28; de chef de groupes, *II Esdr.*, XI, 9, 14, 22; de magistrat, *Is.*, LX, 17; de depositaire de l'argent du Temple, *II Paral.*, XXXIV, 17.

[34] Nonetheless Clement does not quote the LXX verbatim. Compare his 42:5: katastésō toùs episkópous autôn en dikaiosúne kaì toùs diakónous autôn en pístei with *Isaias* 60:17 of the LXX: kaì dósō toús árchontás sou en eirénē kaì toùs episkópous sou en dikaiosúnē (Bible de Jeru.: "Pour magistrature, j'instituerai la Paix et comme gouvernment la Justice.")

[35] Ign. de la Potterie, "L'origine et le sens primitif du mot 'laïc'" in *Nouvelle Revue Theologique*, 90, 1958, p. 844.

[36] *Ibid.*, p. 847.

[37] In the *Epistle of Clement to James*, V.5.

[38] Ign. de la Potterie, *op. cit.*, p. 847.

[39] Namely that described in 42:4 "They preached from district to district, and from city to city, and they appointed their first converts, testing them by the Spirit, to be bishops and deacons of the future believers."

[40] I.e. the bishops and deacons. Note that Clement does not add *leitourgós* to the participle here as he does when speaking of the Old Testament ministers in 41:2: *dià toû archieréōs kaì tòn proeirēménōn leitourgôn.*

[41] G. Kittel (ed.), *TWzNT*, Band 4, p, 235-236: "Dabei ist gewiss nie vergessen, dass mit *leitourgeîn, leitourgía* zunachst einfach Dienst, frommer Dienst den man Gott (*Her.* s.9, 27, 3) und zugleich der Gemeinde (*I Cl* 44,3: *leitourgeîn tô poimníō* und *Did* 15,1) leistet, gemeinst ist."

[42] *Ibid.*, p. 238; also p. 237: including the Apocrypha it appears 14 times in the LXX, three with a strictly sacral meaning(*Is*, 61:6; *Neh.* 10:39 and *Sir.* 7:30).

[43] A.J. Kleist, *op. cit.*, p. 113; *1 Clem* 5:4 reads: "Peter, who because of unrighteous jealousy suffered not one or two but many trials, and having thus given his testimony went to the glorious *place* which was his due." And 5:7:"He (Paul)...gave his testimony before the ruler, and thus passed from the world and was taken up into the Holy *Place*..."; cf. also 2 *Clem.* 1:2 and *Bar.* 19:1.

[44] Note 41:2(place, locality); 8:4, 29:3, 46:3(place in the Scriptures); 7:5(place of repentanee, i.e. possibility of); 63:1(place of obedience).

[45] G.Kittel(ed.) *TWzNT*, Band 8, p. 208; see also *Acts* 1:25a; *Ig.Pol.* 1:2; *Ig.Sm.* 6:1.

[46] J.B. Lightfoot, *The Apostolic Fathers*, Grand Rapids, Michigan, 1967 (from the 1891 Macmillan edition, London), p. 32.

[47] Roberts, Donaldson and Crombie, *The Writings of the Apostolic Fathers*, Edinburgh, 1873, p. 39.

[48] Kirsopp Lake, *The Apostolic Fathers* (Loeb), London, 1912, p. 85; see also Kleist, p. 36.

[49] I. e. 4:4, 10:7, 41:2a, 41:2b, 47:4 (the first four deal with *thusía*).

[50] To which could be added such kindred phrases as 41:1 *enegken thusían*, and 31:3: *proségeto thusían.*

[51] P. Ellis, *The Men and Message of the Old Testament* Collegeville, Minn., 1963, P. 58.

[52] G. von Rad, *Old Testament Theology*, London, 1962, vol. 1, p. 256: "The cereal offering(MNHH) is taken by P as exclusively a gift-sacrifice of victuals consisting of flour, oil, and frankincense. But the history of the cult before the Priestly Document shows no knowledge of the MINeHĀḤ in this specialised meaning: in earlier passages,

and in complete accord with the proper meaning of the word, it was any kind of sacrificial gift, both that with the blood and that without it (*Gen.* 4:3ff; 1 *Sam.* 2:17, 3:14). At times it was even the secular present given between men (e.g. *Gen.* 32:14fi, 43:11ff)."

53 Cf. Hatch & Redpath, A *Concordance to the Septuagint*, Oxford, 1897, vol. 1, pp. 359, 664-5. The 30 are: *Gen.* 4:4 (J), 32:13b-18-20-21(E), 33:10 (J), 43:11-15-25-26 (J), *Jdg.* 3:15-17-18, *1 Sm.* 10:27, *1 Kgs.* 4:21, 8:64 (?), 10:25, *1 Chron.* 16:29, 18:2-6, *2 Chron.* 9:24, 17:5, 28:8, 32:23, *Ps.* 45:12, 72:10, *Is.* 39:1,66:20.

54 And once as booty (*2 Chron.* 28:8). Of the other five cases where *dôron* does represent a material offering made to God, *Genesis* 4:4 included, one is a doubtful reading, viz. *1 Kgs.* 8:64 (possibly a cereal offering!) and another a similie: "And they shall bring all your brethren from all the nations as an offering to the Lord" (*Is.* 66:20). The other two are: *1 Chron.* 16:29 ("Ascribe to the Lord the glory due his name, bring an offering and come before him.") and *2 Chron.* 32:23 ("And many brought gifts to the Lord to Jerusalem.").

55 *Heb*, 5:1: Pâs gàr archireùs ex anthrópōn lambanómenos hyper anthrópōn kathístatai tà pròs tòn theón, hina prosthérē dôrá te kaì thusías hypèr hamartiôn... *Heb, 8*:3: Pâs gàr archireùs eis tò prosphérein dôrá te kaì thusías kathístatai ...*Heb.* 9:9: hétis parabolè eis tòn kairòn tòn enestēkóta, kath' hēn dôrá te kaì thusíai prosphérontai...

56 The RSV footnotes this phrase with "cereal and animal offerings", most likely recalling the meaning of *dôron* via the Hebrew in the Priestly (P) tradition.

57 J.-P. Audet, *op. cit.*, p. 126.

58 Cf. G. Kittel (ed.), *TWzNT*, Band 3, pp. 180-182.

59 O. de Gebhardt & A. Harnack, *PATRUM APOSTOLICUM OPERA: Epistulae Clementis Romani*, fasc. I, part. I, ed. II, Leipzig, 1876, p. 73: "dôrá -Laudes et preces sunt, imprimis in coena sacra celebranda deo offerendae per presbyteros."

60 G. Kittel (ed.), *TWzNT*, Band 3, p. 189: "Opfer sind namentlich die Gebete im Gottesdienst *1 Cl* 40,2ff; 36,1, unter ihnen in erster Linie das Abendmahlsgebet *1 Cl* 44,4; *IgEph* 5,2; *Phld* 4."

61 D. Rudolf Knopf, *op. cit.*, pp. 119-120: "Das *prosphérein tà dôra* besteht in dem Darbringen der Gemeindegebete, besonders derjenigen, die die Eucharistie begleiten, und in der Darbringung der Eucharistie selber."

62 G.G. Blum, *op. cit.*, p. 21.

63 O. de Gebhardt & A. Harnack, *op. cit.*, p. 73.

64 Cf. J.P. Migne, *Patrologiae cursus completus, series graeca*, Paris, 1857, vol. I. cols. 299-300.

65 *Ibid.*

66 CSEL, vol 47-*Opera Tertulliani*(A. Kroymann), p. 442.

67 GCS, vol. 29-*Origenes Werke (W. A. Baehrens)*, p. 274.

68 G.W.H. Lampe, A *Patristic Greek Lexicon*, Oxford, beginning 1961; J.C. Suiceri, *Thesaurus Ecclesiasticus e Patribus Graecis*, Amsterdam, 1682; E.A. Sophocles, *Greek Lexicon of the Roman and Byzantine Periods, From B.C. 146 to A.D. 1100*. New York, 1887; D. DuCange, *Glossarium ad Scriptores Mediae et Infimae Graecitatis*, Lyons, 1688; J.M.S. Baljon, *Grieksch-Theologisch Woordenboek*, Utrecht, 1899.

69 In his *Vita Constantini*, Liber 4, cap. 41, he tells how the Emperor at the Synod of Tyre admonished the bishops that: "It would not be fitting for them to celebrate the divine cult in a state of dissension, since the divine law forbids that they offer *the gifts* to God before the dissenters, having resolved their difficulties, have come to peace and friendship." GCS, vol. 7 (I.A. Heikel), p.133.

70 A compilation of Greek documents dating from the end of the fourth century, the original probably written in Syriac. Liber 8, cap. 5 records with some variations the ordination prayer for a bishop given in Hippolytus: "Grant in Your name, O God, knower

of the heart, to this Your servant, whom You have chosen for the episcopacy, to shepherd Your holy flock and act as Your high priest, blamelessly ministering night and day, for the placation of Your countenance, to gather together the number of those who have been saved and offer to You the gifts of Your holy Church" *(prosphérein soi tà dôra tês hagías sou ekklēsías)*. F.X. Funk, *Didascalia et Constitutiones Apostolorum*, vol. 1 Paderborn, 1905, p. 476. Also in the same Liber 8 *tà dôra* is used twice in cap. 12 (Funk, pp. 494 and 510) and once in cap. 13 (Funk, p. 514) for the Eucharistic elements, and Liber 2, cap. 59 (Funk, p.173) speaks of the Eucharist as "the gift of sacred food" *(trophês hierâs dōreá)*.

71 He relates in his *Oratio 43, In Laudem Basilii Magni*, 52:3, a situation which took place in the Church when Basil was "to have offered the gifts at the holy table" *(tà dôra tê theía trapézē prosenegkeîn)*. F. Boulenger, *Grégoire de Nazianze: Discours Funèbres* (Texte Grec, Trad. Franc., Introd. et Index), Paris, 1908, p. 164.

72 See Note 2.

73 *Hippolyte de Rome: La Tradition Apostolique*, ed. Dom B. Botte, O.S.B., Paris, 1946, pp. 29-30.

74 The word "sacerdotes" does appear once, but in an Old Testament context. Cf. para. 3, ln. 7.

75 Audet, *op. cit.*, p. 125.

76 Küng, H., *op. cit.*, p. 460.

CHAPTER IV

IGNATIUS OF ANTIOCH

OUTLINE

I. BACKGROUND

A. IGNATIUS' LIFE AND FINAL JOURNEY

According to the testimony of Eusebius, Ignatius was installed as bishop of Antioch in 68 C.E.[1] and was, as successor to Evodius, the second person to hold this position, or counting Peter the Apostle the third.[2] John Chrysostom tells us in a homily that Ignatius "conversed with the Apostles."[3]

In his *Chronicon* Eusebius records that during the third persecution of Trajan, i.e. about 108 C.E., Ignatius, the bishop of the church of Antioch, was condemned to be thrown to the beasts at Rome.[4] Ten soldiers — Ignatius calls them "leopards"(*Rom* 5:1) — were assigned to escort him and other prisoners to the Capital. The attempts to reconstruct the precise route they followed are quite conjectural,[5] but we do know from the letters that upon arriving at Smyrna the party rested for some days and Ignatius received Polycarp, the bishop of that city (*Pol* 1:1), and delegates from the neighboring churches of Ephesus (*Eph* 21:1), Magnesia (*Mg* 2:1) and Tralles (*Tr* 1:1). While waiting for a vessel at Smyrna, Ignatius composed four letters: To the Ephesians (*Eph* 21:1), the Magnesians (*Mg* 15:1), the Trallians (*Tr* 12:1) and the Romans (*Rom* 10:1). From Smyrna the group set sail for Troas and for this part of the journey Ignatius had Burrus as his secretary (*Sm* 12:1; *Phld* 11:2). At Troas they were met by Philo, the deacon of Cilicia, and Rheus Agathopous who told them of the end of the persecution in Antioch (*Phld* 11:1). While at Troas Ignatius wrote the last three of his letters: To the Philadelphians (*Phld* 11:2), the Smyrneans (*Sm* 12:1) and to Polycarp (*Pol* 8:1). From Troas they sailed to Neapolis (*Pol* 8:1),[6] then across Macedonia to Philippi (Polyc., *ad Phil.*, ch. 9; 13) and further along the Egnation Way to Dyrrachium.

From there they sailed either to Brundisium (and on to Rome by the Appian Way) or to Ostia as the *Martyrium Colbertinum* reports. At Rome Ignatius was probably led to an arena[7] and there clawed and gnawed to death by the wild beasts.[8] His larger bones were collected and carried back to Antioch where they were buried "extra portam Daphniticam in coemeterio"(Jerome, *De Vir. Ill.* 26).[9]

B. THE LETTERS

Ignatius' Letters, with the exception of those to Polycarp and to the Romans, all follow a general two-part pattern. The first part contains a salutation, expression of thanks and praise, and an exhortation to unity and obedience to the bishop; the second part carries a warning against false teachers and a final paragraph given to personal notes and greetings. The *Letter to Polycarp* differs slightly from this pattern in that the 40-year older bishop first addresses directly to Polycarp five chapters on the duties of a bishop and then three chapters to the Smyrneans themselves wherein he speaks of obedience to the bishop and faithfulness to their baptism. The

Letter to the Romans differs considerably from all the others. Here there is no mention either of heresy or hierarchy. Instead Ignatius explains to the Roman Christians his ardent desire for martyrdom and begs them not to use their influence to deprive him of this honor.

The style used in the letters is by no means classical; crude and enigmatic would be better descriptives considering the frequent repetitions, violent metaphors and unfinished sentences. Still it has to be said that his ideas themselves are sharp and clear, his force of will and intensity of feeling evident, and that this presence of his whole personality is what gives his writings their characteristic note. It is difficult to imagine a better evaluation of the Ignatian letters from a literary point of view than that presented back in 1909 by E. Norden, one of this century's foremost authorities on ancient classic prose:

> Eine bedeutende, mit wunderbarer Schärfe ausgeprägte Persönlichkeit atmet aus jedem Wort; es lässt sich nichts Individuelleres denken. Dementsprechend ist der Stil: von höchster Leidenschaft und Formlosigkeit. Es gibt wohl kein Schriftstück jener Zeit, welches in annähernd so souveräner Weise die Sprache vergewaltigte. Wortgebrauch (Vulgarismen, lateinische Wörter), eigene Wortbildungen und Konstructionen sind von unerhörter Kuhnheit, grosse Perioden werden begonnen und rücksichtslos zerbrochen; und doch hat man nicht den Eindruck, als ob sich dies aus dem Unvermögen des Syrers erklärte, in griechischer Sprache sich klar und gesetzmässig auszudrücken, so wenig wie man das Latein Tertullians aus dem Punischen erklären kann; bei beiden ist es vielmehr die innere Glut und Leidenschaft, die sich von den Fesseln des Ausdrucks befreit.[11]

We have here, indeed, the final attempt of an Oriental Christian mystic whose life has been firmly rooted in everyday pastoral problems to pass on to the Christian communities the tradition and a few of the basic theological insights he stands behind with his life. And yet in a very real sense the uniqueness of Ignatius in his letters is as much that of his own milieu as it is of himself personally, for:

> He is primarily a witness to a type of Syrian Christianity which was known and practiced in Antioch in the early second century, to which he himself had contributed. A recognition of

this fact will do much to explain certain elements in his thought which have been much misunderstood.[12]

C. THE ANTIOCHENE CHURCH

In the second century Antioch was the third city of the Empire after Rome and Alexandria. It had about a half million inhabitants[13] and stood at the center of a network of great roads.[14] Severe earthquakes ravaged the city several times during the first and second centuries C.E.[15] and it appears that the city was continually in the process of being rebuilt. Ignatius must have been quite aware of the constant building for his use of the metaphor of the great derrick (*Eph* 9:1) and the ropes by which heavy stones were drawn into place in the walls suggests how familiar the process was to him.[16] The population of Antioch was cosmopolitan. A Jewish community had been in existence since the city's foundation — 300 B.C.E. by Seleucus Nicator I[17] and Jews were allowed special privileges by the Seleucid rulers. The Roman legions were stationed not far to the north of the city and Roman merchants dominated Antioch's trade and commerce. New groups of one sort or another were continually being attracted to the city, bringing with them their beliefs and ways of life.[18]

The pagan religious activities appear to have been extraordinarily varied. We know of a few of them from coins; others from literary or archeological evidence. They range from worship of the great gods — Apollo, Zeus, Dionysius, Artemis, etc. — to little private cults.[19] From the available data one can safely conclude that around the time of Ignatius the city had about a half dozen large temples and numerous smaller ones.

When Josephus wrote, the Jewish community in Antioch was the largest in any city in Syria.[20] Among them at a very early date in the Christian era the so-called "Hellenists" founded a Christian community. This was a group of Greek-speaking Jews who had been expelled from Jerusalem after the death of their leader Stephen. They had treked north and spread out through Phoenicia, Cyprus and Antioch (*Acts* 11:19). This group of Greek-speaking Jewish Christians had a much stronger awareness of the universality of the Christian message than the Hebrew-speaking Christians and began immediately preaching the Gospel to the pagans,[21] who for the first time gave them the name "Christians"(*Acts* 26). When the Jerusalem church heard of this they sent Barnabas to put a stop to it, but when he himself saw the grace of the Lord at work he recognized the universality of the message and brought Paul to them (*Acts* 11:25-6). Together they spent a full year (probably 45 C.E.) teaching and preaching in Antioch, but even the preaching of Paul was not powerful enough to hold the Hebrew-speaking Christians, who with Peter swung back to the observance of food laws when their consciences were worked on by the men from Jerusalem (*Gal.* 2:11 ff). This situation and the question of circumcision gave rise to the council at Jerusalem. In reading *Acts* and *Galatians* we often tend to assume that the struggle resulted in a victory for the Hellenists; actually there is silence on the matter.[22] We do know that almost immediately after the trip to Jerusalem Paul left Antioch never more to return and that the preaching of the Gospel to the Jews was left to Peter (*Gal.* 2:7-8). What more than likely happened at Antioch was that with the major questions of food laws and circumcision settled to the advantage of the Hellenists, they themselves gladly embraced in charity many other decidedly Jewish aspects in the practice of Christianity. One has only to read the *Gospel according to Matthew* (probably composed in or near Antioch) to see the unmistakable Jewish character the catechesis had taken on in Syria. Nor was it pure chance that Antioch became the great mission sending station of the primitive Church, especially to the East around the Euphrates where large colonies of Jews were living.[23]

Thus by the time of Ignatius it is not surprising that much Jewish and Oriental imagery had found its way permanently into the theology and liturgy in Antioch. Actually the *Odes of Solomon* display this imagery more strongly than Ignatius, although he shows it too in speaking of the "evil odor of the doctrine of the prince of this world"(*Eph* 17:1) and in admonishing the Philadelphians(6:2) to "flee from (the devil's) wicked arts and snares." A positive Jewish influence can be seen in *Mg* 9:2 where Ignatius speaks of Christ raising the Old Testament prophets from the dead and in the story of the star (*Eph* 19). Daniélou has drawn particular attention to three terms employed by Ignatius which show up regularly in Jewish Christian writings: "the name of God"(*Eph* 1:3); "the beloved" as a title for Jesus(*Sm*-Salutation); and "plantation" as a name for the Church (*Phld* 3:1; cf. *Tr* 11:1).[24]

Ignatius also makes frequent reference to the sounds of the ear. The harp suggests the bishop who is "attuned to the commandments as a harp to its strings"(*Phld:*2) or the presbyters attuned to the bishop; "by your concord and harmonious love Jesus Christ is being sung"(*Eph* 4:1). Christians assembled for worship join in this choir to "receive the key-note of God in unison, and sing with one voice through Jesus Christ to the Father"(*Eph* 4:2). Such imagery, which goes beyond anything found in the New Testament, came from Ignatius' Syrian background.[25]

A further use of Jewish imagery can be seen in his reference to the "one Temple of God"(*Mg* 7:2), to the *thusiastérion* (the Court of the People, where the altar of sacrifice stood, and/or the altar itself (*Eph* 5:2; *Tr* 7:2; *Phld* 4; *Mg* 7:2) and especially *Phld* 9:1 where he states that "the [Old Testament] priests likewise are noble, but the High Priest [Jesus Christ] who has been entrusted with the Holy of Holies is greater."

D. THE OPPONENTS

The picture that Ignatius gives us of his opponents is fairly obscure and it is perhaps because of this that for more than a century the question of who precisely his opponents were has been, as Barnard puts it, "a major battleground in Ignatian studies."[26] The issue is important here for the simple fact that Ignatius' articulation of his thoughts on the Church and the ministry will certainly be conditioned, if not determined, by these opponents in (or outside of) the churches of Asia Minor, opponents the like of which he probably had already encountered at Antioch. The letters do show clearly that Ignatius opposed both a Judaizing tendency which extolled certain Jewish practices and observances of the Law (*Phld* 6:1; 8:2; *Mg* 8-11) and a Docetic tendency which denied the reality of Jesus' humanity and taught abstinence from the Eucharist (*Tr* 10; *Sm* 2; 4:2; 5:2; 7:1). The question posed by the experts is whether these two tendencies were incarnated in two distinct heretical groups, i.e. Judaizers and Docetists, or whether there was in fact but one group, i.e. a Judaizing form of Docetism. The answer rests ultimately in the interpretation of certain subtleties in the Greek text and the weight of scholarship today appears to stand behind the single group theory.[27] Grant describes them:

> These people are Judaizing docetists, and at least some of them are gentiles (*Phld* 6:1). They appeal to the Old Testament (*Phld* 8:2), but apparently they treat it in a haggadic manner (*Mg* 8:1) and provide non-Christian exegesis of the prophets (*Mg* 8:2; cf. *Phld.* 9:2). On the other hand, they say that Jesus (or Christ?) merely seemed to suffer his crucifixion (*Sm* 2:1), and they do not admit that he "bore flesh" (*Sm* 5:2). They seem to be concerned with "heavenly matters" such as "angelic locations"

and "archontic conjunctions," which Ignatius also calls "the glory of the angels" and "the archons visible and invisible" (*Tr* 5:2; cf. *Sm* 6:1). They abstain from the Eucharist because they deny that it is the flesh of Jesus, which suffered for sins and was raised by the Father (*Sm* 7:1). Perhaps they even call themselves by the name of some Gnostic teacher (*Mg* 10:1). This teaching is hard to identify with any particular sect we know. Criticism of those who say they are Jews but are not is found in the *Apocalypse* of John (2:9; 3:9); such men belong to "the synagogue of Satan," In *1 John* 4:2 we read of "spirits" which do not confess that Jesus has come in the flesh, and, like Ignatius, John criticises loveless schismatics who have separated from the community (*Sm* 6:2; *1 John* 3:11; 4:11-12; *Eph* 5:3; *1 John* 2:19). But it is not absolutely certain that we know the sect or sects attacked by John, though he may have in mind the Jewish Christian gnosis of Cerinthus. Ignatius may have something similar in view.[28]

It seems to me that there are at least two areas where this opposition could have influenced the ministry as we find it in Ignatius' letters. The first concerns his own adoption of terminology for the Godhead used by different early heterodox sects, namely *sigé* (silence)[29] (*Mg* 8:2; *Eph* 19:1) plus the fact that he singles out the *epískopos* for special awe when he is "keeping silence" *(sigônta)*. And the more anyone sees that the bishop is silent, the more let him fear him"(*Eph* 6:1). What Ignatius is doing according to Chadwick, is attributing the characteristics of God to the bishop.[30] The linking of God, the Silent, with the silent bishop provides one more reason for holding the *epískopos* as the ultimate authority in the Christian community. A second possible area of influence on Ignatius' writing about the ministry and the work of the ministry lies in the fact that he is writing in the full awareness of a strong Judaizing element in Asia Minor. This is one of the factors which is foremost in his thought and his position is clear and positive: "It is monstrous to talk of Jesus Christ and to Judaize. For Christianity did not believe in Judaism but Judaism in Christianity"(*Mg* 10:3). Admittedly it is impossible to determine how much influence this factor had on his presentation of the Christian ministry or the Christian eucharistic celebrations, but it is an important factor to keep in mind when reading the Letters. He is, in any case, certainly not going to make statements or use terminology which he knows the Judaizers would take up and use to their advantage. Perhaps this has

94

something to do with his tremendously sparse use of the Old Testament and his vague treatment of sacrifice.

E. IGNATIUS' THEOLOGY AND SOURCES[31]

One finds in Ignatius, as we have already seen, no systematic theological treatise(s). Forced to take leave of the Christian communities he loves, the future martyr addresses himself in writing to certain problems and certain divisive tendencies present among them. Quite obviously the weight of circumstances leads him to emphasize strongly some theological aspects and leave others (often the very ones we would like to hear about) virtually untouched. In any case, a carefully balanced, well-focused theological panorama of Antiochine theology is out of the question. Nor is it even fair to assume that the theology in Ignatius is the theology of Asia Minor. He seems indeed to have exchanged ideas with the Church leaders of the various great churches there, but how much he has integrated their theological viewpoints into his letters remains an unanswerable question. One thinks, for example, of the 14-chapter *Letter of Polycarp to the Philippians* which never once even mentions the word *epískopos*. The paramount problem for Ignatius, as earlier for Clement of Rome, was to find a way of healing the divisions which were presenting themselves in the Christian communities. He had to make an appeal to them indeed, but on what grounds was he to make the appeal?

> In his time no common creed was yet in existence, and no Christian writings yet possessed sufficient authority. So, being without credal formulas or written documents to appeal to, he could only fall back on the personal element. If some central authority which should command the respect of all parties was essential, it could be looked for nowhere else but in the body of ordained officials. This is the reason for the repeated and insistent exhortations to obey the bishop and his ministry which occur in all the letters except *Romans*. They have led to the frequently expressed view that the keystone of Ignatian theology is the exaltation of the episcopate; but this is a statement that must be received with caution. It does not justify the imputation to Ignatius of any high sacerdotal doctrine, as is sometimes assumed. The importance he ascribes to the bishop's office is no more and no less than a purely practical measure for imposing unity

upon churches which were too often disrupted by internal rivalries and dissensions.[32]

The key to Ignatius' theology lies in what might be called his preoccupation with "unity." The Letters bear witness to this in the continual reappearance of the terms *henótēs (oneness,* unity)[33] and *hénōsis (union,* unity).[34] These concepts form the background upon which most of Ignatius' further theological thinking is projected. His three major concerns: the authority of the bishop and his ministers, hatred of heresy and schism, and the glory of martyrdom are nothing less than the practical conclusions of his theology of unity. Most of what he has to say about God, Jesus Christ, the Church, the ministry and the sacraments is worked out in this context. It is a concept that emerges from his Letters as a deeply felt personal vision of how things are and ought to be. God is *hénōsis, i.e.* "union" or "unity achieved"(*Tr* 11:2), and has created man for this same "union"(*hénōsin:* *Phld* 8:1), a "union" that is promised to those who believe (*Tr* 11:2). It is present in the flesh and Spirit of Christ, in the relation between Christ and God, and in the relation between the flesh and spirit of the believer (*Mg* 1:2; 13:1). In the practical order especially, Ignatius insists on a "oneness" of the members of the community with their ministers (*Eph* 4:2; 5:1; *Phld* 2:2; 3:2; 5:2; 9:1; *Sm* 12:2; *Pol* 8:3) and charges them to "flee division" (*Phld* 2:1; 7:2; *Sm* 7:2) for "where there is division *(merismós)* and anger God does not dwell"(*Phld* 8:1).[35]

The **Christology** of Ignatius can be found rather clearly outlined in seven texts: *Eph* 7:2, 18:2, 20:2, *Mg* 11, *Tr* 9:1-2, *Sm* 1:1-2, *Pol* 3:2, the main thrust of which is to show that the birth, death and resurrection of Christ truly took place and that Christ truly lived as a person. But this person he also calls God (*Eph* 7:2; 18:2) and Son of God (*Eph* 20:2; *Sm* 1). The divine character of Christ also comes out in his use of such words as "uncreated"(*Eph* 7:2), "timeless" and "invisible"(*Pol* 3:2). This identification of Christ with God is also found in the New Testament (e.g. *John* 20:28) but in the context of Ignatius' conception of the "unity" between God and Christ this identification receives a strong foundation.

The Christological formulations clearly stress Christ's being born of Mary (*Eph* 1B:2; *Tr* 9:1; *Sm* 1 "truly born of a virgin) and from the family of David (*Eph* 20:2; 18:2; *Tr* 9:1; *Sm* 1). That He is from God (*Eph* 7:2) or from the Spirit (*Eph* 18:2, comp. *Sm* 1 and *Mg* 8:2) is taken as obvious. The Letters tell further of Jesus' baptism by John (*Sm* 1; comp. *Eph* 18:2) and situate the crucifixion during the reigns of Pilate and Herod the Tetrarch (*Sm* 1:2; *Tr* 9; *Mg* 11). The death of Jesus is seen as a fact that has to be imitated by Christians, i.e. the imitation of Christ unto death is both the end as well as the means whereby a Christian comes to partake in the life of Christ (see *Eph* 1:11; 10:3; *Rom* 6:3; *Mg* 5:2; *Tr* 11:2; *Phld* 4). "To attain to God", "to be truly a disciple of Christ"(*Rom* 4) are in fact the terms Ignatius uses to describe his own upcoming martyrdom. For him "there is but one Teacher"(*Eph* 15:1) and to be a disciple of this Teacher means not only to live one's life in accordance with His life but also to long to have one's life crowned with martyrdom. It is the martyrdom which makes the imitation of Christ complete and perfect (see *Eph* 1:2; *Mg* 9:1; 10:1; *Tr* 5:2; *Rom* 4:4; *Pol* 7:1). Those who are in this process of discipleship are those who "live according to the Spirit" or who "do the things of the Spirit"(*Eph* 8:2). They are also those in whom Christ lives, the bearers of Christ (*Eph* 9:2; 15:3; *Mg* 5:2; 10:1; *Rom* 6:3) and Ignatius himself often in the salutations of his letters makes use of his name Theophóros, bearer of God.

Although Christian tradition is quite present to Ignatius, very much absent from his thought is the preoccupation of later Christian writers for carefully basing each point of their theology on this handed-down teaching. The explanation for this lies in his theology of unity. The community for Ignatius lives primarily not so much out of the past or from what has been handed down in the past but rather it lives here and now in unity with God. This is experienced in a united *ekklēsía* gathered around its one bishop celebrating one eucharist. In a very real sense it is a genuinely simple theology. The systematician will undoubtedly be disappointed with the little concern Ignatius has for finer distinctions. This is a theology, on the other hand, which rather than bog down in an endless dispute with "heretics" could in the fullness of its conviction simply call everyone to the unity of the Church.[36] This call to unity was both his motto and his epitaph, perhaps no better expressed than in his own words: "I then did my best as a man created for unity."(*Phld* 8:1).

Eschatology as such is not treated at much length in the Letters. This is quite understandable when one realizes that Ignatius, the mystic, already sees his own eschatology as realized; he "already lives in the supernatural world in his desire to be with Christ."[37] This psychological state helps to explain why some passages in his Letters, as several scholars have noted,[38] possess an aura of having been written from outside of time. Nonetheless Ignatius does direct a few potent passages to his fellow Christians which speak of "the last times" as well as divine "wrath"(*Eph* 11:1), "judgement"(*Eph* 11:1; & 6:1) and "the unquenchable fire" for the evil-doers and false teachers (*Eph* 16:2). The most striking of these of these is *Eph* 11:1:

> These are the last times *(Éschatoi kairoí)*. Therefore let us be modest, let us fear the long-suffering of God, that it may not become our judgement. For let us either fear the wrath to come, or love the grace which is present — one of the two — only let us be found in Christ Jesus unto true life.

In addition, we find here and there in the Letters eschatological notions of a more general character. Christ has already come "at the end"(*Mg* 6:1), though Christians await his coming(*Pol* 3:2). Now is the occasion for Christians to repent fully (*Sm* 9:1) or perform what God has called them to do (*Rom* 2:1, *Pol* 2:3).39

Ignatius naturally made use of earlier **sources**. Whether they were oral or written is a poor question, not because it is unimportant for us but because it would have been unimportant to Ignatius. He could hardly have been interested in appealing to the authority of a New Testament canon which was at most only beginning to be formed. For him it was simply a question of the Apostolic doctrine, as interpreted in the Church (or as foreshadowed in the Old Testament). Keeping this in mind we can readily see that whether Ignatius in composing his Letters recalls this doctrine from personal contacts with the Apostles, or those who knew them, or from letters or documents penned by the Apostles, or written for them by others, or whether he recalls it as the living Apostolic tradition of the second and third generation Christians he grew up with would not have made an enormous difference to Ignatius. He was in fact not far removed from any of them.

As for the Old Testament, he seems — in stark contrast to Clement — to have made but little use of it. Aside from two quotations from the *Book of Proverbs* (3:34 in *Eph* 5:3, and 18:17 in *Mg* 12) which he introduces with the formula "it is written," we find only allusions to certain Old Testament texts: *Isaiah* 5:26 in *Sm* 1:2, *Isaiah* 52:5 in *Tr* 8:2 and *Psalms* 32:9 in *Eph* 15:1. There could also have been an intended allusion to *Psalm* 57:5 in *Eph* 9:1 and to *Isaiah* 66:18 in *Mg* 10:3. There also seem to be traces of *Wisdom* 7:29f and 18:14f in *Eph* 19; and O. Perler has shown a pervading influence of the Hellenistic Jewish homily throughout the Letters.40

The relation of the Synoptic Gospels to Ignatius' Letters has been the subject of an exhaustive study by H. Köster. In brief, his results show that:

> Ign. weist nie darauf hin, dass ihm ein schriftliches Evangelium bekannt gewesen sei. Sein Gebrauch des Wortes *euaggélion* (*Phld* 5,1-2; 8,2; 9,2; *Sm* 5,1; 7,2) verweist uns in eine Zeit, die schriftliche Evangelien als Autorität noch nicht kannte, sondern mit diesem Wort nur das eigentliche Kerygma bezeichnete, dass in fixierte kerygmatischen Formeln tradiert wurde. ... Doch gibt es Stellen, die es vollkommen sicher machen, dass Ign. wirklich synoptische Überlieferung kannte (besonders *Sm* 3:2f.). Die meisten dieser Stücke zeigen keinerlei für die Redaktionsarbeit der Evangelisten charakteristische Züge, könnten vielmehr in der von Ign. dargebotenen Form bereits aus älterer freier Überlieferung stammen (*Eph* 5,2; 14,2; 17,1; *Pol* 2,2; wohl auch *Pol* 2,1) bzw. von einer solchen alteren Form aus weiterentwickelt worden sein (*Tr* 11,1; *Phld* 6,1).
>
> Alle diese Einzelstellen können für sich genommen, auch wenn sie summiert werden, keine literarische Abhängigkeit von einem Evangelium beweisen. Sie lassen sich sämtlich aus der freien Überlieferung erklären, ohne dass man auf irgendein Evangelium rekurrieren müsste.
>
> Die einzige Stelle, an der sich mit ziemlicher Sicherheit Redaktionsarbeit eines Evangelisten, nämlich des *Mt.*, feststellen liess (*Sm* 1,1),[41] ist nicht von Ign. selbst aus *Mt.* entlehnt, sondern innerhalb einer kerygmatischen Formel von ihm übernommen, ist also auch nicht geeignet, Benutzung des *Mt.-Evangeliums* durch Ign. zu erweisen und damit die Herkunft der anderen sich mit *Mt.* berührenden Stellen aus dem Evangelium wahrscheinlich zu machen. Daraus ist zu schliessen, dass Ign. das *Mt.-Evangelium* nicht benutzt haben wird.
>
> Andere Evangelien kommen für eine Benutzung durch Ign. schon gar nicht in Frage (von *Joh.* ist hier abgesehen). Für *Luk.* sind die Berührungen viel zu schwach. Abhängigkeit des Ign. vom *NE* (Nazoräer-Evangelium) ist so gut wie ausgeschlossen.[42]

The problem of the relationship of the Letters to the Fourth Gospel is a much more complex one and has been widely discussed by patristic scholars for over a century.[43] The Oxford Society of Historical Theology, after a detailed comparative study, posed the problem like this:

> Ignatius use of the Fourth Gospel is highly probable, but falls
> some way short of certainty. The objections to accepting it are
> mainly (1) our ignorance of how far some of the Logia of
> Christ recorded by John may have been current in Asia Minor
> before the publication of the Gospel. If they formed part of the
> Apostle's oral teaching, they must have been familiar to his
> disciples, and may have been collected and written down long
> before our Gospel was composed. (2) The paucity of phrases
> which recall the language of the Gospel, and the absence of
> direct appeals to it; phenomena which are certainly remarkable
> when we consider the close resemblance between the theology
> of Ignatius and that of the Fourth Gospel. It is difficult, for
> example, to think of any reason why Ignatius did not quote
> *John* 20 in *Smyrn.* iii.2.[44]

The answer to the problem, according to Chr. Maurer, who published in
1945 a comprehensive study of the possible Ignatian-Johannine parallels,
was that "Ignatius hat das 4. Evangelium gelesen."[45] J.A. Fischer disagreed:

> Die Frage, ob Ignatius johanneische Schriften gekannt hat,
> darf trotz der Arbeit von Chr. Maurer noch nicht eindeutig
> bejaht werden. Ignatius kann Theologie, wie sie uns bei
> Johannes begegnet; mehr lässt sich kaum mit Sicherheit sagen.
> Falls der Kirchenvater wirklich die johanneischen Schriften,
> besonders das *Jo* in seiner heutigen Gestalt kannte, warum
> tritt dies nicht deutlicher hervor?[46]

R.M. Grant, reiterating Maurer's thesis, maintained that the reason the
Gospel of John does not appear more clearly in the Letters is that Ignatius
does not use it in a consciously literary way:

> But just as Ignatius never mentions any apostles except Peter
> and Paul,[47] and uses formulas of quotation only twice, both in
> reference to the Old Testament,[48] so in making use of the
> Gospel of John he does not speak of its author or use it in a
> consciously literary way. What he knows of John he knows
> from memory; what he knows from memory is, so to speak,
> written in his heart. He does not, and probably would not if he
> could, make use of a book directly.[49]
>
> In any case, Maurer's comparative study remains as the

best we have on the subject, and still we must admit that he has not completely disproved the possibility brought forward by C.C. Richardson commenting on the various Johannine reminiscences in Ignatius: "All of them can be explained by a common religious ethos."[50]

Perhaps we should not exclude another possibility, suggested by W.J. Burghardt, namely that Ignatius knew not the Gospel of John but its author.[51] This cannot be excluded as impossible even though much that has been handed down on the subject may be legendary,[52] nor can it be excluded even if in so saying we are perhaps not even speaking of John the Apostle. Best known to Ignatius of all the New Testament material, though, are the Pauline letters, and especially *1 Corinthians*. A number of years ago H. Rathke produced a monumental work on *Ignatius von Antiochien und die Paulusbriefe*[53] which is clearly the best and most comprehensive study of the influence of Paul on Ignatius in print today. We can do no better here than summarize briefly in Rathke's own words the results of his investigation.

a) Ignatius weiss nach seiner eigenen Aussage (I *Eph* 12,2) von Paulusbriefen und ist mit ihrem Inhalt vertraut.

b) Ignatius sagt nichts über die Zahl der ihm bekannten Paulusbriefe, und er erwähnt auch nicht einzelne dieser Briefe. I *Eph* 12 kann man nicht als Beleg für die Kenntnis eines von Paulus verfassten Epheserbriefes und I *Rom* 4,3 nicht als Hinweis auf den paulinischen Römerbrief ansehen.

c) Die Untersuchung der Ignatiusbriefe auf Zitate aus den Paulusbriefen und Anklänge daran bestätigt die oft festgestellte Tatsache, dass Ignatius den ersten Korintherbrief gekannt und häufig benutzt hat. Dass Ignatius auch die Pastoralbriefe, der paulinische Epheserbrief und die Thessalonicherbriefe bekannt waren, ist auf Grund der vorgefundenen Anklänge nicht zu beweisen, jedoch wahrscheinlich. Dabei bleibt unentschieden, ob Ignatius den Epheserbrief und die Pastoralbriefe als Paulusbriefe ansieht.

d) Die bisherige Untersuchung lässt bereits einige Rückschlüsse auf die Art der Benutzung der Paulusbriefe durch Ignatius von Antiochien zu:

   1. Ignatius benutzt die Paulusbriefe stillschweigend. ...
   2. Ignatius benutzt die Paulusbriefe selbständig. Wir finden kein einziges streng wörtliches Pauluszitat. Der

Hinweis, dass Ignatius eben keine Abschrift der Briefe zur Hand hatte und daher aus dem Gedächtnis ziteren musste, mag das erklären konnen. ...

3. Ignatius ist mit Paulusbriefen sehr vertraut. Es sind nicht einzelne Zitate aus Paulusbriefen, die isoliert dastehen, sondern eine Fülle von Anklängen an die Paulusbriefe durchzieht die Ignatianen.

4. Die Fülle der vielen, oft kurzen Anspielungen auf Paulusbriefe macht es schwer, bei Ignatius von Antiochien zwischen bewusster und unbewusster Benutzung von Paulusbriefen zu scheiden. ...

5. ...Für Ignatius geht es hier nicht um die Autorität der Schriften an sich, wie sie sich später aus ihrer Zugehörigkeit zum Kanon ergab. Der Inhalt der Paulusbriefe ist für Ignatius deshalb von Belang, weil dahinter der Apostel selbst steht, in dem er ein nachahmenswertes Vorbild sieht. ...

6. Bestimmte Methoden der Benutzung von Paulusbriefen bei Ignatius von Antiochien können festgestellt werden. Im ersten Zitat übernahm Ignatius fast wörtlich eine prägnante paulinische Wendung, stellte sie aber in einen neuen Zusammenhang und füllte sie mit einem neuen Sinn. Ähnlich wird im zweiten und dritten Zitat ein Satz- oder Gedankenschema von Paulus übernommen und neu gefüllt. Neben diesem formalen, vielleicht rhetorischen Interesse steht ein inhaltliches Interesse an den Paulusbriefen. Zahlreiche paulinische Begriffe und Gedanken werden übergenommen.[54]

Der Römerbrief wird wegen seiner schwierigen theologischen Gedankengänge von Ignatius weniger verwertet sein, wenn wir auch Zeichen einer Kenntnis dieses Briefes haben. Dafür entspricht das theologische Denkschema der Pastoralbriefe dem Ignatius mehr; ob Ignatius die Pastoralbriefe bewusst benutzt hat, muss trotz vieler Anklänge unentschieden bleiben. Gekannt hat er sie sicher.[55]

Thus, as Johannes Weiss so succinctly put it:

For the first time we have before us an exceedingly intensive influence of the Pauline letters, which is sharply contrasted with the quite external and superficial borrowing in *James* or

First Clement. Ignatius not only knew the Pauline letters, he lived in them completely; his modes of thought and expression are *saturated* with contacts with them.[56]

And yet it is uncertain just how far Ignatius himself penetrated to the depths of Paul's theology. Certain aspects of it, especially the sense of fellowship with the crucified and risen Christ, he understood well. Other aspects seem to have been strange to him.

He never grasped Paul's teaching on justification, on deliverance from *sarx* (flesh), or on the indwelling Spirit. Nor did he penetrate the fullness of Paul's view of faith as receptivity, the opposite of boasting. In Ignatius faith is primarily conviction. Sometimes, indeed, he uses Pauline phrases with meanings that widely differ from the original(e.g. *Rom* 5:1; *Eph* 8:2).[57]

Barnard maintains that for Ignatius "St. Paul was one to be admired as a supreme example of Christian living rather than of reflective thought."[58] Indeed, it would appear that much of his theological interpretation of his martyrdom is due to his identification of himself with Paul — in whose footsteps he hopes to be found.[59]

II. THE MINISTRY IN IGNATIUS

A. TRIPARTITE STRUCTURE

The Letters, *Romans* excluded, present us with a tripartite hierarchy of *epískopos, presbytérion* and *diákonoi.* The *epískopos* functions as the central unifying figure for the community; he is the chief administrator, the over-seer, the one ultimately responsible. The *presbytérion,* the "council of God"(*Tr* 3:1), which takes the place of what Ignatius calls "the council of the Apostles"(*Mg* 6:1) stands on the side of the *epískopos* in the hierarchy and forms an advisory council subject to and representing him. It is thus the *epískopos* together with his *presbytérion* who make up the administrative unit of the community(cf., e.g. *Mg* 6:1; 7:1; 8:1; *Tr* 2:2; 12:21 *Eph* 2:2; *Pol* 6:1). The *diákonoi,* whom Ignatius never mentions as a group without adding the *epískopos* and the *presbýteroi,* are "entrusted with the service of Jesus Christ"(*Mg* 6:1); they are "servants of the mysteries of Jesus Christ" — not "servants of food and drink but servants of the Church of God" who "must please all in every way"(*Tr* 2:3).

On what foundation is this clearly delimited authority structure based? Remarkably enough it is founded on the unity in the Church, on the earthly realization of the heavenly order and unity(*Sm* 8:1; *Mg* 6:1). This is remarkable not because Ignatius is in any way inconsistent in his theology, for he is certainly consistent, but because, unlike most of the Christian writers who come after him, he makes no appeal to apostolic succession as the foundation for ministerial authority, nor does he make mention of the *epískopos* possessing a special charism of the Holy Spirit. Not that Ignatius denies authority based on an historical connection between the *mono-epískopos* and the Apostles;[60] he just has a much more Platonic way of conceiving both the Church and authority in the Church. There is for him a mystical nexus between the earthly Church and the sphere of the divine. This it is that permits him, for example, to urge that deference to the bishop is the same as deference to God.[61] He is not thereby attempting to divinize the bishop or separate the ministry from the community. He is merely giving voice in a practical way to his strong conviction that the divine sphere of complete union and concord is the archtype which must be imitated on earth. This earthly union he has undoubtedly experienced to a profound degree at Antioch in the celebration of the Eucharist with the presbyters, deacons and the whole community gathered around him. This intense union in the community and with himself through the one Eucharist was clearly for him a reflection of the heavenly pattern and apparently remained so until death. Bearing this in mind we can perhaps better understand why for Ignatius the authority of the ministers rests on the united-ness — here and now present — in the local community, and why he repeatedly urges adherence to the bishop and his ministers as an antidote against any lack of union.

Using this teaching as a point of departure, E. Fincke in his *Das Amt der Einheit*[62] has concluded that even in the apparently monarchical church structure of Ignatius the *epískopos* remained completely a part of the community, that not just the ministers but the whole community was seen as "elect and sacred" (*Tr* - Salutation), and that the bearers of authority within this sacral community operated as a "function" of unity. Such a concept of authority presupposes that the *epískopos* especially shoulder an enormous amount of active responsibility, for if he is distinguished in any way, it is not so much by what he is, but by what he for his part must do, namely draw all in the community to that union which reflects the unity of God.

B. *Epískopos*

He must be a person around whom the people will want to be united, a person to "help all men," to "put up with all in love," "to exhort all men to gain salvation"(*Pol* 1:2). He must "speak to each individually after the manner of God," "bear the sicknesses of all" and "be diligent with unceasing prayer" (*Pol* 1:3). "If you love good disciples," writes Ignatius to Polycarp, "it is no credit to you; rather bring to subjection by your gentleness the more troublesome"(*Pol* 2:1). "Let not those that appear to be plausible, but teach strange doctrine, overthrow you"(*Pol* 3:1).

The *epískopos* must protect widows(*Pol* 4:1), show himself especially humble when treating with slaves and not allow them to be puffed up (Pol 4:3), enjoin husbands and wives to ever greater mutual love (*Pol* 5:1) and encourage those who can remain in continence to do so without boasting(*Pol* 5:2).

Then having sketched out for Polycarp the duties of the *epískopos,* Ignatius immediately addresses himself to the whole Smyrnean community: "Give heed to the bishop, that God may also give heed to you. I am devoted to those who are subject to the bishop, presbyters and deacons.... Labor with one another, struggle together, run together, suffer together, rest together, rise up together as God's stewards and assistants and servants"(*Pol* 6:1). This Ignatian norm of union with the *epískopos,* the presbyters and deacons as the will of God for the community and the earthly reflection of the divine sphere reaches its high point in *Sm* 8:1-2:

> See that you all follow the bishop, as Jesus Christ follows the Father, and the presbytery as if it were the Apostles. And reverence the deacons as the command of God. No one should do any of the things pertaining to the church (or assembly: *ekklēsían*) without the bishop. Let that be considered a safe (or sure: *bebaía*) Eucharist which is presided over by the bishop, or by one whom he appoints. 2 Where the bishop appears, there let the people be, just as where Jesus Christ is, there is the catholic Church. It is not right either to baptize or to hold an agape apart from the bishop; but whatever he approves is also pleasing to God — so that everything you do may be *steadfast and sure (asphalès kaì bébaion* [cf. *Heb.* 6:19]).[63]

Ignatius, moreover, sees the bishop's approval not only as a secure guide for pleasing God in the celebration of the Eucharist, Baptism or an agape, but also for the same reason as fittingly extending to Christian marriage: "It is fitting for men and women who marry to be united with the bishop's approval, so that the marriage may be related to the Lord, not to lust."(*Pol* 5:2).

Besides the remarks concerning the *epískopos* in *Sm* 8, there are others which appear terribly extravagant if considered apart from Ignatius' lofty mysticism, his unity theology and the Syrian tendency toward strong metaphors. The *epískopos* is analogous to or, perhaps better said, mystically identifiable with: God (*Mg* 6:1) *the grace* of God (*Mg* 2:1), with the *Father* (*Mg* 3:1; *Tr* 3.1), with *the Lord* (*Eph* 6:1), with *Jesus Christ* (*Tr* 2:1) and with *the "commandment"* (presumably that of God, *Tr* 13:2).[64] All of which would indeed be unusual if we were not dealing with a Syrian mystic on the verge of martyrdom.

But the biggest *novum* concerning the *epískopos,* and the *presbýteroi* and *diákonoi* too for that matter, appears in Tr 3:1:

> Likewise let all respect the deacons as Jesus Christ and the bishop as a type of the Father and the presbyters as the council*(synédrion)* of God and the college of Apostles. Without these the name of "Church" is not given.

To which Ignatius immediately adds: "I am confident that you accept this"(*Tr* 3:2), evidently aware that to say there is no Church apart from these particular ministers is no easy teaching to accept, and possibly alluding to the fact that there were some, other than the Trallians, who did not accept it. The grounds he gives for his confidence that they do is the presence with him of their bishop Polybius who evidently agrees with Ignatius. It is in any case a teaching not found in the New Testament.

Unfortunately Ignatius never tells us exactly how one becomes an *epískopos*. The closest he comes to treating the transmission of the ministry is in *Phil* 1:1:

> I know that your bishop obtained the ministry, pertaining to the whole community, "not from himself or through men"(*Galatians* 1:1) or for vainglory, but in the love of God the Father and the Lord Jesus Christ.

— a comment which only succeeds in submerging the question into deeper mystery. Nor does he ever mention the installation or ordination of presbyters or deacons. Lightfoot commenting on *Tr* 7:1 —"and this will be possible for you, if you are not puffed up, and are inseparable from God, from Jesus Christ, and from the bishop and from the ordinances of the Apostles" — says:

> The reference to the ordinances is doubtless to the institution of episcopacy. Early tradition points to St. John as mainly instrumental in establishing an episcopal organization in Asia Minor, and to him more especially Ignatius may be referring here.[65]

Certainly I would not be the first to say that this comment by Lightfoot seems completely gratuitous and at most drawn from later extrinsic evidence rather than from the text itself.

C. PRESBYTÉRION

The major analogy which Ignatius uses in speaking of the presbyters or the *presbytérion* is the council or college of the Apostles:

Mg 6:1: "the presbyters in the place of the council *(synedríou)* of the Apostles"

Tr 2:2: "to the *presbytérion,* as to the Apostles of Jesus Christ"

Tr 3:1: "the presbyters as the council *(synédrion)* of God and the college *(sýndesmon)* of Apostles"

Phld 5:1: "making the Gospel my refuge as the flesh of Jesus, and the Apostles as the *presbytérion* of the Church"

Sm 8:1: "and the *presbytérion* as if it were the Apostles"

Daniélou thinks that the analogies have to do especially with the number of presbyters:

> Nous avons noté que les *Kerygmes de Pierre* nous montrent les hiérarchies locales de la côte palestinienne et syrienne constituées d'un collège de douze presbytres et d'un évêque. Ignace d'Antioche par ailleurs compare le collège des presbytres au "Sénat des Apôtres" et l'évêque tient la place du Christ. L'allusion aux Apôtres donne à penser qu'il s'agit ici encore d'un collège de douze ou de onze presbytres. ... On sait que l'Église d'Égypte à date ancienne était toute entière gouvernée par un collège de douze entourant l'évêque.[66]

Besides comparing them to the Apostles, Ignatius employs several other picturesque analogies for the presbyters. The Ephesian *presbytérion*, for example, "is attuned to the bishop as the strings to a harp"(*Eph* 4:1); the Magnesians are admonished to be subject "to the *presbytérion* as to *the law of Christ"* (*Mg* 2:1 and "to the *epískopos* as to *the grace of God")*, for their *presbytérion* is the "aptly woven spiritual crown" of the church (*Mg* 13:1).

This latter group of presbyters is also called "holy" for even they "have not taken advantage of his (their bishop's) outwardly youthful appearance, but yield to him in their godly prudence"(*Mg* 3:1).

The Letters tell us further that the *presbýteroi*, just as the *epískopos* and the *diákonoi,* "have been appointed in accordance with the wish of Jesus Christ, whom he has, by his own will, through the operation of his Holy Spirit, confirmed in loyalty"(*Phld* - Salutation; transl. Kleist, p. 85).

Though Ignatius mentions the *presbytérion* and the *presbýteroi* twenty-two times altogether, he says in fact very little about their function. That they form an advisory council for the bishop seems quite clear from *Phld* 8:1:

> But where there is division and anger God does not dwell. The Lord then forgives all who repent, if their repentance lead to the unity of God and the council of the bishop.

Some may want to see in Ignatius' use of *synédrion theoû* (*Tr* 3:1) and *synedríou tôn apostólōn* a clear reference to the Jerusalem sanhedrin who advised the high priest, thus implying a sacerdotal role in the *epískopos* and possibly also in the *presbýteroi*. I think this should be avoided for several reasons. First of all, *synédrion* was the normal classical and *koinë* Greek word for any council or advisory group (Ratsversammlung)[68] and, secondly, because even "the 'Great Sanhedrin' of seventy-one presbyters was recruited both from the Aaronic priesthood and rabbinically qualified laymen,"[69] and the presbyterate in the local Jewish communities was "primarily a civil, a *lay* organization.[70]

D. *DIÁKONOI*

The *diákonoi* are obviously subordinate to the other ministers, for Ignatius says that his fellow servant, the deacon Zotion, "is subject to the bishop as to the grace of God and to the law of Jesus Christ"(*Mg* 2). They appear to be first of all in charge of the more material needs of the community, but Ignatius wants to be sure that their apostolate is not held in distain or that they are looked upon as mere Christian table waiters, "for they are not ministers of food and drink, but servants of the Church of God; ...Likewise let all respect the deacons as Jesus Christ"(*Tr* 2:3; 3:1). The deacons he says "are most dear to me" (*Mg* 6:1), "my fellow servants"(*Sm* 12:2).

And indeed they were for he had three and probably more deacons as personal companions at least in Asia Minor and most likely all the way to Rome: Burrhus from Ephesus who transcribed the letter to the Philadelphians (*Phld* 11:2) and to the Smyrneans (*Sm* 12:1), Philo from Cilicia (*Phld* 11:1) and Rheus Agathopous (*Sm* 10:1). From what he says of Philo in *Phld* ll:1 — "a man of good report, who is at present serving me in the word of God" — and of the deacons in *Tr* 2:3 — "the deacons of the mysteries of Jesus Christ" — one gets the idea that their ministry was indeed a spiritual one as well as material.

E. Tópos

Having taken a look at Ignatius' theology of unity and the tripartite ministerial structure in the Letters, we can turn now to the very important question of the relationship between the ministers and the non-ministers in the comnumity. The points at issue are, first of all, the understanding of "office" *(tópos)* as it appears in the Letters and, secondly, whether and to what degree we can speak of the Letters reflecting a genuine distinction between clergy and laity.

Tópos (place) in the sense of distinction, dignity, office is used but twice by Ignatius: *Sm* 6:1 —

> Let no one be deceived; even things in heaven and the glory of the angels, and the rulers visible and invisible, even for them there is a judgement if they do not believe on the blood of Christ. "He that receives let him receive." Let not *office* exalt anyone, for faith and love is everything, and nothing has been preferred to them.

— and *Pol* 1:2 —

> Vindicate your *office* with all diligence, both as regards its material and spiritual aspects. Make unity your concern — there is nothing better than that.

These uses are much the same as we have already seen in *1 Clement*
40:5 and 44:5 and as also appears in Polycarp's *Letter to the Philippians*
11:1:

> I am deeply sorry for Valens, who was once made a presbyter
> among you, that he so little understands the place *(locum)*
> which was given to him.

Köster, commenting on all three of these texts in his article *Tópos* for
Theol. Wörterbuch z. N.T., states:

> Doch sind diese Belege vereinzelt und bezeugen keineswegs
> einen festen technischen Gebrauch. Es handelt sich vielmehr
> wie schon *Ag.* 1, 25 [Lord...show us which one of these two
> you have chosen to take this *place* of service as an apostle
> which Judas left ... .] um eine gelegentliche Variation der
> dargestellten Bedeutung *rechter Ort, Platz für etwas*.[71]

He also points out in the same article that *tópos* is not found in the
LXX as a technical term for "office." The most we can say for this term at
the end of the first and beginning of the second century is that it stands at
the beginning of a development that with the progression of years will lead
to its meaning "a fixed clerical status" as is indeed found in Eusebius, *The
Apostolic Constitutions*, Origen, Tertullian and Cyprian.[72]

F. *Hoi kat'ándra*

In taking up the question of a distinction between clergy and laity, we
should note first of all that Ignatius does not seem to know the terms *laïkos*
or *laïkos ánthrōpos* which we met in *1 Clement* (40:5). *Klêros* is a term he
uses frequently but then either as the *lot* he wishes to share with a
community(e.g., *Eph* 11:2: "that I may be found in the lot of the Christians
of Ephesus, who also were ever of one mind with the Apostles...") or for his
own lot, his destiny to become a martyr (*Tr* 12:3; *Rom* 1:2; *Phld* 5:1). The
use of *klêros* as in later authors to denote a cleric as opposed to a layman is
not found in Ignatius.

The characteristic Ignatian phrase for speaking of those who are
neither bishop, presbyter nor deacon is *hoi kat'ándra:* "the *individual*
members" of the Church[73] (*Eph* 4:2; 20:2; *Tr* 13:2; *Sm* 5:1; 12:2; *Pol* 1:3)
— an expression which expresses otherness without connoting separation.

110

A designation which clearly harmonizes with his central theological theme of unity. Moreover his way of speaking to them shows how much he himself identifies with them, e.g. *Eph* 3:1:

> I give you no orders as if I were someone great. For even though I am in chains for the sake of the Name, I am not yet perfected in Jesus Christ. Indeed, I am now but beginning to be a disciple, and I speak to you as to my fellow learners, for I need to be anointed by you with faith, encouragement, patient endurance and steadfastness.

And concerning the *hoi kat' ándra,* Ignatius writes to Polycarp(5:1):

> Speak to my sisters that they love the Lord, and be content with their husbands in flesh and in spirit. In the same way enjoin on my brothers in the name of Jesus Christ "to love their wives as the Lord loved the Church."

As a summary of these last two sections, let us consider a comment of H. von Campenhausen on the ministry in the Ignatian letters. He writes: "Ignatios ist in seiner Amtsauffassung eigentumlich 'kirchlich', aber er ist nicht klerikal."[74] This does not say that there were no groups in the churches known to Ignatius. We have just seen them, and we could even add some, e.g. widows, celibates, dissenters, etc. What it does say is that given Ignatius' theology the difference in these groups cannot rest on the grounds of a *status* which makes the one group higher or better, or lower or worse, than the others. It means that if there is a distinction or dignity that redounds to any group in the community to the exclusion of others, it cannot be based on what they are, for they are as all the rest: Christians in a common unity, in community — one community united to God(who is Unity) and to the one bishop in the one Eucharist. And if any group in the community is different, it is because of a ministry, a service in faith and love, which it performs for or on behalf of the community.

The same holds true for the *epískopos* himself. In the Ignatian vision he is far from a lofty honorific titleholder. The *epískopos* is identified in the service he renders the community as its central unifier. His dignity, his *tópos* lies in his doing this. Ignatius never states directly that he is an *epískopos*; he designates himself "a fellow learner" with the community (*Eph* 3:1). Were it not for two third-person statements in Romans (2:2; 9:1) we would be without internal evidence that Ignatius himself functioned as an *epískopos*. That this *tópos* of the *epískopos* is very functional can be seen from the way Ignatius puts his admonition to Polycarp (1:2): "Vindicate your office," into the context of service by immediately adding: "by giving your whole attention to its material and spiritual sides."[75] This is not the way one normally speaks of an honorary distinction or an ontological quality. In short, it seems rather clear that the positing of a fixed clerical "amt" which would make anyone in the community ontologically more or better than his "fellow servants" or his "brothers" or "sisters" would be a belial of the Ignatian task and completely out of consonance with Ignatius' theology.

G. *HIEREÚS*

Those who take up the question of "la condition sacerdotale" in the Letters agree on several points; namely that:
- the technical term for priest *(hiereús)* is not applied to any of the ministers,
- the term, however, does appear twice in the Letters, both times in Phld 9:1:

> The priests *(hiereís)* are noble, but the High Priest (ho ar*chiereús*), who has been entrusted with the Holy of Holies, is nobler and he alone has been entrusted with the secret things of God. He is the door of the Father, through which enter Abraham and Isaac and Jacob and the Prophets and the Apostles and the Church.

- the term *hiereís* in this text applies to the Old Testament priests,[76] the *ho archiereús* to Jesus Christ.

Beyond these points of agreement there are almost as many opinions as there are commentators with regard to the question of a priestly condition for the respective ministers. The reason is that the arguments which could most prove such a condition lie not in *Phld* 9:1[77] — which actually says little more than "the Old Testament was good but the New Testament is better" — but rather in the sacral-cultic interpretation of a whole series of other texts.

J. Colson opens his study of this question by presenting the positions of P. Batiffol, J. Moffatt, G. Bardy and the *Encyclopedia Britannica* (based on Lightfoot) and showing that "les opinions sont contradictoires, et la condition sacerdotale des ministres chrétiens chez Ignace d'Antioche trop vite affirmée ou niée."[78] He himself, although indeed admitting the absence of any explicitly formulated "condition sacerdotale des ministres," attempts a cumulative argument in favor of its implicit presence based on such texts as *Sm* 8:2, *Eph* 5:2, *Mg* 7:1 and *Phld* 4, much the same type of argument K.H. Schelkle works out for the presence of a priestly service in the New Testament writings.[79] This cumulative argument of Colson has to be taken seriously. The possible overtones in the term *thusiastérion* (altar or area around the altar, sanctuary, in the O.T.: Court of the People),[80] the descriptions of the Eucharist as the flesh of Jesus Christ (*Phld* 4; *Sm* 7:1) and the insistence on the *epískopos* as the ordinary minister of the eucharistic celebration all seem to suggest a cultic-sacrificial aspect without ever explicitating it. This was undoubtedly what prompted Moffatt's admission that "in some real sense, which Ignatius does not define, the eucharist denotes sacrifice."[81] The fact remains, for better or for worse, that this is a point Ignatius simply does not work out in any further detail. The two statements he makes wherein the Eucharist is connected with the flesh of Jesus Christ are:

> Be careful therefore to use one Eucharist — for there is one flesh of our Lord Jesus Christ, and one cup for union with his blood... (*Phld* 4).

and

> They [the opponents] abstain from Eucharist and prayer because they do not confess that the Eucharist is the flesh of our Savior Jesus Christ which suffered for our sins, which the Father raised up by his goodness. (*Sm* 7:1)

Ignatius does not call the Eucharist a sacrifice *(thusía)* as later Christian writers readily do.[82] In fact, the word *thusía* appears but once in the Letters: *Rom* 4:2, where Ignatius applies it to his forthcoming martyrdom.

Since ultimately the question of a "condition sacerdotale" in the Letters depends on the presence or absence of certain sacral-cultic conceptions in the text, I think it is best to treat them in a separate section.

III. SACRAL-CULTIC CONCEPTIONS

Let us turn immediately to Professor Colson's argumentation for a "condition sacerdotale" in the Letters. His point of departure is the term *tò thusíasterion* (altar or altar court). To begin with we might note that prior to 534 C.E. the use of this substantive is limited exclusively to Jewish and Christian literature,[83] and is employed by Ignatius five times in five different letters (*Rom* 2:2; *Tr* 7:2; *Mg* 7:2; *Eph* 5:2; *Phld* 4). Colson works with the last four texts:[84]

> Ce sont ces trois fonctions qui constituent dans l'Église, *l'autel:* "quiconque est *à l'interieur* de *l'autel (ho entòs thusiastēríou)* — l'autel, partie principale du sanctuaire prise pour le tout — celui-là est pur *(katharós estin)*, mais quiconque est en dehors de l'autel *(ho dè ektòs thusíastēriou)* n'est pas pur *(ou katharós estin);* ce qui veut dire que celui qui agit *en dehors de l'eveque, du presbyterium et des diacres (ho chōrìs episkópou kaì presbyteríou kaì diakónōn prássōn ti),* celui-la n'est pas pur de conscience"(*Trall.*, VII,2).
> ... Tous, accourez pour vous réunir *comme un seul Temple de Dieu, comme autour d'un seul autel,* en l'unique Jésus-Christ: *pántes hōs eis héna naòn syntréchete theoû, hōs epì hèn thusiastérion, epì héna Iēsoûn Christón. k.t.l (Magn.,* VII, 1-2).

Le Temple et l'autel, c'est donc, en bref, Jésus-Christ et l'Église structurée autour de lui dans l'unité vivante. Cependant, quand Ignace parle de cet "autel unique", ce n'est pas un pur symbole. Il y a référence à l'autel où se célèbre le rite eucharistique autour des ministres de l'Église. Cette référence est sous-jacente lorsque Ignace écrit:"S'éloigner de *l'autel,* c'est se priver du Pain de Dieu: *eàn mè tis ê entòs toû thusiastēríou, hustereîtai toû ártou toû theoû" (Eph.,* V, 2). Le Pain de Dieu, c'est ici, comme au chapitre VI du IVᵉ Évangile, la vraie foi, la doctrine de vérité et le pain eucharistique. Et l'autel est également l'Église unie au Christ autour de ses ministres et la table où est rompu le pain eucharistique. Ce double sens ressort nettement du texte suivant: "Ayez donc soin de ne participer qu'à une seule chair de Notre-Seigneur, une seule *coupe* pour l'union a son sang, un seul autel, comme un seul évêque avec le presbyterium et les diacres" (*Phld.,* IV)
Le caractère sacrificiel de l'eucharistie est, par ailleurs, nettement souligné: "L'eucharistie, c'est la chair de notre Saveur Jésus-Christ, la chair qui a souffert pour nos péchés et

que le Père, dans sa bonté, a ressuscitée" (*Smyrn.*, VII,1). C'est bien là ce qui fait de la table où se célèbre "l'eucharistie, chair de Notre-Seigneur, coupe pour l'union a son sang", un "autel sacrificiel", l'autel d'une *thusía* ou *thusiastérion* (*Phld.*, IV; cf. *Eph.*, V,2)[85]

Building on the aforesaid, he then presents an argument for "la condition sacerdotale des ministres du culte chrétien." This we find in the final section entitled: "Le pouvoir 'divin' de l'évêque et des ministres"(pp. 333-341). First, the "divine power" of the bishop is put forth by recalling the numerous comparisons Ignatius makes between God and the bishop: *Eph* 6:1; 3:1; *Mg* 3:1; 6:1; *Tr* 3:1; *Sm* 9:1. This is followed up by citing the bishop's role as "le centre de tout culte chrétien" ... "Surtout, seule l'eucharistie peut être regardée comme légitime qui se fait sous sa présidence ou celle de son délégué (cf. *Smyrn.*, Vlll)" (p. 339). The next step is to limit "son délégué" to a presbyter or a deacon. To do this Colson points out the texts which show that the *presbytérion* is attuned to the bishop as are the strings to a harp (*Eph* 4:1), that it is "le *sénat de Dieu* et le collège des apôtres"(*Tr* 3:1), and "sa précieuse *couronne spirituelle"*(*Mg* 13:1). The deacons stand in this category of "délégué" too, he notes, for they are to be respected as Jesus Christ himself (*Tr* 3:1), and reverenced as the command of God (*Sm* 8:1), for they are "servants des *mystères* de Jesus-Christ"(*Tr* 2:3). Moreover, according to Colson, this last designation recalls the "Servant of Yahweh" in Isaiah which in the New Testament has a "résonance sacerdotale"(p. 340). Consequently:

le culte chrétien n'est légitime que célebré sous la presidence de l'évêque ou de ses "adjoints" presbytres et diacres. Par contre, tout ce qu'il approuve est agréé de Dieu (*Smyrn.*, VIII,2) ... [and thus] ...
Ici, dans les épîtres de saint Ignace, apparaît nettement en transparence, encore qu'elle ne soit pas explicitement formulée la condition "sacerdotale" des ministres du culte chrétien. (p. 34])

Critique:

While Professor Colson has masterfully pointed out Ignatius' use of sacral-cultic terminology, especially *tò thusiastérion*, in connection with the Christian prayer-gathering and the Eucharist, still it seems that he has on occasion overlooked some important aspects of the texts under discussion and thereby perhaps proved more than the texts themselves contain. Let us reconsider but two of these texts: *Sm* 8:1 and *Eph* 5:2-3.

Sm 8:1 reads:

> Let that be considered a *sure* (or certain: *bebaía)* Eucharist *which is* [held] *under the bishop or him to whom he commits* it *(hē hypò epískopon oûsa è hô àn autòs epitrépsē).*

Remarks:

1. The category in which Ignatius places the Eucharist here is not a legal category; *bebaíos* conveys the idea of that which is safe or sure.[86] Ignatius is primarily interested that what his fellow Christians do be "pleasing to God" and that which is so he calls *bebaíos* (or *asphalés).* Moreover, he asserts that they can he assured of this, if they are guided by the approval of the bishop, for "whatever he approves is also pleasing to God — so that everything you do may be *steadfast and sure" (asphalés kaì bébaion) (Sm* 8:2). Consequently it would have been better had Colson translated the beginning of *Sm* 8:1: *Seule l'eucharistie peut être regardée comme sûre* rather than "comme légitime"(p. 339). Nowhere in the Letters, in fact, do we find Ignatius expressing himself in legal categories.

2. The texts which Colson cites to show that a close relationship does or ought to exist between the bishop and the presbyters and deacons (*Eph* 4:1; *Tr* 3:1; *Mg* 13:1; *Sm* 8:1; 10:1; *Tr* 2:3, etc.) show indeed that it would be logical and fitting for the bishop to appoint a presbyter or deacon to preside at the Eucharist in his absence. We must certainly admit that it seems *a priori* very probable that the *epískopos* would delegate one of the *prokathēménoi (Mg* 6:2). But to prove from the Letters that the bishop *must choose* a presbyter or a deacon is another thing.

This we cannot establish, nor can Professor Colson; it is not in the texts.[87] In short, we must be careful not to misconstrue as establishing a separate clergy Ignatius' assertion that the approval of the bishop assures his fellow Christians that their actions (or celebrations) will be "pleasing to God."

Eph 5:2-3 reads:

Let no one deceive himself: unless a man is within the altar court *(entòs toû thusiastēríou)*,[88] he lacks the *bread of God* (cf. *John* 6:33), for if the prayer *(hē proseukè)* of one or two has such efficacy, how much more has that of the bishop and the whole assembly *(ekklēsías,* the church)!

Therefore he who does not come together (or to *the same place: epì* tò *autò)* is already proud and has separated himself.

Remarks:

1. *Thusiastérion* here is an image which primarily signifies the whole Christian assembly together with its bishop. Colson's contention that here also "Il y a référence à l'autel où se célèbre le rite eucharistique" should be answered, it seems, with the distinction as to whether there were altars, in the literal sense, built in the Christian gathering places or whether Ignatius, besides regarding the whole assembly together with the bishop as a *thusiastérion,* also looks upon the table around which the eucharistic service was held as an altar. Lightfoot[89] and Bauer[90] rule out both cases, but still, given Ignatius' extremely high mysticism, the latter does not seem to be impossible. Perhaps on this point we should give Colson the benefit of the doubt.

2. We can hardly deny that the phrase "bread of God" in this passage contains a reference to the Eucharist, although probably along with other nuances. Colson (above) states, "Le Pain de Dieu, c'est ici, comme au chapitre VI du IVe Evangile, la vraie foi, la doctrine de vérité et le pain eucharistique."[91] Moreover, Ignatius himself refers once again (*Rom* 7:3) to "the bread of God":

> I desire *the bread of God,* which is the flesh of Jesus Christ (who was of the seed of David), and for drink I desire his blood, which is imperishable love *(agápē).*

These two texts on "the bread of God" when confronted with the two most prominent eucharistic texts:

> *Sm* 7:1: They [the opponents] abstain from the Eucharist and prayer, because they do not confess that the Eucharist is the flesh of our Savior Jesus Christ which suffered for our sins... . [and]

> *Phld* 4: Be eager, therefore, to use one Eucharist, for there is one flesh of our Lord Jesus Christ and one cup for union with his blood... .

leave little doubt that Ignatius in *Eph* 5:2, speaking of "the bread of God" in this context of the Christian assembly, is referring primarily to the Eucharist.

3. The clause which immediately follows "the bread of God" here, namely "for if the prayer of one or two has such efficacy, how much more has that of the bishop and the whole assembly"*(ekklēsías)*, has curiously enough not been cited by Colson. This, however, would seem to be very important, for — immediately connected as it is with "the bread of God" — it is the only place in the Letters where Ignatius says anything about how the Eucharist comes about, namely through efficacious prayer, and not just that of the *epískopos*, but "of the bishop and the whole assembly."

The purpose of this critique of Professor Colson's argumentation has been to show that he is correct in concluding from the sacral-cultic imagery in the Letters to an implied "condition sacerdotale" in those who celebrate the Eucharist, but that those who in fact do this are "the bishop and the whole *ekklēsía*" (*Eph* 5.2). Just as Jesus Christ — "the High Priest" (*Phld* 9:1) — is called *thusiastérion* (*Mg* 7:2), so this group: "the bishop and the whole assembly" are called *thusiastérion* (*Tr* 7:2; *Eph* 5:2; *Phld* 4), not just "the bishop, the presbyters and the deacons." We must not forget that we are dealing here with the symbolic application of sacral-cultic imagery, but even so, the extension of the term *thusiastérion* is inclusive of "the bishop and the whole assembly," and exclusive of no one except "he who does not come together" and who is thereby "already proud and has separated himself" (*Eph* 5:3).

The same inclusive thinking we find in *Sm* 8:1 where that Eucharist is to be considered "sure" or "safe" when held under the bishop's leadership "or anyone to whom he has committed it."[92] Here again the categories are neither exclusive nor legal, and we cannot admit that Colson's argumentation changes this, although he does indeed establish — and rightly so — that it would be fitting, logical and most probable for the bishop to choose a presbyter or a deacon. It is quite clear from *Sm* 8 that Ignatius' paramount interest, like that of any truly good bishop, is to see that his fellow Christians do what is "pleasing to God." For them to be "sure" of this, he holds up the "approval of the bishop" as their guideline. But he does not present this as a law coming from himself — for the type of unity he proposes cannot be legislated — but rather as that which will be self-evident and desirable to these who live in faith, love and dedication. Thus for that which comes from himself, he uses such phrases as: "let that be considered"(*Sm* 8:1)[93] or "it is fitting"(*Pol* 5:2; *Mg* 4:1) or "it is profitable for you"(*Eph* 4:2) or "it is better"(*Eph* 15:1) or "Be careful (to use one Eucharist)"(*Phld* 4) or "I do not order you as did Peter and Paul"(*Rom* 4:3).

Consequently, if we must seek in the texts which Professor Colson has employed a "condition sacerdotale" — which would hardly have been an issue for Ignatius — we must admit, if we honor the texts for what they say, that the "condition sacerdotale" which is implied is a collective thing, namely of the whole church gathered together with its bishop, and that the presidency of the bishop at the assembly or his approval for another, functions as the sign of sureness to the community that what is being done is "pleasing to God."

This having been said, perhaps we can suggest a different, possibly more fruitful, approach to Ignatius' use of sacral-cultic conceptions. We might, for example take up a long-standing challenge of H.W. Bartsch concerning the sacrifice-idea in the Letters:

> Davon gibt uns das erfolglose Suchen der katholischen Forcher nach diesem (Opfer-) Gedanken, vor allem im Eucharistieverständnis ein gutes Bild. Sie mühen sich beseichnenderweise, den Opfercharakter der Eucharistie allein aus den Vokabeln *thusía* und *thusiastérion* zu beweisen, können aber nicht den Ort angeben, den der Opfergedanke in der Theologie des Ignatius hat.[94]

Perhaps, to venture a suggestion, the stark reality of Ignatius' own martyrdom was the source of his "Opfergedanken." Merely as a point of departure, suppose we consider for a moment the only *thusíasterion* text that Colson does not employ in his argument for a "condition sacerdotale," namely *Rom* 2:2. It reads:

> Grant me nothing more than to be poured forth to God while an *altar* is still ready, so that forming a chorus in love you may sing to the Father in Christ Jesus that God has judged the bishop of Syria[95] worthy to be found at the west[setting] after sending him across from the east[rising].

Some commentators hold that Ignatius in speaking of being "poured out to God while an altar is still ready so that forming a chorus..." is actually employing the metaphor of a pagan rite of human sacrifice.[96] This argument would be quite convincing had Ignatius used the word for *altar* which dominates Greek pagan literature: *bōmós,* instead of the exclusively Jewish-Christian *thusiastérion.* Here it is not unlikely, though, that he is rather thinking of the Savior — he begs the Romans not to hinder his becoming "truly a disciple of Jesus Christ"(4:2) — whose blood he sees as having been poured out to the Father on the altar of the Cross. Actually Ignatius' high mysticism does everything to confirm this, for he seems here preoccupied in becoming as much as possible like his Lord. In the sentence immediately preceeding *Rom* 2:2, for example, he states:

> For if you are silent concerning me, I am a word of God *(egò lógos theoû);* but if you love my flesh, I shall again be only a cry"(2:1).

In 3:2 he begs the Roman Christians' prayers that "I may not only be called a Christian, but may also be found to be one," and in 4:2 that "I may be found a sacrifice"*(thusía).* The strong implication is that Jesus' martyrdom was a sacrifice and that the martyrdom which Ignatius has already accepted — in fact, he writes: "I long for the beasts"(5:2) — must be allowed by the Roman Christians to also be a sacrifice. As Jesus was a sacrificial victim, so too he wishes to be a sacrificial victim. "Suffer me to follow the example of the Passion of my God," he writes them in 6:3.

But then consider 4:1:

> I am God's wheat, and I am ground by the teeth of wild beasts that I may be found pure bread of Christ,

and 7:3:

> I desire the bread of God which is the flesh of Jesus Christ (who was of the seed of David) and for drink I desire his blood, which is incorruptible love *(agápē).*

All this in a letter that well might have been entitled: "What Martyrdom Means to Me"! Martyrdom for this Syrian mystic means: being a "word of God," being "a Christian," being "a sacrifice," following "the example of the Passion of my God," becoming the "pure bread of Christ." Finally, he climaxes this passionate plea and yearning for martyrdom by identifying it with his desire for all that is contained in the Eucharist and agape. The rest of the letter is aftermath: some instructions and a closing.

Bartsch, had he not been laboring under the "Vorverständnis" that the kind of reconciliation taught by Paul is the only possible kind — which is not necessarily the case — could perhaps have seen that Ignatius does indeed draw his thinking on sacrifice from the fact of his own impending martyrdom, and that his repeated desire to imitate the suffering and death of his Lord shows that he considered the latter as a sacrifice.[97] But this would then, of course, have a bearing on Ignatius' understanding of the eucharistic elements, for "the Eucharist is the flesh of our Savior Jesus Christ which suffered for our sins..."(*Sm* 7:1). Indeed, we would have to admit that Ignatius would confess the eucharistic bread and wine to possess the same sacrificial character as the flesh of Jesus Christ on the Cross. This it seems should be admitted, but then in complete dependence on the sacrificial character of the Lord's suffering and death. Thus the one who gives the eucharistic elements a sacrificial character is Jesus Christ and no one else.

Thus the only place in the Letters where one could deduce theologically a "condition sacerdotale" is in the efficacious prayer "of the bishop and the whole assembly"(*Eph* 5:2), i.e. in "the public *prayer* of the Church, more especially that which accompanied the eucharist."[98] Thus the *thusía* which is offered within the *thusiastérion* (place of sacrifice = "the bishop and the whole assembly") is the public prayer of thanksgiving. This is consonant with the spiritualization of cult which began in later Judaism and carried over into Christianity(cf. *1 Clement* 18:16-17; 35:12; 52:3-4). *Psalm* 49 (50):13-14,23, for example, shows this quite clearly:

> Do I eat the flesh of bulls, or drink the blood of goats?
> Offer to God a sacrifice of thanksgiving, and pay your vows
> to the Most High.
> He who brings thanksgiving as his sacrifice honors me... .

It is through this prayer-sacrifice of the bishop and the whole assembly ("being a priestly body, offering spiritual sacrifices acceptable to God through Jesus Christ"[*1 Peter* 2:5]) that the Lord becomes present —

> For if the prayer of one or two ["two or three" in Mt. 18:20]
> has such efficacy, how much more has that of the bishop and
> the whole *ekklēsía* (*Eph* 5:2) —

and then in the manner which the Lord himself chose as the signs of his remembrance, namely bread and wine.

The presence of a separate priestly class within the Christian community, however, mediating in some way between God and the people, is not present in the Letters not only because there is no explicit mention of it nor use of separative, legal categories which could deliniate it, but also because it would have been completely inconsonant with Ignatius' theology of unity and his own mystical vision of the Church.

This latter, especially, cannot be mentioned enough, for it constitutes the major part of the uniqueness which was Ignatius. In his virtually timeless mysticism, he stands with one foot, as it were, in the supernatural world and one foot firmly — pastorally — planted in the hectic world of the second century, and everywhere he sees indications of the former impinging on the everyday world of time and space. In his vision there is no place for the bishop, the presbyters and deacons who stand like priests of old to mediate between God and man; no, for Ignatius the bishop *is* God, the presbytery *is* the college of the Apostles, the deacons *are* Jesus Christ. Such mysticism, which seems so lofty and exalted in comparison with the struggling conditions of the Church in the early second century, cannot but move us to admiration.[99] Had such a mystical understanding of Church leaders been tenable or credible to later generations of Christians, perhaps the need for a priestly class would have been rendered superfluous.

Ignatius — the leader, the mystic, the martyr — is easy to misunderstand, and if that is the case here, I stand to be corrected; but it is also easy to see that had we understood Ignatius better in the past, fewer arguments for a sacral-cultic priestly class would have been traced back to him, this bishop "who did his best as a man created for unity" (*Phld* 8:1).

IV. CONCLUSION

The rare combination of Christian leadership, Syrian mysticism and an unbelieveable thirst for martyrdom we find in the Ignatian Letters makes it virtually impossible to fit Ignatius into any hard and fast category, although he bears witness primarily to a type of Christianity which was known and practiced at Antioch in the early second century. This Antioch, besides being the mission sending station of the early Church, was the third largest city of the Empire, a metropolis in which pagans, a large Jewish community, Christians from all over the Empire, and a collection of weird Oriental sects lived a strange sort of co-existence dominated by a Roman business monopoly and held peaceful by the Roman legions stationed nearby.

The presence of Judaizing Docetists in some of the Christian communities of Asia Minor as well as his impending martyrdom impel Ignatius to write his Letters. His opponents appeal to the Old Testament; he to the risen Christ. Among others, he employs a concept of God as "union" or "unity achieved"(*Tr* 11:2) which more or less expresses his own mystical experience. To counteract the divisive elements in the Christian communities he knows, Ignatius, working from this concept of God, develops a theology of unity — not systematically but rather in an impassioned rhetorical style — which pleads for unity of the Christians with their local *epískopos* and their presbyters and deacons. The Christian *ekklēsía* in his vision is meant to be a reflection of the divine Unity.

Ignatius' Christology is strongly anti-Docetist; its main thrust is to show that the birth, death and resurrection of Christ truly took place, i.e. that the Savior, though divine, was also truly man.

Eschatology, as such, is not developed at much length in the Letters, but Ignatius does speak of "the last times" as well as the divine "wrath"(*Eph* 11:1), "judgement"(*Eph* 11:1; Sm 6:1) and "the unquenchable fire" for evil-doers and false teachers(*Eph* 16:2).

It is difficult to discern whether Ignatius, who stands so close to the Apostolic tradition, makes use of oral or written sources. Probably a moot question for Ignatius. His use of the Old Testament is indeed rare; of the New Testament tradition he knows Paul best — his foremost source being *1 Corinthians*. But he knows most of the other Pauline letters; in fact, his modes of thought and expressions are saturated with Pauline material. He also knows much of the Synoptic tradition and a Johannine-like theology.

Writing on the tripartite ministry, Ignatius places the *epískopos* parallel with God, the *presbytérion* with the college of the Apostles and the *diákonoi* with Jesus Christ. The authority for this structure he founds on the unity in the Church, on an earthly realization of the heavenly order and unity. There is no appeal made to apostolic succession. Ignatius posits a mystical nexus between the divine sphere and the earthly Church, and thereby comes up with a very Platonic as well as a very sacral concept of the Church. The Christian community is "elect and holy"(*Tr* - Salutation), a reflection of the sacred divine unity which is God. The leaders in the community serve as a function of unity, especially the bishop. He over-sees the celebration of the Eucharist as well as the rites of Baptism and Christian marriage. There is no mention of how the tripartite ministry is transmitted, but Ignatius maintains that without it one cannot speak of Church (*Tr* 3:1).

The term *tópos* (place, "office"), used twice by Ignatius, has not yet taken on the fixed technical meaning of clerical status that is found in later writers, nor is the term *klêros*, which appears four times, used to denote a cleric as opposed to a layman. Ignatius' most common expression for those we today generally call "the faithful" is *hoi kat'ándra,* the individual members of the Church — a phrase which expresses otherness without connoting separation.

The word *priest* appears only in *Phld* 9:1, where Jesus Christ is (indirectly) called "the High Priest" and mention is made of the priests *(hiereîs)* of the Old Covenant. Professor J. Colson, however, has attempted an argument from the Letters for a "condition sacerdotale" in the bishop, the presbyters and the deacons. We have tried to go with him as far as seems possible from the texts themselves, but have pointed out that Ignatius does not express his own convictions concerning Christian "liturgical" functions in legal terminology nor express himself in terms that establish the strict necessity for the bishop to choose only a presbyter or deacon to lead the eucharistic assembly when he himself does not do so, although Colson does establish that it would be logical, fitting and most probable that the bishop would choose a presbyter or a deacon.

We have tried, nonetheless, to show that from Ignatius' use of *thusiastérion* in the Letters, especially *Eph* 5:2, one can reason to a kind of "condition sacerdotale" in "the bishop and the whole *ekklēsía*" who celebrate the eucharistic rite, although admitting that we are reasoning here on the symbolic applications of sacral-cultic imagery from a Christian mystic. Be that as it may, it still does not seem that, so long as we hold to what the texts say, we can arrive at more than a collective "condition sacerdotale," i.e. inclusive of the whole assembly.

It would seem that Professor Colson could have shown more fruitfully that a certain "caractère sacrificiel" is implied in the eucharistic elements had he begun from Ignatius' understanding of his own martyrdom in the *Letter to the Romans*, especially *Rm* 2:2, 4:1-2, 6:3, 7:3, but this would have presented little opportunity to develop an argument in the direction of a "condition sacerdotale."

In short, although the imagery in the Ignatian Letters is often strongly sacral-cultic, we cannot show from the Letters the presence of a separate priestly class within the Christian communities known to Ignatius. The categories that would express this are lacking and it would be completely out of keeping not only with his theology of unity but also with his own mystical vision of the Church and its leadership.

Notes

[1] R. Helm (ed.), *Eusebius Werke* (GCS), Band VII, teil I, *Die Chronik des Hieronymus*, Hinrichs, Leipzig, 1913, p. 186.

[2] E. Schwartz (ed.), *Eusebius Werke* (GCS), Band II, teil I, Hinrichs, Leipzig, 1903, p. 236, lines 14-15; p. 274, lines 17-23.

[3] In *S. Ignatium Martyrem*, 1: Migne, *P.G.*, 50, col. 588.

[4] R. Helm(ed.), *op. cit.*, p. 194. Eusebius also records here that Ignatius' successor at Antioch was named Heron.

[5] Lightfoot sees the journey as probably proceeding from Seleucia (the seaport of Antioch) to Attalia in Pamphilia, then overland through Laodicea, Hierapolis, Philadelphia (the present day Alasehir, Turkey) and Sardis, "It has been seen that at some point in his journey (probably on th banks of the Meander), where there was a choice of roads, his guards selected the northern road through Philadelphia and Sardis to Smyrna. If they had taken the southern route instead, they would have passed in succession through Tralles, Magnesia, and Ephesus, before they reached their goal. It is probable that, at the point where the roads diverged, the Christian brethren sent messengers to the churches lying on the southern road, apprising them of the martyr's destination; so that these churches would dispatch their respective delegates without delay, and thus they would arrive at Smyrna as soon as, or even before, Ignatius himself." Ref. Lightfoot, *Apostolic Fathers*, Part II, Vol. II, London, 1885, p. 2.

[6] "The modern Cavalla, on the coast of Macedonia, between Constantinople and Salonica; the Roman road comes down to the sea there, and is still in fair preservation." Ref. K. Lake, *The Apostolic Fathers*, Vol I, London, 1912, p. 277, note 1.

[7] Cf. Corwin, *St. Ignatius and Christianity at Antioch*, Yale, 1960, p. 22, n. 20: "The Roman and Antiochine Acts both say that he was killed 'in the amphitheater.' H. Delahaye in "L'Amphitheatre Flavien et ses environs," *Analecta Bollandiana*, 16 (1897), 221, 250 ff, points out that there were other places in Rome than the Colosseum where the martyrdom might have occurred."

[8] Cf. Polycarp, *ad. Philip.* 9:2; Irenaeus, *Adv. Haer.* V.28.4:"adiudicatus ad bestias"; Origin, *Hom. VI in Luc.*:"Romae pugnavit ad bestias"; Eusebius, *H.E.* III.36.3

[9] Cf. Migne, *P.L.*, 23, col. 635. Years later in 637 when the Saracens overran Antioch, his remains were taken to Rome and are today claimed to be in the church of San Clemente.

For additional material on Ignatius as well as on the authenticity of the seven letters cf.: B. Altaner, *Patrologie*. 5te Auflage, Herder, Freiburg, 1958, pp. 85-7; O. Bardenhewer, *Geschichte der Altkirchlichen Literatur*, Iter Band, Herder, Freiburg, 1902, pp. 119-146; K. Bihlmeyer, *Die Apostolischen Väter* Iter Teil, J.C.B. Mohr(Paul Siebeck), Tübingen, pp. XXXI-XXXVIII; F. Cayré, *Patrologie*, tom. 1, Desclée et Cie, Paris, pp. 60-70; J. Kleist, *ACW*, Vol. 1, Newman, Westminster, Md., 1946, pp. 53-9; A. Klijn,

Apostolische Vaders, 1, Bosch & Keuning N.V., Baarn, 1966, pp. 14-75; J. Lightfoot, *The Apostolic Fathers*, Part I and of Part II pp. 1-11, Macmillan & Co., London, 1885; H. Musurillo, *The Fathers of the Primitive Church*, New Am. Lib., 1966, pp. 72-4; J, Quasten, *Patrology*, Spectrum, Utrecht, 1950, pp. 63-76.

[10] See, e.g. *Eph* 9:1 where the people = the stones of the Temple; Jesus Christ = the derrick to place the stones; the Holy Spirit = the rope of the derrick, or *Eph* 4:1 where the epískopos = the harp; the presbyters = the harp-strings and the people = the chorus.

[11] Norden, *Die antike Kunstprosa*, II , B.G. Teubner, Leipsig, 1909, pp. 510-11; see also Kleist, *op. cit.*, p. 118.

[12] L.W. Barnard, "The Background of St. Ignatius of Antioch," in *Studies in the Apostolic Fathers and their Background*, B. Blackwell, Oxford, 1966, p. 21.

[13] Klijn, *op. cit.*, p. 21.

[14] Corwin, *op. cit.*, p. 32.

[15] Twice under Gaius and Claudius (in the 40'e), earthquakes and fire under Titus (Josephus, *Bell*. 7.54 ff.) and a still more devestating quake in 115 A.D. while Trajan was there on an imperial visit. Cf. Corwin. p. 32.

[16] *Ibid.*, p. 32.

[17] Corwin, *op. cit.*, p. 32.

[18] Barnard, *op. cit.*, p. 21.

[19] Corwin, *op. cit.*, p. 40.

[20] Josephus, *Bell*. 7.43, quoted by Corwin, p. 46.

[21] Klijn, *op.cit.*, p. 21.

[22] Corwin, *op. cit.*, p. 48.

[23] It was from out of these eastern colonies that such literature as the Odes of Solomon and the Pseudo-Clementine letters came, all embodying the same strong Jewish influence we find in Matthew. Cf. Klijn, *op. cit.*, p. 23.

[24] J. Daniélou, *Théologie du Judéo-Christianisme*, Tournai, 1958, pp. 49-5; cf. also R. Grant, *op. cit.*, vol, IV, pp. 22-24.

[25] Barnard, *op. cit.*, p. 22.

[26] *Op. cit.*, p, 23.

[27] On the side of the two-group theory: C.C. Richardson (*The Christianity or Ignatius of Antioch*, Columbia. Univ. Press, N.Y., 1935, pp. 81-85), H. W. Bartsch (*Gnostisches Gut und Gemeindetradition bei Ignatius von Antiochien*, Gütersloh, 1940, pp. 34-44) and V. Corwin (*op. cit.*, pp. 52-87). Supporters of the single group theory include: T. Zahn (*Ignatius von Antiochien*, Perthe Verl., Gotha, 1873, pp. 356-99), J.B. Lightfoot (*op. cit.*, Part II, Vol. I, p. 361), E. von der Goltz (*Ign. von Antiochien als Christ und Theologe*, Texte und Untersuch., Band 12, Heft 3, Leipzig, 1894, p. 81 ff.), W. Bauer (*Die Briefe des Ignatius von Antiochien und der Polykarpbrief* in *Handb. z. N.T.*, Ergänzungsband: *Die Apostolischen Väter*, Vol. 2, J.C.B. Mohr(Paul Siebeck), Tübingen, 1920, pp. 238-40), R. Bultmann (*Theol. of the N.T.*, Vol. 1, SCM, London, 1965, pp. 171

ff.), E. Molland("The Heretics Combatted by Ign. of Antioch," in *The Journal of Eccles. History*, V, 1954, pp. 1-6), A.J.F. Klijn (*op. cit.*, pp. 56-6) and R.M. Grant (*Gnosticism and Early Christianity*, 2nd ed., Columbia. Univ. Press, N.Y., 1966, pp. 177-181).

28 Grant, *op. cit.*, p. 178.

29 See Barnard, *op. cit.*, p. 27:"If we grant that Ignatius' conception of the Divine Being flows from his own mystical experience yet there remains the possibility that he took over *the terminology* of contemporary speculation. In Valentinian speculation Bythos and Sige beget the aeons Nous and Aletheia who in turn beget Logos and Zoe...According to the Valentinian Theodotus (Clem. Alex. *Exc. Theod.* 29) Sigé is 'the mother of all the emanations from Bythos,' i.e. the parent of all the aeons. Clearly there was considerable speculation, in Valentinian circles, as to the exact status of Sige and the other aeons. The newly discovered Gospel of Truth, which probably represents an earlier stage of Valentinus' thought, speaks of 'the Mind which pronounces the unique Word in Silent Grace'. The association of *Sigé* with the Godhead is not however confined to Valentinianism. It is found in Greek cosmological speculation as early as the comic poet Antiphanes and in the Magical Papyri where Silence is a symbol of the living, incorruptible God. It also occurs in Mandaean and Mithraic speculation. It is also interesting that Gregory Nazianzen gives *Sigé* a place in the systems of Simon Magus, Cerinthus and others (*Orat.* XXV.8.1) while Irenaeus himself states that Valentinus borrowed his theory, with modifications, from earlier Gnostics (*Adv. Haer.* l.II.I)." Hippolytus (*Refut.* VI 18, GCS, p, 144, line 13) also shows that *Sigé* was a concept used by Simon Magus.

30 H. Chadwick, "The Silence of Bishops in Ignatius," *Harvard Theological Review*, XLIII(1950), pp, 169-172.

31 In this section I have made considerable use of the excellent essay by A.F.J. Klijn entitled "De Theologie van de brieven van Ignatius"(*op. cit.*, pp. 64-75).

32 M. Staniforth, *Early Christian Writings: The Apostolic Fathers*, Penguin Classics, Baltimore, 1968, p. 68.

33 Cf. *Eph* 4:2(2x); 5:1; 14:1; *Phld* 2:2; 3:2; 5:2; 8:1; 9:1; *Sm* 12:2; *Pol* 8:3.

34 Cf. *Mg* 1:2; 13:2; *Tr* 11:2; *Phld* 4:1; 7:2; 8:1; *Pol* 1:2; 5:2.

35 The source of Ignatius' idea of *hénōsis* and his emphasis on the "unity of God" (e.g. *Phld* 8:1; 9:1; *Sm* 12:2; *Pol* 8:3) have been widely discussed, for it is clear that we are not dealing here with a reiteration of the Old Testament expressions of the uniqueness of God. H.W. Bartsch sees Ignatius' basic idea as coming from the Gnostic principle of unity which combines theology with soteriology. He holds that "this comprehensive principle was the door through which Gnostic systems and mythical conceptions entered early Christian literature"(*Die Religion in Geschichte und Gegenwart*, III, 3rd ed., Tübingen, 1959, 667; see also *Gnostisches Gut und Gemindetradition bei Ignatius von Antiochen*, Gütersloh, 1940, pp. 8-23; 34-52). T. Preiss has similarly insisted that Ignatius' ideas concerning God are close to Gnosticism because there is "no allusion at all to the idea of creation"(cf. "La mystique de l'imitation du Christ et de l'unité chez Ignace

d'Antioche," in *Revue d'hist. et de philos. rel.*, 18, 1938, pp. 221-225; 239-241). A.F.J. Klijn sees Ignatius' idea of God as *hénōsis* as coming from the Greco-Roman pagan religious culture of that age: "God als 'eenheid' is een gedachte die opkomt in de Grieks-Romeinse cultuur. In de bonte megeling van goden en gedachten die in het Grieks-Romeinse rijk samengestroomd waren, zocht men als vanzelf naar de eenheid. Men wilde een vast uitgangspunt hebben van waaruit men verder kon denken en van waaruit men het geheel kon opvatten. Hierboven is al gezegd hoe dit op godsdienstig terrein aanleiding gaf tot de overdracht van eigenschappen van de ene god naar de andere god. De goden worden verschijningsvormen van de ene allesomvattende macht (*Apostolische Vaders*, 1, Baarn, 1966, p. 66). Klijn has also shown that this concept is not limited only to Ignatius: cf. "The 'Single One' in the Gospel of Thomas," *Journ. of Bib. Lit.*, LXXXI, 1962, pp. 271-278. C. Maurer (*Ignatius von Antiochien und das Johannesevangelium*, Zurich, 1949, pp. 66; 77) believes that a possible connection with *John* 17:21 has been overlooked in the discussion. And R.M. Grant (*Apostolic Fathers. Vol. IV, Ign. of Ant.*, Camden, N.J., 1966, p. 5) maintains that: "It is undeniable that Ignatius' ideas are not exclusively biblical. Instead, they are interpretations of biblical doctrines in new circumstances provided by the Greco-Roman world. The word *hénōsis* (oneness, unity) occurs in the New Testament only in *Ephesians* (4:3 & 13) and *Colossians* (a variant in 3:14), as Bartsch has pointed out; but these letters are part of the New Testament and Ignatius knew both of them."

[36] See A.F.J. Klijn, *Apostolische vaders*, 1, *Ignatius en Polycarpus*, Baarn, 1966, p. 75: "Het is nu ook wel duidelijk waarom Ignatius zo weinig aandacht wijdt aan de traditie. De gemeente leeft niet vanuit het verleden of van wat uit het verleden is overgeleverd. Ze leeft hier en nu in de eenheid met God. Die beleeft ze in een eendrachtige kerk, rondom de ene bisschop en de ene eucharistie waarin ze deelt in het hemels voedsel.

Het enige wat een systematische geest van deze theologie kan zeggen is dat ze vrijwel geen oog heeft voor fijne onderscheidingen. In de eenheid van God waarin Christus, de bisschop en de gemeente delen, vallen de grenzen wel eens weg. Dit nadeel weegt echter nauwelijks op tegen de grote voordelen die deze theologie in de praktijk bood. Het is een theologie die niet verzandde in een woordenstrijd met de ketters, maar die uit de volheid van haar overtuiging de ketters terug kon roepen tot de eenheid van de kerk."

[37] L.W. Barnard, *op. cit.*, p. 21.

[38] E.g., C. Maurer, *op. cit.*, p. 71, where he notes this especially with regard to *Phld* 9: see also Barnard, *loc. cit.*

[39] Cf. R.M. Grant, *The Apostolic Fathers, Vol. IV. Ignatius of Antioch*, Camden, N.J.,1966, pp. 17-18. For other material on the eschatology of Ignatius, see also J.A. Fischer, *Die Apostolischen Väter*, Darmstadt, 1966, pp. 132-133.

[40] Cf. *Rivista di archeologia cristiana*, 25, 1949, pp. 47-72.

[41] I.e., *Mt.* 3:15 in relation to *Sm* 1:1; Jesus was baptized by John "so that all righteousness might be fulfilled by him."

[42] H. Köster, *Synoptische Überlieferung bei den Apostolischen Väter* (TU, 65),

Akademie Verlag, Berlin, 1957, pp. 60-61.

[43] For an historical survey of this literature up to 1940, see W.J. Burghardt, S.J. "Did St. Ignatius of Antioch Know the Fourth Gospel?" *Theological Studies,* I, 1940, pp. 7-26.

[44] A Committee of the Oxford Society of Historical Theology, *The New Testament in the Apostolic Fathers,* Clarendon Press, Oxford, 1905, p. 83.

[45] Chr. Maurer, *Ignatius von Antiochien und das Johannesevangelium,* Zwingli Verlag, Zurich, 1949, p. 100.

[46] J.A. Fischer, *Die Apostolischen Väter,* Darmstadt, 1966, p. 122.

[47] Cf. *Sm* 3:2; *Eph* 12:2; *Rom* 4:3.

[48] Cf. *Eph* 5:3; *Mg* 12:1.

[49] R.M. Grant, *The Apostolic Fathers,* Vol. I, N.Y., 1964, p. 62.

[50] C.C. Richardson, *Early Christian Fathers,* Phila., 1953, p. 79.

[51] W.J. Burghardt, S.J., *op. cit.,* p. 156.

[52] The *Martyrium Colbertinum,* I, III (11th century), for example, speaks of Ignatius as a disciple of John.

[53] H. Rathke, *Ign. von Ant. und die Paulusbriefe* (TU, 99), Akademie Verlag, Berlin, 1967.

[54] Rathke, *op. cit.,* pp. 39-41.

[55] *Ibid.,* p. 65.

[56] J. Weiss, *Earliest Christianity,* Vol. II, Harper, N.Y., 1959, p. 772.

[57] C.C. Richardson, *op. cit.,* p. 78-79.

[58] L.W. Barnard, *op. cit.,* p. 28.

[59] R.M. Grant, *op. cit.,* Vol. IV, p. 24.

[60] Cf., e.g., *Eph* 6:1 which virtually makes the bishop an apostle, or at least one sent by the Lord, and *Tr* 7:1 where "the ordinances of the Apostles" according to Lightfoot refers doubtlessly (?) to the institution of episcopacy.

[61] *Eph* 5:3-6; cf. also Richardson (ed.) *op. cit.,* p. 76.

[62] In *Das Amt der Einheit. Grundlegendes zur Theologie des Bischofsamtes,* Schwabenverlag, Stuttgart, 1964, pp. 140-146.

[63] See also *Eph* 3:2f.

[64] Cf. R.M. Grant, *op. cit.,* Vol. IV, p. 20.

[65] Lightfoot, *op. cit.,* p. 169.

[66] J. Daniélou, "Les Douze," *Bulletin saint Jean Baptiste,* tome IX-2, Dec. 1968, p. 67.

[67] Dix, *op. cit.,* p. 234.

[68] Cf. W. Bauer, *Wörterbuch z. N.T.,* Berlin, 1963, col 1556.

[69] Dix, *op. cit.,* p. 235.

[70] *Ibid.,* p. 233.

[71] *TWzNT* (ed. Kittel), Band VIII: Lieferung 4, p. 208.

130

72   Cf. Lightfoot, *op. cit.*, p. 333-334.

73   Lightfoot, *op. cit.*, p. 41; see also Kleist, *op. cit.*, p. 121. When Ign. speaks of the "whole congregation" meaning the presbyters, deacons and the *hoi kat' ándra* all in union with the *epískopos*, he uses the term *tò plêthos* or *tò pân plêthos* (cf.*Mg* 6:1; *Tr* 1:1; *Sm* 8:2).

74   *Kirchliches Amt und geistliche Vollmacht...*, p. 112.

75   The *epískopos* functioned both as the guardian of the common chest fund for the needy and as the spiritual father of his congregation. Cf. Richardson(ed.), *op. cit.*, p. 118.

76   Cf., e.g., Lightfoot, *op. cit.*, p. 274, Funk, *op. cit.*, p. 272, Campenhausen, *op. cit.*, p. 114, Colson, *op. cit.*, p. 331, Grant, *op. cit.*, p. 106.

77   Working with this understanding of Jesus Christ as High Priest, however, plus Ignatius' analogy of submission "to the bishop as to Jesus Christ" (*Tr* 2:1), one could perhaps possibly come up with at least an analogous type of priesthood for the *epískopos*. The only difficulty with this would be that the deacon (who does not stand on the side of the bishop and presbyters in the hierarchy) would then be just as much a priest as the *epískopos*, since Ignatius also compares the deacons with Jesus Christ (*Tr* 3:1). Nowhere in the Letters are the presbyters compared with Jesus Christ.

78   *Ministre de Jésus-Christ ou le sacerdoce de l'Évangile*, Beauchesne, Paris, 1966, p. 332.

79   *Jüngershaft und Apostelamt*, Herder, Freiburg, 1961, p. 101f.

80   Cf. Bauer, *Wörterbuch z. N.T.*, col. 724-5; Behm, *TWzNT* (ed. Kittel), Bd. III, p. 189.

81   "An approach to Ignatius," *Harvard Theological Review*, 29, 1936, p. 9f.

82   Cf. G.W.H. Lampe, *A Patristic Greek Lexicon*, Fasc. 3, Oxford, 1964, pp. 659-660.

83   Cf. *TWzNT* (ed. Kittel), Band III, p. 182:"Das Subst *tò thusiastérion* begegnet zuerst in der LXX und findet sich vor dem Codex Justinianus I, 12,3,1ff(p. 97f Krüeger) nur in jüd und chr Lit." The Cod. Just. was published by the Emperor Justinianus in 534 C.E. (Ref. Altaner, p. 216).

84   The text he does not use in this argumentation (*Rom* 2:2) speaks of Ignatius' desire "to be poured out to God, while an altar is still ready."

85   Colson, *op. cit.*, pp. 336-337.

86   In French: sûr; in Latin: *stabilis, constans, firmus;* in German: *feststehend, fest, zuverlassig, sicher, glaubhaft, standhaft, dauerhaft.*

87   For an excellent discussion of this problem of the bishop's delegate, see J.F.McCue, S.J., "Bishops, Presbyters and Priests in Ignatius of Antioch," *Theol. Studies*, 28, 1967, pp. 828-834.

88   Commenting on this phrase, Lightfoot (*op. cit.*, pp. 43-44) writes: "The *thusiastérion* here is not the altar, but the enclosure in which the altar stands, as the

preposition *entòs* requires. This meaning is consistent with the sense of the word, which (unlike *bōmós*) signifies 'the place of sacrifice'... The reference here is to the plan of the tabernacle or temple. The *thusiastérion* is the court of the congregation, the precinct of the altar, as distinguished from the outer court. The application of this imagery, which Ignatius had in view, appears from ... *Trall.* 7: "that is to say, whoever does anything apart from the bishop and the presbytery and the deacons is not pure in his conscience." The man who separates himself from the assembly of the faithful, lawfully gathered about its bishop and presbyters, excludes himself, as it were, from the court of the altar and from the spiritual sacrifices of the Church. He becomes as a Gentile (*Matt.* xviii. 17); he is impure as the heathen is impure. Thus *thusiastérion* being at once the place of sacrifice and the court of the congregation, was used metaphorically for the Church of Christ, the *thusiastérion empsukon,* as S. Chrysostom terms it." Cf. also W. Bauer, *Wörterb. z. N.T.,* col. 725: "—a. *entòs (toû) th. eînai: innerhalb des Altarraums... sein,* d.h. in der Kirche, unter Aufsicht ihrer bestellten Leiter bleiben I *Eph* 5,2. I *Tr* 7,2. Dem entspricht bei Ign. d. energische Betonung, das es nut e i n *th.* gäbe I *Mg* 7,2. I *Phld* 4."

89 *Op. cit.,* p. 44: "Thus S. Ignatius does not here refer to a literal altar, meaning the Lord's table.... In fact the imagery here is explained by the following words, where "the bishop and all the Church" corresponds to the *thusiastérion,* while *hē proseukè* [the prayer] is the spiritual sacrifice therein offered; as, e.g. Clem. Alex., *Strom.,* vii.6 and Orig., *c. Cels.* viii.17.... In *Philad.* 4 *thusiastérion* seems to be used ... as here and in *Trall.* 7...."

90 *Handbuch zum Neuen Testament* - Ergänzungsband, *Die Apostolischen Väter,* II, ... p. 205: "Wie man das Wort auch auffassen will, so lehrt es jedenfalls nicht, dass die christlichen Versammlungsstätten der ign. Zeit Altäre aufgewiesen hätten. Das Fehlen solcher, wie das von Götterbildern, Tempeln und Opfern hat den Christen den oft gehörten Vorwurf der Gottlosigkeit eingetragen; vgl. z.b. Minucius Felix, *Octav.* 32,1: *aras non habemus.* Celsus b. Orig., *c. Celsum* VIII, 17; Orig. weiss in seiner Erwiderung nur von unsichtbaren Altären der Christen. *Thusiastérion* ist hier [*Eph* 5:2], wie *Rom* 2:2, *Magn* 7:2, *Phil* 4 (vgl. auch Polyc. *ad Phil* 4:3, Clemens Alex. *Strom.* VII,6; 31 und Chrysostomus, *Hom XIII in Jo.* ed. Bened. VIII, 74f.), bildlich zu fassen. Der Aufenhalt im *Altarraums* bedeutet nach dem Zusammenhang und der gleichgearteten Ausführung *Trall.* 7:2 das Bleiben in der kirchlichen Gemeinschaft unter der Autorität ihrer Leiter."Note that Bauer leaves out all connection between *thusiastérion* and the fact that Ignatius is speaking here especially of the Christian prayer-gathering.

91 The phrase "bread of God" appears in the N.T. only in *John* 6:33, shortly before the eucharistic texts begin. The verse reads: "For the bread of God is he who(or/ "that which") comes down from heaven and gives life to the world." That in the account Jesus at first seemed to be speaking of the manna in the desert but actually was speaking of himself can be seen from the later question of the crowd: "How, then, does he say, 'I have come down from heaven'?"(John 6:42).

S.M. Gibbard("The Eucharist in the Ignatian Epistles," *Stud. Patr.* VIII [TU, 93], Berlin, 1966, pp. 214-215) has noted that "he [Ign.] uses the terms the flesh and blood of Jesus, not only of the eucharistic elements, but also in wider senses to denote faith, love and the gospel: "Be renewed in faith, which is the flesh of the Lord and in love, which is the blood of Jesus Christ"(*Trall.* 8.1):"I found mercy, making the gospel my refuge as the flesh of Jesus"(*Philad.* 5.1)..."

92 Transl. J.A. Kleist, S.J., *op. cit.,* p. 93.

93 The phrase with perhaps the strongest legal connotation in the Letters also appears, however, in this pericope (*Sm* 8:2), where Ignatius states: *"It is not allowed* (or *it is not right: ouk exón estin)* either to baptize or to hold an "agape" apart from the bishop." There is every reason to believe, though, that Ignatius here is not presenting this prohibition as directly from himself (although he obviously stands behind it) but rather as an already accepted norm in the Church and as an echo of Pauline tradition. Paul had himself addressed some strong words to the Corinthians who had abused the Christian communal meal (*1 Cor.* 11:20-22) as well as to those who apparently had misunderstood the function of the one who had baptized them (*1 Cor.* 12-17). Thus it seems very probable that Ignatius' statement is a reiteration of a long-standing norm among Christians, at least those of Antioch.

94 H.W. Bartsch, *Gnostisches Gut und Gemeindetradition bei Ignatius von Antiochien,* Bartelsmann, Gütersloh, 1940, p. 82.

95 Scholars intepret this phrase differently. Lightfoot (*op. cit.,* p. 201) holds that it means "the bishop belonging to Syria, i.e. 'from the distant East'; the genitive denoting, not the extent of his jurisdiction, but the place of his abode." E. Schweizer(*op. cit.,* p. 139) states that "Der Bischof ist, mindestens in der Theorie des Ignatius, nicht nur monarchischer Gemeindeleiter, sondern schon so etwas wie ein Metropolit. Der Bischof von Antiochia ist zugleich Bischof von Syrien, ohne ihn ist die Gemeinde in ganz Syrien bischofslos (*Rm* 9,1; vgl. *Mg* 14; *Tr* 13,1)." R.M. Grant (*op. cit.,* Vol. IV, pp. 87-88), who agrees with Schweizer on this point, notes: "In this passage Ignatius refers to himself as 'the bishop of Syria'(not 'the Syrian bishop,' cf. 9:1). It would therefore appear that he was the metropolitan of Syria as bishop of Antioch; his letters to the various churches and to a bishop suggest that he was not unaccustomed to writing epistles. This is to say that the see of Antioch was essentially patriarchial at the beginning of the second century as well as toward the end, when we find Serapion of Antioch directing the affairs of the nearby seacoast town of Rhossus (Eus., *H.E.,* 6,12,3-6)."

96 K.F. Hermann, *Gottesdienstl. Altherth.,* ii, para. 29 (quoted by Lightfoot, *op.cit.,* p. 201); also K. Lake, *The Apostolic Fathers,* I(Loeb), p. 193; R.M. Grant, *op. cit.,* Vol. IV, p. 87.

97 Bartsch's reasoning (*op. cit.,* p. 82) runs as follows. "Es fehlen bei Ignatius die Kategorien, die der Opfergedanke erfordert: "Sünder" —"Gerechter." Mit ihnen wird das Verhältnis zwischen Gott und Mensch beschrieben, wenn man den Opfergedanken

kennt. Für Ignatius ist Gott nicht in erster Linie der Gerechte, dem gegenüber der Mensch Sünder ist, sondern Gott ist der *Eine*, von dem der Mensch getrennt ist. Nicht gerecht zu werden ist darum die Sehnsucht des Ignatius, sondern zu Gott zu gelangen, mit ihm vereint zu werden. Auf die Übernahme des paulinischen Begriffs *dikaioûn* und seine durch das Fehlen des Verständnisses bedingte Wandlung haben wir schon oben(S. 41f) hingewiesen. Wir können darum das Auftauchen des Opfergedankens nicht so erklären, dass Ignatius tatsächlich unter diesem Gesichtspunkt sein Martyrium verstanden habe, sondern die dahinzielenden Aussagen sollen lediglich die Gleichförmigheit seines Leidens mit dem Leiden Christi. erweisen. Daraus folgt, dass der Opfergedanke auf das Leiden Christi bezogen, zum Gut der Gemeinde gehört. Das erweist schon das bekannte Wort *Mk* 10, 45: *lútron antì pollôn.*"

[98]   J. Lightfoot, *op. cit.*, p. 257.

[99]   Cf. L.W. Barnard, *op. cit.*, p. 19.

CHAPTER V

THE LETTER(S) OF POLYCARP TO THE PHILIPPIANS

OUTLINE

I. Background
    A. The Harrison thesis; the Barnard correction
    B. Sources and Doctrine
II. Ministerial Functions
III. Sacral-Cultic Conceptions
IV. Conclusion

I. BACKGROUND

We learn from Irenaeus (*Ep. ad Florinum* [Eus. *H.E.*v. 20])[1] that Polycarp, who was bishop of Smyrna in the first half of the second century, wrote numerous letters of encouragement and admonition to churches and individuals; the only one Irenaeus cites specifically, however, is the Letter to the Philippians (*Adv. Haer.* iii. 3.4).[2] The Philippian Letter is also the only work of Polycarp known to Eusebius, who quotes chs. 9 and 13 (*H.E.* III. 36=13-15).[3] Jerome mentions that the Letter was read even to his day at Christian gatherings *in conventu Asiae (De Vir. Ill.* 17).[4] Today the Letter's authenticity cannot be seriously questioned, although it has been at various times in the past.[5] Unfortunately the complete original Greek text of the Letter has not been preserved.[6] The manuscripts which we have go only up to ch. 9:2; from there the gaps must be filled in by the quotations from Eusebius mentioned above, or with the help of the oldest Latin translation.[7] So completed it forms a missive of about 1750 words.

On the grounds of the text C.C. Richardson has written a telling analysis of the man who stood behind the Letter:

> Brief as it is, Polycarp's letter gives us the measure of the man. He was simple, humble and direct. There was nothing subtle about him, or pretentious. He does not appear to have had much in the way of formal education. His Greek is without style, without the faintest touch of rhetoric, without learned allusion. He is not versed, as he himself admitted, in the Scriptures, i.e., the Old Testament. But he had meditated much on Christian writings; his letter is a veritable mosaic of quotation and allusion to them. Modern critics are fond of calling him "unoriginal." It is true; he shows not the slightest interest in theological or philosophical speculation.[8]

The Letter can be briefly outlined as follows:

Introduction

Ch. 1: Praise of the Philippians for their hospitality to the martyrs and for their faith, well-rooted from early times.

Ch. 2: Exhortation to faith, hope, the practice of virtue and keeping of the Lord's teaching.

Ch. 3: Polycarp's reason for writing: the invitation of the Philippians.

Ch. 4 - 6:2: Exhortation to virtue for married women, widows, deacons, young men, virgins and presbyters.

Ch. 6:3 - 7:2: Warning against heresy.

Ch. 8 - 9: Exhortation to hope and perseverance motivated by:
A. the example of Christ,
B. the example of the martyrs.

Ch. 10: Exhortation to brotherly love and good works.

Ch. 11: Concerning the fall of the presbyter Valens.

Ch. 12:1: The need for forgiveness.

Ch. 12:2 & 3: Prayer for blessing.

[Ch. 13: Promise to forward their letter to Antioch and mention of the letters of Ignatius accompanying this letter to them.]

Ch. 14: Request for their kindness to the bearer of the letter (Crescens) and to his sister. Farewell.

A. THE HARRISON THESIS; THE BARNARD CORRECTION.

From the time that Polycarp's Letter was first printed in Latin by Faber Stapulensis (Paris, 1498) up to 1666 when the French savant Daille produced his *magnum opus*,[9] the authenticity of the Letter was discussed and disputed on the presupposition that one was dealing with an integral letter penned from start to finish (14 chapters) at one and the same time. Daille's work presented the first serious challenge to the integrity of the Letter. He pointed out a contradiction in the text which to his day had gone remarkably unnoticed, namely that ch. 9 speaks of Ignatius as already dead while in the last sentence of ch. 13 he is still alive. The solution of Daille was simply that ch. 13 should be considered as spurious. And this marked the beginning of a long line of more or less unsatisfactory interpolation theories. Every competent critic from his time until Lightfoot was forced to make some attempt to account for the contradiction.[10]

In 1936, P.N. Harrison of Cambridge University produced a long scholarly study in which he sought to solve the contradiction by positing that ch. 13 (and possibly 14) formed an earlier "cover letter" to a package of Ignatius correspondance which Polycarp sent to the Philippians before the news of and particulars concerning Ignatius' death had reached him, and that the first twelve chapters made up another letter which Polycarp addressed to them some twenty-five years after the martyrdom of Ignatius, i.e. about 135 C.E.[11] Today many patristic scholars endorse the "two letter" theory, although not all are disposed to accept it precisely as proposed by Harrison.

Briefly put, the problem centers around the last line of ch. 13, only extant in Latin: Et de ipso Ignatio et de his, qui cum eo *sunt,* quod certius agnoveritis, significate.[12] The verb "to be" here clearly signifies that Ignatius is still alive, but ch. 9 reads:

> I exhort all of you, then, to obey the word of righteousness and to exercise all endurance, which you also saw before your eyes not only in the blessed Ignatius and Zosimus and Rufus, but also in others from among you and in Paul himself and in the rest of the apostles; being persuaded that all these did not run in vain, but in faith and righteousness, and that they are in their due place beside the Lord with whom they also suffered. For they did not love the present world but him who died for us and was raised by God because of us.

In this chapter Ignatius and his companions are clearly among the dead. Harrison rejected the interpretation of Lightfoot that in ch. 13 the Greek of *qui cum eo sunt* would have been *tois syn autō,* a temporally neutral phrase whose tense would be governed by the context. According to Lightfoot, the original Greek would have meant "(those) who *were* with him," signifying that although Polycarp is aware of Ignatius' death (ch. 9), full particulars *(certius)* have not yet arrived.[13] Today a scholar such as W.R. Schoedel — one of the more recent commentators on Polycarp's Letter — who fundamentally agrees with Lightfoot on the unity of the Letter, rejects Lightfoot's interpretation of ch. 13 as "very artificial even if the retranslation is correct. It is more likely that the *qui cum eo sunt* refers to the living —or, *more precisely, to those still most vividly remembered as alive;* if so, Polycarp writes (both here and in 9:1) before the news of Ignatius' death had arrived but after it might reasonably be held that he had been martyred."[14]

L.W. Barnard and K. Lake, among others, agree with Harrison's "two letter" thesis. The former states that "this explanation fits in much better with the background of ch. xiii than Lightfoot's theory that Polycarp is taking the final completion and sequel to Ignatius' journey as a foregone conclusion yet strangely makes no mention of it."[15] Lake remarks concerning Harrison's work: "For the future, I shall certainly regard Dr. Harrison's theory as the almost certain explanation of an otherwise insoluble problem."[16] Barnard, considering Eusebius' way of handling passages from Polycarp, adds still a further argument to support the "two letter" thesis:

> It would seem that Harrison's theory can be further strengthened. He failed to notice a small but significant fact which in the event is a strong confirmation of his thesis. Eusebius, in his *Ecclesiastical History* iii. 36. 14-15, quotes both Chs. ix and xiii of Polycarp's Epistle in the original Greek with only the connecting link *kaí hexês epiphérei*. After recording the deaths of the blessed martyrs Ignatius, Rufus and Zosimus in Ch. ix Eusebius quotes Ch. xiii in full, *but significantly omits the last sentence,* which is now only extant in the Latin quoted above. Why did Eusebius omit this when he had the original Greek before him? The only feasible explanation is that he saw that in the original, Chs. ix and xiii were in dire conflict, the one recording the death of Ignatius and the other presupposing he was still alive. Accordingly, as befitting one who assumed the unity of the Epistle, Eusebius removed the contradiction. Lightfoot's view that the original Greek contained no time reference and therefore could refer to a period after the death of Ignatius was not therefore the view of Eusebius, who after all had the original Greek before him which the modern scholar has not. (The only way of avoiding

this conclusion is to assert that the Latin is a later interpolation. But I know of no competent authorities prepared to support this.) This would therefore appear to be a further support for Harrison's theory that the references in Chs. ix and xiii are in fact irreconcilable and belong to two distinct letters written at different times. It is extraordinary that Harrison, with his accute perception, while repeatedly referring to Eusebius' quotation of Ch. xiii, made no reference to the omission of the last sentence.[17]

Still although Barnard agrees with the fundamental thesis set forth by Harrison, he does not agree with the latter's dating of chapters 1-12 at about 135 C.E. and in this he is not alone.[18] Harrison maintained that:

The date of Polycarp's 'Crisis Letter'(chs. i-xii) can be determined, on our hypothesis, within fairly narrow limits, by the reference to Marcion. For the False Teaching here specified (ch. vii) is clearly, not fully developed Marcionism, but that earlier phase which, as we saw reason to believe, must have preceded Marcion's admission to the Roman Church in the last year of Hadrian. If his activities at Philippi followed his rejection by the leaders of the Church in Asia, this fixes the Philippians' appeal to Polycarp within a year or so of A.D. 135-137.
Other indications within the body of this letter point in the same direction. The very numerous phrases taken, with or without modification, from Christian writings known to Polycarp, and presumably to his readers, prove that the process which ended in the formation of our canonical New Testament had advanced appreciably further then we have any evidence that it had gone in Trajan's time... While it is not wholly impossible, nor without precedent, that a man in his forties might have attained the very exceptional influence and reputation implied by the Philippians' request for Polycarp's intervention in their affairs at such a critical juncture, it is much more natural to suppose that this happened when he was twenty years older.[19]

Thus Harrison's main arguments for a 135 C.E. dating for chs. i to xii are: (a) that Marcion who was propagating at Philippi an earlier phase of what later became Marcionism had caused a crisis situation in that community and this could not have happened before 135 C.E.;

(b) That the use of the canonical New Testament by Polycarp shows that the formation of the canon had gone appreciably further than we have any evidence it had gone in the reign of Trajan;

(c) that the frequent echoes in the Letter from the Ignatian Epistles show that it must have been written at a time when the writer could have presumed that the Philippians would have been long familiar with the Ignatian phraseology, i.e. many years after Ignatius' martyrdom.

(d) that, when Ignatius passed through Smyrna, Polycarp was only in his middle forties but the Philippians request for him to intervene in their difficulties "suggests that he must have been by this time a man of wide influence, ripe experience and advanced age."[20]

Barnard discusses each of these arguments.

(A) On the question of false teaching, both he and E.J. Goodspeed[21] hold that Harrison emphasized the crisis situation too much. Says Barnard:

> Heretical teaching was not the foremost reason why Polycarp wrote to the Philippians. He says that he writes "concerning righteousness, not at my own instance, but because you first invited me"(iii.1). In Ch. iv he warns against the love of money and in Ch. v gives Christian obligations to a virtuous life; in Ch. vi come the duties of the presbyters — especially are they to be compassionate, merciful and forgiving. The fair name of the Philippian church had been sullied by the sin of one Valens, a presbyter, and his wife, who had apparently been guilty of some act of fraud and diahonesty(Ch. xi).[22]

Furthermore, only in Ch. 7 is one to find "a warning against heretical teaching of a Docetic type similar to that found elsewhere in early Christian literature" (e.g. *1 Cor.* 15.12; *2 Tim.* 2.18; *1 Jn.* 4.2-3; *2 Jn.* 7; *Rev.* 2-6 & 14ff. & 2Off.; Ign. *ad Smyrn.* 1-7)[23] The reference to Marcion, according to Harrison, occurs in ch. 7.1 which reads:

> For everyone who does not confess that Jesus Christ has come in the flesh is an anti-Christ; and whoever does not confess the testimony of the Cross is of the devil; and whoever perverts the oracles of the Lord for his own lusts, and says that there is neither resurrection nor Judgement, this man is a first-born of Satan.

On this text Barnard makes the following significant comments:

There is nothing specifically Marcionite in the doctrine attacked in this passage. Marcion's dualism, his doctrine of the two gods, his rejection of the Old Testament nowhere appear. Neither did Marcion deny the judgement — in fact he held as firmly as any Catholic that men would be rewarded or punished hereafter according to their deeds in this life, although it would be the Demiurge who would be their Judge. The death of Christ was very important to him although he was a Docetist (note Harnack in *Marcion* [1924 edn.], p. 125:"To conclude from this that the sufferings and death of Christ were to him a mere shadow-show is incorrect."). Moreover Marcion excised rather than perverted the scriptures and he certainly did not do this for his own lusts *(pròs tàs idías epithumías)* which denotes the antinomian license known to have been practiced by certain Docetic groups. Marcion's conduct was above suspicion and even Tertullian, his doughty opponent, bears decisive witness to his moral rectitude(cf. *de praescr. haer.* XXX; *adv. Marc.* I,1,29; IV,11). Harrison attempted to get around these damaging facts by arguing that Ch. vii referred to an earlier phase of Marcion's teaching before he went to Rome, where he derived his characteristic doctrines from Cerdo. But we have no other information as to this earlier phase of his activity or that he had ever been at Philippi... This is the weakest part of Harrison's notable book and it seems inconceivable that he would have put it forward save for the reference to 'a first-born of Satan'. It is quite true that Polycarp's choice of this epithet seems appropriate to Marcion, as later on a famous occasion (Iren. *adv. haer.* iii.3.4). Yet there is surely no difficulty in believing that Polycarp may have used the phrase as a general term of abuse against Docetic heretics (is it significant that there is no definite article in the Greek?) and later in his life applied it specifically to Marcion... In any event the teaching of Ch. vii is so at variance with the characteristic teaching of Marcion that it is difficult to find in it any reference to the arch-heretic. Docetism was rampant in Asia Minor in the late first and early second centuries and it is against this that Polycarp warns the Philippians.[24]

It should be noted that all of Harrison's arguments for the later dating of chs. 1-12 are pitched against the unity of the Letter supposedly written and dispatched within a month or so of Ignatius' last visit to Smyrna. This holds true especially for what was then perhaps his strongest argument, (B) namely that Polycarp's use of the books of the New Testament betrays a stage that the formation of the canon seems to have reached at a much later date. Barnard, who does not negate Harrison's contention that the use of books in the New Testament canon is too much to expect in the period around Ignatius' martyrdom, maintains that recent discoveries show that the formation of the canon had reached a sufficiently advanced stage to admit a dating of the Letter at about 120 C.E. He notes that:

> Recent discoveries at Nag Hammadi, and in particular the *Gospel of Truth,* have shown that the formation of the New Testament canon was not a late development belonging to the mid-second century but had begun at an earlier date. Polycarp's quotations of the New Testament, if such they are, in Chs. i-xii, are quite consistent with a date c. 120. A further significant fact is that while Polycarp is familiar with the *Corpus Paulinum* he shows no acquaintance with the fourfold Gospel which a Christian leader in Asia Minor writing c. 135 would have been expected to have known.[25] (The widespread influence of the fourfold Gospel in the period 120 - 160 is evidenced by its use in *Papias, 2 Peter, the Gospel of Peter,* the *Epistola Apostolorum* and the writings of Justin Martyr).[26]

Thus primarily on the grounds that Polycarp does not quote the fourfold Gospel, and the fact that the formation of the New Testament canon had begun fairly early in the second century, Barnard opts for a dating of the first twelve chapters of the Letter at approximately 120 C.E.[27]

(C) Moreover, by this date not only can we reasonably assume that the Philippians will be familiar with the allusions which Polycarp makes to Ignatius' ideas,

(D) but by 120 C.E. Polycarp would have already been well into the fifties,

> and as a direct link with our Lord's Apostles (cf. Iren. *adv. haer.* iii.3.4; Tert. de *praescr. haer.* 32) would have been venerated as a source of trustworthy information concerning the first age of the Church. We are expressly told that even before his hairs were grey he was treated with every honour by those about him (*Mart. Polyc.* xiii). It was natural for such a leader to be asked for advice by the Philippians, who may not have had a bishop of their own.[28]

Consequently, as to the problems of unity and dating of the Letter, it would seem that the better solution is to accept ch. 13 as a 'cover letter' to a collection of Ignatian letters which Polycarp sent to the Philippians before the news and particulars concerning Ignatius' martyrdom had reached Polycarp, and to take chs. 1-12 as another letter written by Polycarp to the community at Philippi about a decade later at their request. Ch. 14, the conclusion, would seem to be more likely that of chs. 1-12, as Kleist and Fischer have printed it,[29] although this can hardly be considered a major issue.

B. SOURCES AND DOCTRINE

According to C.C. Richardson, "the principal interest of Polycarp's letter is his use of early Christian writings."[30] Anyone working with a well-annotated text, such as Funk-Bihlmeyer, sees this immediately; in fact, one gets the idea that there is hardly an idea to be found which was not already expressed in an earlier Christian classic. A. Puech states simply that as a letter "elle est faite, pour une bonne part, de citations ou de souvenirs."[31] Grant calls it "the mosaic of Polycarp,"[32] the pieces of which come for the most part from the New Testament. The Old Testament however, as J. Weiss has noted, is rarely used:

> Polycarp cites the Old Testament very little. The most obvious quotation is in 10:2, from *Tobit* 12:9, "Alms rescues from death"; in 11:2, *Jer.* 5:4 is used in much freer form: "They know not the way nor the judgement of the Lord." There are still other allusions here and there to the Old Testament, in language and religious formulae, but they are all quite general, and the brief expressions are completely worked over into the writer's own idiom. From these observations of course one cannot conclude in the slightest that Polycarp or his readers depreciated or discarded the Old Testament as did the Gnostics. The Bishop of Smyrna is however obviously not well acquainted with the sacred scrolls, as he himself expressly says, "I am certain that you are well read in the Holy Scriptures and that nothing escapes you; *to me, of course, this has not been vouchsafed"* (12:1). The meagre Old Testament learning of Polycarp may be due in large part to the fact that he was not Jewish by birth but had come from a Greek family of Asia Minor.[33]

Harrison devoted a long chapter of his book to a learned and detailed expose of Polycarp's use of New Testament and extra-canonical sources;[34] more recently J.A. Fischer has prepared a summary of these sources which effectively reiterates Harrison's finds:

> Von den synoptischen Evangelien ist vor allem wieder Mt verwendet, vielleicht Lk sowie die Apg dieses Verfassers; von Mk finden sich auch hier keine deutlichen Spuren. Auffallenderweise scheidet wohl, wenigstens was eine ausdrükliche Benutzung betrifft, Jo aus, bestimmt die Apk. Aus dem Corpus Paulinum ist mit Sicherheit eigentlich nur von Philem kein Anzeichen wahrzunehmen; dass alle übrigen Briefe benutzt wurden, ist jedoch mit Bestimmtheit nicht zu sagen. Deutlich tritt begreiflicherweise vor allem der paulinische Phil hervor. Für die Geistlichkeit Polykarps ist bezeichnend, dass er die spekulative Theologie des Apostels jedoch nicht heranzieht. Die Verwandtschaft von Phil mit den Pastoralbriefen veranlasste v. Campenhausen a.a.O. zu der Vermutung, Polykarp oder jemand aus seinem Klerus könnte deren Verfasser sein, eine Hypothese, die mehr Fragen weckt als sie, ohne zu befriedigen, zu lösen versucht. Das 1 Petr verwendet ist, hat schon Eusebius bemerkt (Kirchengesch. IV 14,9). Über Jak und Jud ist nichts Bestimmtes auszumachen, noch weniger über 2 Petr. Dagegen ist 1 Jo benutzt worden (Da 1 Jo zeitlich nicht welt vom Johannesevangelium entfernt sein kann, ist es wahrscheinlich, dass Polykarp auch das Jo nicht unbekannt war.), vielleicht auch 2 Jo und 3 Jo.
>
> In der Kombination von Bibeltexten (Phil 5,3; 7,1f; 8,1; 10,1f; 12,1; 12,3) hatte Polykarp ein gewisses Vorbild u.a. im Klemens-Brief (Doch überwiegen bei Polykarp die ntl Texte, und unter diesen Stellen aus den ntl Briefen). Phil 2,3a ist eine rhythmisch-gereimte Zusammenstellung von Vorschriften der Berg-(Feld-) Predigt bzw. aus ihrem Geist; wahrscheinlich fand sie Polykarp bereits mnemotechnisch gestaltet (für katechetisch-homiletische Zwecke) vor; die Form ist gegen über Klem 13,2 einerseits geschliffener und kürzer, andererseits wortgetreuer.
>
> [Was betrifft die Frage eines ntl Kanons]... erscheint die Sammlung der Paulus-Briefe im Phil wohl so gut wie abgeschlossen, was aus Ignatius noch nicht zu entnehmen war und daher an und für sich für eine spätere Abfassung dieses Briefes sprechen könnte, aber keineswegs sprechen muss; Polykarp setzt auch voraus, dass die Adressaten in Philippi

die Briefsammlung kennen und an erkennen (vgl. das wiederholte, auf nachfolgende Paulus-Zitate bezogene *eidótes, hóti* . Phil 1,3; 4,1; 5,1; s.a. 9,2; 11,2).

Konnte für die Ignatianen die Benutzung des Klemens-Briefes wahrscheinlich gemacht werden, so verwerter Polykarp diesen sehr deutlich und ausgiebig; er entnimmt ihn, freilich ohne diese Quelle zu nennen, eine Reihe von Ausdrucken, Wendungen und Gedanken; der Bischof von Smyrna ist der älteste sichere Zeuge für die Verbreitung des Klemens-Briefes. Ausserdem schöpfte Polykarp aus den Ignatianen.

In Phil 2,1; 7,1 und 9,2 klingen vielleicht auch frühe Glaubensformeln an; ob diese auf schriftlichen Vorlagen beruhten, entzieht sich unserem Wissen. Sonstige literarische Quellen sind nicht erkennbar.[35]

Thus we can say that Polycarp supplies us with the broadest range of New Testament source material found in the Apostolic Fathers. Most likely he had a great many of these documents at his immediate disposal. C.C. Richardson has suggested that "his conflation of quotations may have been due to his citing them from memory."[36] And L.W. Barnard develops a point also noted above by Fischer, namely the possibility of Polycarp's drawing from a pre-prepared body of catechetical material:

> Recent studies of the background of early Christian writings (especially P. Carrington, *The Primitive Christian Catechism,* and E.G. Selwyn, *The First Epistle of St. Peter*) have shown that a large body of catechetical material, in oral and written forms, circulated in the early Church and was used by teachers, catechists and writers as 'pegs' on which to hang their own theological interpretations. It is not therefore to be supposed that a Christian writer is always quoting verbatim from an earlier document when similarity of subject matter occurs. It seems possible that a few of the 'quotations' from the New Testament in Chs. i-xii of Polycarp's Epistle may in fact come out of a wider background of catechesis.[37]

As a theologian Polycarp is weak; to give but one example of this that touches on our subject matter: in 5:3 he repeats almost literally a statement of Ignatius on the ministry ("It is necessary.... to be subject to the presbyters and deacons as to God and Christ.") without ever giving any of the Ignatian background for this statement nor for that matter giving his own reasons for endorsing it. But then again Polycarp is a Christian leader and shepherd primarily engaged in imparting requested pastoral advice. Camelot notes this clearly:

> A vrai dire, le contenu doctrinal en est assez pauvre .... Polycarpe est un pasteur zélé, ferme dans la foi, certes, on l'a vu, mais plus moraliste que docteur. Il nous donne donc un bon chapitre de théologie pastorale, où les differentes conditions reçoivent des conseils appropriés. On y remarquera l'exhortation à la patience (8,2; 9,1), au pardon des injures (6,2), à la douceur et à la modération envers les coupables eux-mêmes (11, le cas de Valens), à la prière pour tous, pour les rois, les magistrats, les princes (12), et surtout l'insistante exhortation à fuir la cupidité et l'amour de l'argent, qui sont la source de tous les maux (4,1, citant *1 Tim,* 6,10) et qui furent vraisemblablement l'occasion de la chute du presbytre Valens (11,1).
>
> L'enseignement dogmatique de la lettre est assez sommaire: on se contentera d'y relever deux traits ... — C'est la foi, solennellement affirmée, à "Dieu, le Père de notre Seigneur Jésus-Christ", et au Christ lui-même, "grand-prêtre eternel, fils de Dieu" (12,2). On retrouve ici une formule assez étroitement inspirée de saint Paul (*Rom.* 15,6; *2 Cor.* 1,3; 11,31; *Eph.* 1,3; *Col.* 1,3; cf. *I Petr.* 1,3). Quant à l'affirmation du sacerdoce éternel de Christ, elle vient de l'Épître aux Hébreux, et se retrouve dans l'Épitre de Clément (36,1; 61,3; 64): c'est encore un des points de contact de notre lettre avec ce dernier texte. La prière de Polycarpe avant son martyre exprime une théologie analogue (v. *Mart. Polyc.* 14,1-3). La résurrection de Jésus est le témoignage éclatant de sa filiation divine (1,2; 2,1; 12,2; et cf. *Act.* 2,36; *Rom.* 1,4, etc.).[38]

Still, in spite of the theological poverty of the Letter, there is a brilliant find on Polycarp's part recorded in ch. 8. He appears to have been meditating on *1 Peter* 2:21-24 and writes:

> Let us persevere, then, constantly in our hope and the pledge of our righteousness *(arrabôni tês diakaiosúnēs hēmôn),* which is Christ Jesus, who "bore our sins in his own body on the cross"(*1 Peter* 2:24), "who did no sin, not was any deceit found in his mouth"(*1 Peter* 2:22); but he endured all things for us "that we might live"(*1 Peter* 2:24) in him. 2. Let us be imitators, then, of his endurance, and if we suffer for his name, let us glorify him. For this is the "example"(*1 Peter*

2:21; cf. also *1 Clem.* 16-17) which he gave us in himself and
in which we have learned to put our faith.

Polycarp sees the Crucified Lord as the *"arrabôn,"* as the pledge of (or first
instalment or down payment on)[39] our righteousness. And he connects this
"pledge" with our own perseverance in righteousness. W.R. Schoedel
comments:

> Faith and righteousness are to be understood in terms of
> "endurance" — even to the point of martyrdom if necessary.
> Polycarp clearly feels that the whole line of early Christian
> martyrs [— from Paul to Ignatius —(9:1)] lends support to his
> interpretation of the faith.[41]

Thus, since the Crucified Lord has given himself as the down payment on
our righteousness through his own endurance in righteousness unto death,
we through "the example which he set in himself" are challenged to
persevere in righteousness in imitation of him. "This adds weight to the
suggestion that Polycarp understood the Docetism of the errorists as leading
to undisciplined living."[42] In any case, "Christ Jesus" as "the pledge of our
righteousness" is indeed an unexpected insight that must be original.[43] One
wonders if this interpretation of the enduring Christ as "the pledge of our
righteousness" is not the most needed one for our own age.

II. MINISTERIAL FUNCTIONS

When we reflect that Ignatius of Antioch apparently knew of a
threefold hierarchy *(epískopos, presbýterion* and *diákonoi)* existing at
Ephesus, Magnesia (on the Meander), Tralles, Philadelphia and Smyrna,[44]
it seems a bit strange that Polycarp, who was clearly *the* bishop of Smyrna,[45]
never uses the term *epískopos* (singular or plural) in his Letter(s) to the
Philippians; nor does he name anyone who may be assumed to be the bishop
at Philippi. In 5:3 where, as we have already seen, he leans most closely on
Ignatius and would have most probably mentioned the *epískopos* if anywhere,
he writes: "Be subject to the *presbýteroi* and *diákonoi* as to God and
Christ."[46] From this, as well as his remarks in 5:2 and 6:1, it is clear that
Polycarp knows only of presbyters standing at the head of the Church in

148

Philippi, with deacons as their helpers. As to these latter, J. Weiss notes:

> In our other sources these church officials [the deacons] always
> appear in connection with the bishops, as in the address of the
> letter which St. Paul addressed to this very church (*Phil*, 1:1).
> If Polycarp diverges from this apparently established usage, the
> reason is perhaps that he at least cannot speak of bishops in the
> plural when he has in mind the officials of one and the same
> church. If, accordingly, the leadership of a church lies in the
> hands of more than one, as is the case in Philippi, Polycarp can
> speak only of 'presbyters' and he must place the deacons
> alongside the presbyters. The deacons were the younger
> assistants who stood by to 'serve' the presbyters in the conduct
> of their office. In 5:2 the letter gives the model for deacons to
> follow: they must be blameless before the righteousness of
> God, as servants of God and not of men; they must not be
> slanderers, not double-tongued, lovers of money, but on the
> contrary temperate in all things, merciful, painstaking, living
> according to the truth of the Lord, who became the servant of all.[47]

The only real information Polycarp gives us about presbyters is
found in chs. 6 and 11. The first part of ch. 6 contains a sort of "Haustafel"
of virtues which he obviously expects to find in his own presbyters at
Smyrna and which he sees as worthy of practice by the presbyters at
Philippi:

> And let the presbyters also be compassionate, merciful to all
> men, bringing back those who have erred, caring for all the
> weak, neglecting neither widow, nor orphan nor poor, but ever
> providing for that which is good before God and man, abstaining
> from all anger, human respect, unjust judgement, being far
> from all love of money, not quickly believing evil of any, not
> severe in judgement, knowing that we are all debtors of sin.

This remarkable passage, with few parallels either in the New Testament or
in the other Apostolic Fathers, appears to be a direct composition of Polycarp
himself. A high percentage of the characteristics which Polycarp sees as
desirable in the presbyters point in the direction of a sort of role as judges in
forgiveness. He gives, however, no description of a concrete function in
which these virtues are to be exercised, but follows immediately in 6:2 with:
"If then we pray the Lord to forgive us, we also ought to forgive, for we stand

before the eyes of the Lord and of God..." The overall suggestion seems to be that in cases where serious evil has been done to and/or within the community, it should be the presbyters — clothed with the abovementioned virtues — who would decide the steps to be taken. And this is all the more understandable when we consider that the community at Philippi was facing precisely such a case, namely that of Valens and his wife who apparently had embezzled some of the church's money. In ch. 11 Polycarp writes:

1. I am deeply sorry for Valens, who was once made a presbyter among you, that he so little understands the place (locum) which was given to him. I advise, therefore, that you keep from avarice, and be pure and truthful. Keep yourselves from all evil.

2. For how may he who cannot attain self-control in these matters enjoin it on another? If any man does not abstain from avarice, he will be defiled by idolatry....

4. Therefore, brethren, I am deeply sorry for him and for his wife, and "may the Lord grant them true repentance" (2 Tim. 2:25). Therefore be yourselves moderate in this matter, and "do not regard such men as enemies" (2 Thess. 3:15), but call them back as weak and erring members "that you may preserve your body in its entirety"(1 Clem. 37:5). For by doing this you build up one another.

This story of Valens and his wife suggests another function of a presbyter, namely the control and disposition of the church's money. Polycarp says nothing, however, of obligations which they might have had with regard to the worship of the church.

In addition to presbyters and deacons, the Letter also makes mention of apostles and prophets. The prophets clearly belong to the Old Testament period for they are "the prophets who proclaimed beforehand the coming of our Lord"(cf. Acts 7:52). Like Ignatius, Polycarp has no mention of New Testament prophets. Apostles are mentioned twice: 6:3 speaks of "the apostles who preached the Gospel to us;" and 9:1 mentions "Paul himself and the rest of the apostles." This last instance of "the apostles" could mean "the Twelve," although it is more probable that in both cases Polycarp is using the Pauline concept of "apostle."

The widows spoken of in ch. 4 seem to have a special office of prayer, and are compared by Polycarp to "an altar of God." We will discuss them in the following section.

III. SACRAL-CULTIC CONCEPTIONS

There are but two instances of genuine cultic terminology in Polycarp's letter: his mention of Jesus Christ as eternal high priest (*sempiternus pontifex*)[48] and his metaphor applied to the widows, namely "that they are an altar of God *(thusiastérion theoû)* and that all offerings are carefully inspected."[49] There is no mention whatsoever of communal worship, although prayer is frequently recommended (4:3; 6:2; 7:2; 12;3).

From Polycarp's extensive use of *1 Clement* it would appear that his reference to Jesus Christ as "eternal high priest" is an echo of Clement's three such references,[50] although possible acquaintance with the *Epistle to the Hebrews* cannot be excluded. There can be little doubt that Polycarp's use of this title (12:2) plus his strong emphasis on the Crucifixion as the salvific moment in history —"Christ Jesus, who bore our sins in his own body on the tree ... for our sakes, that we might live in him"(8:1) — plus his admonition "to be subject to the presbyters and deacons as to God and Christ"(5:3), sets up a network of relationships which could very well develop into a ministerial priesthood. There is, however, no evidence that this was already the case.

In 4:3 where the widows are called "the altar of God" we have to do, according to W.L Schoedel, with:

> A figurative use of the term attested to here for the first time. Elsewhere altar is used of the pure heart and mind.[51] ... Widows in particular may be connected with the altar because of their concern with prayer (cf. *Rev.* 5:8; 8:3,4; 11:1); note the Rabbinic teaching that prayer is of a value equal to that of the cultus (*Sifre on Deuteronomy* 41, f.80a [G.F. Moore, *Judaism* (Cambridge, Mass., 1927), II, 218: "Just as the worship of the altar is called worship, so *prayer* is called worship).[52]

The fact that Polycarp immediately adds the phrase "that all offerings are carefully inspected" *(mōmoskopeîtai)*, recalling *1 Clement* 41:2, shows clearly that we have to do with a metaphorical recollection of the Old Testament sacrificial system. There is nothing that suggests a real altar in the Christian community.

The use of *locus* when speaking of the "place" which Valens had been given as a presbyter, like *tópos* in the Ignatian letters, can hardly be regarded as having reached the stage of representing a *terminus technicus* for the clerical state.[53]

IV. CONCLUSION

This *Letter of Polycarp to the Philippians* could, I think, best be seen as composed of [1] a covering note to some of Ignatius' letters, i.e Polycarp's ch. 13, and [2] twelve (possibly thirteen) chapters of a longer letter. The 'cover letter' was written no doubt a fairly short time after Ignatius had passed through Smyrna on his way to martyrdom at Rome (about 108-110 C.E.); the longer letter in the light of what we presently know about the development of the New Testament canon could best be dated about 120 C.E., although a dating one or two decades later cannot be definitively excluded.

The longer Letter (chs. 1-12) is a rather bland mosaic of quotations, but the panoramic use of New Testament literature is extraordinary. *1 Peter,* the *Pauline corpus* and *1 Clement* are the most cited early Christian writings. One could perhaps best typify the theology in the Letter as a repetition of several major Pauline points with ideas from *1 Clement* worked in. Refreshingly original, though, in this highly unoriginal document is Polycarp's insight that "Christ Jesus" is "the pledge of our righteousness"(8:1).

The great historic Pauline church at Philippi had solicited his advice "concerning righteousness" and more especially concerning the embezzling presbyter Valens and his wife. Polycarp answers their plea simply and humbly, drawing on much of the tradition which he has received. He is himself the leader of the presbyteral college of the church at Smyrna, although he chooses not to make use of the term *epískopos* — singular or plural — in his Letter.

From Polycarp's remarks it appears that the church at Philippi has an exclusively presbyterial Church organization with deacons. There is nothing in the Letter to suggest that theirs was a separate cultic ministry; in fact, there is no mention whatsoever of communal worship. Still it is clear that presbyters and deacons constitute two groups within the community given to pastoral service with a broad social dimension, especially care for widows, orphans and the poor. The presbyter Valens is spoken of as having little understood "the place (or position: *locum)* which was given to him"(11:1). The context suggests that at least one of the functions of one of the presbyters, or perhaps of the whole group, was to control and dispose of the church's money. Something that Valens apparently did for his own advantage! Another possible function of the presbyters may be alluded to in

6:1 where in the "Haustafel" of presbyteral virtues we find such terms as "compassionate, merciful," refraining from "unjust" and "hasty judgement" connected with "the debt of sin" which "we all owe." This suggests vaguely and without any further detail on Polycarp's part that the presbyters, either individually or as a group, function in some way or another as judges in questions which call for forgiveness. Most likely this serves as an introduction to the case of their fellow presbyter which Polycarp takes up in ch. 11. The deacons are to function as "the servants of God and Christ... walking according to the truth of the Lord, who was the servant of all" (5:2).

There is reason to think that Polycarp's strong emphasis on the Crucifixion as *the* salvific moment in history (8:1) plus his mention of Jesus Christ as "eternal high priest"(12:2) plus his admonition "to be subject to the presbyters and deacons as to God and Christ"(5:3) could lead, given certain needs and developmental factors, to the establishment of presbyters as priests for the community. There is, however, no evidence that this was already the case, nor that Polycarp had any such thing in mind.

Aside from the Letter's mentioning Jesus Christ as "eternal high priest," the only other sacral-cultic term appears in the metaphor of the widows who are compared to "the altar of God"(4:3). The phrase following this metaphor which speaks of the careful inspection of the offerings shows that we are dealing here only with a figurative remembrance of the Old Testament sacrificial system. The prayers of the widows are like the material sacrifices under the Old Law, and they themselves like "the altar of God" must remain particularly holy, "being far from all slander, evil speaking, false witness, love of money, and all evil"(4:3). It appears that they possessed a sort of contemplative office in the church at Philippi, "praying ceaselessly for all men."

NOTES

1   See J.B. Lightfoot, *The Apostolic Fathers. Part II. S. Ignatius. S. Polycarp.* *Vol. I*, Macmillan & Co., London, 1885, p. 538.

2   *Ibid.*, p. 537.

3   Cf. C.C. Richardson, *Early Christian Fathers. Vol. I* [Library of Christian Classics], Westminster Press, Philadelphia, 1953, p. 124.

4   See K. Bihlmeyer, *Die Apostolischen Väter*, Erster Teil, J.C.B. Mohr (Paul Siebeck), Tübingen, 1956, p. XXXXIX.

5   Cf. Lightfoot, *op. cit.*, pp. 562-587.

6   Cf. Richardson, *op. cit.*, p. 124:"These are contained in nine late Greek manuscripts, in which ch. 9:2 is followed immediately by an incomplete text of the Epistle of Barnabas which begins at ch. 5:8. All these manuscripts are derived from a single archetype. The 11th century *Codex Vaticanus Graecus* 859 is the best of the group."

7   "Preserved with the Latin manuscripts that contain the longer recension of the Ignatian epistles. Comparison with the extant Greek pieces shows that the Latin version is a trustworthy translation of the original." Ref. Richardson, *op. cit.* p. 124.

8   *Ibid.*, p. 123.

9   Joannes Dallaeus (Daille), *De Scriptis quae sub Dionysii Areopagitae et Ignatii Antiocheni nominibus circumferuntur...*, Geneva, 1666, lib. II, cap. xxxii, pp. 425-9.

10   For the history of this criticism cf. P.N. Harrison, *Polycarp's Two Epistles to the Philippians*, Cambridge Univ. Press, 1936, pp. 28-42.

11   *Ibid.*

12   Cf. K. Bihlmeyer, *op. cit.*, p. 120.

13   See Lightfoot, *op. cit.*, pp. 572-573.

14   W.R. Schoedel, *The Apostolic Fathers. Vol. 5. Polycarp, Martyrdom of Polycarp, Fragments of Papias*, Nelson & Sons, Camden, N.J., 1967, p. 40; see also A.C. Headlam's article in *Church Quarterly Review*, 141, 1945, p. 7.

15   L.W. Barnard, "The Problem of St. Polycarp's Epistle to the Philippians," in *Studies in the Apostolic Fathers and their Background*, Blackwell, Oxford, 1966, p. 32.

16   K. Lake in *Journal of Biblical Literature*, LVI, 1937, p. 73.

17   Barnard, *op. cit.*, pp. 32-33.

18   Cf., e.g. C.J. Cadoux reviewing Harrison's book in *Journal of Theological Studies*, 38, 1937, p. 270; H.-Ch. Puech in *Rev. de l'hist. des rel.*, 119, 1939, p. 102; H.D. Simonin in *Rev. des sciences phil. et théol.*, 27, 1938, pp. 258-260; E.J. Goodspeed, *A History of Early Christian Literature*, Chicago, 1942, p. 25; P. Th. Camelot, O.P., *Lettres: Ignace d'Antioche, Polycarpe de Smyrne; Martyre de Polycarpe* (SC, 10), du Cerf, Paris,

154

1951, 2e édit. revue et augmentée, p. 195; J.A. Fischer, *Die Apostolischen Väter* (Schriften des Urchristentums, 1), Wissensch. Buchgesellsch., Darmstadt, 1966, p. 237.

[19] Harrison, *op. cit.*, pp. 315-316.

[20] *Ibid.*, p. 268; see also p. 283.

[21] Goodspeed, *op. cit.*, p. 25.

[22] Barnard, *op. cit.*, p. 34.

[23] *Ibid.*, p. 34.

[24] *Ibid.*, pp. 34-35.

[25] Here Barnard cites the authority of E.J. Goodspeed, *op. cit.*, p. 25.

[26] Barnard, *op. cit.*, p. 36.

[27] *Ibid.*, pp. 36-37.

[28] *Ibid.*, p. 39.

[29] See J. A. Kieist, *op. cit.*, p. 75; J. A. Fischer, *op. cit.*, p. 246.

[30] Richardson, *op. cit.*, p. 125.

[31] Puech, *op. cit.*, p. 68.

[32] R.A. Grant, *The Apostolic Fathers Vol. 1. An Introduction*, Nelson, N.Y., 1964 p. 67.

[33] J. Weiss, *op. cit.*, p. 825.

[34] Cf. Harrison, pp. 285-310.

[35] Fischer, pp. 238-239.

[36] Richardson, p. 125.

[37] Barnard, pp. 197-198.

[38] P.-Th. Camelot, O.P., 197-198.

[39] See W. Bauer, *Wörterbuch zum NT*, Berlin, 1963, p. 217, resp. "Anzahlung," "Angeld"; comp. *Gen.* 38:17-20.

[40] Cf. T.F. Torrence, *The Doctrine of Grace in the Apostolic Fathers*, Oliver & Boyd, Edinburgh, 1948, p. 92: "Christ is thought of as the pledge of a righteousness which we must persevere to fulfill."

[41] W.R. Schoedel, *op. cit.*, p. 28.

[42] *Ibid.* p. 27.

[43] The term for "pledge" — *arrabôn* — is not found elsewhere in the Apostolic Fathers and only twice in the NT: in *2 Cor.* 1:22 where it is said that God "has given us His Spirit in our hearts, as His pledge;" and in *Eph.* 1:14 where the author says that "through union with him(Christ) you have been marked with the seal of the Holy Spirit that was promised, which is the pledge of our inheritance..."

[44] See, e.g., Ign. *ad Eph.* 4:1;2:1; *ad Magn.* 6:1; *ad Trall.* 7:2; *ad Philad.* Salut.; *ad Smyrn.* 8:1.

[45] See Ign. *ad Polyc.* Salut.; *Mart. Polyc.* 16:2; comp. Ign. *ad Smyrn.* 12:2.

[46] Ignatius had written: "Likewise let all respect the deacons as Jesus Christ, even as the bishop is also a type of the Father, and the presbyters as the council of God and the college of the Apostles" (*ad Trall.* 3:1); and in *ad Magn.* 2:1:"... subject to the bishop as to the grace of God, and to the presbytery as to the law of Jesus Christ;" and in *ad Eph.* 6:1:"Therefore it is clear that we must regard the bishop as the Lord himself."

[47] J. Weiss, *op. cit.*, p. 821.

[48] Polyc. *ad Phil.* 12:2.

[49] *Ibid.* 4:3.

[50] *1 Clem.* 36:1; 61:3; 64.

[51] Here Schoedel cites "Sextus 46b[Pythagorean parallels in H. Chadwick, *The Sentences of Sextus* (Cambridge, Engl., 1959), 166], Philo, *De Specialibus Legibus* 1.287[note that a nearby passage, 1.294-295, offers one of the best parallels to vs. 1 — that is, *1 Tim.* 6:7]; Clement, *Str.* 6.60.2; 7.14ff; 7.32.5."

[52] W.R. Schoedel, *op. cit.*, p. 18.

[53] See Chapter II, Section II, E: *Tópos.*

CHAPTER VI

THE EPISTLE OF BARNABAS

OUTLINE

I. Background
    A. Origin, Dating, Author
    B. Nature of the Work, Contents, Method
    C. The "Two Ways"
II. Kind of Christianity Represented
    A. Christology
    B. Eschatology
    C. Basic Sacramental Theology
III. Possible Hints at Church Organization and Ministry
IV. Conclusion

I. BACKGROUND

A. ORIGIN, DATING, AUTHOR

In the so-called Epistle of Barnabas we have an approximately 6600-word Christian document which pre-dates the middle of the second century. It has repeatedly defied attempts of the critic to date it precisely, to locate its place of origin and destination, or to suggest what type of person might have been its author.[1] There was a fairly widespread agreement of scholars for an Alexandrian origin of the Epistle on the grounds of its extensive allegorical exegesis,[2] at least until 1961. In that year Pierre Prigent published an extensive study of the Epistle and its sources[3] in which he opted for Syria as its place of origin due to the comparable doctrines and striking parallels to it found in *The Ascension of Isaiah, The Gospel of Peter,* and *The Odes of Solomon,* all apparently Syrian documents. But even this may be a too simple solution to the complex problem of where such different materials came to be combined in such a peculiar way. R.A. Kraft, summing up an eleven-page essay on the Epistle's origin, presents an hypothesis which while perhaps not completely satisfying seems at least to take in most of the factors involved:

> Barnabas is the work of a Christian teacher whose thought, in general, is oriented toward Alexandria, and whose area of ministry is in northeast Egypt. He was not trained in the "classical" Philonic tradition, however, but in a related "school" which had both profited from that approach (or vice versa) and which was steeped in apocalyptic eschatology — a school which had access to a large stock of "ancient" Jewish sources alongside of the Old Testament. Perhaps it was a Christianized offspring of a Qumran-like Judaism in Greek dress — Philo attests the existence of certain Hellenistic Jews living near Alexandria (and elsewhere — also in Asia Minor?) who had several such "Qumranic" traits (the "Therapeutae" of *De Vita Contemplativa*), and the Qumran caves themselves have produced a few scraps of Greek literature, which suggests the existence of Greek speaking sister communities. Barnabas' relationship to Asia Minor may then be explained by positing a widespread influence of such a school, or by suggesting that Pseudo-Barnabas had also studied (directly or indirectly) under and Asian teacher.[4]

Scholars generally agree on the limits for dating at least the first seventeen chapters of the Epistle. The year 70 C.E. marks the *terminus a quo* for 16:3-5 presupposes that "the city and the Temple" have been destroyed "because of their making war," and that the Temple site was still in ruins. The *terminus ad quem* is generally considered to be 135 C.E. when Hadrian's workmen erected a Roman Temple to Zeus-Jupiter on the same site. Moreover the Epistle makes no mention of the revolt of Bar-Cocheba in 132, when Jerusalem was destroyed by the Romans a second time, and it is hardly conceivable that such an event so apt to the writer's purpose would have been ignored had he known of it. In any case, after the year 135 the question of the Temple was pretty much a dead issue so far as Judaism and Christianity were concerned. The respected Barnabas scholar L.W. Barnard dates the whole Epistle at 117-119 C.E.[5] The limits of 70-135 C.E., however, are sufficient for our purposes here.[6]

Who the person was that put the Epistle into its final form remains an open question. From the text itself we learn only that he is a "Teacher," although even here he says he does not wish to address his readers in this formal capacity (see 1:8; 4:6b, 9a). Going on the Epistle itself, F. C. Burkitt describes him as "an artless writer, not ill-informed or stupid, but with very little power of expression and liable to continual digressions."[7] J. Muilenburg, K. Thieme and L.W. Barnard believe he was a converted Rabbi.[8] Others guess him to have been a pagan convert to Christianity; still others conjecture that he was a former proselyte to Judaism who became Christian. According to R.A. Kraft:

> One view that is almost universally shared by recent scholarship is that the "apostle" Barnabas did not write the epistle. Although some of the reasons advanced have been less than "scientific" (e.g., Barnabas 10 is "unworthy of an apostle"!), it can scarcely be denied that the cumulative evidence does not favor the traditional attribution -- the post-70 date and the possibly non-Jewish authorship[9] are probably the strongest single obstacles. But it should also be emphasized that the "apostle" Barnabas is an almost unknown figure to us, and that even what little information is contained in Acts is not entirely above suspicion. There is no legitimate way to exclude this possibility that an early missionary-apostle named Barnabas who once traveled with Paul is responsible for transmitting some, or even much, of the material now contained in the epistle, perhaps by way of a sort of "Barnabean school," which preserved and promulgated his teachings (and from which *Hebrews* also came?). But this can neither be "proved" nor "disproved" with the available evidence, and it best accords with both the situation and the modern critical temperament to refer to the author-editor as Pseudo-Barnabas.[10]

B. Nature of the Work, Contents, Method

Actually these questions of higher criticism regarding the Epistle's origin, dating and authorship would probably take on much greater importance were it not for the type of document we are faced with. Kraft calls it "evolved literature," i.e. a work which shows clear evidence of being the product of a developing process, as opposed to writings which have a single author in the modern sense of the word.[11] Prigent states:

> Il faut donc parler d'éditions successives d'un écrit qui se voit
> amplifié peu à peu par celui-là même à qui l'on doit attribuer
> la paternité du traité primitif.[12]

In this sense, then, the Epistle's final form-giver is at best an author-editor
who reproduces and reworks older material.

> He may add certain of his own insights and emphases; he may
> apply the materials to new situations and embody them in new
> contexts; he may apply his own judgement as to what is or is
> not relevant. But he does not rise above his tradition to appear
> as a clearly defined personality who has produced a piece of
> original literature in accord with our usual ideas of authorship.
> He has not consistently digested his materials so that they
> become part of him; he has not integrated them by means of a
> perspective which may be called, in a special way, his own.
> Rather, his tradition speaks through him. *It* is of prime
> importance. He is its *vehicle*, but the focus remains on the
> traditional material, not on the author-editor.[13]

The *form* of "evolved literature" we find in Pseudo-Barnabas is that of an
epistle-homily. It contains several personal touches combined with a vast
amount of traditional instruction and was most probably intended originally
to be read to a particular (Egyptian?[14]) community. Its use in the early
Church, however, appears to have gone far beyond this, for:

> The fourth-century Codex Sinaiticus[15] ranks the Epistle among
> the canonical books of the New Testament and lists it
> immediately after the *Apocalypse* of St. John. Clement of
> Alexandria culls from it many quotations which he credits to
> the Apostle Barnabas. Origen calls it *katholikè epistolé* and
> numbers it among the books of Sacred Scripture. Eusebius
> relegates it to the controverted writings and Jerome counts it
> among the apocryphal works.[16]

L.W. Barnard has advanced some strong arguments in an attempt to show that

> the Epistle was designed to be read at the paschal Feast which
> culminated in the Easter baptism and eucharist — a solemn
> occasion when large numbers of Christians were gathered
> together; and that the writer has adapted older catechesis and

homiletic material (based on Jewish models) with this Feast in mind.[17]

This is certainly a very reasonable and quite probable standpoint, at least for some sections of the Epistle, and one that would be even stronger were we able to find some direct reference to the eucharist. This latter, however, is lacking.

In his text the author-editor spotlights the Church's relationship with Judaism, a problem which apparently had reached acute proportions in a community which he knows. The answer given is direct and uncompromising. Any historical link between Judaism and the Gospel is flatly denied. He maintains that the Old Testament rites and ceremonies had been intended by God simply as mystical pointers to Christ and that the Jews had been seduced by an evil angel into a literal rather than spiritual understanding of them (9:4). This had led them to regard the fulfillment of the Law as an end sufficient in itself. Indeed there were a few righteous men such as Moses, David and the Prophets who did grasp the true meaning of the Law, but Israel by and large failed to understand it correctly and consequently forfeited their claim to the possession of the Covenant which was reserved instead for the Christians. Pseudo-Barnabas exposes this alleged misconception of the Old Testament in an elaborate series of allegorical interpretations, attempting to show in every case that the ancient Hebrew institutions prefigured their spiritual counterparts in the Christian dispensation. The Cross of Christ, especially, he shows as having been prefigured from the beginning under a variety of types.[18]

The Epistle contains approximately one hundred explicit quotations from the Old Testament, one-fourth of which can be traced to the book of Isaiah. These Isaiah references are reasonably close to our LXX texts, whereas the quotations from the Pentateuch and the other Prophets are very often hardly recognizable.[19] Most of the time the writer is content just to give the general meaning of a text and has regrettably few scruples about altering or adding to Scriptural text to strengthen his argument.[20]

Besides the Scriptures, it is clear that Pseudo-Barnabas made use of various other sources, i.e. certain blocks of traditional material to which he had access. What the precise nature and form of this material was, is a question that has held the limelight in Barnabas studies for decades — the question of the *testimonia*. It actually plays no central role in our study here, but anyone interested in an in-depth investigation of Barnabean sources will find helpful material in the excellent analyses of Barnard[21] and Prigent.[22] The following brief outline shows the variety of subjects the author-editor has chosen to treat and the order in which he handles them.

1:1	Greetings.
1:2-5	An expression of gladness over the spiritual condition of his readers and a longing to write to them.
1:6 to 2:3	Through the Prophets the Lord has made known the past, present and future.
2:4-11	God does not desire sacrificial victims, burnt offerings or gifts.
3:1-5	God does not desire fasts.
3:6 to 4:5	Flee from wicked deeds.
4:6-8	The Covenant is for the Christians.
4:9-14	Be vigilant now that the last days have come.
5:1-4	The Prophets were also writing for us.
5:5-14	Christ appeared in the flesh to destroy death and establish a new people.
6:1-4	Christ is the "Stone" the Prophets spoke about.
6:5-10	Concerning the Prophets who speak about a land "flowing with milk and honey."
6:11-19	The Christians are created anew and led into the land "flowing with milk and honey."
7:1-5	Concerning Christ's drinking of "vinegar and gall."
7:6-11.	Concerning the sacrificing of two goats.
8:1-7	Concerning the sacrifice of a heifer.
9:1-9	Concerning circumcision.
10:1-10	Concerning impure food.
10:11-12	Concerning pure food.
11:1-11	Concerning water.
12:1-7	Concerning the Cross.
12:8-11	Jesus is the Son of God.
13:1-7	The Covenant is for the Christians.
14:1-9	The Jews have lost the Covenant.
15:1-9	Concerning the Sabbath.
16:1-10	Concerning the Temple.
17:1-2	Conclusion of the first part.
18:1-2	Introduction to the "Two Ways."
19:1-12	Concerning the Way of Light.
20:1-12	Concerning the way of the "Black One."
21:1-8	An appeal for obedience.
21:9	Close.[23]

In spite of this rather untidy potpourri of topics the writer works with an explicit purpose in mind and employs a variety of methods to get his material across. He tells his audience in 1:5 that he is writing to them "in order that your knowledge *(gnôsin)* may be perfected along with your faith." The purpose,then, of the Epistle is to impart *gnôsis*.

> It is because Pseudo-Barnabas has witnessed for himself that his readers have already received from the Lord a generous "implantation of the pneumatic gift" (1:2f.; see 9:9) that he feels justified in helping to bring their gnosis to perfection (1:5; cf. 13:7b).
> There is nothing strange or illegitimate about referring to this attitude as "gnostic." In fact, Pseudo-Barnabas probably would not have hesitated to use the word of himself, just as his admirer, Clement of Alexandria, later does. It is true that this is not the "Gnosticism" which developed among certain second-century groups and which came to be condemned by the developing "orthodox" church for its differentiation between the hidden God of Jesus and the inferior creator God of the Jews, its obsession for cosmological-theological speculation, and so forth. ...
> But gnosis for Barnabas is not an end in itself. The term is used technically to refer to two closely related ideas: "exegetical gnosis," which enables the recipient better to understand salvation-history (see 6:9; 9:8; 13:7), and "ethical gnosis," which is the correct understanding of the Lord's requirements for conduct (see 18:1; 19:1; 21:5)[24]

The latter ethical "knowledge" appears to be drawn more from tradition; the former deals more with a personal but "given" exegetical insight. In the ethical context the writer speaks of the "knowledge of the way of righteousness" (5:4) and the knowledge of the "Two Ways" (18:1). Here his methodology generally follows the Old Testament "commandment" pattern "Thou shalt not ..."

The exegetical *gnosis* he speaks of is quite different from this. It is a knowledge given on a more personal level, an insight into what God actually intended when He spoke in the Law and the Prophets. There one finds things hidden of which not everyone has knowledge, things which according to the Epistle are only made known to him who "is wise, and learned, and a lover of his Lord" (6:10).

It is remarkable that its author hardly draws on New Testament ideas of knowledge; we find no subordination of knowledge to love and no focusing of knowledge upon the person of Christ. Indeed most of what is said about knowledge in the Epistle might have been written by a Palestinian Jew rather than a Christian. It is a reasonable inference that the author brought over his conception of knowledge into Christianity from Alexandrian Judaism.[25]

In any case, the writer is convinced that he has the correct insight into God's purposes. One gets this insight by approaching the Old Testament in a particular way. In this, however, he does not limit himself to any one method. To get the Scripture to say what, according to him, it was meant to say, he employs four methods:[26]

1. The typological method — where a particular person or happening in the Old Testament stands as a profiguration, as a type of what is coming and really is. Most of these types have to do with the circumstances under which Jesus was put to death: the sacrifice of Isaac (7:3), the offering of two kids (7:7, 10-11), the offering of one heifer (8:1), and Moses who stretched out his arms over the people of Israel (12:2, 5-6). Not directly related to the Cross is Joshua (12:10) whose name in Greek is Jesus — i.e. "the savior" and who prefigures the saving work of Christ. Also the fact that Jacob blesses with crossed arms the two sons of Joseph stands as a type showing that the role of the Jews and the Gentiles would be exchanged in God's plans.

2. A second method is that of spiritualization. According to the writer the fault of the Jews lay in their strictly literal understanding of the laws. But the person with insight knows, for example, that the food laws point in fact to particular virtues or vices (ch. 10), and that the question of circumcision has to do not with the body but with the heart (ch. 9). This insight will also show one that the sabbath really refers not to a weekly day of rest but to the rest at the end of time (ch. 15), and that the Temple rather than being a structure of stone is the heart of the individual wherein God desires to dwell (ch. 16).

3. Another method is the writer's repeated use of *testimonia* material (see note 22). Often it is easy to see in these a direct parallel with the life of Jesus, for example, the citation of Isaiah 53 concerning the Suffering Servant (5:2). Less direct parallels of this sort in the *testimonia* blocks have to do the manifold use of the word "stone," when one remembers that

Jesus in the New Testament speaks of himself as "the stone which the builders have rejected" (*Mt.* 21:42 [*Ps.* 118: 22-23], cf. *1 Peter* 2:4,6-8).

4. A final method is based on the writer's contention that some texts of the Old Testament were especially written for the Christians who would later inherit the Covenant. To the Jews ("to them"), for example, God said that He had no need of sacrifices (2:4), but to the Christians ("to us") was said that the true sacrifice is a "broken spirit: an aroma pleasing to the Lord is a heart that glorifies its Maker" (2:10). "To them, He says" that they need not fast (3:1); "to us He says: 'Behold, this is the fast with which I am pleased:

> destroy every unjust bond;
> untie the knots of extorted contracts;
> set the oppressed at liberty,
> and tear up every unjust promissory note.
> Break your bread to feed the hungry,
> and when you see someone naked, clothe him;
> take into your home the homeless;
> and when you see one who is lowly,
> do not despise him ..."(3:3)

For still further examples see 5:2, 5:11, 14:5, 4:8, 14:3. J. L. Koole rightly calls this particular approach "a highly peculiar method of explaining Scripture."[27]

The other methods, however, were not uncommon in the early Church. Typological interpretation appears in the New Testament (e.g. *Rom.* 5:14 and *Gal.* 4:25-26). An opening to the spiritual interpretation of Jewish institutions goes as far back as *Deut.* 30:6, and the existence and use of *testimonia* in the first century is readily attested by the Qumran finds. Indeed, the primitive Church working especially with typology and the spiritualization of institutions had found a way to accept the Jewish Scriptures. The text itself remained, but it was given a very definite interpretation. Thus the Old Testament became a "Christian" book in which all the important things to be said about Christ could in one way or another be found.

C. The "Two Ways"

Chapters 18 to 21:9 of the Epistle presents the "Teaching of the Two Ways," which also appears in a slightly different form at the beginning of the *Didaché*. Scholars disputed for years whether Barnabas depended on the latter, whether the *Didaché* was a re-writing of Barnabas, or whether they both depended on a third source. By the mid-3O's a number of key scholars (Armitage Robinson, J. Muilenburg, F. C. Burkitt, R. H. Connolly, *et.al.*) agreed that the didachist had edited and modified at least part of the *Barnabas* text.[28] Their main argument was the silence of Jewish sources as to the existence of a Two Ways manual and the alleged chaotic order of the *Barnabas* Two Ways section which in the *Didaché* is brought into a more formal order by careful rearrangement. Today, as L.W. Barnard has pointed out, this first point is no longer valid. The *Manual of Discipline* of the Qumran scrolls has a section comprising lists of virtues and vices entitled "Of the Two Spirits in Man," which was in all probability an expository sermon used by the priests of the community. A comparison of *Barnabas* with the *Manual of Discipline* does not provide parallels close enough to prove that the writer of *Barnabas* was directly acquainted with the Qumran version, but the *Manual* is of great value in demonstrating, for the first time, that a *written* Two Ways manual was known in Judaism in the pre-Christian era.[29] Today most scholars presume that both the Didachist and the author-editor of *Barnabas* drew from an earlier Christian Two Ways manual which followed to some extent existing Jewish style patterns.

II. Kind of Christianity Represented

A. Christology

The Epistle reveals what might be called a rather traditional second century Christology, leaning more in the Johannine direction than in that of the Synoptics. H. Windisch comments:

> Auch in Barn. ist die Christologie auf der Lehre von der *Gottheit Christi* aufgebaut. Seine *Präexistenz* ist deutlich ausgesprochen: Chr. ist bei der Weltschöpfung beteiligt(5:5,10; 6:12), hat mit Moses gesprochen(14:3), die Propheten inspiriert (5:6) und vor der Menschwerdung empfängt er seinen Auftrag vom Vater (14:6). So sind die die ihm gebührenden Prädikate *huiòs toû Theoû*[im vollen Sinn des Worts](7:2; 12:8,10; 15:5) und *pantòs toû kósmou kúrios* (5:5). ... So wird er denn

auch ganz mit Gott zusammengeschaut: er ist Herr der Welt
(5:5)wie Gott (21:5), Offenbarer im A.T. und Inspirator der
Exegeten(5:3,6)wie Gott(1:7), Bereiter des neuen Volkes (5:7)
wie Gott (3:6) und künftiger Weltrichter (5:7; 15:5) neben
Gott (4:12); Gottes Reich (21:1) ist auch sein Reich (7:11; 8:6
vgl. 4:13).[30]

Pseudo-Barnabas tells us more than the other Apostolic Fathers
about the life of Jesus, but even this is quite limited. From him we learn that
Jesus did wonders in Israel and that he preached (5:8). He knows that Jesus
gathered a group of apostles around himself and that they in turn preached
the Gospel (5:9). He tells that at the Crucifixion Jesus was given vinegar and
gall to drink (7:3).

> Most important, however, is the fact that he "endured suffering
> in the flesh" at the hands of men, to bring forgiveness (5:1),
> to destroy death and exhibit the resurrection (5:5; see 15:9,
> where Easter Day and the ascension are noted), to fulfill the
> promise to the fathers and prepare the new people (5:7;
> 14:1b,6), and to bring to a grand total the sins of those who
> oppose God's agents (5:11; 14:5a).[31]

Still there is nothing in the Epistle that would evidence a widespread use of
any one or more of the written Gospels. Chapter 6:13: "The Lord says, "See,
I make the last things as the first" — could certainly be a re-writing of
Matthew 19:30 and 20:16, however; and a few words in 4:14 would seem to
establish that *Pseudo-Barnabas* knew at least some form of Matthew's
Gospel as Scripture:

> Since you see that Israel, even after such great signs and
> wonders were wrought, still was rejected, let us beware lest as
> it was written (*hōs gégraptai*) "Many are called, but few are
> chosen" (*Matt.* 22:14), may not be verified in us.

Barnabas 5:9 —"He came not to call the righteous but sinners." — also
appears in the Synoptic tradition (*Matt.* 9:13 and parallels). And there is the
possibility that the information about Jesus' having been given vinegar and
gall to drink came from Matthew's Gospel (27:34, 48). Still aside from these
few contact points and occasional word correspondances[32] there is little to
show of a profound contact with the New Testament corpus.

The most frequent designation for Jesus is "Lord," especially in the material that emphasizes his suffering (chs. 5-8; see also 1:1; 2:6; 14:4, etc.), although, as we have seen, the same title is also used freely for God — a fact which makes precise interpretation difficult in many passages (e.g. 8:7; 16:8; 19:9; etc). Jesus' functions often seem to overlap with those of God. Another notable title for Jesus is that of "Beloved One" in 3:6; 4:3,8.

> "Christ" occurs as a name (with Jesus) in the Greek textual tradition only at 2:6, where it might well be secondary....The contrast drawn in 12:10 between "man's son" and "Son of God" is not necessarily a conscious reflection of the (Synoptic Gospels') title "Son of man," although such a possibility cannot be excluded entirely. Notice that in the same context," Son of David" is rejected as an appropriate title! "Servant" is applied to Jesus only in quotations (6:1; 9:2; cf. 5:2), and quotations also supply such titles as "Stone/Rock" (6:2f), "Day" (?6:4), and "Righteous One" (6:7). The shorthand title "the Name" is employed only in 16:8b....[33]

God is the eternal (18:2) and universal sovereign (16:2; 21:5), the creator of the universe and man (2:10; 5:5; 15:3; 16:1) who rules the course of history (see, e.g. 12:5; 19:6; 4:3; 15:4). He is also called "Lord" (e.g. ch. the "Father" (2:9; 12:8; 14:6), "Master" (1:7; 4:3), and the "Patient One" (3:6), the one who sent his Son Jesus for men's salvation (14:7). As to the Holy Spirit, nowhere in *Barnabas* is there an unambiguous reference to the "Spirit" as a separate entity/person/hypostasis of the Godhead.[34]

B. ESCHATOLOGY

Pseudo-Barnabas seems to have been a millenarianist, a teaching not uncommon the early Church which held that the duration of the world is symbolized and determined by the "days" of Creation. Every "day" of Creation was seen as equivalent to a thousand years. Therefore, the world would last six thousand years. Since the Lord rested on the seventh day, so He would come to destroy the world, judge the wicked, change the sun, moon and stars, and then rest — for the seventh millenium — together with the just. After the seventh millenium, i.e. in the eighth, a new world would begin (15:3-9). Pseudo-Barnabas obviously believed that the end of the sixth millenium, and consequently the second coming of Christ, was near (4:5; 21:3).

The entire atmosphere in which Pseudo-Barnabas exists is charged with a view of "the last times" which borders on the apocalyptic and which makes the task of paranesis all the more important and urgent. These are "the last days," the climax of evils which will usher in the "age to come" (2:1; 4:1,3,9; 16:5ff). The Christian must walk in this present wicked world, but he must walk carefully and perform his righteous task with deliberate haste (19:1b, 21:7b) as he continually looks forward to the imminent holy age (8:6; 10:11, 21:1,3). The Lord is about to judge (4:12, 5:7; 7:2; 15:5, cf. 10:5; 12:9) and the Christian must be prepared for this "day of recompense" (11:8; 19:10 ff; 20:2c, 21:6).[35]

C. THE CROSS AND BAPTISM: THE EPISTLE'S BASIC SACRAMENTAL THEOLOGY

At first reading one gets the idea that Pseudo-Barnabas knows but one sacrament — Baptism, and that in the narrowest of relationships with the Cross. P. Meinhold writes:

> Wie das Kreuz und der rettende Glaube an den Gekreuzigten vielfache Vorbilder im Alten Testament haben, so finden sich in gleicher Weise Hinweise auf die Taufe; denn auch "in Bezug auf das Wasser hat es dem Herrn — *kýrios* — gefallen, im Voraus eine Offenbarung zu geben"(11,1). Die Taufe erscheint für Barnabas bei den Propheten an jenen Stellen, an denen von der "Quelle des Lebens", von dem "zuverlässigen Wasser", von dem fruchtbringenden Baum gepflanzt an "Wasserbächen", überhaupt vom "Fluss", also von Bildern die Rede ist, die sich auf das Taufwasser beziehen lassen (11,2). So weist das Alte Testament nicht nur auf die Tatsache der Taufe hin, es deutet zugleich an, wie die Juden die Taufe zur Vergebung der Sünden nicht annehmen werden (11,1). Die Wirkung der Taufe bestehen in der Vergebung der Sünden und damit in der inneren Erneuerung des Menschen: "Das meint der Prophet: wir steigen wohl hinunter in das Wasser, voll von Sünden und Schmutz, aber wir steigen hinauf und tragen Früchte im Herzen und haben im Geiste die Furcht und die Hoffnung zu Jesus"(11,11).[36]

From this last *Barnabas* citation as well as from 11:8 — "Blessed are those who, having placed their hope in the Cross, descended into the water."

— it appears that Baptism by immersion was the common practice in the Barnabean milieu. The writer has no express treatment of Baptism as an inauguration into the Christian community, though one could see it as implied. His main purpose seems rather to lie in reasserting a Baptism for the forgiveness of sins which the Jews had rejected — thus the repeated tie-in with the Cross.

> Since then He made us new by the remission of sins, He made us another type, that we should have the soul of children, as though He were creating us anew (6:1).

Later in the Epistle's Two Way material we find what might be called a follow-up to the Christian's Baptism unto the forgiveness of sins. The writer states simply, with no comment and no development:

> Confess your sins. Do not come to prayer with a guilty conscience. (19:12)

The parallel text in the *Didache* reads:

> In the Church, confess your transgressions and do not betake yourself to prayer with an evil conscience. (4:14)

In neither instance is the *modus quo* of this confession discussed, but from the latter it would seem that it was not just a private affair between God and the individual but that some ceremony or ritual was involved.

The question of a Eucharistic theology in Barnabas is a more difficult problem. There is no explicit statement about the Eucharist in the Epistle but authors such as Barnard, Prigent and Daniélou find indirect references to it in the much repeated theme of the "land flowing with milk and honey" Barnard, as we have already seen in part, has presented a reasonable cumulative argument to show that Psuedo-Barnabas was writing a Paschal homily to be delivered before a Christian community celebrating a baptismal-eucharistic celebration, i.e. like that described in Hippolytus (*Trad. Apos.* 23:2) where the newly-baptized received three cups in succession — of water, of milk mixed with honey, and of wine.[37] To this latter Prigent adds similar citations from the *Odes of Solomon* (4:10) and from Hippolytus' *Elenchos* (5:8), concluding as Barnard that:

> Dans cette perspective la promesse de la terre où coulent le
> lair et le miel vise tout naturellement la première eucharistie
> paschale dans laquelle du lait et du miel sont offerts au
> nouveau baptisé. En vérité cette terre est la chair du Christ.[38]

Daniélou bolsters the same position with further evidence from Clement of
Alexandria (*Ped.* I,6; GCS, 110, 26-31) and Tertullian (*Adv. Marc.* I, 14),
noting especially that the latter attests to the practice among the Marcionites
of administering the cup of milk and honey to the newly baptized.[39] This
would at least situate the practice in the first half of the second century, i.e.
in the time of the writing of our Epistle. Nonetheless the fact still remains
that, aside from these very probable eucharistic allusions, there is not a
single instance in the Epistle where the Eucharist is explicitly mentioned —
an odd fact indeed if the text (or part of the text) of this copious compendium
of teaching was meant to be proclaimed at a eucharistic celebration.

In any case, we must admit that whatever there is of explicit
sacramental theology in the Epistle arises from a Baptism for the forgiveness
of sins which is firmly rooted in faith in the Cross. There is no development
of a theology of the Eucharist or of Penance and were it not for the
above-mentioned allusions and the hint at some sort of confession practice
in 19:12, we might be inclined to think that the Eucharist or forgiveness for
sins after Baptism was not available for the Christians of the Barnabean
Church. But still an even bigger problem remains to be faced: trying to find
in the Epistle some hint concerning the organization of the Christian
community and its ministry.

III. Possible Hints at Church Organization and Ministry

The bold fact is that Church organization and ministry are virtually
ignored in the *Epistle of Pseudo-Barnabas.*

> Nulle part, le didascale qu'il prétend bien être, en dépit de ses
> déclarations répétées d'humilité, ne mentionne la hiérarchie.
> Il n'est question, dans sa lettre, ni des évêques, ni des presbytres
> ou des diacres. Seul compte le docteur qui doit donner à ses
> disciples une connaissance approfondie de l'Écriture et de ses
> mystères. Cela est déjà assez inquiétant. Il n'y est pas davantage

question de l'Église: le mot *ekklēsía* est employé deux fois: la première, dans une citation de l'Ancien Testament(VI, 16); la second, avec un sens tellement général qu'il perd toute sa valeur(VII, 11). Ses destinataires sont d'ailleurs des chrétiens vivants et réels. Ils sont l'objet de son affection, de ses louanges: ce sont des enfants de joie et d'allégresse. Ils constituent un groups fidèle, nettement déterminé et leur maître est conscient des responsabilités qu'il encourt s'il ne leur donne pas la formation spirituelle à laquelle ils ont droit.[40]

While Bardy's analysis here is for the most part accurate, there is certainly more that can be said concerning the corporate Church in the Epistle than the fact that the word *ekklēsía* only appears at two places in the text. The Church for *Barnabas* is more than just an assembly *(ekklēsía)*. It is a *people (laós)* — "the people He prepared in his Beloved"(3:6; cf. also 13:1), in fact, a *new* people — "that He himself might prepare this new people" *(tòn laòn tòn kainòn)* (5:7) — the new heirs of the Covenant (4:6-8; 6:19; 13:1ff). Moreover, the word *ekklēsía* is not the only means of conveying the idea of a Christian assembly, as can be seen from 4:10:

Do not by retiring live alone as if you were already made righteous, but come together *(epì tò autò synerchómenoi)* and seek the common good.

And while it is true that the use of *ekklēsía* in 6:16 appears "dans une citation de l'Ancien Testament," when we read this citation in its full context, we see that it is clearly applied to the Christian community, to the "we" to whom *Barnabas* writes:

6:13 Again I will show you how he speaks to *us*. In the last days he made a second creation; and the Lord says, "See, I make the last things as the first." To this then the Prophet referred when he proclaimed, "Enter into a land flowing with milk and honey, and rule over it." See then, *we* have been created afresh, as he says again in another Prophet," See," saith the Lord, "I will take out from them" (that is those whom the Spirit of the Lord foresaw) "the hearts of stone and I will put in hearts of flesh." Because he himself was going to be manifest in the flesh and dwell among us. For, my brethren, the habitation of our hearts is a shrine holy to the Lord. For the

Lord says again, "And wherewith shall I appear before the
Lord my God and be glorified?" He says, "I will confess to
thee in the *assembly* of my brethren, and will sing to thee in the
midst of the *assembly* of saints." [cf. *Ps.* 22:23] We then are
they whom he brought into the good land.

R.A. Kraft has made an analysis of the Barnabean *ekklēsía* that goes
a bit deeper than that of Bardy. Concerning the recipients of the Epistle, he
writes:

Clearly they are a community (or group of communities),
a fellowship of believers — and are exhorted to remain so
and not to slip into individualism (4:10; 6:16; 16:8 19:10
[=*Did.* 4:2]; 21:2,4). If the Two Ways tradition is
characteristic of this community — and this cannot be
taken for granted — their social concern approached the
communal life of *Acts* 2-5, at least in terms of sharing
possessions (19:8f [= *Did.* 4:8,5]; cf. 21:2b). [But] ... Apart
from the references to the ministry of the "teachers," there
are only vague allusions to "those in authority" (or perhaps,
"those economically prosperous"? [21:2]) and to those
"who proclaim the Lord's word" (19:9b [= *Did.* 4:1]; cf.
10:11c; 16:10). Sunday seems to have been observed
(weekly?) as a "day of rejoicing" in commemoration of
Jesus' resurrection, apparently to the exclusion of the
traditional Jewish Sabbath-rest (15:8f).[41]

Although, as we have seen, the Epistle does not present an ordained ministry
within the Christian community, there are nonetheless clear implications of
Christian leaders at work. Someone (or ones) would have to shoulder the
responsibility for gathering the people "together to seek out the common
good" (4:10). Someone would have to baptize. Someone would have to
"proclaim the Lord's word" (19:9). Someone would have to preside at
communal gatherings (on the "day of rejoicing"). There would have to be
those whose function it was to keep the community together and foster the
social implications found in the Two Ways material. Indeed, we do not find
such persons (or groups) spoken of categorically in the Epistle, but
Pseudo-Barnabas clearly expects things to take place in the Christian
community to which he writes that do, in fact, call for organizational and
leadership qualities on an evangelical level.

In addition to these implications of local ministry, we find in ch. 8 a rather clear allusion to the original Apostolic ministry:

> But what do you think is typified by the injunction to Israel: men already grown grey in sin shall offer a heifer, and slay and burn it; then small boys are to collect the ashes and put them into vessels, and to tie the scarlet wool and hyssop around a piece of wood — note here again the type of the Cross and the scarlet wool! — and with this the boys are to sprinkle the people one by one, that they may be sanctified by the remission of their sins? Observe how plainly He speaks to you: The calf is Jesus; the sinners who offer it are those who brought Him to the slaughter. And now — gone are the men; gone is the glory of the sinners! The small boys who did the sprinkling are those who brought us the good tidings of the forgiveness of sins and the sanctification of the heart — those whom He empowered to preach the Gospel. They were twelve in number to represent the Tribes of Israel, which were twelve. But why are the sprinklers three boys? To represent Abraham, Isaac, and Jacob, since these men were great in the sight of God.

Commentators generally admit the "boys" in this passage to be the Apostles.[42] They are "those who brought us the good tidings of the forgiveness of sins and the purification of the heart — those whom He empowered to preach the Gospel.[43] This is certainly the fundamental Apostolic ministry we find in the Gospels and *Acts.*

It is upon this allusion to the Apostles that Colson bases his argument for the presence of a sacerdotal function in the Epistle. Perhaps it is best to let him speak for himself.

> En résumé, d'apres l'épître de *Barnabé,* c'est ainsi que par la croix et le baptême, qui en applique les fruits rédempteurs: purification, rémission des péchés, Dieu a fait alliance avec un Peuple nouveau, un Peuple saint qui, à la place du sabbat, lui rend un culte nouveau au "Jour du Seigneur". Et dans la constitution, par purification, de ce Peuple saint appelé à rendre à Dieu le culte "spirituel", les apôtres apparaissent comme les "enfants qui aspergent", c'est-à-dire mettent en oeuvre l'efficacité rédemptrice du sacrifice du Christ, en proclamant la rémission des péchés et la purification du coeur, fruits de ce sacrifice. Et, par le fait même, ils

apparaissent comme exerçant une fonction "sacerdotale". ...
De part et d'autre, les apôtres apparaissent comme *substitués
au sacerdoce lévitique*, mais *dans une perspective
spiritualisée: Ils ne succèdent pas* aux *hiereîs* juifs. Ils ont
comme "ministère sacerdotal" l'Evangile, pour constituer le
Peuple des sanctifiés et construire ainsi le Temple spirituel.[44]

Colson would obviously like to see a priestly act in *Barnabas* 8:3, i.e. in the
sprinkling by the small boys (viz. the Apostles) of the people with a mixture
of water and ashes. This is however not the case. The "boys" in *Barnabas*
8:3 are set parallel in *Numbers* 19 — the Old Testament basis for this
passage —not to the Levitical priest in 19:4 but to "a person who is clean,"
i.e. in the
state of ritual purity, in 19:19. F. X. Funk mentions this in his commentary:

> Barnabas non loquitur de aspersione sanguinis vaccae rubrae,
> quae a sacerdote solo fiebat (*Num.* 19,4), sed de aspersione
> aquae cinere permistae, quae a mundo quoque (*Num.* 19,19)
> fieri potuit. Cf. *Mischna Parah* 3, 3.4.[45]

This can perhaps be seen even more clearly from the excellent comparative
chart which Prigent has prepared to show the relationship between *Barnabas*
8 and *Numbers* 19. He adds *Mischna Parah* 3 as a third column to the chart
to show that *Barnabas* knew some further details which have only been
preserved for us in this particular rabbinical tradition.

In short, that "les apôtres apparaissent comme *substitués au sacerdoce
lévitique*, mais *dans une perspective spiritualisée*" can be proved neither
from the *Barnabas* parallels in *Numbers* nor from those in the *Mischna
Parah*. What can be proved by a comparison of the texts is a parallel
relationship between "les enfants" i.e. the Apostles, and "un homme en état
de pureté," a state to which every good Israelite aspired every day of his life.
But even though we cannot accept Colson's argument for the presence of a
sacerdotal function in the Epistle, this should not keep us from investigating
further.

176

Barnabe 8	Nombres 19	Parah 3
Une génisse	Offrande d'une génisse rousse	Offrande d'une génisse rousse
est offerte par des hommes en qui sont des péchés parfaits.	L'eau lustrale obtenue avec les cendres sert à purifier quiconque a eu contact avec la mort.	
Ils l'égorgent	On l'immole hors du camp	
la brûlent	On la brûle.	
Des enfants	Un homme en état de pureté	Des enfants prennent de l'eau dans les vases
recueillent les cendres dans des vases	recueille les cendres et lea place en un lieu pur	et y mêlent les cendres
et enroulent la laine pourpre sur le bois et l'hysope laine	La génisse a été brûlée avec du bois de cèdre, de l'hysope et de la	La génisse a été brûlée avec du cèdre, de l'hysope et de la
Puis les enfants aspergent tout le peuple pour la purification des péchés.	pourpre. Un homme en état de pureté prend l'hysope, la plonge dans l'eau lustrale et asperge gens et choses souillés par le contact avec la mort.	pourpre. Les enfants s'aspergent.[46]

We read in 15:9:

> Wherefore we also celebrate/observe *(ágomen)* with gladness the eighth day in which Jesus also rose from the dead, and was made manifest, and ascended into Heaven.[47]

Are there perhaps texts which could possibly carry some type of allusion to a Christian cultic assembly on "the eighth day"?

The author-editor does use the verb *eucharisteîn* twice in the Epistle:

5:3 Therefore we ought to give great thanks
(hyper-eucharisteîn) to the Lord that he has given us knowledge
of the past, and wisdom for the present, and that we are not
without understanding for the future.
7:1 Understand therefore, children of gladness, that the good
Lord has revealed everything to us in advance, that we may
know Him to whom we ought to give thanks and praise for
everything *(ho katà pánta eucharistoûntes opheílomen aiveîn)*.

Both of these sentences are sort of interjectory statements in the text; they
are neither explained nor developed by the contexts in which they stand.
Moreover both are in the first person plural and attach a genuine "oughtness"
to the giving of thanks. The point which defies proof here is whether the
verb "to give thanks" *(eucharisteîn)* had come to be used for a Christian
eucharistic assembly/meal in the community to which *Barnabas* writes. It
appears to be possible but unlikely.[48]

One consideration, and a very strong one, which makes it unlikely
that *eucharisteîn* has to do with an organized Christian cult in the Epistle,
lies in the enormously strong "anti-cultic" sentiment expressed in the first
main section (beginning at 2:4)[49] The text presents a categorical rejection
of the Mosaic sacrificial cult and calls for a thorough spiritualization,
actually an intense personal interiorization of the concept of sacrifice.

2:4 For He made it clear to us through all the prophets that He
needs neither sacrifices *(thusiôn)* nor whole burnt offerings
(holokautōmátōn) nor offerings in general *(prosphorôn)*— as
He says in one place:
5 What good is the multitude of your sacrifices to me? says
the Lord.
I am full of burnt offerings of rams and the fat of lambs, and
I do not want the blood of bulls and goats — not even if you
come and appear before me: For who has required these things
from your hands? Do not continue to tread my (Temple) court
(mou tèn aulèn). If you bring finely ground flour, it is in vain;
offering of incense is an abomination to me, I cannot bear your
new moon festivals and sabbaths (cf. *Is.* 1:11-13).

Barnabas immediately adds the reason for this:

6 Therefore He set these things aside, so that the new law of the Lord Jesus Christ,[50] which is not tied to a yoke of necessity (cf. *Acts* 15:10), might have its own offering *(tèn prosphorán)* which is not man-made *(mē anthrōpopoíēton).*[51]

F.X. Funk explains this latter Christian "offering which is not man-made" as a:

sacrificium ne in rebus externis versetur nec manibus hominibus paretur vel offeratur, sed spirituale sit et in virtutibus consistat, ut in versibus sequentibus exponitur.[52]

7 And again He says to them, "Did I command your fathers when they came out of the land of Egypt to offer me burnt offerings and sacrifices?
8 Nay, but rather did I command them this: Let none of you cherish any evil his heart against his neighbor, and love not a false oath."
9 We ought then to understand, if we are not foolish, the loving intention of our Father, for He speaks to us, wishing that we should not err like them, but seek how we may make our offering to Him *(pôs proságömen autô).*
10 To us then He speaks thus: "Sacrifice *(thusía)* for the Lord is a broken heart, a smell of sweet savor to the Lord is a heart that glorifies him that made it."

Thus while the material sacrifices of the Old Law are indeed rejected, the concept of sacrifice is not. The corrective proposed by *Barnabas* is that of a personal sacrifice in the spiritual order involving love of neighbor, faithfulness to one's word, humility and praise of the Creator. This is, in fact, the same spiritualization of the Old Testament sacrifices based on *Ps.* 51 that we have already seen in *1 Clement* 18:16-17. *Barnabas,* however, goes beyond *1 Clement* in that he extends this spiritualization also to fasts (ch. 3), circumcision (ch. 9), food laws (ch. 10), the Sabbath (ch. 15) and the Temple (ch. 16). Perhaps the most important point here is the fact that *Barnabas* retains and passes along to the Christian community the concept of sacrifice in a spiritualized, internalized form, a form which, if it became general Christian practice in the years following, could have called for collective expression in an external Christian ritual.

IV. Conclusion

In the *Epistle of Barnabas* we encounter a fairly early second-century Christian document from Egypt or possibly Syria. Who the final redactor was remains to this day a mystery, but since we actually know so little about the Apostle Barnabas, there is no way to disprove his having had something or much to do with the material ultimately contained in the Epistle even should this be by way of a "Barnabean school." The text itself, actually a sort of epistle homily, has been shown to be an example of 'evolved literature' which means that whoever gave the Epistle its final form was at most an author-editor who reproduced and reworked older material, such as *testimonia* collections (including Scripture quotations), Jewish apocalyptic writings, Two Ways material, 'targumic' paraphrases, etc. Regardless of its development, the Epistle was highly respected in the early Church, especially by Clement of Alexandria and Origen and was included in the *Codex Sinaiticus* immediately after the canonical books of the New Testament.

The theme of the Epistle is the relation of Christianity to Judaism. Denying any historical link between Judaism and the Gospel, the author-editor posits that all rites and ceremonies of the Mosaic Law were intended by God as mystical pointers to Christ and that the Jewish people who had been seduced by an evil angel (9:4) settled for a literal rather than a spiritual understanding of them. Consequently, according to the writer, they lost their claim to the possession of the Covenant and it was thenceforward reserved for the Christians. To impart more in detail this exegetical and ethical knowledge *(gnosis)*, Pseudo-Barnabas, as he is generally called in patristic literature, makes use of a somewhat complex methodology: 1) typological interpretation of Old Testament texts and personalities, 2) spiritual interpretation of Old Testament institutions, 3) fairly extensive use of *testimonia* and other earlier material, and 4) a personally unique twist in Scripture interpretation — the insistence that certain sections of the Old Testament were directly and explicitly written for the Christians.

The kind of doctrinal Christianity presented by Pseudo-Barnabas moves strongly in the Johannine direction without really evidencing any genuine contact with the New Testament corpus aside from a citation of *Matt.* 22:14 and a few occasional word correspondences. The *Matthew* quotation, however, is prefixed with the canonized phrase denoting Sacred Scripture: *hōs gégraptai.* For Pseudo-Barnabas Christ is divine and pre-existent; in fact, His functions often seem to overlap with those of God the Father. There is indeed more in the Epistle about the life of Jesus than in the other Apostolic Fathers, but even this is quite limited: He did wonders and preached; He gathered about Himself disciples and sent them out to preach; He was given vinegar and gall to drink and crucified to bring forgiveness of sins, to destroy death, to show forth the resurrection, to fulfill the promises to the fathers and to prepare for Himself a new people. The Epistle contains no clearly discernible theology of the Holy Spirit; on the other hand, a strong millenarian eschatology makes itself felt throughout the whole work and gives a genuine urgency to the writer's desire to impart his teaching.

In terms of sacraments, the spotlight centers on Baptism for the forgiveness of sins which Pseudo-Barnabas firmly links with the Cross, the source of this forgiveness. One finds also in the Two Ways material an isolated admonition to confess one's sins (19:12), but this without any further comment. The arguments of Barnard, Prigent and Daniélou to show that certain references within the Epistle, especially those to a "land flowing with milk and honey" point to a Paschal eucharistic celebration at which catechumens were baptized cannot be taken lightly, but the absence of a clear reference to the eucharistic celebration — especially if this Epistle in whole or in part was to have been the homily at that celebration — make them less than completely convincing.

Perhaps the most difficult problem is trying to find some hint of Church organization or Christian ministry in the Epistle. There is no explicit mention of *epískopoi, presbýteroi* or *diákonoi*. In fact, the only ministerial function Pseudo-Barnabas seems to know explicitly is his own — that of "teacher." Nonetheless there are clear implications of Christian leaders at work. Someone (or ones) would have to gather the people "together to seek out the common good" (4:10). The same holds true for baptizing, proclaiming the Lord's word (19:9), presiding at communal gatherings and fostering the social implications put forth in the Two Ways material. In ch. 8:3 we find an allusion to the Apostles:

> The boys who sprinkle [the ashes of the heifer mixed with water] are they who preached to us the forgiveness of sins, and the purification of the heart, to whom He gave authority to proclaim the Gospel, and there are twelve as a testimony to the tribes, because there are twelve tribes of Israel.

We can see here that the original Apostolic ministry, at least as Pseudo-Barnabas understood it, centered in the authority to preach the Gospel which included the forgiveness of sins and the purification of the heart. J. Colson has attempted to find a Christian sacerdotal function in this passage for, according to him, the Apostles "apparaissent comme *substitués au sacerdoce lévitique* mais *dans une perspective spiritualisée.* A comparison of ch. 8 with Pseudo-Barnabas' obvious source material in *Numbers* 19 and *Mischna Parah* 3, however, shows that the parallel is not between the "boys" and the Levitical priest in *Num.* 19:4, but between the "boys" and "a person in the state of (ritual) purity" (*Num.* 19:19), a state to which every good Israelite constantly aspired.

The search for some sort of Christian cultic ritual considering the remark in 15:9 that "we also observe with gladness the eighth day in which Jesus rose from the dead," yields a few possibilities but nothing that can be considered conclusive proof. The verb *eucharisteîn,* for example, appears twice (5:3; 7:1) and indeed in statements sufficiently isolated in their contexts to possibly carry a cultic significance were we able to prove that "to give thanks" had already become a technical term for the Christian eucharistic celebration in the community in which or to which Pseudo-Barnabas wrote. The presence of an organized Christian ritual cultus in the Epistle, however, is rendered unlikely not only by the radically anti-cultic stand taken in the first main section of the Epistle but also by the writer's call for a spiritualization of the Mosaic notion of sacrifice along the lines of *Ps.* 51 (cf. also *1 Clement* 18:16-17), a call for the personal interiorization of sacrifice. Still the concept of sacrifice itself is not rejected and perhaps it was the practice of this spiritualized, internalized form of sacrifice among Christians which in a later era would call for external expression in a Christian ritual cultus.

Thus while there are some implicit suggestions that a Christian ministry is operative in the community to which Pseudo-Barnabas writes, a curtain of silence unfortunately lies over any further precision in the matter.

182

NOTES

[1] R. A. Kraft,"Barnabas' Isaiah Text and the 'Testimony Book' Hypothesis," *Journal of Biblical Literature*, 79, 1960, p. 336.

[2] For these arguments as well as a critique of Prigent's position cf. L.W. Barnard, "Judaism in Egypt C.E. 70-135," *Studies in the Apostolic Fathers and their Background*, Blackwell, Oxford, 1966, p. 46, and R.A. Kraft, *Journal of Theological Studies*, 8, 1962, p. 406.

[3] P. Prigent, *Les Testimonia dans le christianisme primitif: L'ÉPÎTRE DE BARNABÉ I-XVI ET SES SOURCES* [Études Bibliques], Gabala, Paris, 1961, (Syrian origin: p. 219).

[4] R.A. Kraft, *THE APOSTOLIC FATHERS: A New Translation and Commentary, Vol. 3, Barnabas and the Didache*, Nelson, New York, 1965, p. 55.

[5] See Barnard, *op. cit.*, pp. 57-72.

[6] For discussions on a more precise dating of the Epistle one can confer: L.W. Barnard, *Journal of Egyptian Archeology*, 44, 1958, p. 101 ff; F.X. Funk," Die Zeit des Barnabas briefes," *Kirchengeschichtliche Abhandlungen und Untersuchungen*, t. 11, Paderborn, 1899, pp. 77-108; M. d'Herbigny, "La date de l'épître de Barnabé," *Rech. de science relig.*, 1, 1910, pp. 417-443, 540-566; J. Muilenburg, *The Literary Relations of the Epistle of Barnabas and the Teaching of the Twelve Apostles*, Marburg, 1929, p. 167; A.L. Williams, "The Date of the Epistle of Barnabas," *Journal of Theological Studies*, 34, 1933, p. 344.

[7] Barnabas and the Didache "*Journal of Theological Studies*, 33, 1932, p. 26.

[8] Cf. Muilenburg, *loc. cit.*; Thieme, *Kirche und Synagoge*, Olten, 1945, also J. Oesterreicher & K. Thieme,"Um Kirche und Synagoge im Barnabasbrief," *Zeitschr. fur kathol. Theol.*, 74, 1952, pp. 63-70; Barnard, "Judaism in Egypt..." *op. cit.*, pp. 47-51.

[9] Cf. Kraft, *op. cit.*, p. 39:" The contrast between 'us' and 'there' (Israel) is repeatedly drawn (3:6; 4:6-8; 5:2-8, 12; 6:7; 8:1-3; 9:4f), and the community is expressly identified with uncircumcised Gentiles (13:7; 14:5-8; cf. 3:6; 16:7-9). Nowhere does the author-editor attempt to distinguish himself from them in this respect (see e.g., 16:7), but writes as one of them (1:8; 4:6).

[10] R.A. Kraft, *op. cit.*, p. 44.

[11] *Ibid.*, p. 1; see also note 1.

[12] P. Prigent, *op. cit.*, p. 13; cf. also H. Windisch, *Der Barnabasbrief. Handb. z. N.T.-Ergänzungsband: Die Apostolischen Väter*, III, J.C.B. Mohr (Paul Siebeck), Tübingen, 1920, pp. 408-413.

[13] R.A. Kraft, *op. cit.*, p. 2.

[14] "Some commentators, however, suggest that the epistle may have been written to Rome (Volkmar, Lipsius), Asia Minor (Muller), or Syria (Pfleiderer). V. Bartelet, 'Papias's *Exposition;* its Date and Contents,' in *Amicitiae Corolla*, ed. H. G. Wood, p. 20, suggested that Barnabas was written ca. 70-79 C.E. "by an Asian teacher to Christians in Alexandria." Ref. R.A. Kraft," Barnabas Isaiah Text..." *Journ. Bib. Lit.*, 79, part II, 1960, p. 336, note 2.

[15] Until the 19th century we knew the Epistle only in a Latin version of the first 17 chapters. The discovery of the Codex Sinaiticus in 1859 revealed for the first time the Greek text of the Epistle in its entirety.

[16] J. Quasten, *Patrology*, Vol. I, Spectrum, Utrecht, 1950, p. 85.

[17] "Is the Epistle of Barnabas a Paschal Homily?" *Studies in the Apostolic*

Fathers, p. 74.

18   Cf. M. Staniforth, *Early Christian Writings. The Apostolic Fathers*, Penguin Classics, Baltimore, 1968, p. 189.

19   Cf. R.A. Kraft, "Barnabas' Isaiah Text..." *Journal of Bib. Lit.*, 79, 1960, p. 237.

20   Cf. M. Staniforth, *op. cit.*, p. 191.

21   Barnard, "The Use of Testimonies in the Early Church and in the Epistle of Barnabas," *op. cit.*, pp. 109-135.

22   Prigent, *op. cit.*, pp. 217-220: He unravels four groups of "testimonies" in the Epistle: A. *Anti-cultic* (not *per se* anti-Jewish) *testimonies:* based on LXX quotations, probably a single collection from Syria with affinities to the views of Stephen (2:5; 2:7-8;2:10; 3:1-5;9:1-3; 9:5; 11:2-3; 14:1-3; 15:1-2; 16:1-3; also 4:7-8). B. *Midrashic testimonies* which give Christian allegorical interpretations to O.T. institutions (6:8-19 [&11:9]; 7;8; 9:7-9; 1 1:4-8; 12;13). C. *Messianic testimonies,* divided into "Christological" (5:2, 12ff; 6:1, 2-4, 6-7; 8:5; 12:1-4) and "universal" (12:10-11,14:6). And D. *other kinds of source material* including references to Jewish apocalyptic writings, Two Ways material and 'targumic' paraphrases (e.g., 4:4-5; 15:8; 16:5-6).

23   Cf. A. F. J. Klijn, *op. cit.*, p. 15ff.

24   R.A. Kraft, *Apostolic Fathers. Vol. 3. Barnabas and the Didache*, pp. 23-24.

25   Barnard, "The Dead Sea Scrolls, Barnabas, the *Didache*...," *op. cit.*, p. 92.

26   The following is a summary of the excellent analysis by A. F. J. Klijn, *op. cit.*, pp. 17-19.

27   J.L. Koole, *De Overname van het Oude Testament door de christelijke Kerk*, Hilversum, 1938, p. 140.

28   Cf. J.A. Robinson, *Barnabas, Hermas and the Didache*, London, 1920; J. Muilenburg, *The Literary Relations of the Epistle of Barnabas and the Teaching of the Twelve Apostles*, Marburg, 1929; F. C. Burkitt, "Barnabas and the Didache," *Journal of Theological Studies*, 33, 1932, p. 27; R. H. Connolly, "The *Didache* in Relation to the Epistle of Barnabas," *JTS*, 33, 1932, p. 247; see also Connolly, "Barnabas and the Didache," *JTS*, 38, 1937, pp. 165-167.

29   L.W. Barnard, "The Dead Sea Scrolls, Barnabas, the *Didache*..." *op. cit.*, p. 93-94, 97; see also the older but still quite valid essay of Windisch, *op. cit.*, pp. 404-406.

30   H. Windisch, *op. cit.*, p. 374.

31   R.A. Kraft, *op. cit.*, p. 35; A. F. J. Klijn, *op. cit.*, p. 20:" Op een punt lijkt de schrijver een van de latere orthodoxie afwijkende mening te hebben. Hij spreekt namelijk niet over de vleeswording van Christus maar van een 'in het vlees komen' (5:6&11). Er ontstaat zo een verschil tussen de Geest en het licham van Christus.... Het is de vraag of deze scheiding van vlees en Geest als 'docetisch' kan worden betiteld. Bij het oudchristelijke docetisme wordt deze scheiding tot een leer, waarbij verondersteld wordt dat Jezus 'in schijn' geleden heeft omdat nu eenmaal God of het goddelijke niet lijden kan. Van een dergelijke leer is hier evenwel niets te bespeuren."

32   See Verzeichnis der Schriftstellen in Funk-Bihlmeyer, *Die Apostolischen Väter*, Tübingen, 1956, pp. 153-4.

33   R.A. Kraft, *op. cit.*, p. 36.

34   *Ibid.*, pp. 37-38.

35   *Ibid.*, p. 27.

36   P. Meinhold, "Geschichte und Exegese im Barnabasbrief," *Zeitschrift für Kirchengeschichte*, LIX, 1940, pp. 280-281.

37   L.W. Barnard, "Is the Epistle of Barnabas a Paschal Homily?" *op. cit.*, pp. 73-85, esp. pp. 82-84.

38   P. Prigent, *op. cit.*, p. 87.

[39]   J. Daniélou, *Théologie du Judéo-Christianisme*, Désclée, Paris, 1958, p. 389; see also N.A. Dahl, "La terre ou coule le lait et le miel," in *Aux Sources de la Tradition chrétienne* (Mel. Gogel), Neuchâtel, 1950, pp 62-70.

[40]   G. Bardy, *La Théologie de l'Église de saint Clément de Rome à saint Irénée* (Unam Sanctam, 13), du Cerf, Paris, 1945, pp. 159-160.

[41]   R.A. Kraft, *op. cit.*, pp. 38-39.

[42]   Cf., e.g., H. Windisch, *op. cit.*, p. 349: "Deutung der Knaben = 12 Apostel. ... Zum erstenmal in der urchristl. Literatur wird hier die Zwölfzahl der Apostel ausdrüklich mit der Zwölfzahl der Stämme (Sir. 44,23) in Verbindung gebracht vgl. Mt. 19, 28=Lc. 22,30. ... Eine zweite Deutung der Knaben, auf der willkürlichen Annahme einer Dreizahl beruhend, die Num. 19 nicht angegeben ist und auch zu 3 nicht passt. Wenn die Dreizahl (vgl. 1,6; 10,1 u. ö.) von Anfang an festgestanden hätte, wäre die Deutung auf die zwölf Apostel unmöglich gewesen. Wir haben es hier also mit einer anderweitigen, nachträglich beigefügten Deutung oder einer Glosse zu tun." See also Kleist, *op. cit.*, p. 174.

[43]   The Epistle has one direct mention of the Apostles as historical figures (5:9). They are called "sinners above every sin" evidently as a proof that the Lord "came not to call the righteous but sinners." The text adds little aside from establishing the Apostles as historical figures in Barnabas' viewpoint.

[44]   J. Colson, *Ministre de Jésus-Christ ou le sacerdoce de l'Évangile*, pp. 298-299.

[45]   F.X. Funk, *Opera Patrum Apostolicorum*, Tübingen, 1878, p.26.

[46]   P. Prigent, *op. cit.*, p. 110.

[47]   Comp. Ign. *ad Magnesios*, 9:1.

[48]   Another possible but unlikely allusion to a Christian cult appears in a textual variant in 1:7 of the old Latin version. The Sinaiticus reads: "We ought to be all the more generous and inspired in our effort to advance in fear of Him *(proságein tô phóbō autoû)*. The old Latin version (L) ends this sentence with: *accedere ad aram illius*. Windisch (o.c., p. 307) comments: "L hat am Ende von 7 *accedere ad aram illius*, scheint also *proságein tô bōmô autoû* (statt *t. phóbō aut.* SC) gelesen zu haben vgl Philo de spec. leg. II 162 p. 294. Ich glaube nicht, dass Barn. ohne nähere Ausdeutung vom 'Altar' gesprochen haben sollte. Ganz unverdächtig ist der griechischen Texte freilich auch nicht. *Proságein* ist intransitiv wie 2,9 und Jos. 3,9 u.ö." Scholars generally prefer the Sinaiticus reading because it is correlated by the Codex Hierosolymitanus, although A. Hilgenfeld, writing in the years shortly after the publication of the Sinaiticus, retains the reading "to His altar" (cf. his *Barnabae epistola* ..., Lipsiae, 1866). If the literal reading of the old Latin could in some way be proved as original we would indeed have to reckon with a Christian cult and probably priesthood as early as Barnabas. Lampe's *Patristic Greek Lexicon* (Fasc. 2, p. 306) shows that *bōmos* meaning literally a Christian altar shows up rarely even in the 5th and 6th centuries, although Clement of Alexandria and Origen did use it in a metaphorical sense.

[49]   R.A. Kraft reviewing Prigent's book in *JTS*, 8, 1962, p. 405 notes: "It is not difficult to show that many of the 'anti-cultic' criticisms raised in Barnabas' letter were also current in *Jewish* circles which were critical of the Jerusalem cultus." See also Kraft, *The Apostolic Fathers. Vol. 3. Barnabas and the Didache*, p 84.

[50]   The only occurrence of the full name "Jesus Christ" in the Epistle.

[51]   H. Windisch, *op. cit.*, states that *mē anthrōpopoíēton* "meint den geistigen Gottesdienst in Werken der Liebe Jac 1,27 gegenüber den äusserlichen kultischen Zeremonien; doch kann auch gedacht sein, dass das neue Gesetz göttliche Offenbarung ist, während das jüdische Opfergesetz Menschengebot war Js 29,13 = Mc 7, 6f. Par." Colson, *op. cit.*, p. 284, commenting on the same text writes: "Avec *anthrōpopoíēton*, nous demeurons en plein domaine de polémique traditionnelle. 'Fait par les hommes'

(anthrōpopoíētos, cheiropoíētos) est un leitmotiv de la polémique juive contre les idoles païennes *(Théod.* V; I *Hen.* XLVI, 7; II *Hen.* LXVI, 5; *Sap.* XIII, 10; *Sib.* III, 587, 606, 618, 722; IV, 6...), plus rarement employé contre le Temple et son culte: cf. cependant JOSÈPHE, *Ant. jud.*, VIII, 227ss., qui raconte ainsi l'origine du Schisme de Jéroboam bâtissant un Temple rival de celui de Jérusalem en disant que la présence de Dieu n'est pas liée a un endroit déterminé ... c'est un homme qui a édifié le Temple de Jérusalem. Cf. *Mc.* XIV, 38; *Act.* VII, 48; XVII, 24; *Heb.* IX, 11-24, où *cheiropoíētos* est appliqué au Temple de Jérusalem et à la circoncision."

52   F.X. Funk, *op. cit.*, pp. 42-43.

CHAPTER VII

THE SHEPHERD OF HERMAS

OUTLINE

I. Background
    A. Literary Genre and Sources
    B. Writer(s), Composition and Dating
    C. Content Outline
II. Doctrine
    A. The Call to *Metánoia* and other moral teaching
    B. Christological Concepts and Eschatology
    C. Ecclesiology
III. Ministerial Functions in the Shepherd
    A. *Apóstoloi*
    B. *Didáskaloi*
    C. *Prophétai*
    D. *Epískopoi* and *Presbýteroi*
    E. *Diákonoi*
IV. Sacral-Cultic Conceptions?
V. Conclusion

I. BACKGROUND

The *Shepherd of Hermas*[1], the longest — roughly 39,000 words — and certainly the most enigmatic of the Apostolic Fathers, was composed at Rome[2] during the first half of the second century. It recounts five Visions, twelve Commandments and ten Parables (or Similitudes) in a simple and direct style. The language is the *koinē* of the people[3], written often with linguistic simplifications that would undoubtedly scandalize a cultured hellenist[4] and so mixed with a variety of Latinisms that such scholars as C.H. Turner and C. Mohrmann have voiced their suspicions that although the author wrote in Greek, he probably thought in and spoke Latin[5].

In the Church of the later second century, "the *Shepherd* was one of the most widely read of the 'popular' writings,"[6] and was widely accepted as inspired.[7] With the passing of the ages, however, the *Shepherd* was to meet a rapid decline. During the third century the Roman church quickly lost its former confidence in the work and eventually even the church in Alexandria became doubtful.[8] St. Jerome, writing in the latter half of the fourth century, was most unenthusiastic about Hermas, to whose Visions he referred. For him it was an apocryphal book full of stupidity and practically unknown among Latin readers.[9] Still, as H. Chadwick has commented:

> Hermas fall from grace did not much matter. For theologically the *Shepherd* had achieved exactly that end which the author had designed it to attain. It enjoyed an authoritative status for long enough in ecclesiastical circles of sufficient importance to exercise an epochmaking influence upon subsequent doctrinal developments. By the time that the Church had decided that it could not be used to settle disputed points of doctrine, not being divinely inspired revelation, its teaching had already been absorbed and set in a wider context both in Rome and in Alexandria. It is perhaps ironical that a work which in its time made an impression on Catholic doctrine quite as far reaching as many books safely within the New Testament canon should have been so diminished in status that the complete Greek text has failed to survive.[10]

A. Literary Genre and Sources

Thousands of pages have been written about what the *Shepherd* is in form and in fact. Several scholars have posed the problem of literary genre as a clear disjunction: "The Shepherd of Hermas: Apocalypse or Allegory?"[11] The danger with such an approach is the presumption that we are dealing with a single literary form and that having identified what the Shepherd is in form we will have established what it is in fact. This is not necessarily the case. Moreover, there is clear evidence that the author of the *Shepherd* made use of a variety of literary genres.[12]

Perhaps a better approach is to begin with the "raw materials" from which the *Shepherd* arose. Who and what are we dealing with? We have here a man[13], a Christian[14] whose name could or could not have been Hermas[15], living in the first half of the second century in a Jewish Christian milieu[16] who in one way or another finds himself inspired to announce in

Jewish-Christian forms and symbols[17] a message of repentance[18] first of all to that section of the Church which he knew, and ultimately to all the churches. To gain acceptance for his message he makes use of the forms, symbols and experience at his disposal.

One of the literary forms at his disposal was the apocalyptic. This genre he makes use of principally, although rather clumsily, in the VISIONS.

> In fact, his use of the apocalyptic is in direct contradiction to its form. Apocalyptic intends to communicate a revelation in the face of the end time. Hermas communicated a possibility because the time is not yet. His message is more: "Repent for the kingdom of God is not yet at hand." This centrality of repentance is demonstrated by his breaking of the apocalyptic form with a confession of sins, an element impossible for the "saints" who normally receive apocalyptic visions.[19]

Nonetheless R. Joly has noted that we still find many of the hallmarks of the classic apocalyptic form incorporated into the work:

> On retrouve donc ici les conventions les plus typiques de ce genre traditionnel, ce qui explique la parenté secondaire, qu'on peut remarquer entre le *Pasteur* et par exemple des textes hermétiques: usage du symbole, de la vision, du récit à la première personne, du dialogue fort inégal entre un Révélateur loquace et un privilégié très modeste; aspect imposent ou effrayant du Révélateur, aveux d'ignorance, insistence pour obtenir de nouvelles révélations, remonstrances de la part du Révélateur, mission d'apostolat dont est chargé le privilégié.[20]

The question of why the author of the *Shepherd* chose to use this apocalyptic form stimulated an exceptionally wise observation on the part of Kirsopp Lake. He speaks more of the overall work than of the specific literary genres, but the remark bears mentioning:

> It is an apocalypse, but a practical apocalypse, and although the writer chose to express himself in this, as it were, old-fashioned and conservative form, it is plain enough that he was really a progressive thinker, and deliberately chose this form of expression, because he knew that human nature will often listen to a reformer who wishes to change either appearance or substance, but not to one who attacks both simultaneously.

That is why progress is never direct but spiral: one generation alters the substance, but leaves the appearance; the next sees the inconsistency, and changes the appearance as well.[21]

The MANDATES evidence another literary genre. It will be strikingly apparent if in reading them one thinks of the relatively short admonitory sermons that Catholics were often subjected to in past decades. G.F. Snyder, drawing strongly on H. Thyen's *Der Stil der Judisch-Hellenistischen Homilie*[22], maintains that:

the mandates of the Shepherd participate in a *widespread form of Jewish-Hellenistic homily,* especially in the diminutive address(most often *tekna mou*), the commandment and the homily. The closing formulas, the blessings and curses, may simply be a general form of authority used by the author to ensure a hearing and not something organically connected to the form of the homily,[23]

It was undoubtedly the sermon form the author knew his audience would be most familiar with and consequently most apt to accept.[24]

The SIMILITUDES — at least in the light of modern criticism — contain two closely related literary genres: the "true" parable (*Sim.* I-VII) and the allegory (*Sim.* VIII-IX), both abundantly sprinkled with moral admonitions and exhortations generally spoken of as *parenesis.* A parable is generally understood as a short fictitious narrative from which a moral or spiritual truth is drawn.[25]

A *true* parable, however, is much more than an anecdote since, implicitly at least, detail for detail in the parable is parallel with the situation which calls forth the parable for illustration. Parables are in this sense allegories.[26]

And in this sense we could call all the Similitudes in the *Shepherd* allegories, for the author consistently gives each detail in his stories an explicit meaning. There is, however, a distinguishing factor between a "true" parable and an allegory, namely length. An allegory is an "extended metaphor;"[27] a parable "a *short* narrative." Thus, all things being equal, *Sim.* VIII (roughly 4,200 words) and *Sim.* IX (about 11,000 words) would normally be regarded as allegories. The author follows the same pattern with the allegories as with the genuine parables by explaining the meaning of each detail, thus leaving little to the imigination of the reader. This is not always done nor always expected for an allegory, but it has the advantage of increasing considerably the clarity of the author's often abstruse metaphors and the readability of his text.

In short, then, we can delimit four predominant literary genres: the apocalyptic (or visionary) form, the second century Jewish-Hellenistic homily, the "true" parable and the allegory. The *parenesis* which runs throughout the *Shepherd* actually functions more to set the overall moral tone than as a separate genre.

It is, however, one thing to make a judgement as to the one or more literary forms employed; it is another to say, granted or in spite of the forms, what the document itself in fact is, or was for its age. Since the Visions appear to have been imparted in dreams or dream-lie trances we can hardly speak of arriving at objective truth. Nonetheless, from the document itself, from Hermas' style, manner, humility, trials and difficulties we can affirm that he appears as sincerely recounting what he in one way or other experienced. Says Van Deemter:

> Ob Hermas wirklich Prophet ist oder ob alles nut Einbildung ist, kann nicht wissenschaftlich entschieden werden. Aber für diese Anschauung ist der Verfasser wenigstens subjectiv-wahr. Er *ist völlig aufrichtig und betrachtet selber, was er sagt, als die Wahrheit.* Sein Werk ist für ihn eine Apokalypse.[28]

To this we can add that his audience — from the middle of the second century on into the third — accepted what the author wrote as true and credible, and that the work was recognized as divinely inspired Scripture during that time (by Irenaeus, Clement of Alexandria, Origen, the young Tertullian, and *a fortiori* by the common people as well).[29] It appears that anti-Montanist bias, distance of the final publication from the Apostolic period and the appeal of later heretics[30] to certain passages of the *Shepherd* had more to do with its exclusion from the canon and subsequent decline than doubt concerning the author's integrity.

Generally speaking, then, we can say that we are dealing here with a practical moral apocalypse which, after a long history as inspired Scripture, came to be regarded as apocryphal. The apocalyptic genre which predominates in the Visions was somewhat artificially extended to cover the Mandates and Similitudes, whereas in fact the Mandates take the form of the then widespread Jewish-Hellenistic homily and the Similitudes comprise two allegories and a collection of "genuine" parables.

SOURCES

The *Shepherd* is a document which does not make an appeal to the accepted authority of the Scriptures. Its authority lies in the revelator — be that the elderly Lady(the Church) or the Angel of Repentance(the Shepherd). It is the message of these two in separate dialogue with Hermas which the reader is invited to accept. Nonetheless biblical words and phrases show up frequently in the text — G.F. Snyder has found 183 examples, but, says he:

> one cannot be certain of any direct quotations from or allusions to the Old or New Testament. On the other hand, there is much in the *Shepherd* that has no parallel in biblical tradition or early Christianity. This material reflects the environment of the author, for, like the biblical phrase, his use of other material seems subconscious rather than deliberate.[31]

This disuse by the *Shepherd* of direct Old Testament quotations differs strongly from Clement of Rome and the writer of *Barnabas* whose epistles, as we have seen, are steeped in LXX citations. It is interesting to note further that most of the Old Testament words and phrases which do come up in the *Shepherd* are drawn from the *Psalms* and Wisdom literature. This would seem to indicate a general immersion in the Old Testament and Jewish piety rather than an attitude to the Law as authoritative.[32] J.-P. Audet writes of the author that:

> Son curieux judaïsme, détaché de la nation et de l'observance légale, le pénètre jusqu'à la moelle.[33]

As to the New Testament writings — the influence of *James* and the Johannine corpus seems to be the strongest.

> The use of *James* by the author of the *Shepherd* has been generally assumed, but once again any concrete evidence is lacking. The several individual similarities could be explained by the common ethos of Hellenistic-Judaism. But in the case of *James* at least two concerns are also central to the *Shepherd*:

(a) the *dipsychos* of *James* 1:8 is a man alienated from God because of conflicting loyalties (and two conflicting spirits) in his life. Such a man is the chief concern of the *Shepherd* (*Mand.* IX,1-2), though he connects it with repentance in a way quite unrelated to *James*. (b) The debate with those who believe in faith without works (*Jas.* 2.14-26) is reflected frequently in the *Shepherd* (*Sim.* VIII,9,1; 10,3; IX,19,2; 21,2; cf. *Vis.* III,6,1-4; *Mand.* X,1,4f.)[34]

In the Johannine corpus:

The phrase "enter the kingdom of God"*(John* 3:6) especially spoken of those who must pass through the water of baptism (*Sim.* IX,16,2-4), and the reference to Christ as the *pulë* (*John* 10:9) in the vision of the tower and the rock(*Sim.* IX,12,1) are the most likely references to *John*, though the dwelling of the spirit *(logos)* in the flesh of Jesus (*John* 1:33; 59:5) and the theology of the name (*John* 17:6,11,12,26; *Hermas:Sim.* IX,12,4-8) may indicate dependence or similarity in source. Granting that some phrases are borrowed from the Johannine tradition, still the Christian life *(zên tôi theô)* in the *Shepherd* has no formal relationship to the participation of the Christian in the incarnational existence of the Son (as in John).[35]

There are 43 similar word combinations in the *Shepherd* that also appear in the Synoptics and *Acts*, but still no clear evidence that the author made use of these books. The closest parallels appear in *Sim.* V(the parable of the slave) where certain details from the parable of the vineyard in *Mark* 12:1-11 (and parallels) and the story of the slave and the master in *Luke* 17:7-10 also appear.

Pauline influence is fairly negligible in the case of the Shepherd. On this Snyder remarks:

While there are several phrases which sound Pauline (the one-body theme of *Eph.* 4:3-6 and the admonition to "be at peace" in *1 Thess.* 5.13), the form of the *Shepherd* and its content has nothing to do with that of Paul.[36]

The *Apocalypse* and the *Shepherd* both make use of the vision form and the same sort of closing blessings and curses, plus the image of the Church as a bride *(Apoc.* 21:2; 23:1; *Vis.* IV,2,1), but beyond this they have little in common.

In fact, we actually do wrong to seek in the *Shepherd's* form, structural elements or theology a development stemming from the Old or New Testaments. The work is too much a child of its own milieu. G.F. Snyder has pointed this out very clearly:

> The most important consensus of recent research on the *Shepherd* is to place the writing squarely in the milieu of Jewish-Christianity. Regardless of whether the author writes this way because of training or by deliberate literary design, the conclusion remains that the *Shepherd* is not a watered-down version of Christianity which marks the failure of Pauline thought and the beginning of early Catholicism. Its form — visions, mandates and parables — is Jewish-Christian. Its structural elements — angels, the glorious angel as the Son, the revelator as an aged woman or as a bride, the Two Spirits — all are aspects of Jewish-Christianity. Its theology — the pre-existence of the spirit and the church, the Son as the holy Spirit, the emphasis on *kúrios* and the name — is derived from the same source. Understood in this way, then, the *Shepherd* ought not to be judged in terms of the development of Johannine or Pauline theology but in terms of that Christianity from which came *James, 2 Clement,* the *Testament of the Twelve Patriarchs, Barnabas, Didache, Enoch*(?) and finds its roots in a Judaism like that of 4 *Ezra* and the scrolls of Qumran.[37]

The study of the immense network of relationships between the *Shepherd* and this abovementioned Jewish and Jewish-Christian literature has fairly well dominated the *Hermas* research of the past several decades. R. Joly has found so many resemblances in detail between the *Shepherd* and 4 *Ezra* that he has concluded to a conscious imitation of it by the author of the *Shepherd*[38] J.-P. Audet has discovered undeniable affinities between the pneumatology and dualism of *Hermas* and the instruction on the Two Spirits in the Qumran *Manual of Discipline*[39] to mention but two examples.

Another possible but certainly negligible influence on the author of the *Shepherd* could have been the heresy of Gnosticism. M. Dibelius insists that the author of the *Shepherd* knew Gnostics.[40] On this point, R. Grant comments that:

> Hermas seems to have attacked Gnostic doctrines. In *Sim.* IX,22 he criticizes those who lay false claims to knowledge,

and in *Sim.* V,7,2 he opposes those who say that the flesh is perishable and that therefore sins of the flesh have no importance. Such men may advise against repentance (*Sim.* VIII, 6,9). But Hermas can hardly have found Gnosticism a matter of cardinal importance.[41]

Since the turn of the century a great deal of interest has been shown in the possible pagan literary influences in the Shepherd. The facts are quite obvious.

> The author lived in a segment of society that was deeply immersed in Roman culture and he utilizes this environment as a means of communicating his message of repentance. Not only does he use illustrations from his social milieu(the tree and the vine), but he even makes reference to Hellenistic and Roman religious structures. He confuses the elderly woman with the Sibyl (*Vis.* II,4,1) and reveals *Similitude* IX in the famous Arcadia(1,1-2).[42]

Research in this area began to gain momentum when in 1904:

> R. Reitzenstein offered the suggestion that Hermas had borrowed his Shepherd from the Poimandres, the first and presumably earliest of that small collection of pagan religious documents ascribed by the ancients to Hermes Trismegistus and hence known to modern scholars as the 'Corpus Hermeticum.'[43]

The gist of Reitzenstein's argumentation was that the Shepherd of *Vision* V was this very Hermes, and Arcadia was mentioned in *Sim.* IX,1,4 because it was his home. This was then connected to the *Poimandres* of the *Corpus Hermeticum.* The connection with Hermes and the *Poimandres* as a "direct" source relationship in the *Shepherd of Hermas* was later carefully rejected by Bardy[44] and Dibelius[45] but not without admitting certain literary parallels.[46]

The piece of pagan literature that comes closest to winning the approval of scholars as a direct literary model for the Shepherd, however, is the *Tabula of Cébès,* "a short writing the origin of which is quite unknown."[47] G. Bardy describes it as an "ouvrage pythagoricien,"[48] and R. Joly writes:

D'ailleurs qu'est-ce que le *Tableau*? Une oeuvre stoïco-cynique, répond-on d'ordinaire. Nous avons essayé de montrer, dans un mémoire inédit, que cette oeuvre syncrétiste et populaire, à côté d'élements stoïciens fort pâles et de notions cyniques plus consistantes, mais transposées, contient surtout un message de philosophie religieuse, de teinte fortement néo-pythagoricienne, prêchant d'une facon énigmatique, mais fort reconnaissable, l'immortalité céleste des initiés.[49]

The resemblances, briefly, are these:

(1) "The twelve virgins of *Similitude* IX and their names have no Judeo-Christian counterpart, but do closely resemble the maidens and their names in the *Tabula* of Cebes (e.g. XVII-XX)."[50]

(2) "Le Daímōn, dans Cébès, tient un livre dans une main (4, 3) et le vieillard qui explique le tableau se sert d'un bâton (4, 2). L'Église, dans le *Pasteur* tient un livre (*Vis.* 1,2), puis un bâton (*Vis.* III, 2, 4). Le socle de *Paideia* (18, 1) est un symbole de sécurité, comme le *sympsélion* à quatre pieds en *Vis.* III, 13, 3.

(3) "Mêmes images: anodíai, plános(Cébès, 27, 3; *Pasteur,* 15);

(4) "même sens eschatologique de *bíos* et de *thánatos*."[51]

(5) The account of the work of the Angel of Punishment in Sim. VI has an almost exact parallel in Cebes10.

(6) "Quoi qu'il en soit d'ailleurs, le centre doctrinal du *Tableau* est dans les notions de *kathársis* et de *metánoia* ... et précisément la *kathársis* et la *metánoia* sont des themes fondamentaux du *Pasteur*."[52]

Joly who states: "Je crois fermement pour ma part qu'Hermas connaît le *Tableau* du ps.-Cébès et s'en inspire,"[53] admits clearly however that "Hermas n'emprunte aucune doctrine à Cébès."[54]

In short, although the only literature the author of the *Shepherd* directly quotes is the lost book of *Eldad and Modat* (*Vis.* II,3,4), the text reflects a clear awareness of the Old and New Testament tradition and an acquaintance with the forms and ideas of the contemporary Jewish-Christian and Hellenistic-pagan literature. Furthermore, there are good reasons to believe that the author of the *Shepherd* consciously used such works as *4 Ezra* and the *Tabula of Cebes* as literary models.

B. WRITER(S), COMPOSITION AND DATING

These three interrelated problems because of the lack of sufficient second-century data are the most disputed and most difficult problems in *Hermas* studies. As early as 1860 the German theologian H. Hagemann could write concerning the *Shepherd:*

> Es giebt kein zweites Buch in der kirchlichen Literatur ... über welches die Ansichten der Gelehrten so schnurstracks einander entgegen laufen wie über dieses Buch.[55]

In the years since then, the literature on these three problems has grown so voluminous[56] that one is almost at odds to choose a point of departure. Perhaps the best way to begin is with the two contemporary authors who have written most about these problems: Stanislaus Giet and Robert Joly. The former, of the Catholic theology faculty in Strasbourg, published in 1963 a 333-page linguistic analysis of the *Shepherd* in which he opted for a plurality of authors, works and dates.[57] The latter, who prepared the *Sources chrétiennes* critical edition *Hermas: Le Pasteur*, has strongly opposed this thesis of Giet.[58]

Let us turn first to Giet's analysis. L.W. Barnard summarises it well:

> Giet holds that the existing text of *Hermas* consists of three different works by three authors who wrote at different times. The first and oldest work comprised *Vis.* 1-4 and was probably written by Hermas himself. It is this work that contains the reference to a certain Clement *(Vis.* 2,4) whom it seems best to identify with the Clement who wrote the well-known letter to the Corinthians c.C.E. 96. ...He would date *Vis.* 1-4 early in the second century. The fifth *Vision* is an introduction to the *Mandates* or *Commandments* which follow in the text of the *Shepherd.*
>
> The second work, according to Giet's theory, comprised *Sim.* 9 and this, he thinks, was probably written by the brother of Pius, bishop of Rome *c.* 140-50. It is to this that the Muratorian Fragment on the Canon refers when it says that the *Shepherd* was written 'quite lately in our times' (Pastorem vero nuperrime temporibus nostris in urbe Roma Hermas conscripsit, sedente cathedra urbis Romae ecclesiae Pio episcopo fratre eius)....
>
> The third work, according to Giet, was of distinctly

Jewish-Christian tendency and was written several years after *Sim.* 9, i.e. c. 155-160. This comprised the remainder of the work, viz. the *Mandates* and *Sim.* 1-8 and 10. The unknown author Giet calls Pseudo-Hermas who passed himself off as the original Hermas of the Visions. It is this third work which contains a Christology of an adoptionist tendency — e.g. the Son of God is identified with the Spirit (*Sim.* 5,6).[59]

Giet recounts that his desire to make a deeper study of the *Shepherd* was stimulated when, in reading through the text, he was struck by the rather clumsy transitions and apparent interpolations between the first four Visions and the Mandates and before and after the ninth Similitude.[60] He proceeded to a study of the anomalies and incoherences in the "three parts of the text" both as to doctrine and as to word usage. This study convinced him that his first suspicion was correct, *viz,* that the *Shepherd* contains three separately written works by different authors writing at different times. This study, however, did not convince Joly. He writes concerning Giet's thesis that his "désaccord est profond, pour ne pas dire complet."[61] He admits indeed a certain incoherence in the doctrine of the Shepherd as well as incontestable differences in vocabulary "dans leur matérialité,"[62] and states assuredly that a careful critical examination of Giet's arguments will, in fact, reveal whether one must thereby necessarily conclude to a triple authorship.

One of Joly's biggest disappointments with the work of Giet is that "il étudie le Pasteur exclusivement en lui-même."[63] While this is perhaps a bit exaggerated considering Giet's six two-column pages of authors cited, it may indeed be true as to his study of second-century apocalyptic works. Giet, lining up sixteen connective passages to show their resemblances and repetitive character, notes: "On pensera peut-être que l'auteur manque surtout d'imagination."[64] Joly points out, on the other hand, that this same repetitive connective style is found in *Enoch,* the *Ascension of Isaias* and in the *Apocalypse of Peter,* and claims that "le genre apocalyptique valorise singulièrement la technique de la répétition."[65]

For Giet, the fundamental doctrinal anomaly,"une opposition décidée," lies in the adoptionist Christology of the *Mandates* and *Similitudes* I to VIII and X, and the type of pre-existent Christology evidenced in the rest of the work. Joly sees this not so much as an opposition or contradiction but as a complementarity. He writes:

Les *Paraboles* V et IX sont-elle en contradiction sur le plan de la christologie? Je ne vois pas en quoi. Hermas ne répète pas dans la neuvième *Parabole* l'expose doctrinal de la cinquième, mais il ne le contredit pas non plus. Ces textes, une fois de plus, sont complémentaires. Le Fils apparaît en Similitude IX comme le maître de l'Église et comme le médiateur unique et universel: tout cela était clairement indiqué en *Sim.* V,6,2-4.[66]

There is reason to think, however, considering the whole atmosphere of theological thinking in the first half of the second century, that neither the age nor the author would have consciously regarded these two ideas either as decidedly opposed or as clearly complementary. L.W. Barnard has seen this perhaps more clearly than either Joly or Giet. Reviewing Giet's book he writes:

> One cannot help feeling that Giet is looking at the *Shepherd* through twentieth-century eyes and with a rigid idea of the difference between 'orthodoxy' and 'heresy'. But it is not certain that these were opposing poles as early as the mid-second century. The church was then only beginning to grapple with the great heresies. Moreover the *Shepherd* is a rambling prophetic work which cannot easily be systematized. It may be that we should not expect to find a coherent theology running through it any more than in the Visions of such mystics as St. Teresa or St. Catherine of Sienna. Thus a Jewish-Christian Christology of an adoptionist tendency could be held side by side with a theologically more advanced Christology which asserted that the Son of God was older than creation. What to us seems a contradiction was not so thought of in an age when much fluidity in doctrine and practice prevailed.[67]

This being the case, perhaps it is more realistic to regard the Shepherd's doctrinal statements as expressions of various theological currents known to the author which he simply took up and incorporated into his message, into his call to metánoia.

Aside from the issue of doctrinal anomalies, Giet draws support for his thesis from the unavoidable differences in vocabulary found throughout the *Shepherd*. Joly's analysis of Giet's study in this area bears mentioning:

Les arguments tiré du vocabulaire ne me paraissent pas plus convaincants. Je ne retiendrai que quelques exemples: les mêmes remarques s'appliqueraient aux autres cas.

Le mot *díabolos* n'apparaît que dans les *Préceptes*. C'est peut-être qu' Hermas ne parle pas, ne sent pas le besoin de parler du diable ailleurs. S'il le faisait en lui donnant un autre nom, le cas mériterait plus d'attention En réalité, le mot apparaît aussi en *Sim*. VIII,3,6, mais M. Giet ne l'a pas retrouvé, mon index mentionnant par erreur *Sim*. VI,2,6.

Il en est de même *pour sphragís*, qu'on ne trouve que dans les *Paraboles*. Si Hermas emploie dans les *Visions* le verbe *baptízein*, il n'utilise pas d'autre substantif pour désigner le baptême.

Prenons un cas plus intéressent: les chrétiens sont désignés dans les *Visions* surtout par *eklektoí* et *hágioi*, qui n'apparaissent pas ou très peu ailleurs. Dans la neuvième *Parabole*, Hermas ecrit *hoi pisteúsantes* un grand nombre de fois. Ce dernier point devient beaucoup moins impressionnant si on constate que *hoi pisteúsantes* revient toujours dans la même formule, qui introduit chaque fois le commentaire des collines; la formule n'est abandonée qu'à la fin de ce commentaire, en *Sim*. IX,25,2.

Cet emploi, qui paraît étendu, dépend donc avant tout de la technique de répétition. On admettra aussi qu'un auteur n'est pas, dans un tel cas, tenu de n'employer pour une oeuvre très longue qu'un seul terme, quand s'offrait à lui une riche gamme de vocabulaire.

Voici un exemple étranger à Hermas et qui n'a que le mérite de me tomber sous la main. Lisant l'*Hénoch* grec, je constate d'abord d'innombrables répétitions. Je remarque ensuite que, dans une section homogène comme 21-36, le verbe voir est d'abord rendu par *tethéamai* ou *etheasámēn*, puis à partir de 26,3, par *eîdon*; il n'y a plus qu'un *tethéamai* en 32,1.

L'étude de la langue n'aboutirait, à mon avis, qu à une seul conclusion légitime, qui est confirmée d'ailleurs par des données littéraires et doctrinales et qui n'est pas nouvelle: un certain intervalle de temps sépare la composition — je ne dis pas l'édition — des *Visions* et l'achèvement de l'oeuvre. Mais Hermas s'est visiblement attaché a intégrer les *Visions* dans l'ensemble et il y a largement réussi.[68]

Now in spite of the almost diametrically opposed positions of Joly and Giet, both do agree that the first four *Visions* were composed separately from the rest of the work. They also accept the Hermas who appears there as the most probable author for these *Visions*. Let us, then, accept these two points as the first step towards a working hypothesis.

Joly's overall position is clear. He upholds along with many of the early commentators, such as Funk, Link and Baumgärtner[69], the "Einheit" of the *Shepherd*. He rejects — as do virtually all scholars today — the hypothesis of Origen[70] that the author was the "Hermas" of *Romans* 16:14, and also rejects the identification of the Clement in *Vis.* II with the famous Clement of Rome as well as a very early second-century dating based on such an identification. In last analysis he chooses to accept the testimony of the *Muratorian Fragment* and dates the publication of the work at about 140 C.E.[71]

My own thinking about this problem began to crystalize on reading an excellent chapter by R. van Deemter[72] in which he dismisses with clear arguments the hypothesis that Hermas, writing for publication about 140 C.E., to gain near-Apostolic authority for his work deliberately antedated it by including Clement of Rome in the second *Vision*. Van Deemter ends his chapter as follows:

> Es gibt eine *vierte* Möglichkeit. Beides ist ja möglich: Clemens ist der berühmte, und, obgleich Hermas nicht züruckdatierte, hat doch der Kanon recht. Harnack hat einen Versuch gemacht, in dieser Weise die Schwierigkeiten zu lösen: Das "Buchlein" im 2. Gesicht "fällt bereits in die trajanische Zeit[98-117 C.E.], spätestens um das Jahr 110",... "das (ganze) Werk ist um das Jahr 140 publicirt." Zwar sagt Bardenhewer:" Seltsamerweise glaubt Harnack die Angabe des Fragmentisten und das Selbstzeugnis der Verfassers mit einander vereinbaren zu können.... aber die Voraussetzung, Klemens habe noch um 110 gelebt, fusst auf sehr fragwürdigen Kombinationen. Die Überlieferung sagt, Klemens sei 101 gestorben....(und) das Jahr 155 hat ganz denselben Anspruch, als Jahr der Abfassung zu gelten, wie das Jahr 140", aber doch scheint hier der richtige Weg gewiesen zu sein. Wir glauben zwar nicht, dass nur das "Büchlein" aus der 2. Vision so früh geschrieben wurde, aber es lässt sich doch beweisen,— und fast alle sind darüber einig — die Schrift ist allmählich entstanden. Namentlich die 9. Similitudo ist wahrscheinlich aus viel späterer Zeit. Die Worte des Kanons lassen sich ganz gut erklären, wenn man sie nur bezieht auf die Schlussredaktion. Wir denken uns Anfang und Schluss des

Werkes zwischen 100 und 135. Wie dem aber sei, und welche Lösung man sich denke, fest steht, dass die Argumente, welche den Nachweis der Zurückdatierung führen sollen, unzulänglich sind: Von Pseudonymität lässt sich keine Spur im Hirten finden.[73]

Suppose, then, having accepted a double composition[74] and Hermas as author of the first four *Visions*, we add the *terminus a quo* and *ad quem* suggested by van Deemter, *viz.* 100-135 C.E. Within this framework what would be the constants and the non-constants? As constants, or perhaps better said — as "givens" we have:

(1) the witness of the *Muratorian Canon* — "a tradition that seems to be repeated with slight variations in the *Liberian Catalogue* of the bishops of Rome and in the anonymous *Carmina adv. Marcionem*, iii, 294f,"[75]

(2) the mention of a certain Clement in *Vis*. II whose duty it was to send communications to the cities abroad, and

(3) the not absolutely certain but highly probable tradition that Clement of Rome died in 101 C.E.

As non-constants we can list:

(1) the precise dates for the "episcopacy" of Pius, mentioned in the *Muratorian Canon* as the brother of Hermas, and

(2) the precise life-span of Hermas.

Now if we admit the dates of Pius' "episcopacy" as after 135 and before 155 C.E. — this is quite probable, although the various manuals disagree on more precise dating within this period — and if we assume that Hermas lived 75 to 80 years, then the *Muratorian Canon* could have been quite correct as to when the final text was completed and the Clement of *Vis*. II could have been *Clemens Romanus*. This would mean that Hermas as a man of about forty, perhaps not terribly long after becoming a Christian, wrote down the first four *Visions* at approximately the turn of the first century while Clement lived and functioned as the encyclicist for the Church complex at Rome. Then in the course of the next thirty-five to forty years Hermas in an agglutinative manner and in pace with the age, its literature and its theological development could have composed the *Mandates* and *Similitudes,* possibly from time to time re-editing them as well as the previously composed *Visions*. Finally as an elderly man, at a time when his brother was (one of) the bishop(s) of Rome, he could have completed the final redaction and allowed the work to be published.[76]

This hypothesis presupposes (a) that the Hermas of the *Shepherd* was a real and thus not a fictitious person, and (b) that he was at least the primary author of the work. On these points I would fall back on the scholarship of Zahn, von Strom, van Deemter, Joly and Audet.[77] The latter states clearly:

> Sauf corrections textuelles autorisées par la *transmission*, et compte tenu de l'histoire intérieure de l'écrit, le *Pasteur* doit être accepté en toutes ses parties comme l'oeuvre du chrétien Hermas.[78]

This hypothesis also accepts the witness of the *Muratorian Fragment* — and the corroborative evidence in the *Liberian Catalogue,* although this could be dependent on the former, i.e. that (a) Hermas, the author of the Shepherd, was the brother of Pius I, and that (b) Hermas wrote the *Shepherd,* i.e. produced the final work, during the time when Pius held office in the church at Rome.

Concerning the *Muratorian Fragment (circa* 200 C.E.), however, it seems clear that one must be prepared to admit in it certain strong anti-Montanist tendencies which would have immediately cast suspicion on a visionary work such as the *Shepherd* and which would have undoubtedly found expression in the desire to establish that it was sufficiently removed from the near-Apostolic time to assure its apocraphal and decidedly non-Scriptural value.[79] It seems to me that one could also accept the proposition of Joly that the *Muratorian Fragment,* having been written at a time when a *mono-epískopos* was surely present at Rome, possibly could have projected this form — perhaps on solid grounds: indeed Pius could have been one of the foremost or the best known or the most respected of the *epískopoi* in the era prior to the mid-second century — back to the time when the *Shepherd* first appeared as a completed work.[80]

In conclusion, I have taken as a final working hypothesis for this study — clearly aware that it is just that — a single authorship of a two-part work, the former *(Vis.* I-IV) composed at the beginning of the second century within a fairly short period of time, the latter (*Vis.* V and following) composed more gradually during the following three-and-a-half to four decades with the publication of the final text between 135 and 140 C.E. How much editing was actually done by Hermas on the original compositions or how much interpolation by others we have no idea. It seems clear, in any case, that before the work reached its present literary form it passed through a state of conscious reflection.[81] Still the problems, multiple and complex as they are, remain to this day. They can hardly be called settled. Perhaps the most that can be said for the solution offered here is that it gives us a working hypothesis to go further. And this is no small step when to go further means first situation in history the utterances of a possibly Latin-speaking, Jewish-Christian thinking, Greek-writing author in the historically most obscure era in Church history.

C. Content Outline

Before turning to the delicate questions of doctrine in the *Shepherd* and its whole approach to ministry, let us survey briefly the actual contents of the work. In doing so it is good to keep in mind that although it is presented in the form of *Visions, Mandates* and *Similitudes,* logically seen the *Shepherd* is divided into two prolonged and often interrupted conversations: the first between Hermas and the Church in the guise of a lady who becomes younger as the conversation progresses, and the second between Hermas and the Shepherd who identifies himself as the Angel of Repentance.

Part 1: The Church Speaks with Hermas

Vision 1 On his way to Cumae, Hermas falls asleep and in a dream sees Rhoda, a Roman matron whose slave he once was. She accuses him of the sin of once having had an evil desire towards her. She exhorts him to repent and then disappears. Later there appears to him an aged white-haired lady seated in a chair holding a book in her hand. She:

- makes known to Hermas that the Lord is angry with him because of his evil desire and because of his neglect in raising his children properly;
- promises that the Lord will have mercy on him and his family provided he correct his children and that they do penance;
- reads from the book terrible threats against the pagans and the apostates.

Vision 2 After a year's interval, Hermas again sees the same lady, now much younger but still wrinkled and white-haired. She gives him a book to copy letter for letter which he does without understanding one word of its contents. Fifteen days later, the contents of the book are made known to him. In substance, it stated that the Lord would pardon the sins of the faithful if they repented with all their heart. Later a handsome young man appears and tells Hermas that the aged lady is the Church. She then again appears to him and says that after she has added certain passages to the book, he is to make two more copies. One for Clement who will then send it on to the other cities and one for Grapte who works with widows and orphans. He himself, however, is to read the book "in this city" along with the *presbýteroi* who preside over the church.

Vision 3 Shortly afterwards, the Church, now a young and joyous woman, appears to Hermas and shows him a large tower that is being built over the waters by six youths and a myriad of men, who carry to it many stones of different sizes and quality. Around the tower stand seven women. Hermas is then told the explanation of the vision. The tower represents the Church; the waters, Baptism; the six youths, the superior angels; the myriads of men, the lower angels; the different stones, the different categories of Christians; the seven women, the seven virtues of Faith, Continence, Simplicity, Knowledge, Innocence, Chastity and Charity. Lastly, a young man explains to Hermas the three different forms in which the woman (the Church) appeared to him; the first state indicated the Church under the weight of the sins of the Christians; the second, the Church repentent; the third, the Church of the forgiven.

Vision 4 Twenty days later Hermas has another vision in which he sees a terrible monster rushing towards him to devour him. Assured by a mysterious voice, he walks up to the monster which immediately falls to the ground. A short distance away Hermas sees a maiden dressed as a bride. She, who represents the Church washed of all sin, explains that the monster is a sign of an imminent persecution.

PART 2: THE SHEPHERD SPEAKS WITH HERMAS

Vision 5 The young man who had previously appeared to Hermas appears again and identifies himself as the Shepherd "to whom you were handed over." He wishes Hermas to write down a series of commandments and parables. This Hermas does. In brief they are as follows.

The Mandates (Commandments)
1. Have faith in the one God, Creator of all, and fear Him.
2. Have simplicity and be innocent.
3. Love truth and let only truth proceed from your mouth.

4. Live chastely whether this be within or outside of marriage.[82]
5. Be patient and courageous in suffering and restrain your temper.
6. Believe in the Spirit of Righteousness but disregard the Spirit of Iniquity[83]
7. Fear God and keep His commandments but do not fear the devil.
8. Let your temperance neither refrain you from doing good nor hinder you from avoiding evil.
9. Do not be double-minded but trust in the Lord.
10. Cast away grief from yourself and put on all joyfulness.
11. Avoid false prophets.
12. Eradicate all evil and envious desires from your heart and fill it with goodness and joy.

The Similitudes (Parables)

I. "You know that you who are the servants of God dwell in a strange land, for your city is far away from this one." Do not make then expensive preparations to remain in the city where you now dwell but use what wealth you have to do good as befits the servants of God, nor should you be concerned about another's wealth.

II. As the vine clings to the elm and adorns it with fruit, so the poor man clings to the rich and helps him with prayers.

III. As in winter, live trees cannot be distinguished from dead ones, so in this world the just cannot be distinguished from the wicked.

IV. But as in the summer, the leaves and the fruit distinguish the live from the dead trees, so in the next world, the good deeds of the just will distinguish them from the wicked.

V. Outward fasting should be accompanied by inward reform and the money saved in the usual daily expenditure should go to the poor.

VI. Christians are like a foolish flock in danger of being lost. The Angel of Desire leads them to evil; the Angel of Punishment leads them back to the right path.

VII. The afflictions brought upon Hermas by the Angel of Punishment were just because of his own sins and those of his family. But he must now persevere in humility and in serving *(leitourgôn)* the Lord with a pure heart, with both his children and his household, and in keeping the commandments and then the affliction will depart.

VIII. A willow tree, sheltering all Christians, represents the law of God. The Angel Michael cuts its branches and gives one to each Christian. Those who after a while have persevered in keeping their branches green, or whose green branches now have leaves or fruit, are sent into the tower. The Shepherd then takes the other branches, plants and waters them. Some become green, and their owners are saved; others do not, and their owners are lost.

IX. The symbol of the tower is fully explained. In the middle of the plain there stands a rock (the Son of God) in which there is a door (the Son of God made man) surrounded by twelve virgins (the 12 Christian virtues). The angels build the tower (the Church) upon the rock with stones (the faithful) which they obtain from the streams (Baptism) or from the twelve mountains (the whole world) and which all go in through the door. Suddenly the work is stopped; the Lord comes to test the quality of the stones. Many of them are cast aside and given to the Shepherd to be properly shaped by repentance, after which many of them are used in the building of the tower. The rest are taken away by the twelve wicked and beautiful women dressed in black (the 12 vices).

X. Hermas is exhorted to cleanse his house by repentance and to call all others to repent before the construction of the tower is completed, for then it would be too late for repentance.

II. Doctrine

A. The Call to *Metánoia* and other moral teaching

The message which Hermas is charged with conveying in the *Shepherd* is a call to *metánoia* or repentance. This is the central theme of the work and that towards which all the *Visions*, *Mandates* and *Similitudes* converge.[84] How one is to interpret this call to *metánoia*, however, has long been a theological battleground. The center of conflict is *Mand.* IV,3 which reads as follows:

> "Sir," I said, "I have heard from certain teachers that there is no other repentance except that one when we went down into the water and received forgiveness of our former sins." He said to me, "You have heard correctly for that is so. For the one who has received forgiveness of sins ought never to sin again, but live in purity. But since you inquire so precisely into everything, I will explain this also to you without giving an excuse to those who in the future shall believe or to those

who have already believed in the Lord. For those who have already believed or shall believe in the future, have no repentance of sins, but have remission of their former sin. So for those who were called before these days the Lord established repentance; for since the Lord knows the heart and knows everything beforehand, he knew the weakness of men and the cunning of the devil, that he would do something evil to the servants of God and act wickedly toward them. So being full of compassion, the Lord had mercy on what he had made and established this repentance, and authority over this repentance was given to me[i.e. the Shepherd]. But I tell you," he said,"after that great and holy calling, if anyone sins who has been tempted by the devil, he has one repentance. But if he continually sins and repents, it is of no advantage to such a man, for he will hardly live." I said to him, "I was given new life when I heard these things so precisely from you; for I know that if I no longer continue in my sin, I will be saved." "You will be saved," he said, "and everyone else who does these things."

In spite of what Hermas says to the Shepherd, "these things" are *not* "so precisely" said at all. The major problem, though, is obvious. A pagan or a catechumem is told that for him there is no post-baptismal forgiveness; a Christian fallen into sin is told in fact that what does not exist for the pagan or the catechumen does exist for him. Is then the message one of rigorism[85], of laxism[86], or are we simply dealing with an untenable contradiction?

One of the clearest explications of the problem is that presented by A. Benoît.[87] He maintains that the "certain teachers" from whom Hermas had heard the traditional teaching of his age were in all probability catechists, who would of course stress the necessity of a single lasting repentance at Baptism for their pupils. Hermas, however, also knows another group: those who out of fear have postponed their Baptism (*Vis.* III,7,3). And there is abundant evidence in the text of Christians, indeed ministers of the Church, who have fallen into sin (Cf., e.g., *Sim.* IX,26,2). In any case, Hermas, clearly aware of both the common doctrine as well as the abundant mercy of God, seeks for a solution which while confirming the former in a lasting repentance, also holds out the hope of salvation to the latter. In a certain sense, it is for Hermas more a seeking for the *via media* than actually finding it. Benoît writes:

Théoriquement, Hermas adopte l'attitude rigoriste, qui paraît avoir été predominante à l'époque. Mais pratiquement, il cherche à tenir compte de la possibilité d'une pénitence renouvelée, possibilité qui avait aussi, nous venons de le voir, ses partisans.

Il adopte donc l'idée, non pas d'une pénitence indéfiniment renouvelée, mais d'une seconde pénitence exceptionnelle après le baptême. Il n'arrive pas à tenir cette position médiane et ses affirmations oscillent entre la notion d'une pénitence unique et celle d'une pénitence qui se renouvelle et se prolonge jusqu'à l'avènement du Royaume.[88]

Ainsi, quand nous considérons comment Hermas réalise pour lui-même son message de pénitence, l'image qu'il nous présenté n'est pas une. Il oscille entre la conception d'une pénitence limitée et temporaire, et celle d'une pénitence envisagée comme un état durable.[89]

G.F. Snyder, who interprets the message of the Shepherd very much as Benoît, stresses especially the dialectic aspect of the repentance. He notes:

The position of Hermas is neither legalism nor laxity. It is more correct to take the admonition to perfection as incumbent on all believers ([as in] *Matt.* 5:48), and the possibility of repentance for "fallen Christians" only. This is clear in *Mand.* IV,3. Those who teach that there is no other repentance are correct according to the *Shepherd* (IV,3,2). However, when one is in sin, alienated from God, there is repentance (IV,3,4f.). But this is not a system or teaching on repentance —when you repent, you must repent on the assumption that forgiveness brings with it the command of perfection (IV,3,6), otherwise repentance is in vain. For Hermas, repentance is the dialectic between the perfection of man in the kingdom (church, tower) and God's mercy for man caught between the kingdom and the world.

Only the one who has experienced repentance can understand its dialectic: the standard and counsel of the church is perfection only, but still there is the mercy of God (cf. *Mand.* IV,2,2; X,1,6; *Sim.* IX,22,4; also *Sim.* V,4,3f.)

Though poorly stated at times, the teaching of the *Shepherd* moves on this dialectic without fail.[90]

While the original forgiveness of sins through Baptism appears clearly to have been through the Church, there is nothing in the text of the *Shepherd* to suggest that the *metánoia* was in any way mediated through the Christian community or its ministers.[91] Says K. Rahner:

> Hermas will nicht die kirchliche Busse schildern, sondern das Gewissen der Sünder erschüttern, er ist Bussprediger, nicht Dogmatiker und Kanonist.[92]

Although most of the moral teaching of the *Shepherd* is polarized around the question of *metánoia*, we do find several "asides" concerning moral teaching. *Mand.* IV,4 contains a rather developed and precise teaching on marriage; *Sim.* V,3,3 has a treatment of supererogatory works. The former has been neatly summarized by R. Grant:

> Desire for women other than one's own wife leads to sin, which can be prevented by remembering one's own wife. But what if the wife herself is committing adultery (she is assumed to be the Christian wife of a Christian)? The Angel of Repentance answers this question in considerable detail. (1) As long as the husband is ignorant, he does not sin. (2) If he knows of the sin, he implicitly participates in it; he must separate from her, but he cannot remarry. (3) If after separation the wife repents, she is to be received back by her husband — but only once. This looks like a paraphrase and expansion of the rules expressed by Paul in *1 Corinthians* 7:10-16. Again, second marriages are permissible, but it is better for a widower or a widow to remain single — as in *1 Corinthians* 7:40. The questions Hermas asks may conceivably suggest the existence of certain difficulties with his own wife. More probably they show that the Church is gradually developing a kind of canon law, or a pre-canonical kind of law.[93]

The *Shepherd* also makes the distinction between commandment and counsel (i.e. *opera obligatoria* and *supererogatoria*). In *Sim.* V.,3,3 Hermas is told by the Shepherd:

> I will show you His commandments and if you do anything good beyond the commandments of God, you will gain for yourself greater glory and be more glorified before God than you were destined to be.

This is said in relation to their discussion on the nature of true fasting, and is meant undoubtedly to pertain primarily to fasting. It would seem, however, that it also applies to martyrdom (cf. *Sim.* IX,28,1-4) and if the statement that the wife of Hermas is "about to be his sister" *(Vis.* II,2,3) regards their marital relations[94], then perhaps it refers also to sexual abstinence.

B. CHRISTOLOGICAL CONCEPTS AND ESCHATOLOGY

The present-day Christian standing atop a veritable mound of developed Christological doctrine can hardly help finding the Christology of the *Shepherd* quite unique and to say the least "très déficiente."[95] "But," as G. Snyder has remarked, "if the anthropology of *Hermas* is relatively unique *(Mand.* VI,2 [where each man has within him two angels, one of righteousness, one of wickedness]), one should not be surprised to find a rather unique Christology."[96] Nonetheless, it is indeed a surprise to find no mention at all either of the life and works of the historical Jesus, nor even of the words "Jesus," "Christ"[97] or "the Word. One finds rather "Lord"[98] and "the name of God"[99] — vague titles — but also "Son of God."[100] This latter appears at first sight to be the least equivocal of the three, that is, until one reads *Sim.* IX,1,1: "For this Spirit is the Son of God," where "this Spirit" is expressly identified as *tò pneûma tò hágion.* Joly, however, has pointed out that this identification of the Holy Spirit and the Son of God in a document from the first half of the second century should hardly surprise us, for although:

> La christologie d'Hermas est *pneumatique* et *binitaire,* ... cette christologie est loin d'être aussi exceptionelle qu'on voudrait parfois le faire croire. Le binitarisme — qui confond le Fils et l'Esprit — est monnaie courante à l'époque, bien des témoignages l'attestent.[101]
>
> Les doctrines de Justin et de Tatien par exemple sont caractéristiques à ce point de vue et la christologie des *Actes de Paul* est exactement celle du *Pasteur.*[102]

But in addition to this Spirit-type of Christology, L. Pernveden has shown that we can also find a *nomos*-Christology, an *angel*-Christology and a *wisdom*-Christology.[103] In *Sim.* VIII,3,2 "the law" is identified with "God's Son preached to the ends of the earth." On this Pernveden remarks that:

> Hermas comes closer to the rabbinically inclined
> Torah-Christology of Matthew than to the Pauline
> Wisdom-Christology. ...Whereas Paul says that Christ is the
> wisdom of God, Hermas says that the Son of God is the
> law.[104]

But there is a sense in which the Son of God in the *Shepherd* is connected with Wisdom personified. The Son of God "is older than all his Creation, so that he was the counsellor of his Creation to the Father"(*Sim.* IX,12,2) — "these concepts," writes Pernveden:

> have their origin in Jewish sapiential speculation, which, although in another way, also lies behind the Christology in *Sim.* V. Wisdom is also a firstling in creation *protéra pántōn éktistai sophía* (*Sir.* 1:4), she was also present at the creation. In *Hermas*, however, it scarcely seems to be a question of a direct reproduction of the Jewish Wisdom. *Hermas* seems rather to fit into a tradition, which has left several testimonies in early Christian literature and even in the Jewish literature which was contemporary with it. In *I Cor.* 10:4 Paul presents Christ as a rock. And if we turn to Philo, this water-giving rock, of which Paul speaks, is said to be the Wisdom of God (*Legum allegor. lib.* II, 86).[105]

Finally, one can also find a type of angel-Christology in the Shepherd. It has perhaps best been summarized by G.F. Snyder:

> While Christological titles are vague, it is clear that Christological functions are carried out by various angels or holy(divine in *Mand.* XI) Spirit *(Mand.* V,1,2-4; 2,5; X,2,1-2 & 4; 3,2; XI,8f.; *Sim.* V,5,2; 6,5f.; 7,2; IX,1,1; 25,2). They are pre-existent *(Vis.* III,4,l; *Sim.* V,5,3); they give the law *(Vis.* V,5; *Sim.* V,5,3; VIII,3,2); they bring repentance (*Vis.* V,7; *Mand.* XII,4,6f.; 6,1-3; *Sim.* IX,14,3); they build *the* church (*Vis.* III,4,1); they are the Lord of creation (*Vis.* III,4,1; *Sim.* V,6,5); they define the Incarnation *(Sim.* V,6). The *Shepherd* has a Christology expressed by the activity of the spirit and the angels in creation.[106]

Thus even when working with the clearest Christological title in the *Shepherd*, i.e. "Son of God," we come up with four Christologies, or perhaps better said — four Christological concepts which stress respectively the

Spirit, the law, wisdom and the work of the angels. In his Christology especially it is obvious that the author of the *Shepherd* knows nothing of a closed doctrinal system. Nor should we expect this in a document composed roughly two hundred years before Nicea. In any case, Pernveden is certainly correct when he writes that the concept of the Son of God in the *Shepherd* cannot be contained in any of the traditional Christological models and that even if we try to do this with the help of new concepts, we still cannot arrive at an adequate solution, especially if we try to characterize it with a single term.[107]

Still, in spite of the problems involved here, the Christological thinking of the *Shepherd* appears to have been judged by its contemporaries and also later generations of Christian scholars as an area worthy of being passed over in silence. R. Joly presents an explanation for this:

> Il est étonnant à première vue que les conceptions christologiques d'Hermas n'aient pas soulevé de protestations dans les siècles suivants: aucun Père n'a jamais fait allusion à la christologie du *Pasteur*. La raison, cependant, en est simple: c'est le moraliste qui a toujours retenu l'attention, et à bon droit. Hermas est et se veut moraliste, il ne s'affirme pas théologien. Les quelques explications christologiques qu'il a cru donner sont noyées dans la parénèse.Il est fort remarquable aussi que la *Sim.* V soit expliquée dans sa portée morale (*Sim.* V,3,3) bien avant de l'être dans sa portée théologique.[108]

Although *Eschatology* plays a rather ambiguous role in the *Shepherd*, it is clear enough that the author thinks in eschatological terms.

> He announces the forgiveness of sins committed "up to this day," mentions "the last day," and speaks of "the great tribulation which is coming" (*Vis.* II,2,4-7). For the elect there will be eternal life in the age to come (*Vis.* IV,3,5); it can be compared to summertime; but for the others it will be winter, though they will be burned (*Sim.* IV,1,2; 4,4). The master will come (*Sim.* V,5,3), though the Son of God has (already?) been made manifest "at the end of the days of the Consummation"(IX,12,3). The present period is that in which the Church is being built, and the traditional sayings about entering the kingdom of God are referred to entering the Church. Hermas calls upon the unworthy ministers to repent before the Church is completed (IX,26,6). True believers

already have a place with the angels — if they continue serving the Lord until the end(IX,27,3).[109]

Perhaps more important to this whole context, however, is the author's constantly reiterated formula for the redeemed life: "living to God" — Zên tô theô. The formula does not appear at all in the first four Visions but shows up thirty times from Vis. V to Sim. VIII, appearing in all the Mandates except V and XI. In the ninth Similitude we find it six times (20,4; 22,4; 28,8; 29,3; 30,5; 33,1).[110] The formula has for the most part, been taken eschatologically. This is, in fact, not always the case as G.F. Snyder has shown,[111] but its use in Sim. IX appears clearly to refer to the life to come. In general, however, the term seems to be one of realized eschatology which covers one's human life from the time of metánoia up to and through death to a life to come. In this sense, then, perhaps the best translation of the formula would be "living in relatlon to God." This is the proposal of F. Barberet, who writes:

> Puis, le contenu de cette vie s'est précisé:'vivre à Dieu', c'est 'adhérer' à Dieu à travers son Église ou, réciproquement, c'est vivre dans l'unité de l'Église grâce à une communauté de vie avec Dieu par la médiation de son Fils; c'est un rapport bilatéral de l'homme à Dieu, tel que l'homme mette Dieu en son coeur, et que Dieu habite en lui et y répande son esprit.[112]

In any case, it is clear that the overall eschatological thinking in the Shepherd must be seen in relation to the fundamental message of metánoia.

> For Hermas' admonition to metánoia is presented as if it is necessary to hurry (Sim. VIII,8,3 & 5; 9,4; IX,19,2; 20,4; 21,4; 26,6) and this haste is caused by the fact that the building of the tower is about to be completed. ...[Moreover] The Lord of the Church may suddenly return and therefore the building of the Church has to take place in a hurry (Vis. III,8,9; Sim. IX,10,2; cf. Sim. IX,9,4). Waiting for the parousía and completing the Church form the dominating elements in Hermas' concept of metánoia.[113]

With all of this it is interesting to note that the punishments which are mentioned do not seem to purdure beyond the éschaton. L. Pernveden discusses this point briefly:

. The punishments Hermas talks of in *Sim.* VI do not seem to be thought of as eternal punishments *after* the judgement. Instead they lie before the judgement, are limited in time and aim at leading the sinner back to *metánoia.* Persisting in evil does not bring prolongation of the punishment but death *(Sim.* VI,5,7). And according to *Sim.* IV the sinner's punishment is not thought of as lasting; instead they "shall be burnt, because they sinned and did not do *metánoia,* and the heathen shall be burnt, because they did not know their Creator" *(Sim.* IV,4). It seems undeserved that the heathen shall experience this fate. The thought behind it can only be that after the end of time nothing else can remain but the Church. Everything else has then fulfilled its task since it was created for the sake of the Church.[114]

C. Ecclesiology

In the first Vision of the *Shepherd* the elderly lady in shining white garments who appears to Hermas, reads the following to him from a book:

Behold the Lord of hosts, who in his invisible power and might and great wisdom has fashioned the universe and has clothed his creation in loveliness following a glorious design. He has fixed the heavens with his word of power, established the earth upon the waters, and fashioned his holy Church by his wisdom and foresight, and also blessed it." *(Vis.* I,3,4)

From this it seems that one of God's first works was the creation of and blessing of his holy Church. This same idea reappears in *Vis.* II,4,1:

And a revelation was made to me, brethren, while I slept, by a handsome young man who said to me, "Who do you think that the elderly lady was from whom you received the book?" I said, "the Sibyl." "You are wrong," he said, "she is not." "Who is she then?" I said. "The Church," he said. And I said to him, "Why then is she an elderly lady?" "Because," he said, "she was created the first of all things. For this reason is she old; and for her sake was the world established."

We appear, indeed, to be confronted here with a concept of the Church as, to use the words of Joly, "une réalité transcendante, métaphysique." He adds:

> Cette idée, qui a des antécédents juifs se trouve peut-être dans
> l'*Épître aux Ephesiens;* on la rencontre dans la *IIᵃ Clementis*
> (XIV,1-2-3) et fréquemment dans Clément d'Alexandrie. Mais
> c'est chez certains gnostiques qu'elle prend tout son
> développement, par exemple chez Valentin, qui devait être à
> Rome à peu près au moment où Hermas composait son
> ouvrage.[115]

But the author of the *Shepherd* also presents another aspect of the Church,
practically the more important.

> Dans la Vision II et la Sim. IX, l'Église est réprésentée sous
> la forme d'une tour en construction. Elle n'est pas achevée,
> elle ne le sera qu'au dernier jour, lors de la Parousie, qui
> d'ailleurs est imminente. Cette Église sera la société des
> saints: c'est une réalité eschatologique. Autour de lui, Hermas
> voit cette Église se faire progressivement et aussi — helas! —
> se défaire. Les fidèles de Rome sont loins de former déjà une
> société de saints. Ils comprennent certes des saints, mais aussi
> des pecheurs et Hermas insiste assez là-dessus. ...
>   Ainsi, Hermas conçoit l'Église sous deux aspects: c'est
> une réalité transcendante, créée avant toute chose; c'est aussi
> une réalité eschatologique en devenir. Le premier aspect n'est
> mentionné qu'incidemment: il plaisait à Hermas dans la mesure
> où il conférait a l'Église un prestige peu commun, mais il
> n'engage pas sa doctrine réfléchie. Il en va autremant pour le
> deuxième: le thème de la tour en construction ne s'étale pas
> seulement dans la plus importante Vision et la plus longue
> Similitude; c'est encore une sorte de leitmotiv qui revient
> ailleurs *(Vis.* IV,3,3; *Sim.* VIII, 2,1; 3,5 & 6, etc.); là s'exprime
> la pensée profonde de l'auteur.[116]

Pernveden in his detailed work on *The Concept of the Church in the
Shepherd of Hermas* pictures the ecclesiology of the *Shepherd* in much the
same way as Joly, but stresses perhaps more strongly than Joly the oneness
of the Church. He maintains that loosing sight of this point has made some
scholars too prone to divide the Shepherd's concept of the Church into an
ideal, pre-existing Church and an *empirical,* human community on earth
(among these with certain qualifications he mentions Zahn, Stahl, Dibelius,
Optiz, Grotz and Loisy).[117] Pernveden speaks rather of three "stages of the

Church in the *Shepherd* — roughly the same but a bit less categorically expressed than the "deux aspects" of Joly:

> We designate them as the pro-existent, the existent or manifested and the post-existent or eschatological stages. Then we only have to bear in mind that these stages are not to be seen as periods of time that follow upon each other. In any case one must say that the post-existent stage enters into the existent one.[118]

Seen in this way, Pernveden maintains, the continuity and identity of the Church in the *Shepherd* are completely preserved.

How then are these three stages related? In the pro-existent stage, says Pernveden, the Church belongs entirely to the divine and celestial world, but it is impossible to know anything about that order except by the revelation that takes place through the Church after it has taken on shape in the human world. But the Son of God is the eternal foundation of the Church and consequently the Church's transition to the manifest stage is indissolubly linked with his manifestation. With his coming and the proclamation of his commandments, the Church takes form on earth and in history. This then becomes the Church which is depicted under the image of continuous building. In this stage teachers especially play an important role in furthering the manifestation of the Church and constant cooperation between God and man brings it towards its completion. The third stage of the Church in the *Shepherd,* according to Pernveden, lies in the eschatological future when the hope is that men will be found to belong to the Church. This eschatological stage is not fully realized until the end-time, although it already affects the manifested stage of the Church. Thus *Hermas'* message of *metánoia* aims at fulfilling this eschatology and it is consequently a mistake to interpret him as a founder of a penitential system. He wished rather to awaken men to insight about their chance of sharing in the salvation available in the Church.[119]

On the concrete level of the actual Christian community in which the author lived and wrote, there are several important points to be considered. The document is undoubtedly Roman, as we have already seen,[120] but the actual audience is less clear. G.F. Snyder speaks about "the unwritten fiction of a 'church at Rome.'"

We find it impossible to believe that a document written for the "Roman church" between 110 and 140 could be so totally ignorant of what had gone before and what transpired at that moment. Where is there a hint of other documents for and from Rome: Paul's letter to Rome, Ignatius' letter to Rome, *Mark, 1 Peter, 1 Clement*? Where is the influence of persuasive teachers at Rome: Justin, Marcion, Valentinus?

The problem is not so much the simplicity and ignorance of Hermas as it is the "church at Rome" fiction. Rome was far from a uniform city. The city was flooded with foreign elements who maintained their own language and customs.[121]

Because of the imperially illegal position of the Christians and the "underground" existence of the Church in the second century, it is impossible for us to come up with exact data on the number of Christians in Rome at that time. "The Church at Rome," in any case, still appears to be in the period of "house-churches," i.e., gatherings in private homes. The transition to larger "church houses" and fixed chapels would seem to have taken place later.[122] Still from the size of Rome at the middle of the second century, from the fact that Hermas can distinguish twelve different categories of Christians in the church which he knows, and from the presence of a large Christian community at Rome from the time of Paul, we can conclude to a considerably large and quite differentiated Christian population there when the *Shepherd* was composed, and because of these circumstances not unreasonably to a plurality of "house-churches." It was probably in one of these "house-churches" that the community to which Hermas belonged gathered for their Christian services (or due to the Jewish background of the community perhaps by some arrangement in a synagogue building[123]). Aside from the fact that this congregation preferred Jewish-Christian forms and imagery, we know too that:

> It was wealthy and wealth, or preoccupation with business concerns, was a major problem for the congregation (*Vis.* III,6,5f.; 9,3-6; *Mand.* X,1,4f.; *Sim.* I,1-6; II,5; VIII,9,1; IX,19,3; 20,1-3; 30,4f.; 31,2). The situation of this congregation sounds very much like that period of economic affluency which followed Trajan and Hadrian, when many of the lower *bourgeoisie* tried to move into the ranks of the upper class.[124]

On this practical communal level, some have seen the *Shepherd* as a vast examination of conscience for "the Church at Rome."

> On a pu dire du *Pasteur* qu'il est "un vaste examen de conscience de l'Église romaine" (L. Duchesne, *Hist. anc. de l'Église*, I, Paris, 1906, p. 230). Il y a des divisions et des querelles, beaucoup d'attachement aux biens du monde, d'hésitation dans la foi *(dipsychía)*; même dans le clergé, on voit des prêtres [!] négligents, ambitieux, injustes, des diacres qui détournent l'argent destiné aux veuves et aux orphelins.[125]

W.J. Wilson has suggested that the pointed allusions to ecclesiastical strife and the *Shepherd*'s scathing rebuke of the selfish ambitions of church leaders (*Vis.* III,9,2 & 7-10) could have been in part or in whole directed against the schism at Corinth in the time of Clement. If directed against the presbyters of his own community:

> the passage lacks tact, to say the least. But if *Vis.* III is really contemporaneous with *1 Clement*, the warnings take on another significance. Hermas probably heard the letter to the Corinthians read before the ... congregation, was impressed with the gravity of the schism, and felt moved to do his part also toward correcting the situation. It was indeed just at this time that his ambition became world-wide; *Vis.* II, 4, 2 sets forth a plan to make known these revelations to "all the elect."[126]

III. MINISTERIAL FUNCTIONS IN THE *SHEPHERD*

Of all the Apostolic Fathers, the *Shepherd* presents us with the richest vocabulary of ministerial functions: *apóstoloi, didáskaloi, prophétai, epískopoi, presbýteroi, poímenes* (shepherds), and *diákonoi,* plus various other more general terms for leadership.

A. *APÓSTOLOI*

"The apostles" — always in the plural — appear five times in the *Shepherd,* once in *Vis.*III and four times in *Sim.* IX. The texts read as follows:

Vis. III,5,1: "The stones that are square and white and fit into their joints are the *apostles* and bishops and teachers and deacons, who have walked according to the holiness of God, and who have sincerely and reverently served the elect of God as bishops *(episkopēsantes)* and teachers *(didáxantes)* and deacons *(diakonēsantes).* Some have fallen asleep while others are still living."

Sim. IX,15,4: "And the forty (stones) are the *apostles* and teachers of the proclamation of the Son of God."

Sim. IX,16,5: "Because," said he, "these *apostles* and teachers, who preached the name of the Son of God, having fallen asleep in the power and faith of the Son of God, preached also to those who had fallen asleep before them, and themselves gave to them the seal of the preaching."

Sim. IX,17,1: "Listen," he said, "these twelve mountains are the twelve tribes which inhabit the entire world. So the Son of God was proclaimed among-them-by the *apostles*."

Sim. IX,25,1-2: "And from the eighth mountain ... are such believers as these: *apostles* and teachers who preached to the whole world, and taught the word of the Lord reverently and sincerely, and misappropriated nothing at all for the sake of evil desire, but always walked in righteousness and truth, just as they had received the Holy Spirit."

Thus, "the apostles" are those "who have walked according to the holiness of God," who "preached the name of the Son of God" "to the whole world" — or, figuratively speaking, "to the twelve tribes who inhabit the whole world" — and who even after their death preached to and baptized those who had preceded them in death.[127] In short, they are the heralds of the fundamental Christian kerygma. Can we, however, correctly limit the meaning of "apostles" in the *Shepherd* to "the Twelve"? This seems to be the case rather clearly in *Sim.* IX,17,1, but in the other four citations there is no indication whereby we can say with any certainty that the author meant only "the Twelve." We do know that St. Paul had a wider concept of "apostles" than just "the Twelve."[128] We know, too, that the *Didache* mentions "apostles"(11:3-6), who have been identified by J. Daniélou as "clergé missionaire."[129] Nonetheless, our precise understanding of these *Didache* "apostles" has not been completely settled.[130] The term could mean about the same as "evangelist" in *Ephesians* 4:11.[131]

In any case, whether the extension of the term "apostles," outside of *Sim.* IX,17,1, goes beyond "the Twelve," or beyond the Pauline idea of apostle, or as far as Daniélou's interpretation of "apostles" in the *Didache*, it is at least clear that they were primary officers of the Church who needed no legitimation[132], and that they were the first or among the first to preach (the name of) the Son of God —generally in conjunction with the *didáskaloi* — to all the world, a task which the author of the *Shepherd* apparently knows them to continue, along with baptizing, after their deaths for those who departed this life prior to the Christian era.

B. *DIDÁSKALOI*

Teachers are coupled with "apostles" in three of the texts we have already seen *(Sim.* IX,15,4; 16,5; 25,2). The picture is one of non-residential kerygmatics and catechists who preached "to the whole world." This combination plus prophets seems, at least according to St. Paul, to have been the earliest make-up of Christian ministry. "God has sent ... first apostles, secondly prophets, thirdly teachers" (1 *Corinthians* 12:28). But apparently by the second century the role of prophets especially in long-established Christian communities like that of Hermas at Rome had diminished considerably, and even become suspect.[133] In the *Shepherd* they are no longer grouped with the apostles and teachers.

Moreover, it would seem that in the *Shepherd* the at one time primary role of the *didáskaloi* has now been fitted into the institutional framework. Note, for example, the order of functions in *Vis.* III,5,1: *apóstoloi, epískopoi, didáskaloi, diákonoi,* where the participial forms of the last three are also repeated in that order. The once travelling charismatic preachers appear to have become residential catechists.

So far we have considered four of the references to the *didáskaloi;* there are two more.

> *Mand.* IV,3,1: "I have heard, sir," said I, "from certain *teachers* that there is no second repentance beyond the one given when we went down into the water and received remission of our former sins."
> *Sim.* IX,19,2(3): "And from the second mountain, the bare one, are such believers as these: hypocrites and *teachers* of wickedness...(3) and each one taught according to the desires of sinful men."

The value of the first of these statements is to corrorborate the fact that although some of the *didáskaloi* spoken of must belong to a past generation, their function is indeed carried on in the local community which Hermas knows. One also finds teachers who appeal "to the desires of sinful men." These are probably the persons tagged with the hapax *ethelodidáskaloi* in Sim. IX,22,1-3. Concerning them the *Shepherd,* says:

> [They were] believers, but slow to learn and presumptuous, and pleasing themselves, wishing to know everything, and yet they know nothing at all. Because of this presumption of theirs understanding has departed from them, and senseless folly has entered into them, and they praise themselves for having understanding and they wish to be teachers (*ethelodidáskaloi*) in spite of their folly. For this high-mindedness therefore many have been made worthless by exalting themselves, for presumption and vain confidence is a great demon. Many of these therefore were rejected, but some repented and believed, and some submitted themselves to those who have understanding, recognizing their own folly.

Using this hapax as a point of departure, L. Pernveden makes an excellent analysis of the function of the *didáskaloi* as it was probably known at Rome when the *Shepherd* was being composed:

> In *Sim.* IX, 22:2 some that have not been officially appointed by the Church are called *ethelodidáskaloi*. They regard themselves as having understanding, *sýnesis,* and their self-assumed position is characterized by the expression "exalting themselves". This indicates three important factors that seem to determine the function of the teacher.
> 1) A teacher has understanding. The *Shepherd* tells us of understanding that it belongs to God, that it is where the Lord dwells, and that it is given to men. It is given to anyone who does *metánoia* and can also be said to be *metánoia* itself. Anyone who is the servant of God and has the Lord in his heart asks for understanding and receives it. Thereby he also wins the ability to interpret and understand parables. On this point the teacher does not differ in principle from the believer in general.
> 2) The teacher is regarded as somehow qualified in relation to other believers, since the self-assumed practice of the teaching function on the part of the false teachers is regarded as an exaltation. It is not only these false teachers

who are said to exalt themselves. It is also said with reference to the false prophet. To hold a ministry should, then, simply mean occupying a special position. We can also note that it is said of those believers who did *metánoia* and believed, that they subordinated themselves to those who have understanding. This should mean that they acknowledged the authority of the teachers.

3) The teacher does not have a self-assumed task but has been invested with it. We know nothing of how this occurred. But as it appears from *Vis.* III,9 as if the Church were ultimately giving the teaching, it is surely not unreasonable to imagine that the task of teaching was delegated by the Church through its *proēgoúmenoi* and *prōtokathedrítai*. Perhaps we have to look for teachers amongst the presbyters, as they are the first to hear Hermas' prophetic proclamation and evidently to impart it to the Church. All of those persons mentioned serve to some extent an educative function and the teaching is *one* very important aspect of this upbringing.

It seems on the basis of what has been said so far, as if the teachers held an established position in the Church and carried out locally organized ministerial functions. Daniélou's opinion that they were "missionaires itinérants", may be valid for the *Didache* — we make no decision with regard to this problem — but it seems hardly possible to extend it so that it becomes valid for Hermas. Their function was too important simply to depend on more or less temporary "performances". How and under what circumstances it was practised, it is not possible to decide completely, but there is no doubt that it belongs to the Church together with other functions mentioned here.[134]

In short, the *didáskaloi* in the *Shepherd* represent, on the one hand, when coupled with the "apostles," those charismatic teachers who laid the foundations of the Church in the earliest Christian era; on the other hand, *didáskaloi* also exist — both good and bad ones — in the local community known to the author, although apparently in a much less mobile and charismatic capacity.

C. *Prophétai*

In the *Shepherd* the discussion of prophecy, and particularly of false prophets, is neatly limited to *Mand.* XI.[135] This phenomenon, which does not appear in the roughly contemporary writings of Ignatius, is treated at length in the *Shepherd*, although as Pernveden has noted:

> it seems rather as if prophesying were exceptional and occurred through persons that more or less momentarily came under the influence of the spirit of prophecy. The fact that a fairly thorough teaching is given in how to distinguish between true and false prophets, indicates that prophetship cannot have been a fixed element in the normal life of the community. On the other hand this teaching could hardly have been given if prophetship had been unknown or only belonged to the past.[136]

The two key passages are *Mand.* XI, 7-9 and 11-13. Note especially that the context in which the prophesying is ultimately to be judged true or false is "a meeting *(synagōgè)* of righteous men." The passages read as follows:

> "How, then," said I, "sir, shall a man know which of them is a true prophet and which is a false prophet?" "Listen," said he,"concerning both the prophets, and as I shall tell you, so you shall judge the true prophet and the false prophet. Test the man who has the Divine Spirit by his life. In the first place, he who has the spirit which is from above, is meek and gentle, and lowly-minded, and refrains from all wickedness and evil desire of this world, and makes himself poorer than all men, and gives no answers to anyone when he is consulted, nor does he speak by himself (for the Holy Spirit does not speak when a man wishes to speak), but he speaks at that time when God wishes him to speak. Therefore, when the man who has the Divine Spirit comes into a *meeting (synagōgè)* of righteous men who have the faith of the Divine Spirit, and intercession is made to God from the assembly *(synagōgês)* of those men, then the angel of the prophetic spirit rests on him and fills the man, and the man, being filled with the Holy Spirit, speaks to the congregation *(plêthos)* as the Lord wills." [*Mand.* XI,7-9]
> "Listen, now," said he,"concerning the spirit which is earthly, and empty, and has no power, but is foolish. In the first place, that man who seems to have a spirit exalts himself and wishes to have the first place *(prōtokathedrían),* and right away he is bold and shameless and talkative, and lives in great luxury and in many other pleasures, and accepts pay for his prophesying. And if he does not receive, he does not prophesy. Is it possible, then, for a Divine Spirit to accept a salary for prophesying? It is not possible for a prophet of God to do this,

but the spirit of such prophets is from the earth.

Next, on no account does he come near to an *assembly* of righteous men, but shuns them. But he cleaves to the double-minded and empty, and prophesies to them in a corner, and deceives them by empty speech about everything according to their lusts, for he is also answering the empty."[*Mand.* XI,11-13]

From the texts, then, it appears that a true prophet must possess "the Divine Spirit" habitually, i.e. be living a righteous life. When this is so and such a man enters "a meeting[137] of righteous men who have the faith of the Divine Spirit," where "intercession is made to God from the assembly," it can happen that "the angel of the prophetic spirit...[here apparently equated with the Holy Spirit] fills the man" and he is able to impart to this group the will of the Lord for them. The false prophet, whose life shows he does not possess "the Divine Spirit," is unable to do this. Nonetheless, it seems that he is indeed able to threaten the position of those who hold the "first places" (*prōtokathedrítai*) and to exert a strong influence on the *dípsychoi*.

In any case, the mediation of the Spirit to the people through Christian prophets appears here to be much more limited than in the Pauline era. Bardy's comment on the place of the prophet in the *Shepherd* reveals this very clearly:

A vrai dire, le rôle du prophète, tel qu'il l'indiqué, semble assez restreint. Celui-ci n'est pas, dans la communauté, un personnage de premier plan. Lorsqu'il paraît dans l'assemblée et qu'il y élève la voix, on l'écoute avec respect comme le porte-parole de l'Esprit. Mais on n'a pas besoin de lui; il ne tient pas de place dans la liturgie; il n'est pas indispensable pour l'enseignement de la doctrine; à plus forte raison ne compte-t-il pour rien dans l'administration de la communauté. Bien plus encore, il appartient à l'Église de contrôler la vérité de ses paroles et de juger son message.[138]

Christian tradition, nonetheless, has generally looked upon the author of the *Shepherd*, because of his visions and revelations, as himself a prophet. Indeed, according to E. Dorsch, "mit ausdrüklichen Worten finden wir ihn (Hermas) als Prophet bezeichnet in der Aufschrift der äthiopischen Übersetzung seiner Schriften."[139] Although one of the most recent commentators, G.F. Snyder, thinks that "he is a teacher who uses the prophetic form even against the prophets of his day.[140]

D. Epískopoi and Presbýteroi

The term *epískopoi* — always plural — appears but three times in the document. The first of these, *Vis.* III,5,1, we have already seen in conjunction with the "apostles," where *epískopoi* are mentioned after them and before "teachers and deacons" as those "who sincerely and reverently watched over *(episkopésantes)* the elect of God." This can hardly be anything less than "eine besondere Stellung"[141] of Christian service. The two other uses of the term appear together in *Sim.* IX,27,1-3:

> And from the tenth mountain, where trees were giving shade for some sheep, are believers such as these: *bishops* and hospitable persons who were always glad to entertain, without hypocrisy, the servants of God in their homes. And the *bishops* in their service, always sheltered the destitute and widows without ceasing and always conducted themselves with purity. All these, then, will always be sheltered by the Lord.

Here the "Stellung" of the *epískopoi* to watch over the elect of God is functionally worked out in terms of hospitality and material help especially to the very poor and to widows.

> *Philoxenía* [hospitality] was a mark of the leader from the beginning of the Church *(Tit.* 1:8; 1 *Tim.* 5:10; cf. *Rom.* 12:13; *Heb.* 13:2; *1 Pet.* 4:9; *1 Clem,* 10:7, etc.). It was surely a practice of charity, but also a very important means of spreading the Gospel in the early days of the Church *(Did.* 11-13; 2 and 3 *John.*).[142]

Indeed, the "office" of the *epískopoi* appears to be one of taking the lead in works of practical charity. Pernveden remarks:

> The function of the bishop does not seem to have been of a cultic and sacramental kind. In any case nothing is mentioned about such tasks. On the contrary, the bishop had to concern himself with practical matters such as receiving travelling fellow-believers and taking care of widows and people who needed help. Perhaps this means a different form of the episcopacy than otherwise was usual. And perhaps that explains why Ignatius does not mention the bishop in his epistle to the Romans, although he does this in his other epistles.[143]

Before turning to the *presbýteroi,* let us take up briefly a question which can hardly be avoided in a study of this sort, namely that of a *mono-epískopos* in the Roman church-life known to Hermas. R. Joly has written several poignant paragraphs on this:

> Parmi une multitude de points importants, je n'en vois même qu'un sur lequel se soit faite une unanimité bien affirmée: il n'y a dans le *Pasteur* aucune mention de l'épiscopat monarchique. L'evidence, aussi bien, est formelle. Chaque fois qu'Hermas parle des autorités religieuses, il emploie le pluriel sans aucune exception. Nulle parte n'émerge une individualité privilégiée parmi des *epískopoi*... .
> Mais déjà, l'interpretation de ce fait n'est plus unanime. Certains exégètes sont d'avis que le silence d'Hermas ne prouve pas du tout que l'épiscopat monarchique soit inconnu à Rome de son temps, vers 140.[144] Il est, en vérité, bien difficile de les suivre, car ils me semblent abuser singulièrement de l'argument *e silentio. Si Hermas ne parlait jamais des autorités ecclésiastiques,* on aurait le droit de prétendre que son silence ne prouve rien. Mais, au contraire, Hermas ne cesse d'en parlet; il a un vocabulaire plus riche à ce sujet que les autres "pères apostoliques" et, répétons-le, il emploie le pluriel avec une persévérance jamais en défaut. Les mêmes exégètes répètent a l'envi une note de Turner [*Journal of Theological Studies,* 1920, p. 194] qui déclare en substance ceci: il est absurde d'accepter les renseignements chronologiques du *Canon de Muratori,* qui fait d'Hermas le frère de l'évêque Pie, et de se servir ensuite du *Pasteur* pour démontrer l'inexistence à cette époque de l'épiscopat monarchique. Le dilemme dans lequel on vent nons enfermer par là peut paraître inconsistant: le *Canon* en question, rédigé à la fin du second siècle, à une époque où l'épiscopat monarchique existait certainement à Rome, ne pouvait pas omettre de transposer cette institution assez récente dans un passé plus lointain et d'attribuer ainsi à Pie—très discrètement d'ailleurs — une prééminence qu'il n'avait pas eue; mais cette adaptation n'entraîne pas que les autres renseignements soient faux.[145]

While Joly's textual information is quite exact and while his suspicion about the *Muratorian Canon* could well be correct, there is a chance that he has arrived at a wrong conclusion because of not taking into account the overall ecclesiology in the *Shepherd*. Pernveden, who has taken the concept of the Church as the central point in his study, has still wiser words to say on this problem:

> The fact that he [Hermas] does not mention the monepiscopacy, does not necessarily mean, however, that it did not exist. For the Church in *Hermas* is not the locally organized Church that it is, for example, in Ignatius, but an entity that is essentially celestial and independent of every local confinement with world-wide and universal purpose. Thus when one talks about the episcopacy of the Church this must be described in the plural, in so far as this Church has concrete form in a great number of places. Moreover, partly as a result of this, Hermas does not only talk about the present situation of the Church; he talks to the Church in its present situation and does it from the point of view of the reigning situation. But his concept of the Church is just as little tied to time as it is to locality, and even if he only referred to the episcopacy in Rome he would have had to speak of it in the plural since it would have been impossible for there to have been only one bishop in Rome up to Hermas' time.[146]

Consequently the important point to be made here, in spite of the argumentation of Joly, is that because of the way in which the author of the *Shepherd* expresses his concept of the Church, it is impossible for us to use his document either to prove or to disprove the presence of a *mono-epískopos* at Rome during the time he was writing.

The first mention of the *presbýteroi* occurs in *Vis*. III,1,8, where the ancient lady, who represents the Church, invites Hermas to be seated on an ivory couch upon which lay a linen cushion covered with a veil of fine linen. Hermas answers: "Lady, let *toùs presbytérous* sit first." Aside from the fact that this takes place in a field in the country and Hermas says explicitly "we were alone," one wonders just what *presbytérous* is meant to signify here. Actually though a small point, it is important. Pernveden, for example, states: "Thus he [Hermas] has noted a distinction between them [the presbyters] and himself indicating that he has subordinated himself to them. The members of the Church are not equals amongst themselves."[147] Lake, on the other hand, remarks that, "The meaning is obscure: 'the elders' is often explained as 'the Elders of the Church,' but it is more probably a mere formula of politeness 'seniores priores.'"[148] Snyder maintains that "Hermas recognizes the couch as an elder's bench," like the *subsellium* in *Mand. XI* "on which those men sit who are listening to the false prophet."[149] This point would indeed be more convincing if we could prove that the men in *Mand.* XI were clearly "elders of the Church." Joly thinks that the couch has another meaning.

> Il faut retrouvér ici le thème du "siège vide"(cf. *L'AntiquitéClassique* 1953, pp. 425-426). Le siège vide, pour Dieu invisible, a reçu un culte en Orient (cf. J. Auboyer, *Le trône dans la tradition indienne*, in *Cahiers Archéologiques*, VI, 1952, pp. 1-9), mais aussi en Grèce et à Rome (cf. désormais Ch. Picard, *Le trône vide d'Alexandre dans la cérémonie de Cyinda et le culte du trône vide à travers le monde gréco-romain*, in: *Cahiers Archéologique*, VII, 1954, pp. 1-17). Le christianisme l'a ensuite adopté: on connait des fresques chrétiennes où les Apôtres entourent un siège vide, celui du Christ (cf. Pauly-Wissowa, *R.E.*, VI, 606, v° *thrónos*).[150]

In the conversation which follows, the martyrs because of their great sufferings may sit on the right-hand side of "the holy place" *(hagiásmatos)*[151]; Hermas, however, may only sit on the left and finally the lady sits on the right-hand side. All of this seems to be conducted very much in the treint of *Matthew* 25:33-41 where the Son of Man sitting on the throne places the good on his right and the bad on his left, or like *Matthew* 20:21 where the mother of the sons of Zebedee asks Jesus to allow her sons to sit one on the right and one on his left when he comes into his glory. In any case, it would seem that Joly's interpretation of the couch best explains both Hermas' panic at first seeing it as well as the conversation which follows. Still it does not explain Hermas' response to the lady's invitation to be seated in which *toùs presbytérous* is mentioned. Although Funk, Lightfoot, Giet, Pernveden and Snyder more or less presume that we have to do here with the presbyters of the Church, it seems to me that Kirsopp Lake has come up with the more reasonable solution. Standing alone in a field with the elderly lady — her elderliness is expressed more than a dozen times in the Visions — and being asked by her to be seated on the linen-covered couch, Hermas as a gentleman and as a much younger person, in all politeness — not wishing to emphasize her elderliness — simply remarks in the plural: "Lady, let those who are elder sit first," i.e. "if it is a question of being seated, I beg you to be seated first."

The term *presbýteroi* appears only two other times — in *Vis.* II,4,2-3:

> The ancient lady came and asked me if I had already given the book to the *presbytérois*. I said that I had not given it. "You have done well," she said, "for I have words to add. When, therefore, I have finished all the words they shall be made known by you to all the elect. You shall therefore write two little books and send one to Clement and one to Grapte. Clement shall then send it to the cities abroad, for that is his duty; and Grapte shall exhort the widows and orphans; but in this city you shall read it yourself with the presbyters who are in charge of the church *(metà tôn presbyterōn ton proïstaménōn tês ekklēsías)*.

And with this *Vis.* II comes to an end. There is no further context here whereby we might establish more precisely what is meant. Since *presbýteroi* and *epískopoi* are never mentioned together in the *Shepherd,* the traditional guess at the meaning has been:

> This must show that bishops and presbyters, as in Clement's letter, are practically identical; it also suggests that no one presbyter was called *the* bishop.[152]

This is undoubtedly a reasonable guess, but perhaps it would be better to say that if there was a distinction between *presbýteroi* and *epískopoi* at the time of *Hermas*, there is not sufficient evidence in his text to allow us to discern it. But these remarks concerning presbyters in *Vis.* II,4,2-3 still leave an enormous number of questions unanswered. To list but a few:

Does the last phrase mean that some presbyters were in charge of the church and some were not?

Was there a distinction of functions within the presbyters?

Is it here a question of all the Christian communities in Rome?[153]

Was there perhaps a central committee of presbyters chosen from the presbyters of the individual Christian communities?

Were the *presbýteroi* the administrators both of the individual communities and of the larger municipal complex that made up "the Church of Rome"?

And if this were the case, did the *epískopoi* have a part in this administration? Or were they the spiritual fathers, the shepherds of the Christians?

And if this were the case, was there just one *epískopos* in each Christian community or many? etc., etc.

And all of these questions, as important as they are, are not answered in the Shepherd. There is indeed mention made of the *leaders* of the Church --

> **Vis. II, 2,4:** "You shall say, then, to the leaders *(proēgouménois)* of the Church, that they reform their ways in righteousness, to receive in full the promises with great glory."
>
> **Vis. III,9,7-10:** "Therefore I speak now to the leaders *(proēgouménois)* of the Church and to those 'who have/take the first seats' *(prōtokathedrítais)*. Be not like the poisoners. For while the poisoners carry their drugs in bottles, you carry your drug and poison in your heart. You have become callous, and do not wish to cleanse your heart and mix your wisdom together in a pure heart in order that you may have mercy from the great King. See to it then, children, that these dissensions of yours do not turn you away from your life. How do you expect to teach the elect of the Lord if you yourselves do not have training? Teach one another therefore and have peace among yourselves."

— but the term remains vague and any further precision is lacking here. One also finds mention of *shepherds* —

> **Sim. IX,31,5-6:** "And he(God) will rejoice, if all are found safe, and none of them are missing. But if some of them are found missing, woe to the *shepherds (poimésin)*. But if the *shepherds* themselves are found missing[i.e. found fallen away], what shall they answer to the master of the flock? That they are missing because of the sheep? They will not be believed, for it is incredible that a *shepherd* should be harmed by his flock."

— but here again the same applies. These texts on leaders and shepherds do show, however, that there were dissensions among them — the chance that the shepherds themselves would be scattered. The cause(s) of the dissensions is not given, but from what is said about teaching and training it would seem that they were of a doctrinal nature. The "leaders of the Church" could mean the *epískopoi,* and the *prōtokathedrítai* the *presbýteroi,* but again this is not certain. There is another mention of dissensions in the community *(Sim.* VIII,7,4-6) concerning the question of "first places" which might possibly refer to the dissensions among the leaders, although it appears that they were past by the writing of *Sim.* VIII. The text reads:

> And they who give up their sticks green with cracks, these were ever faithful and good, but had some jealousy among themselves about first places (prōteíon) and about glory of some kind or other *(perì dóxés tinós).* But all these are foolish who quarrel among themselves about first places. But these also when they heard my commandments, because they were good, purified themselves and quickly repented; so their dwelling was in the tower. But if any of them turn again to dissension, he shall be cast out of the tower, and shall lose his life. Life is for all those who keep the commandments of the Lord. And in the commandments there is nothing about first places or about glory of any kind, but about man's longsuffering and humility. In such men, therefore, is the life of the Lord, but in factious and lawless men is death.

This could, of course, apply to the community-at-large, but E. Schweizer thinks that it "ist vermutlich eher innerhalb der Gruppe der Amtsträger zu suchen."[154]

E. *DIÁKONOI*

Aside from the fact that deacons are mentioned in *Vis.* III,5,1 after apostles, bishops and teachers and are there said to serve *(diakonésantes)* the elect of God, there is in fact nothing further we can say with complete certainty about deacons in the *Shepherd.* The only other statement about *diákonoi* appears in *Sim.* IX,26,1-2:

> And from the ninth mountain, which was desert, and had in it creeping things and wild beasts which devour men, are such believers as these: Those with spots are *diákonoi* who served *(diakonésantes)* badly and stole the livelihood of widows and orphans, and made gain for themselves from the ministry *(diakonías)* which they had received to administer *(diakonêsai).* If, then, they persist in the same desire, they are dead and there is no hope of life for them. But if they turn and fulfill their ministry *(diakonían)* in holiness, they will be able to live.

The question here is whether these *diákonoi* are the same as the group denoted with this term in *Vis*. III,5,1. The *diákonoi* here do appear to possess a particular ministerial task, but the reference could be to a wider group. Lake translates the term here as "ministers,"[155] and Grant remarks that:

> It is not clear whether anything specific is said here about the deacons; those called *diákonoi* who have robbed widows and orphans and made gain from their ministry may be 'ministers' in general.[156]

And it is indeed true that *diakonein* and its derivitives are used widely throughout the document in the more general sense of "ministry" and "service"(cf. *Mand*. II,6; XII,3,3; *Sim*. I,9; II,7 & 10; VIII,4,1-2; IX,27,2).

On the other hand, if we take the *diákonoi* here to be the same as the deacons of *Vis*. III,5,1, then the pattern of *Sim*. IX would be maintained, i.e that apostles and teachers are treated in *Sim*. IX, 25, deacons in 26, and *epískopoi* in 27. This latter position, which is supported by Lightfoot, Joly, Giet and Snyder, appears to be the more probable one, in which case the function of the deacons would have been a charitative one of caring for, at least, widows and orphans, even though some of the ones known to Hermas did not fulfill this service very nobly.

This completes our survey of the ministerial functions in the *Shepherd*. The text shows us that they were primarily preaching, teaching, pastoral care and administration. The *Shepherd* gives us the widest range of ministerial categories in the Apostolic Fathers but precious little to distinguish the one from the other. The impression created is one of a Church community in which, as Schweizer has noted, "noch vieles im Fluss ist."[157] Nonetheless ministerial groups clearly exist, and appear to have "service" as their common denominator.

IV. SACRAL-CULTIC CONCEPTIONS?

So far we have taken a long, hard, look at the major problems and difficulties concerned with the origin, doctrine and ministerial functions of the *Shepherd*. This prepares us to pose in the case of the *Shepherd* the central question of our study, namely how the Old Testament and pagan nomenclature for the priestly class found its way into the Church, and along with it the sacral-cultic conception of Christian ministry and, in fact, of Christianity itself.

We can begin by noting that the terms for high-priest, priest, priesthood, and "to offer (sacrifice)," i.e. *hiereús* or any of its derivitives, appear nowhere in the *Shepherd*. The same applies for such terms as *klêros* or *laïkos* or such expressions[158] which would distinguish a separate sacral group from the rest.

Perhaps our study of the moral teaching, the ecclesiology and the understanding of Baptism can shed some light on the reasons for this. Baptism was for Hermas as much a forgiveness rite as it was an initiation rite. It was "when we went down into the water and received forgiveness for our former sins"(*Mand.* IV,3,1). It was an adult experience which brought with it not only membership in the Church but also a calling (*klêsis: Mand.* IV,3,6) to sinless perfection, the alternative to which was a loss of salvation. And the practice of the Church at that time, which the Shepherd admits as true was that after Baptism there was no further chance for forgiveness (*Mand.* IV,3,2). Hermas recognizes the inadequacy of this teaching, seeks to rhyme it in some way with the mercy of God, but does not, in fact, arrive at rejecting it. Thus it is abundantly clear that being a baptized Christian in the age of the *Shepherd,* because of the sheer finality of it all, already carried with it a certain genuine sacrality or personal sacredness, the understanding of which we have long since lost sight of. Note that the Church is called "holy" (*Vis.* I,1,6; 3,4; IV,1,3) and its members referred to as "saints" or "saints of God" (*Vis.* I,3,2; II,2,4-5; III,3,3; 6,2; 8,8-9 & 11; IV,3,6; *Sim.* VIII,8,1) or "the elect"(*Vis.* I,3,4; II,1,3;2,5; 4,2; III,5,1; 8,3; 9,10; IV,2,5; 3,5).[159] Now so long as the alternatives for the baptized Christian are sinless perfection or a loss of salvation with no further chance after Baptism, and so long as there are those who admit this as too high a calling and consequently postpone their Baptism (*Vis.* III,7,3), the psychological ideal of "those closer to God," of "the elect," is already present, both in doctrine and practice, in the body of baptized Christians. They are themselves, to borrow a phrase from *1 Peter* 2:9: "a priestly community." To add a further ideal within this context would be quite unnecessary, although that too was present in the possibility of martyrdom and the lady in the *Visions* makes it quite clear to Hermas that "it is given to them (i.e. the martyrs) to be on the right hand of the Holiness" (*Vis.* III,2,1), they are the closest to God.

The point to be made is that, given the doctrine and practice of the Church in the first half of the second century, the problem of the sacred and the profane was not an internal one, for the members of the Church, the baptized, were sacred and those not yet members were profane. This is clear from the tower allegory in *Sim.* IX.

The importance of the *Shepherd* was to point out that the problem of the sacred and the profane was *indeed* an internal one; there were sinful members of the Church who robbed widows and orphans, who were selfish and greedy and who caused dissensions. To these Hermas' call to *metánoia* is directed. We could say that in the long run the *Shepherd* forced a shift in the ecclesiological thinking of the age which finally resulted in admitting the Church to be both sinful and sacred. As a consequence of this shift of thinking about the Church would introduce another chance for forgiveness after Baptism and eventually develop a detailed penitential system. In those ages, when the problem of the sacred and the profane would be clearly admitted as an internal one for the Church, new ideals of "those closer to God" would be needed. Then, with the ecclesiological door open and the need present, a separate sacred group within the Church would develop. But history shows that when it does develop its separateness lies in the exclusive right to preside at the eucharistic celebration. This is one of the most puzzling points of the *Shepherd,* for nowhere is there mention of an action that could be associated with a celebration of this sort. There is no mention of a communal meal, or of "the breaking of the bread" or of an "agape."[160] The verb *eucharisteîn* appears five times (*Vis.* IV,1,4; *Sim.* II,6; V,1,1; VII,5; IX,14,3) but always in terms of a private prayer of thanksgiving. The only gathering of persons that could even approximate this is the *synagōgè andrôn dikaíōn* in *Mand.* XI, but this appears to be primarily a prayer service and there is nothing that even hints at a celebration of the Eucharist. Still Justin Martyr writing at Rome about 165 C.E. can write a rather detailed description of the eucharistic celebration.[161]

The question of repentance presents the same problem. Nowhere in the *Shepherd* do we find any evidence that a post-baptismal forgiveness of sins could be mediated through anyone in the Church.[162] In fact, just the opposite is true.

> But do you pray to God, and He shall heal the sins of yourself and of all your house and of all the saints (*Vis.* I,1,9).[163]

The truth of the matter is that the only rite clearly mentioned in the *Shepherd* is Baptism. It is the sign of Christian initiation, or "seal" *(sphragís)*,[164] and the paramount opportunity for forgiveness of sins. It is seen as absolutely necessary and indispensable for the salvation of the individual. Indeed, even those who died before the Christian era would have to receive "the seal" in order to be saved. This the *Shepherd* solves by having the "apostles and teachers" descend after their own deaths to the place of the dead to preach and baptize *(Sim.* IX,16,5). On this A. Benoît notes:

> On ne sait l'origine d'une conception si curieuse. Mais elle a été reprise par Clément d'Alexandrie *(Stromates* II,44,1), puis par Origène. Ce dernier a pensé qu'après sa mort, Paul était devenu l'apôtre des païens, des Israélites, et peut-être aussi d'autres êtres invisibiles *(Commentaire sur les Romains,* II,13). Mais cette théorie ne persistera pas, elle sera remplacée par la descente de Christ aux enfers et sa prédication aux morts (Cf. *1 Pierre* 3,19).[165]

J. Colson makes use of *Sim.* IX,16,5 in working out an interesting argument concerning a sacerdotal function in the *Shepherd*. He first states:

> La purification, la rémission des péchés sont, nous l'avons vu dans la première partie de cette étude, une fonction éminemment sacerdotale qui caracterise le sacerdoce du Christ.[166]

The argument then runs as follows:

> Baptism is clearly necessary for salvation *(Sim.* IX,16,2-4) Because of this the Apostles and teachers after their deaths preached also to those who died prior to the Christian era and gave them the "seal" of the preaching.
> Therefore, because this purification, the remission of sins, is an eminently sacerdotal function which characterizes the priesthood of Christ, the Apostles and teachers in preaching to and baptizing the souls of the dead appear to have been performing a sacerdotal function.[167]

This is as far as the argument can go, for nowhere else in the *Shepherd* are any other ministers connected with the administration of Baptism.[168] It is

not a strong argument. One wonders if the preaching to and baptism of the
dead by other dead is not tenuous ground upon which to base anything, let
alone a sacerdotal function in the living Church.[169] R. Joly in his edition of
Hermas: Le Pasteur has written a sufficient comment on the above argument
as presented by Colson:

> C'est sur ce passage [*Sim.* IX,16,5] que se fonde
> essentiellement J. COLSON, *Ministre de Jésus-Christ ou le
> sacerdoce de l'Évangile*, p. 326 sq. pour admettre, au point de
> vue qui le retient, un progrès de la IXe Parabole par rapport
> aux *Visions* "dans la prise de conscience du rôle sacerdotal des
> ministères, en relation avec la fonction sacerdotale de
> Purificateur qui est celle du Christ dans sa mort et au-delà de
> sa mort"(p. 328). Remarquons qu'il ne s'agit ici que des
> apôtres et des didascales et que, pour Hermas, ils appartiennent
> au passé. J. Colson admet que l'idée qu'il croit dégager n'est
> qu'implicite (p. 327) et, dans sa conclusion, p. 328, il s'exprime
> au conditionnel.[170]

The *Shepherd* contains several sacral-cultic conceptions, though,
which call for investigation. They are: *thusía*: sacrifice (*Sim.* V,3,8) and
thusiastérion: altar (*Mand.* X,3 [3x]; *Sim.* VIII,2,5). The former comes up
in a discussion between the Shepherd and Hermas on the nature of true
fasting. The Shepherd explains that the correct way to fast is to take nothing
but bread and water and then give the price of the food saved that day to the
poor, after which he adds:

> If then you thus fulfill the fast as I commended you, your
> *sacrifice* shall be acceptable to God. [Cf. *Ecclus.* 32:9;
> *Philippians* 4:18] and this fast shall be written down to your
> credit, and the service which is thus done is good and joyful
> and acceptable to God.

The most we can say is that *thusía* here appears to be part of a remembrance
of phrases from Scripture and that true fasting would seem to be approved
as one possible substitute on a personal level for the Jewish Temple cult.

Thusiastérion in *Mand.* X,3 is used in a discussion of the value of the
personal prayer of a mournful or grieving person.

> [Shepherd:] "For the prayer of a mournful man never has the power to ascend to the *altar* of God." "Why," I said, "does not the prayer of one who is mournful ascend to the *altar* of God?" "Because," he said, "grief sits in his heart, so when mixed with prayer, grief does not allow the prayer to ascend in purity to the *altar*, for just as vinegar and wine mixed together do not have the same pleasant taste, so also grief mixed with the Holy Spirit does not have the same appeal."

This is obviously the Old Testament image of the burnt-offering's aroma rising into the heavens to God. It is interesting to note that the author, writing several generations after the destruction of the Temple, knows that the altar which still represents the presence of God[171] is now in the heavens. The concept of prayer as a spiritual sacrifice we have already met in *1 Clement* (18:16-17; 35:12; 52:3-4) and *Barnabas* (2:10), all of which reflect a spiritualization of the Temple cult going back to *Psalms* 50 and 51. There is nothing here that might suggest the presence of a Christian altar or of an altar ritual.

In *Sim.* VIII,2,5, *thusiastérion* appears once again. The Angel of the Lord says to the Shepherd:

> "I am going away, but you shall send these [ones with the branches] within the walls, according as any is worthy to dwell there. But consider their branches carefully and thus let them go, but look carefully. See to it that none pass you," he said, "but if anyone pass you I will test them at the *altar*."

Most likely the meaning here is the same as in the other three uses of *thusiastérion*, i.e. that the Angel is going away, but if any unworthy ones pass unnoticed into the tower, he will test them when they come into "the presence of the Lord." This, however, is not certain. The remark is a strange one, and is neither preceded nor followed by contextual statements which might shed some light on its interpretation. Had the Angel of the Lord said: "I am going into the tower (the Church), instead of the indeterminate: "I am going away," there might be reason to think of "the altar" in a more physical sense and as within the Church. The remark that he would "test them at the altar," however, might refer to the inspection by the Jewish priests of the offerings brought for sacrifice. A description of this we have already seen in *1 Clement* 41:2 where it is stated that the "high priest and other ministers" "examined" the offerings "at the altar." The parallel is a bit forced but if one thinks of the branches that are carried as symbolic of the life the person has lived up to that time which must now be judged, just as the offerings, as either acceptable or not before God, then the ideas at least are similar. In this case one might possibly see the Angel of the Lord, who in *Sim.* VIII,3,3 is identified as Michael, as exercising a certain sacerdotal function in terms of the Old Testament cult, but it is highly improbable that this could have any bearing on a cultus in the Christian community.

V. CONCLUSION

In the light of our whole study of the *Shepherd,* then, what are the conclusions that can be drawn with regard to the introduction of sacerdotal terminology and sacral-cultic concepts of Christian ministry or of Christianity itself. Let us begin with what is perhaps the most important consideration.

1. The Ecclesiology of the Shepherd. A propos, several remarks of Pernveden:

> For Hermas... the Church is not founded on the suffering of the Son of God or on His work at all, as is the case in the earlier Apostolic tradition, but instead on creation.[172]
> Given the clear and realistic proclamation of the act of Christ in the preceding and contemporary traditions, it is admittedly a little surprising to find that Hermas does not even mention this main article of early Christianity; but he has in fact not even named Christ or Jesus of Nazareth at all.[173]
> In Hermas there is no expression of the idea of Christ's death and its importance in the history of salvation, and so there is no concept of an atonement theology in the New Testament sense. The incorporation of God's people in the death and resurrection of Christ, and the element of sacrifice, both of which play such a dominant role in the New Testament, are absent in Hermas.[174]
> Hermas, the apocalypticist and visionary, is not historically orientated in the way of other early Christian writers, a characteristic which, incidentally, he shares with the writer of the New Testament apocalypse. His efforts are not directed towards approaching earthly reality, but rather towards transcending it. A consciously argued theology of atonement has no place in such a point of view. The act of salvation must be given another form.[175]

This other form we saw in our investigation of the Spirit/wisdom/*nomos*/ angel Christology of the *Shepherd*. The Christ-function of taking away sin, rather than being rooted in a once-and-for-all act of salvation, is taken to be an on-going process dating from Creation and based on the work of the holy angels, of the Holy Spirit and of the law(meaning the one Covenant newly opened to all people).[176]

The importance of this for our central problem is obvious. A soteriology which does not focus on the Crucifixion as the central salvific act in history, which does not see the death of Jesus as either an atonement or as a sacrifice, will hardly feel the need either for a separate sacral-cultic priestly class or for sacral-cultic rites whose purposes in one way or another would be to mediate this unique saving event to the Christian people. Consequently it should hardly be surprising that we find nowhere in the *Shepherd* any mention of the Old Testament or pagan nomenclature for the priestly class.

2. The understanding of Baptism and the penitential teaching of the age.The *Shepherd* shows that the acceptance of Baptism was a mature human act which brought with it membership in the Church and forgiveness of sins. Christians by virtue of their Baptism belong to a select group, not in the sense of a social or snobistic *status* but simply because Baptism was the sign of a "great and holy calling"(*Mand.* IV,3,6). "In the circle to which Hermas belonged the belief obtained that Christians after Baptism were capable of leading sinless lives, and that if they fell they could not again obtain forgiveness."[177] They are called "the saints" or "the saints of God"(*Vis.* I,3,2; II,2,4-5; III,3,3; 6,2; 8,8-9 & 11; IV,3,6; *Sim.* VIII,8,1) or "the elect"(*Vis.* I,3,4; II,1,3; 2,5; 4,2; III,5,1; 8,3; 9,10; IV,2,5; 3,5). And Hermas clearly knows of those who have postponed their Baptism (*Vis.* III,7,3). Apparently only those more pleasing to God than the baptized are the martyrs who have suffered "stripes, imprisonments, great afflictions, crucifixions, wild beasts, for the sake of the Name. Therefore it is given to them to be on the right hand of the Holiness"(*Vis.* III,2,1).

The point is that to be a baptized Christian, because of the definitive personal demands and responsibilies, already carried with it something of the sacred, the holy and the elect. Consequently it should not come as a surprise that we find nothing in the *Shepherd* to suggest a clergy-laity distinction, even though there were those in the community who argued about "first places" (*Sim.* VIII, 7,4-6), nor that the ministries are by and large spoken of in terms of pastoral care or charitative social service.

3. The ministries. Although the *Shepherd* uses eight different terms for Christian ministry, past and present,[178] nowhere is there any mention of how individuals or groups are installed in their function and precious little is given whereby we might distinguish one group from the other. In fact, "we do not seem to have any fixed concept of ministry."[179] There are, however, certain lessons to be learned from the little that is said about the ministries. From "the apostles and teachers" of past generations we learn the centrality of the Christian preaching and the world-wide dimension it was clearly meant to have. We learn, too, that in Rome qualified teachers or catechists form part of the community known to Hermas. From the work of the *epískopoi* we learn the high value placed by the second-century Christians on the virtue and practice of hospitality. From what is said of the prophets we learn that the high regard for these charismatic figures possessed by earlier Christian generations is now on the wane and that a type of pre-Montanistic suspicion for things visionary and prophetic is beginning to grow. Of the *presbýteroi* we learn only that they are a group holding a position of leadership and responsibility *(proïstámenoi)*. From the intended work for the *diákonoi*(and the *epískopoi*) we learn of a fairly widespread program of social care within the Christian community known to Hermas.

Given the Jewish-Christian soteriology of the *Shepherd,* one is left to guess what form the Eucharist of this milieu actually took. There is, in any case, no mention of a common meal, nor of "the breaking of the bread," nor of an "agape."[180] In fact there is not even the vaguest suggestion of a table or altar ritual. The several uses of the terms *thusiá* and *thusiastérion* refer either to personal fasting or private prayers of thanksgiving or an "altar" in the heavens representing the presence of God; there is nothing given whereby they might be connected with a communal Christian cultic act.

The only rite clearly mentioned is Baptism. It is "when we went down into the water and received forgiveness of our former sins"*(Mand.* IV,3,1) or were "baptized in the name of the Lord" *(Vis.* III,7,3), but the *Shepherd* does not mention the one or ones who administered this rite in the Christian community — we might guess, however, that it was the *presbýteroi* of *Vis.* II,4,3. Nonetheless, the only ministers clearly mentioned in connection with Baptism are "the apostles and teachers" of past generations "who preached the name of the Son of God, [and who] having fallen asleep in the power and faith of the Son of God, preached also to those who had fallen asleep before them, and themselves gave them the seal of the preaching" *(Sim.* IX,16,5). On this G.F. Snyder comments:

> In Similitude IX the author is quite conscious of the ecclesiastical requirements for entering the tower. Baptism is one of the essentials (16,2). This poses a problem for the patriarchs and prophets of the OT (15,4). Therefore the author makes their eschatological seal a type of baptism given by the leaders of the early church (16,5).[181]

Colson has attempted to find in *Sim.* IX,16,5 a progress in the "prise de conscience" of a sacerdotal function based on the purifying function of these "apostles and teachers" which would ultimately be founded on the priestly activity of Jesus Christ. His attempt is praiseworthy insofar as he has seen that if such an argument is viable at all it can only be so here, for this is the only place in the *Shepherd* where any group of ministers is clearly connected with an apparent "sacramental" rite. Still, when we consider (a) how far the soteriology of the Shepherd is removed from anything that would suggest the "priestly activity of Jesus Christ," (b) the theological reasoning which produced the supposition that the deceased "apostles and teachers" preached to and baptized the deceased of pre-Christian ages, as well as (c) the totally indefinable type of "baptism" that this might have been, we have to admit that this type of argumentation is too tenuous upon which to base any concrete conclusion, let alone a sacerdotal function in the living church.

Notes

[1] Two excellent critical editions are M. Whittaker, *Die Apostolischen Väter I. Der Hirt des Hermas* (GCS, 48), Akademie Verlag, Berlin, 1956, and R. Joly, *Hermas: Le Pasteur* (SC, 53bis), Éditions du Cerf, Paris, 1968. English translations used in preparing this chapter: K. Lake, *The Apostolic Fathers*, II (Loeb, 25), 9th ed., Heinemann, London, 1965; J.B. Lightfoot, *The Apostolic Fathers*, Baker, Grand Rapids, 1967(reprint of Macmillan, London, 1891); A. Roberts, *The Writings of the Apostolic Fathers* (Ante-Nicene Chr. Libr.), Clark, Edinburgh, 1873; and G.F. Snyder, *The Apostolic Fathers*. Vol. VI. *Hermas*, Nelson, Camden, N.J., 1968.

[2] Cf. G.F. Snyder, *op. cit.*, p. 19:"The Shepherd was written at Rome. The geographical references will have it no other way (*Vis.* I,1,3; II,1,1; IV,1,2). Several illustrations appear Roman: the elm and the vine (*Sim.* II) as an agricultural device was practiced in central Italy, the two cities (*Sim.* I) may point to the intense power of Rome. Tradition offers no other origin for the *Shepherd* than Rome: the Muratorian canon considers Hermas the brother of the Roman bishop Pius, while Origen links him to the Hermas of *Romans* 16:14. Some consider the Clement of *Vis.* II,4,3 the author of *1 Clement* and bishop of Rome."

[3] Cf. J. Lebreton, *Histoire de l'Église. Vol. I. L'Église Primitive*, Bloud & Gay, Paris, 1946, p. 348.

[4] Cf. A. Puech, *Histoire de la littérature grecque chrétienne*, II, Paris, 1928, pp. 94-5.

[5] C.H. Turner,"The Shepherd of Hermas and the Problem of its Text," *Journal of Theological Studies*, XXI, 1920, p. 198; C. Mohrmann, "Les origines de la latinité chrétienne à Rome," *Vigiliae Christianae*, 3, 1949, pp. 74-78.

[6] H.A. Musurillo, S.J.,"The Need for a New Edition of *Hermas*," *Theological Studies*, XII, 1951, p. 383, also:"The distribution of the manuscripts of the Latin versions, and of the Coptic, Ethiopic and middle Persian versions, reveals how widely *Hermas* was read in Egypt, Europe and Asia." Cf. also the remark of H. Chadwick, "The New Edition of *Hermas*," *Journal of Theol. Studies*, VIII, 1957, p. 275:"It is at first sight a surprising fact that no Syriac version appears to have been made; nor, to the best of my knowledge, is any quotation from Hermas found in any native writer. The *Shepherd* passed from Rome to Alexandria and Egypt, where Clement and Origen were profoundly influenced by it; to them it was congenial not only for its ascetic tone, but also for its subtle and revolutionary doctrine of the Church as a school for sinners and its consequent conception of divine punishment as purification, with the corollary that the *eschaton* will come when the Church is purged, complete, and perfect. But outside Egypt the Eastern churches did not hold it in respect."

[7]   Irenaeus prefixes a quote from it in his *Adv. Haer.* IV, 20, with the words:"Well said the Scripture." Clement of Alexandria cites it frequently as Scripture. Origen holds the author to be the Hermas of *Rom.* 16:14 but admits that not everybody held this opinion. In the early 4th century Eusebius noted it was read publically in the churches and used for instruction but that some doubted its inspiration. He classed it as non-canonical along with *Barnabas* and the *Didache.* Athanasius excluded it from the canon but included it among works to be used for catech. instruction. In the *Codex Sinaiticus* a portion of the *Shepherd* (up to *Mand.* IV,3,5) is appended to the *NT* after *Barnabas.* The author of the *Muratorian Fragment* (c. 200 C.E.) calls Hermas the brother of Pius I and refuses to admit the work as inspired. Tertullian in his catholic period considered it Scripture but later as a Montanist referred to it as "the Shepherd of adulterers" and relegated it to the apocrypha. Later in the early 7th century we find 15 references to it (*Visions* excluded) in the *Pandectes* (150 "homilies") of the Palestinian monk Antiochus. For references and further witness to the *Shepherd* in the Fathers see: *Dict. théol. cath.,* t.6, cols. 2269-71.

[8]   H. Chadwick, *op. cit.,* p. 279.

[9]   R. Grant, *The Apostolic Fathers,* Vol. I. Introduction, Nelson, N.Y., 1964, p. 20.

[10]   H. Chadwick, *op. cit.,* p. 279.

[11]   Cf. K.D. Macmillan's so-entitled article in the *Princeton Theol. Review,* 9, 1911, pp. 61-95 and R. van Deemter's doctorate thesis *Der Hirt des Hermas: Apokalypse oder Allegorie?,* Delft, 1929. The former concludes that the *Shepherd* is an allegory, the latter that it is an apocalypse. See also A. von Ström, *Der Hirt des Hermas. Allegorie oder Wirklichkeit?* [Arbeit. und Mitteil. aus dem NT-lichen Sem. zu Uppsala], III, 1936.

[12]   Cf. S. Giet, *Hermas et les Pasteurs,* Presses univ. de France, Paris, 1963, p. 309.

[13]   Or perhaps several authors. We shall take up this problem in the next section.

[14]   Cf. R. Joly, "Judaism, Christianisme et Hellenisme dans le *Pasteur d'Hermas,*" *La nouvelle Clio,* V, 1953, p. 406:"L'élement chrétien est prédominant; les autres, juif et hellénique, sont consciemment et fort visiblement christianisés..."

[15]   H. Musurillo, S .J., *The Fathers of the Primitive Church,* Mentor-Omega, N.Y., 1966, 87.

[16]   See G.F. Snyder, *op. cit.,* p. 16; J.-P. Audet,"Affinites litteraires et doctrinales du Manuel de Discipline,"*Revue Biblique,* LX, 1953, pp. 41-82; L.W. Barnard, "Hermas, the Church and Judaism," *Studies in the Apostplic Fathers and their Background,* Oxford, 1966, pp. 151-163; J. Daniélou, *Théologie du Judéo-Christianisme,* Tournai, 1958, p. 48ff. and "Trinité et angélologie dans la théologie judéo-chrétienne," *Rech. de sc. rel.,* 45, 1957, pp. 5-41; R. Joly, *Hermas: Le Pasteur* (SC, 53), Paris, 1968, p. 47, and "Judaïsme, christianisme...*loc. cit.,* pp. 394-406.

[17] D.W. Riddle in the *Anglican Theol. Review*, 9, 1927, p .275; and K. Lake in *Harvard Theol. Review*, 4, 1911, p. 26ff.

[18] See A. Puech, *op. cit.*, p. 79.

[19] G.F. Moore, *Judaism*, I, Cambridge (Mass.), 1927-1930, p. 517, cited by Snyder, *op. cit.*, p. 10.

[20] R. Joly, *op. cit.*, pp 11-12.

[21] K. Lake, "The Shepherd of Hermas and Christian Life in Rome in the Second Century," *Harvard Theol. Review*, IV, 1911 pp. 26-27.

[22] Göttingen, 1955, pp. 88-105.

[23] G.F. Snyder, *op. cit.*, p. 11 [my italics].

[24] Snyder (*ibid.* pp. 10-11) outlines the correspondances as follows:

	Shepherd	J.-H. Homily Form
1.Recipient is addressed in diminutive by revelator	*Mand.*X,2,cf. *Vis.* III,9,1.	*Jas.* 2:20; *Did.* 3:1; *Test. of Reuben* 2:1; *Doct.* 12 *Apost.* 3:1.
2.Commandment in the imperative	*Mand.* II,1,etc.	*Test. Reub.* 3:9; *Did.* 3:1; *Barn.* 19:2-12; *Jas.* 2:1.
3.Homily or dialogue on the commandment:		
(a) An explanation of its importance	*Mand.* II:2-6; III, 1-4.	*Did.* 16:1-8; *Test of Judah* 14:2-8.
(b) The psychology of choice(i.e. the Two Spirits or Two Ways)	*Mand.* V,2-6; VI,2,3-7; VII, 1-4.	*Test. of Asher* 1:3 to 6:6; *Manual of Disc.*(1QS) 3:13 to 4:26.
(c) The effect, way or power of the command (i.e., vice or virtuelist)	*Mand.* V,2,1-7; VIII,2-11.	*Doct.* 12 *Apost.* 3:1-10; 5:1f. *Barn.* 20:1f.
4.Blessing for the recipient if he keeps the commandment	*Mand.* V,2,8; VIII,12; XII,2,2.	*Test. of Naphtali* 10:10; *Doct.* 12 *Apost.* 6:1f.
5.Curse on the recipient if he fails to keep the commandment	*Mand.* IV,1,2; IV,3,6; XII,2,3.	*Doct.* 12 *Apost.* 6:1f.
6.Blessing on the reader if he keeps the commandments	*Mand.* X,3,4; XII,3,1.	*Test. of Issachar* 6:3; *Rev.* 22:7
7.Curse on the reader if he fails to keep the commandment	*Mand.* VII,5	*Rev.* 22:18f

[25] Webster's *New Collegiate Dictionary*, Merriam Co., Springfield (Mass.), p. 608.

[26] W.F. Thrall, *A Handbook to Literature*, Odyssey, N.Y., 1960, p. 339.

[27] Thrall, *op. cit.*, p. 7.

[28] R. van Deemter, *op. cit.*, p. 2

[29] See note 7.

[30] Athanasius criticized both the Arians (*de decretis nicaen. synod.*[P.G. 25,456A]) and the semi-Arian Eusebians (*ad Afros*[*P.G.* 26,1037B]) for their use of the first Mandate. Cited by R. Grant, *op. cit.*, p. 19.

[31] G.F. Snyder, *op. cit.*, p. 13; see also pp. 161-164 for his index of biblical phrases.

[32] *Ibid.*, p. 13.

[33] J.-P. Audet, "Affinites litteraires...," p. 44

[34] G.F. Snyder, op. cit., p. 15

[35] *Ibid.*, p. 14

[36] *Ibid.*, p. 14.

[37] *Ibid.*, pp. 16-17.

[38] R. Joly, Hermas: *Le Pasteur* (SC, 53bis), p. 47

[39] J.-P. Audet, "Affinites litteraires....," pp. 41-82.

[40] M. Dibelius, *Der Hirt des Hermas,* Tübingen, 1923, p. 630.

[41] R. Grant, *op. cit.*, p. 100.

[42] G.F. Snyder, *op. cit.*, p. 17.

[43] W. J. Wilson, "The Career of the Prophet Hermas," *Harvard Theol. Review,* XX, 1927, p. 37, referring to Reitzensteins's *Poimandres: Studien zur griechisch-ägyptischen und frühchristlichen Literatur,* Leipzig, 1904, pp. 11-13; 33-35.

[44] G. Bardy, "Le Pasteur d'Hermas et les livres herémetiques," *Revue biblique,* VIII, 1911, pp. 391-407.

[45] M. Dibelius, "Der Offenbarungsträger im Hirten des Hermas," *Harnack-Ehrung.,* Leipzig, 1921, pp. 105-118, esp. p. 116.

[46] Cf. R. Joly's evaluation of their answers to Reitzenstein in *Hermas: Le Pasteur* (SC, 53bis), Paris, 1968, pp. 49-50; see also H. Musurillo, S.J., "The Need for a New Edition of Hermas," *Theological Studies,* XII, 1951, p. 382, note 3.

[47] L. Pernveden, *The Concept of the Church in the Shepherd of Hermas* (Studia Theologica Lundensia, 27), Gleerup, Lund, 1966, p. 198.

[48] G. Bardy, *op. cit.*, p. 401.

[49] R. Joly, *op. cit.*, p. 53.

[50] G. Snyder, *op. cit.*, p. 18.

[51] R. Joly, *op. cit.*, p. 51.

[52] R. Joly,"Judaïsme...," *loc. cit.*, p. 404; see also Ch. Taylor, "Hermas and Cebes," *Journal of Philology,* XXVII, 1901, p. 276ff; *ibid.,* XXVIII, 1903, p. 37ff & 95ff.

[53] R. Joly, "La doctrine pénitentielle du Pasteur d'Hermas et l'exégèse récente," *Revue de l'histoire des religions,* t. 147-148, 1955, p. 34.

[54] R. Joly, *Hermas: Le Pasteur* (SC, 53bis), p. 53.

[55] H. Hagemann, "Der Hirt des Hermas," *Theol. Quartalsch.,* 42, 1860, p. 38 (quoted by R. van Deemter, *op. cit.*, p. 8)

[56] W.J. Wilson, *op. cit.*, p. 33, gives a brief sketch of some of this literature prior to his own work in 1927: "The suggestion that the Visions were written by the apostolic

Hermas of *Rom.* 16,14, and the rest of the book by the brother of Pius, seems to have been made independently by Thiersch, *Die Kirche im apostolischen Zeitalter*, Frankfurt, 1858, p. 352f., and by de Champagny, *St. Cécile et la Société Romaine aux deux premiers siècles*, 2nd ed., 1874, p. 132f, 197f. Haussleiter, "De versionibus Pastoris Hermae latinis," in *Acta seminarii philologici erlangensis*, 1884,III, p. 423f., assigned the Visions to a later date than the Shepherd proper. A. Hilgenfeld, *Hermae Pastor*, 2nd ed., Leipzig, 1881(an entirely different work from his editions of 1853, 1856, 1873), p. 138f suggested three different authors, making another division between *Sim.* VII and VIII. Spitta, "Studien zum Hirten des Hermas," in *Zur Geschichte und Litteratur des Urchristentums*, Göttingen, 1896,II, pp. 241-437, believes the basal work to have been Jewish, but with large Christian redactions; and in this he was followed by D. Völter, *Die Visionen des Hermas*, Berlin, 1900; *Die apostolischen Väter*, Leyden, 1904, I, p. 170f; *Die älteste Predigt aus Rom*, Leyden, 1908, pp. 60-69; and Völter's pupil, H.A. van Bakal, *De Compositie van den Pastor Hermae*, Amsterdam, 1900. H. von Soden, in the *Theologische Literaturezeitung*, XXII, 1897, pp. 584-587, threw out the suggestion that *Hermas* had passed through first a Jewish and then a Christian stage; whereas the anonymous *Antiqua Mater: A Study of Christian Origins*, 1887, had denied that there was anything Christian about the book. Weinel, in Hennecke's *Handbuch zu den neutest. Apokryphen*, commenting on *Vis.* V, propounded a theory not of divided authorship but of divided personality. Grosse-Brauckmann, *De compositione Pastoris Hermae*, Göttingen, 1910, finding no possibilities left in the way of redactors, interpolators, or separate authors, conceived the novel idea that Hermas had revised himself, the original visions having been applicable to the prophet and his immediate family but expanded for presentation to the Church at large. Jean Réville, *Le valeur de témoignage historique du Pasteur d'Hermas*, Paris, 1900, defended the unity of authorship, but regarded the prophet's family as symbolizing the church at Rome, and the various other persons as standing for abstract qualities. K.D. Macmillan, "The Interpretation of the Shepherd of Hermas," in *Biblical and Theological Studies by the Faculty of Princeton Theological Seminary*, Princeton, 1912, pp. 492-543, reverted to the theory that the *Shepherd* is an edifying fiction. A. Link, *Die Einheit des Pastor Hermae*, Marburg, 1888, and still more effectively P. Baumgärtner, *Die Einheit des Hermasbuchs*, Tübingen, 1889, defended the unity of authorship on grounds of style and vocabulary.

[57] S. Giet, *Hermas et les Pasteurs*, Presses univ. de France, Paris, 1963. His other articles on the *Shepherd* in order of publication are: "L'Apocalypse d'Hermas et la pénitence," *Studia Patristica*, III(TU, 78), Akademie Verlag, Berlin, 1961, pp. 214-18; "Les trois auteurs du Pasteur d'Hermas," *Studia Patristica*, VIII(TU, 93), Akademie Verlag, Berlin, 1966, pp. 10-23[a summary of his book]; and in the same vol.: "De trois expressions: Auprès de la tour, la place inférieure et les premiers murs, dans le Pasteur

d'Hermas," pp. 24-29; "Un courant judéochrétien à Rome au milieu du IIe siècle?" in *Aspects du judéo-christianisme. Colloque de Strasbourg*, Paris, 1965, pp. 95-112; "Pénitence ou repentence dans le *Pasteur d'Hermas*," *Revue de droit canonique*, XVII, 1967, pp. 15-30.

[58] Cf. esp. "Hermas et le Pasteur," *Vigiliae Christianae*, 21, 1967, pp. 201-218; his other articles on the Shepherd: "Judaïsme, christianisme et hellénisme dans le Pasteur d'Hermas, *La nouvelle Clio*, 5, 1953, pp. 394-406; "Philologie et psychanalyse, C.G. Jung et le Pasteur d'Hermas," *L'Antiquite classique*, 1953, pp. 422-428; "La doctrine pénitentielle du Pasteur d'Hermas et l'exégèse récente, *Revue de l'histoire des religions*, CXLVII, 1955, pp. 32-49. His *Source chrétiennes* critical edition (SC 53 bis) appeared in 1958 from Les Éditions du Cerf, Paris.

[59] L.W. Barnard, "The Shepherd of Hermas in Recent Study," *Heythrop Journal*, 9, 1968, pp. 29-36.

[60] S. Giet,"Les trois auteurs..," p. 12.

[61] R. Joly, "Hermas et le Pasteur," *Vig. Christ.*, 21, 1967, p. 201.

[62] *Ibid.*, p. 205

[63] *Ibid.*, p. 203

[64] Giet, *Hermas et les Pasteurs*, p. 99.

[65] Joly, *loc, cit.*, p. 206

[66] *Ibid.;* see also Joly, *Hermas: Le Pasteur* (SC, 53 bis), p. 33.

[67] L.W. Barnard, *op. cit.*, p. 32.

[68] R. Joly, *Vig. Christ.*, 21, 1967, pp. 214-215. *A propos* of Giet's analysis of word usage, J.R. Michaels ("The 'Level Ground' in the Shepherd of Hermas," *Zeitsch. für NT Wissensch.*,59,1968,pp. 249-250) has made a *Hermas* study of the word *homalós*. Although not uncommon in classical Gk, it appears neither in the LXX, the NT, nor the other Apost. Frs. except for *Hermas* where it shows up in all three of Giet's divisions: *Vis.* I,1,3; I,3,4; *Mand.* II,4; VI,1,2; 1,4; *Sim.* IX,10,1. R. Grant, opposing Giet's thesis, notes that the word *agathós* appears 21 times in *Romans* but not once in *I Corinthians*, nor does the word *pistós* appear at all in Paul's Epistles. This does not, however, diminish the fact that Paul wrote them. (*Gnomon*, 1964, pp. 357-359 [cited by Joly, *loc. cit.*, p. 218]). Moreover, such a key term in *Hermas* as *dípsychos* (19x as adj., 21x as cognate verb, 16x as substantive) is found abundantly throughout all Giet's divisions.(Cf. O.J.F. Seitz,"The Relationship of the Shepherd of Hermas to the Epistle of James," *Journ. of Bib. Lit.*, LXIII, 1944, p. 131ff.)

[69] Cf. F.X. Funk, "Die Einheit des Hirten des Hermas," *Theol. Quartalsch.*, 1899, pp. 321-360; A.V. Link, *Die Einheit des Pastor Herma*, 1888; P. Baumgärtner, *Die Einheit des Hermasbuchs*, 1889.

[70] In his commentary on *Romans*. "Puto tamen, quod Hermas iste sit scriptor

libelii illius, qui Pastor appellatur"(X, 31-P.G. 14, 1282), but it is likely a reflection of his desire to consider it an apostolic witness("et ut puto divinitus inspirata"). Cf. G.F. Snyder, *op. cit.*, p. 22.

71 R. Joly, SC, 53 bis, p. 14.

72 *Der Hirt des Hermas: Apokalypse oder Allegorie?* Delft, 1929, pp. 43-59.

73 R. van Deemter, *op. cit.*, pp. 58-59; Lightfoot, Lebreton, Altaner and Quasten follow more or less the same train of thought. Cf. *Catholicisme*, 19, col. 667.

74 W.J. Wilson, who also supports a double composition, (*op. cit.*, p. 31)holds that "the Visions were originally designed for oral presentation; their publication in book form was something of an afterthought. But the Mandates and the Similitudes show every indication of having been literary creations from the start. They are unquestionably from the same mystical prophet, and they often show vision-like qualities, as if some dream or trance lay at the basis of them, but they are no longer addressed directly to the 'brethren.'"

75 *Ibid.*, p. 27, note 4.

76 We do know that the work was well-known and popular in the latter half of the century and we have a full Latin translation from the end of the second century.

77 Cf. Th. Zahn, *Der Hirt des Hermas*, Gotha, 1868; A. von Ström, *op. cit.;* R. van Deemter, *op. cit,;* R. Joly, *opera cit.;* J.-P. Audet, *op. cit.*

78 J.-P. Audet, "Affinites litteraires...," p. 43.

79 Cf. *Frag. Murat.*:"Et ideo legi eum quidem oportet, se publicare vero in ecclesia populo neque inter prophetas completum[l. completos] numero neque inter apostolos in fine temporum potest," Ref. F.X. Funk, *Patres Apostolici*, I, Tübingen, 1901, CXXIII.

80 R. Joly, "La doctrine penitentielle...," p. 32.

81 L.W. Barnard, "The Shepherd of Hermas in Recent Study," *Heythrop Journal*, 9,1968, p. 29.

82 Cf. K. Lake, *op. cit.*, p. 79f; "This mandate is really explaining the practical problem which arose from the conflict between the Christian precept against divorce (*Mk.* 10,11f) and the equally early precept against having intercourse with immoral persons. As the inserted clause "except for the cause of fornication" in the Matthaean version of *Mk.* 10,11f. (*Mt.* 19,9; cf. *Mt.* 5,32 and *Lc.* 16,18) shows, the latter precept was regarded as more important, and immoral wives were put away, but Hermas and other writers always maintained that this was not strictly divorce, as the innocent party was not free to remarry in order to give the other the opportunity of repenting and of returning.

83 Actually an expansion of the first Mandate.

84 Cf. A. Benoît, *Le Baptême chrétien au second siècle*, Presses univ. de France, 1953, p. 115: "La révélation qu'Hermas est chargé de communiquer aux chrétiens a pour objet la pénitence. C'est là le seul et unique thème de son ouvrage, thème vers lequel

convergent les *Visions,* les *Préceptes* et les *Similitudes.*"

85   As hold, e.g., J.A. Robinson, *Barnabas, Hermas and the Didache,* London, 1920, p. 28; and A. Nygren, *Agape and Eros,* Philadelphia, 1953, p. 262.

86   Such is the position of: T.F. Torrence, *The Doctrine of Grace in the Apostolic Fathers,* Edinburgh, 1948, pp. 111f., 115, 124; H.B. Swete, *Patristic Study,* London, 1902, p. 25; E.J. Goodspeed, *A History of Early Christian Literature,* Chicago, 1942, p. 47.

87   A. Benoît, *op. cit.,* Chap. VI, pp. 115-137.

88   *Ibid.,* p. 135.

89   *Ibid.,* p. 126.

90   G.F. Snyder, *op. cit.,* pp. 70-71.

91   Unless one wants to read some special meaning into *Vis.* II,4,3 where Hermas is told to read the little book himself at Rome "with the *presbýteroi* who are in charge of the Church."

92   "Die Busslehre im Hirten des Hermas," *Zeitsch. für kath. Theol.,* 77, 1955, p. 418; aside from those already mentioned, some other notable articles on the penitential teaching in the *Shepherd* are: P. Batiffol, "L'Église naissante. Hermas et le problème moral au second siècle," *Rev. bib.,* 10, 1901, pp. 337-351; H. Koch "Die Bussfrist des Pastor Hermä, *Festgabe Harnack,* Tübingen, 1921, pp. 173-182; J. Hoh, *Die kirchliche Busse im zweiten Jahrhundert,* Breslau, 1932, pp. 10-34; A. d'Ales, *L'édit de Calliste,* Paris, 1914, pp. 52-113; P. Galtier, *Aux origines du sacrement de pénitence,* Rome, 1951, p. 133; B. Poschmann, *Penance and the Anointing of the Sick,* N.Y.,1964, pp. 28-35.

93   R. Grant, *op. cit.,* pp. 187-188.

94   The meaning of this puzzling statement is disputed. For an analysis of the pertinent literature cf. G.F. Snyder, *op. cit.,* p. 35

95   See *Catholicisme,* 19 (Paris, 1958), col. 668 (by Th. Camelot, O.P.)

96   G.F. Snyder, *op. cit.,* p. 107; cf. also K. Adam, "Die Lehre von dem hl. Geiste bei Hermas und Tertullian," *Theol. Quartalsch.,* 1906, p. 61.

97   Except in *Vis.* II,2,8 of the *Codex Sinaiticus* where *christon* replaces *filium* in the Old Latin, and Ethiopic translations; and in *Vis.* III,6,6 of *Athous* where *christô* replaces *kyriô* of all the other manuscripts.

98   Cf. G. Snyder, *op. cit.,* p. 37: "The Son is mentioned only once in *Visions* I-IV and is infrequent elsewhere (*Sim.* V,5,2f.; V,6,1f.; VIII,3,3; 11,1) except for *Similitude* IX. ... The question remains whether *kúrios* is a Christological title. *Theós* and *kúrios* are interchangeable as far as the author is concerned (IX,23,4). In fact, there are some 32 times in the text of the Shepherd where the two names are variants (Audet [*op. cit.*], p.48; Joly prefers *theós, Vis.* I,1,3; III,3,1; III,5,2; IV,1,8; *Mand,* X,3,2; XII,4,4). Audet, p. 50, in his attempt to demonstrate the strong Judaistic character of the *Shepherd,* concludes that *kúrios* never refers to Christ. There are few passages to disprove his thesis. Here [i.e. in

Vis. II,2] *kúrios* appears to be Christ, because the persecution would be at the point of affirming or denying Jesus as Lord (*qui negaverit se christianum esse* ... *veniam ex paenitentia impetret,* Pliny, Ep. X, 97). In *Vis.* III,7,3 baptism "in the name of the Lord" ought also to refer to the early confession (*Rom.* 10:9), but references to the word of the Lord (*Sim.* IX,25,2) or the name of the Lord in general (especially *Sim.* IX,12-17) could, in Jewish theology, designate the presence of God (see Giet, pp. 164-167; Daniélou, pp. 151-153). *Kúrios,* then, is not a Christological title in the *Shepherd,* but so nearly represents that presence of God which in the NT is the Son, that it can approximate a Christological meaning."

99   *Ibid.,* p. 107: "The "name of God," a Jewish circumlocution for God's presence (for Christ: *Acts* 10:43; *1 Cor.* 1:10) is frequent in the *Visions* and *Similitudes* (*Vis.* II,1,2; III,4,3; 5,2;7,3; IV,1,3; *Sim.* VIII,6,2 & 4; IX,12,8; 14,3; 18,5; 28,6; absolute: *Vis.* III,1,9; 2,1; *Sim.* VIII,10,3; IX,13,2f.; 19,2; 28,3 & 5), but except for baptism "in the name of the Lord" (*Vis,* III,7,3), need not be Christological. In *Similitude* IX the Christology is explicit with "the name of the Son of God"(12,4;13,3 & 7; 14,5-6; 16,3 & 5 & 7; 17,4; 28,2), but the Son himself is unclear (contrast Daniélou, pp. 147-157)."

100   *Ibid.,* pp. 107-108: "The Son occurs only once before *Similitude* V (*Vis,* II,2,8), briefly in *Similitude* VIII (3,2; 11,1) and then frequently in *Similitude* IX. In *Similitude* VIII the Son is the "law of God" (3,2;) much like *Sim.* V,5,3. In *Similitude* IX the Son is the rock(12,1 — 16,7) as well as the portico (12,1) and the glorious man (12,8) otherwise identified as the archangel Michael (*Sim.* VIII,3,3)."

101   R.Joly, "La doctrine pénitentielle...," p. 35; see also K. Adam, *op. cit.* p. 60: "Hermas lehrte einen ewigen Geist Gottes der zugleich dessen Sohn ist, also einen hypostatischen Ausdruk der vollen göttlichen Wesenheit mit Ausschluss jeder dritten göttlichen Person"

102   R. Joly, SC, 53 bis, p. 32.

103   L. Pernveden, *op. cit.,* pp. 52-69.

104   *Ibid.,* p. 57.

105   *Ibid.,* p. 66

106   G.F. Snyder, *op. cit.,* p. 108; see also Pernveden, pp. 58-64.

107   Pernveden, p. 70.

108   R. Joly, SC, 53 bis, p. 33

109   R. Grant, *op. cit.,* p. 113.

110   Cf. S. Giet, *Hermas et les Pasteurs,* p. 269

111   Snyder, p. 64: "The definition of life with God — life which results from keeping the commandments — is present (in *Mand.* VII,5). In the parable of the sticks to "live to God" is repentance (*Sim.* VIII, 11,1) and every believer is in some state of life or death (*Sim.* VIII,2,9;8,1 & 5) except for the *dípsychos,* who is neither alive nor dead (*Sim.*

VIII,7,1), i.e., not faithful, but not lost. ...As a result of faith and obedience, "living to God" is also eschatological (*Sim*. IX,28,8), but the references to purely eschatological life are rare."

[112] F. Barberet, "La formule *Zên tô theô* dans le Pasteur d'Hermas," *Rech. de sc. rel.*, 46, 1958, p. 395; he also points out (p. 397f.) that this formula does not appear in the Qumran texts, the Apocrypha or the other Apost. Frs. "Dans le NT au contraire on a quelques rares emplois de l'expression... et de tournures similaires"(*Lk*. 20:38; *Rom.* 6:10-11; 14:7-8; *2 Cor.* 5:15; *Gal.* 2:19; 5:25; *1 Pet.* 2:24).

[113] G.F. Snyder, *op. cit.*, p. 64.

[114] L. Pernveden, *op. cit.*, p. 299

[115] R. Joly, *op. cit.*, p. 34.

[116] *Ibid.*, pp. 35-36

[117] L. Pernveden, *op. cit.*, pp. 293-294.

[118] *Ibid.*, p. 295.

[119] *Ibid.*, pp. 295-298; also see L.W. Barnard's analysis of his work in "The Shepherd of Hermas in Recent Study," *Heythrop Journal*, 9, 1968, 33-34.

[120] See note 2.

[121] G.F. Snyder, *op. cit.*, p. 19

[122] Cf. C.J.A.C. Peeters, *De Liturgische Dispositie van het Vroegchristelijk Kerkebouw*, Van Gorcum, Assen, 1969, pp. 18-19: "Maar dat deze dienst, met zijn direct, pragmatisch, on-emotioneel en exclusief huislijk karakter, plaats placht te vinden in particuliere huizen van christenen, heeft, volgens de acten van zijn proces in 165, Justinus zelf getuigd in zijn verhoor door de prefect Rusticus, wanneer hij bevestigt, dat hij woont en zijn leerlingen ontvangt bij een zekere Martinus, die boven een particulier badhuis woonachtig is, en dat, in het algemeen, de vergaderingen der christenen plaats vinden waar zij willen en mogen samenkomen. Aan vaste vergaderplaatsen denkt men zeker wanneer men leest, dat Minucius Felix te Rome in zijn *Octavius* (tweede helft 2e eeuw) de christelijke vergaderplaatsen *sacraria* noemt. Een eeuw later spreekt Porphyrius van *megístous oíkous* door de christenen voor hun eredienst benut.... De oudste stadtsbasilieken van Rome, de *tituli*, zijn vóór een deelde opvolgsters van kerkhuizen die reeds vóór de Kerkvrede, in de 3e en in het begin van de 4e eeuw, gesticht zijn. Het zijn er later een vijfentwintig geworden, waarvan hoogstens tien mogelijk enige sporen nagelaten hebben... ."

[123] Cf. note 137.

[124] G.F. Snyder, *op. cit.*, pp. 20-21.

[125] *Catholicisme*, 19, col. 668 (par P.-Th., Camelot, O.P.).

[126] W.J. Wilson, *op. cit.*, p. 29, note 5.

[127] K. Lake, *The Apost. Frs.*, II, p. 263, notes: "Cf. *1 Peter* 3,19, *Gospel of Peter*

ix and the Descensus ad inferos in the *Acta Pilati*. The idea that hearing the Gospel and Baptism is necessary for salvation of the righteous dead of pre-Christian times is common, but it is more usually Christ himself who descends..."

[128] Cf. J. Weiss, *Earliest Christianity*, II, Harper, N.Y., 1959, pp. 673-687.

[129] J. Daniélou, *op. cit.*, p. 407.

[130] See R. Grant, *op, cit.*, p. 161.

[131] Cf. J. Weiss, *op. cit.*, p. 683.

[132] G.F. Snyder, *op. cit.*, p. 47, note.

[133] Cf. D. van den Eynde, *Les Normes de l'Enseignement chrétien dans la littérature patristique des trois premiers siècles*, Gabala, Paris, 1933, p. 91: "Au reste, le prophète ne joue pas, dans le livre, un rôle saillant. Si Hermas le dépeint, c'est pour l'opposer au pseudo-prophète plus que pour relever son importance. Il est en effet remarquable qu'aucune vision de la tour, symbole de l'édifice de l'Église, ne mentionne les prophètes; ils ne constituent plus dans la communauté une catégorie à côté des apôtres, des docteurs, des évêques et des diacres."

[134] L. Pernveden, *op. cit.*, pp. 148-149.

[135] Prophets are mentioned in *Sim.* IX 15,4, but they are clearly those of the OT.

[136] L. Pernveden, *op. cit.*, p. 150.

[137] Three times in these two passages we find the only mention in the *Shepherd* of an actual gathering of persons. It appears to be a prayer meeting, since "intercession is made to God from the assembly." Aside from prayer, there is no further mention of cultic or ritual action. While the use of *synagōgè* could simply mean a gathering of Christians as in Ignatius' *ad Polyc.* 4:2, here, considering the Jewish-Christian milieu, the term could also carry a local nuance, i.e. a synagogue meeting of Jews who were also Christians but still accustomed to attend synagogue or who made use of a synagogue for their meetings. This nuance could also be present in *James* 2:2.

[138] G. Bardy, *La Théologie de l'Église de saint Clément de Rome à saint Irénée* [Unam Sanctam, 13], du Cerf, Paris, 1945, p. 141.

[139] E. Dorsch, S.J., "Zur Hierarchie des Hirten," *Theol. Quartalschr.*, 1904, p. 278.

[140] *Ibid.*, pp. 47 and 150.

[141] H. von Campenhausen, *op. cit.*, p. 91.

[142] G.F. Snyder, *op. cit.*, p. 153.

[143] *Ibid.*, p. 146.

[144] Here he mentions: A. Lelong, *Le Pasteur d'Hermas*, 1912, p. LXXXII; G. Bardy, *op. cit.*, p. 120; J. Colson, *L'évêque dans les communautés primitives*, Paris, 1951, pp. 77-78.

[145] R. Joly, "La doctrine pénitentielle du Pasteur d'Hermas et l'éxègese récente,

Revue de l'histoire des religions, t. 147-148, 1955, p. 32.

[146] L. Pernveden, *op. cit.*, p. 145.

[147] *Ibid.*, p. 144.

[148] K. Lake, Apost. Fathers, II (Loeb), p. 29.

[149] *Ibid.*, p. 41n; see also E. Stommel,"Die bischöfliche Kathedra im christlichen Altertum," *Münchener Theol. Zeitschr.*, 1952, p. 21; K. Lake, *op. cit.*, [ctd. below].

[150] R. Joly, SC, 53 bis, pp. 100-101.

[151] Lightfoot (*op. cit.*, p. 171) and Lake (*op. cit.*, p. 31) translate *hagiásmatos* as "the Holiness."/149 (ctd.) p. 117, note 1, states: "*sumpséllion* here cannot he translated by the same word as in *Vis.* III,1,4. Here it is the 'bench' of the learner as opposed to the 'chair' of the teacher."

[152] R. Grant, *op. cit.*, p. 165; see also E. Schweizer, *op. cit.*, p. 144 and H. von Campenhausen, *op. cit.*, p. 91.

[153] We know from Tacitus that as early as 64 C.E. there was already an "ingens multitudo" of Christians in Rome. Cf. Poulet-Raemers, *Church History*, I, 1935, p. 31.

[154] E. Schweizer, *op. cit.*, p. 144.

[155] K. Lake, *op. cit.*, p. 281.

[156] R. Grant, *op. cit.*, p. 165.

[157] E. Schweizer, *op. cit.*, p. 141.

[158] E.g. *tópos* (place) which is occasionally used in Hellenistic-Jewish and for the most part later Greek-Christian literature to denote a separate sacral "Amt" (cf. W. Bauer, WzNT, col. 1628) appears 37 times in the *Shepherd*, but never once with this meaning.

[159] They are also called *pisteúsantes* (believers) 21 times and *doûloi* (servants) 37x.

[160] Although *agápē*, meaning "love," occurs six times (*Vis.* III,8,5 & 7; *Mand.* VIII,9; *Sim.* IX,15,2; 17,4; 18,4).

[161] *Apologia* I, 65,1-67,8 (P.G. 6, 428-429; G. Krüger, 56-58)

[162] Cf. S. Giet, "Pénitence ou repentence...," *Rev. de droit canon.*, XVII, 1967, pp. 29-30; J. Hoh, "Die Busse im Pastor Hermae," *Theol. Quartalsch.*, 1930, p.278; A. Lelong, *Le Pasteur d'Hermas* [*Les Pères Apost.*,IV], Paris, 1912, p. LXX; and A. d'Ales, "La discipline pénitentielle...," *Rech. de sc. rel.*, 1911, p. 258.

[163] See also *Sim.* IX,33,3.

[164] Cf. A. Benoît, *Le Baptême chrétien au second siècle*, Presses univ. de France, Paris, 1953, p. 122, n. 16, and for a detailed treatment on the "seal" pp. 131-2; see also A. Hamman, "La signification de 'sphragís' dans le Pasteur d'Hermas," *Studia Patristica*, IV (TU, 79), Berlin, 1961, pp. 286-290. Both authors stress that the relation with Baptism, while primary, must not be taken too exclusively or too narrowly.

[165] A. Benoît, *op. cit.*, p. 135.

166 J. Colson, *Ministre de Jésus-Christ...*, Paris, 1966, p. 323.

167 *Ibid.*, pp. 326-328.

168 Although, since Hermas speaks of his own Baptism as "when we went down into the water" (*Mand.* IV,3,1), it is reasonable to believe, even without it being mentioned, that there were those in the community known to Hermas whose function it was to baptize the living.

169 In a personal discussion with Abbé Colson on this point, he stressed rather the necessity of seeking the foundation of Christian priesthood in the Apostolic preaching.

170 SC, 53 bis, Paris, 1968, p. 439 (as addition to original text p. 328, note 1).

171 Cf. R. de Vaux,O.P., *Hoe het oude Israel leefde*, II, Romen, Roermond, 1962 (Dutch transl. L. Grollenberg), p. 322: "Het altaar is een teken van de aanwezigheid van God."

172 L. Pernveden, *op. cit.*, p. 78

173 *Ibid.*, p. 79.

174 *Ibid.*, p. 76; nonetheless the preconceived divine plan of "the Lamb of God who takes away the sins of the world"(*Jn.* 1:29)— freely as an act of obedience — which forms the background of the New Testament soteriology (cf. *Mt.* 1:21; *Rom.* 4:25; 8:3; *1 Cor.* 15:3; *Gal.* 1:4; *Heb.* 2:17; *1 Jn.* 4:10), is found more or less clearly stated in other Apostolic Fathers (*Barn.* chs. 5 to 7; *1 Clem.* ch. 16; Ign. *Eph.* 18:2), where the reference to Christ's suffering and the importance of His blood is a frequently recurring theme (*1 Clem.* 7:4; 12:7; 21:6; *Barn.* 5:1; 12:1; Ign. *Eph.* 1:1; *Smyrn.* 1:1f.; ch. 2; Pol. *Phil.* 1:2).

175 *Ibid.*, p. 79.

176 See citation and note 106.

177 K. Lake, *op. cit.*, p. 2.

178 *Apóstoloi, didáskaloi, prophétai, epískopoi, presbýteroi, poímenes, diákonoi and proēgouménoi.* No other Apostolic Father nor any single book of the NT contains such a wide variety of ministerial terms.

179 L. Pernveden, *op. cit.*, p. 155.

180 If one knew for certain that eucharistic celebrations were held in the milieu described by the *Shepherd*, one would guess them to take place either at the *"synagōgē andrôn dikaíōn"* where " intercession is made to God from the assembly of those men" (*Mand.* XI,9) [see note 137], or in the homes of the *"epískopoi* and hospitable persons who were always glad to entertain (i.e. receive), without hypocrisy, the servants of God in their homes"(*Sim.* IX,27,2).

181 G.F. Snyder, *op. cit.*, p. 146.

THE DIDACHE

OUTLINE

I. BACKGROUND

For centuries patristic scholars had known of but possessed no complete text of a work called "The Teaching *[Didache]* of the (Twelve) Apostles," which was mentioned and in part quoted by various early and some later Christian writers, e.g. Eusebius, Athanasius, Lactantius, Nicephorus, Rufinus,[1] as well as the medieval Rhineland preachers, Boniface of Mainz and Severianus of Cologne.[2] Until the modern period it was generally considered that this "Teaching", like so many other ancient works, had perished in the wreck of history. Then, in 1873, Philotheos

Bryennios, bishop of Seres (Macedonia), later metropolitan of Nicomedia, found a 120-page Greek parchment codex[3] in the library of the Jerusalem Patriarch at the hospice of the Holy Sepulchre in Constantinople.[4] The codex was dated June 11, 1056, by a scribe, Leo, who signed himself as a notary and a sinner. Included in it were *1* and *2 Clement,* the *Epistle of Barnabas* (which were published in 1875), the *Letters of Ignatius* ("long" recension), Chrysostom's *Synopsis of the Old and New Testament* (incomplete), two other shorter, hitherto unknown documents, and the *Didache* which Bryennios published separately in 1883.[5]

The world-wide wave of popular and scholarly interest that followed the publication of the *Didache* has only been equalled in our day by the discovery of the Dead Sea Scrolls. Immediately the antiquity of the text was recognized and scholars began to include it among the Apostolic Fathers.

The *Didache* is listed in the index of the Bryennios codex and at the beginning of the text itself under the brief title: *Didachè tôn dódeka apostólōn;*[6] the apparently "complete title" given second at the beginning of the text, however, reads: *Didachè toû kyríou dià tôn dódeka apostólōn toîs éthnesin,* i.e. The Teaching of the Lord (as handed on) through the Twelve Apostles to the Nations/Gentiles. This latter title, as J. Armitage Robinson noted years ago,[7] calls to mind the instruction of the Lord in *Matthew* 28:19: "Go, and make disciples of all the nations/gentiles (*pánta tà éthnē*), baptizing them ... and teaching *(didáskontes)* them to observe whatsoever I have commanded you." Still, even though the *Didache* purports to carry the very teaching of the Lord destined for the nations/gentiles through the Apostles, we are hardly justified in concluding either to Apostolic authorship or to a mission carried on directly by the Apostles among the Gentiles.[8]

A. Form, Style and Content

The *Didache* presents itself in the form of a small(2190 words),[9] impersonal[10] community manual[11] on morals, ritual and Church order. It appears to be, in spite of its rather isolated position among early Christian documents, a predecessor — in one way or another — of the great Church manuals of the third and fourth centuries, several of which have taken over *Didache* material — e.g., the *Didascalia Apostolorum* (3rd c.), the *Canones Ecclesiastici* (early 4th c.) and the *Constitutiones Apostolici* (4th c.).[12] This latter contains virtually all of our *Didache* in its chapter VII: 1-32.[13]

Most patristic scholars today will admit that the *Didache* is an example, to use Kraft's term, of "evolved literature." That is to say, the *Didache* (as we possess it) shows clear evidence of being the product of a developing process. Some individual, it is true, has put it into the form preserved for us, but he/she is at best an author-editor.[14] The question of the various steps in this "developing process" is disputed and forms part of the larger problem of the document's higher criticism, but it is clear that the basic inspiration is Jewish. A Jewish "Two Ways" tradition somewhat like that in *Did.* 1-6 was found in the Qumran *Manual of Discipline* (I QS iii.13 — iv.26)[15]; Rabbi G. Klein has shown the clear relationships between the Jewish blessings at table and the liturgical prayers of *Did.* 9-10;[16] and, A. Benoît has pointed out the remarkable parallels between the Didache's prescriptions for Christian baptism and those for Jewish proselyte baptism.[17]

In his style and choice of words the didachist displays a certain taste for order and clarity; he composes methodically and expresses himself with lucid simplicity.[18] E. Jacquier has noted that:

> La langue et le vocabulaire de la Didachè sont, à très peu de différences près, ceux du Nouveau Testament, et en particulier ceux de l'Évangile selon saint Matthieu. La langue est le grec appelé ordinairement héllénistique. ... Dans les Septante, cette langue héllénistique était déja d'une construction plus simple que le grec classique, était surtout moins chargée de propositions incidentes; elle devint, dans quelques écrits du Nouveau Testament et en particulier dans la Didachè, une langue dont la construction est toute hébraïque. C'est une suite de propositions, unies par une simple copule, qui ne les relie pas par un lien solide, mais les juxtapose plutôt les unes à la suite des autres. Les mots sont grec, mais la pensée et le style sont hébraïques. Les phrases sont courtes, sentencieuses, sans développements incidents. Le style est simple, naturel et populaire. C'est une oeuvre qui a dû être parlée avant d'être écrite.[19]

As to content, the Bryennios text can be roughly divided into three parts, devoted respectively to catechesis, ritual and church order. *Part I* is an epitome of Christian morality, suited to pagan candidates for baptism. This catechetical section (chs. 1-6) inculcates, under the form of the Way of Life and the Way of Death, the practice of Christian virtue and enumerates the vices to be shunned. Its starting point is the double commandment of the love of God and of neighbor, and the Golden Rule in its negative wording. *Part II* (chs. 7-10) is a ritual or liturgical summary. It first explains the rite of baptism (ch. 7)[20] both by immersion and by aspersion (infusion), then treats the Christian practice of fasting and prayer (ch. 8), and finally records an early liturgical prayer for the giving of thanks *(Eucharistía)* which take up chs. 9 and 10. *Part III* (chs. 11-15), the "canonical" section, broadly outlines Church organization and Church life. It distinguishes three classes of ministers (ch. 11): "apostles" or itinerant missionaries; "prophets" or those charismatically gifted to speak "in the Spirit"; and "teachers" or catechists. It lays down principles (ch. 12) for according or refusing hospitality to travelling brethren, and urges the support of prophets (ch. 13). It makes reference to the Sunday observance (ch. 14), and advises the election of and proper respect for *epískopoi* and *diákonoi* (ch. 15). The treatise closes with an exhortation (ch. 16) to take life seriously in view of the impending judgement and the end of the world.[21]

Schematically, then, the document has the following appearance:

Introduction (1:1-1b)

I. Catechesis (The Two Ways)
    A. The Way of Life (1:1c - 4:14)
    B. The Way of Death (5:1-2)
    C. Conclusion to the Two Ways (6:1-2)
    D. Excursus on food (6:3)
II. Ritual and Liturgy
    A. Concerning Baptism, fasting and prayer (7:1 - 8:3)
    B. Concerning *Eucharistía* (9:1 - 10:8)
III. Church order
    A. The approved teacher (11:1-2)
    B. Concerning apostles and prophets (11:3 - 12)
    C. Hospitality towards travelling Christians (12:1-5)
    D. Material support for prophets and teachers (13:1-7)
    E. The Sunday community "sacrifice" (14:1-3)
    F. Call to elect and respect *epískopoi* and *diákonoi* (15:1-2) G. Community discipline and conduct (15:3-4)
        —Eschatological admonition (16:1-8)—

B. APPROACH TO CHRISTIAN LIFE; THEOLOGICAL POINTS

Despite the high regard for the charismatic workings of the Spirit and the great liberty accorded the prophets in the Didache, the work itself as a whole represents a rather rigorous ethical, or perhaps better "canonical" approach to Christianity. The material is presented as a very definite teaching which is to be carefully guarded. It is normative and authoritative, and its recipients are to: "See that no man leads you astray from this Way of the Teaching, since any other teaching takes you away from God"(6.1). Back in 1922, P. Batiffol analyzed the Didache's approach to Christian life as follows:

> On ne se tromperait pas de beaucoup en supposant qu'elle s'inspire, du moins dans sa partie éthique, de ce moralisme juif dont l'épître de saint Jacques est un si remarquable écho, état d'esprit assez proche de celui du prosélytisme des *phoboúmenoi tòn theón*. Il n'y est point question de "sagesse", come dans l'épître de saint Jacques, ni non plus de "Loi", mais bien de "crainte de Dieu". Le fidèle devra instruire ses enfants dès leur bas âge de "la crainte de Dieu" (*Did.* IV,9). Il devra commander sans amertume à ses serviteurs "qui espèrent dans le même Dieu", de peur, par de mauvais traitements, de les détourner de "craindre Dieu"(IV,10). Peut-être ces préceptes ont-ils été pris à une sorte de catéchisme moral à l'usage des prosélytes: ce sont des préceptes juifs d'esprit et d'expression.
> Sur ce moralisme juif se superpose le christianisme, un christianisme qui n'a rien de cet enthousiasme charismatique que quelques textes ont pu faire croire prédominant et entraînant tout dans les communautés chrétiennes primitives: c'est, au contraire, un christianisme fait de préceptes nets et autoritaires fondés sur la parole du Seigneur. "Vos prières, vos aumônes, toutes vos actions, faites-les ainsi que vous avez vu dans l'Évangile de Notre-Seigneur"(XV,4). "Tu n'abandonneras pas les commandements du Seigneur, tu observeras ceux que tu as reçus, n'y ajoutant rien, n'y supprimant rien" (IV,13). L'inspiration individuelle, vînt-elle de l'Esprit saint, est subordonnée à des commandements reçus, établis, souverains. "Si quelqu'un vient à vous et vous enseigne tout ce qui est dit ici, écoutez-le: mais si, à l'encontre, il vous enseigne une doctrine autre et dissolvante, ne l'écoutez pas"(XI,1-2). Il y a donc une *didachè*, une doctrine, réglée déjà et come définie, une doctrine contre laquelle rien n'est recevable.[22]

In short, it seems that we have in the *Didache* one step — although difficult to situate in history — toward what later was to become a complete systematization of Christianity. Looking back from our vantage-point today, this approach appears to be quite disadvantageous for the history of Christianity, but it is not so easy to say that this was also the case for the milieu toward which the *Didache* was directed, for, as one writer put it:

> The *Didache* was widely received in the Church, venerated almost as Scripture by some, and incorporated into later works, so it must have struck a chord in general Christian sentiment.[23]

The *Didache* itself gives us a hint as to why such "un christianisme fait de préceptes nets et autoritaires fondés sur la parole du Seigneur" might have been quite acceptable to its recipients. That milieu for which the Didache was originally intended (whenever and wherever that may have been) was one in which the spontaneity of the Spirit, although it was highly appreciated — as is evidenced by the central place given to the prophets — was nonetheless on the wane. The whole series of "practical and hardheaded, but somewhat simple-minded expedients"[24] for testing the true prophet bears witness to this. "The older system of dependence on prophets and teachers is breaking down; but bishops and deacons have not yet taken their place."[25] In such an uncertain situation, where the known and respected itinerant charismatic ministry was dying out, there is every reason to believe that a simple, apodictic manual of clear "apostolic" teaching would have been quite welcome.

In any case, it is quite obvious that the *Didache's* approach to Christian life centers more on the regulation of practice than on the deepening of insight. "Theology, even in a rudimentary sense," remarks R.A. Kraft, "is almost completely lacking."[26] While this is not *exactly* the case, it is true that if we seek the kind of Christianity represented by the *Didache* we do much better to look first at the practices which it prescribes. Here we have a fairly wide variety; outlined briefly, they run as follows:

(1) Careful basic moral instruction before Baptism (7:1; 11:1);

(2) Prebaptismal fasting, both by those to be baptized as well as by the baptizer (7:4);

(3) Baptism in the Trinitarian formula (7:1,3), although Baptism in the "name of the Lord" is also mentioned (9:5);

(4) Possibly a special Eucharistic meal with the initiants after the baptismal service (9:1 - 10:6 [?]);

(5) Possibly an anointing with oil following this meal — or perhaps directly

after the Baptism (10:8 variant; cf. the Coptic fragment);

(6) Regular fasts on Wednesdays and Fridays (8:1; cf. 1:3), as opposed to the Jewish fasts on Mondays and Thursdays.

(7) Meetings on the Lord's Day (14:1-3; 16:2), which included the *fractio panis* and tharksgiving prayers with some form of confession of transgressions beforehand (14:1).

(8) Recitation of the "Lord's Prayer" three times daily (8:2-3), following the Jewish three special times for prayer;[27]

(9) Possibly also a daily community gathering (4:2; see 16:2);

(10) Regular attention to community discipline and prayer (15:3ff; cf. also 1:3; 2:7; 4:3; 4:14), acts of charity, such as almsgiving, etc. (15:4; see also 1:5-6; 4:4-8; 11:12; 13:4), as well as the regular contribution of "first fruits" to the prophet, if the particular community had one (13:3-7).

(11) The extending of hospitality to travelling Christians, and their leaders (11:3-12:5).

What there is of theology in the *Didache* has been included more or less *en passante* among the precepts and prescriptions, and has to be gleaned from the text. The eschatological ch. 16, however, is something of an exception to this. Leaving aside for the time being questions on ministry and Eucharist, we can consider briefly those remarks in the *Didache* which would generally fall under Christology, ecclesiology and eschatology.

The *Didache's* CHRISTOLOGY rests mostly in the titles employed. "Jesus" is mentioned by name only in the liturgical prayers and there in the thrice repeated phrase "through Jesus your Servant/Child *(dià Iēsoû toû paidós sou* [9:2 & 3; 10:2][28]). In 10:4 we find "through Jesus Christ." This is the only appearance of the title "Christ", although in 12:4ff reference is made to "Christian" and "Christ-peddler." By far the most employed Christological title, however, is *kýrios*. It is applied unambiguously to Jesus ten times in the text, and there are an additional ten uses of the term, all more or less ambiguous, which could apply to Jesus depending on how the final author-editor understood the tradition he had received.[29] R.A. Kraft maintains that by and large:

> The most that can be said is that Christology is incidental to the Didache — it is echoed, in various forms, especially in the liturgical passages, but this cannot be called "theological reflection." In general, the identity of "Jesus" and "Lord" is simply assumed. He is never explicitly called "God," and his functions are seldom defined with any precision (e.g. 16:7f.

describes his apocalyptic role, but nowhere is he pictured as creator or revealer or savior — *there is no reference to his blood, suffering, death,* etc.)[30]

As to *Ecclesiology,* aside from questions of ministry, it is important to note that the *Didache's* concept of *ekklēsía* is both local (4:14) and universal (9:4; 10:5; 11:11). Transgressions are to be confessed "in church"(4:14), but the prayer over the bread in 9:4 asks that just as the multitude of grains were once scattered upon the hills and yet became one bread, "so may Thy Church be gathered from the ends of the earth into Thy kingdom."

And in 10:5 we find the following petition:

Remember, O Lord, Thy Church: deliver her from all evil, perfect her in Thy love, and from the four winds assemble her, the sanctified, in Thy kingdom, which Thou hast prepared for her.[31]

The *Eschatology* of the *Didache* is limited for the most part to chapter 16, the epilogue — an apocalyptic exhortation to faithfulness strongly reminiscent of the apocalypse in the Synoptic tradition.[32] This is not to say that eschatological notions are completely absent in the rest of the work, but only that we do not find there the same pervading eschatological orientation as we meet, for example, in the *Epistle of Barnabas.* Kraft has brought this out quite clearly in his analysis of the *Didache's* eschatology; he points out:

It is true that the Two Ways section alludes to "the reward" (4:7b; 5:2c = *Barn.* 19:11a; 20:2c), and the prayers repeat traditional language about the coming "kingdom" and the activity of "evil" or the "Evil One" (8:2; 9:4; 10:5), the passing away of "this world" and the coming of the Lord (10:6), but these are extremely faint echoes and inspire no confidence that the community which used them was waiting with bated breath for the consummation.[33] Apart from chapter 16 we find that such matters as "the Lord's return," resurrection, judgement, and final salvation have no real role in the *Didache.* There are a few references to "judgement" in *Didache* 1-15, but none of them are strictly eschatological (4:3; 5:2; 11:11f.). The "resurrection" is mentioned only in 16:6f. There is no clear concept of a new creation in the last days (cf. 4:10[?]), but only general exhortations to "watch" and "be ready"(16:1) so as to be "perfect" (16:2; see 1:4; 6:2; 10:5) and "endure" to salvation (16:5; cf. 1:4 var.; 5:2; 8:2; 10:5).[34]

Furthermore, although the traditional categories of SOTERIOLOGY — sin, repentance and satisfaction — are not absent (cf., e.g., 4:6; 4:14; 10:6; 14:1; 15:3), it is nonetheless quite striking that these are never treated in relation to the Crucifixion.

The general prerequisite to participation in the community life appears to have been baptism "in the Lord's Name", but the theological significance of baptism is never treated (explicitly or implicitly). There is no indication in the *Didache* that an initial repentance connected with the idea of personal sinfulness for which Jesus' death atones was considered basic to the Christian life.[35]

C. THE DIDACHE AND SCRIPTURE

The most conspicuous aspect when we compare the *Didache* with Scripture is the predominant presence of the Matthean tradition. K. Bihlmeyer records more than 45 word resemblances or allusions to the Gospel according to *Matthew*.[36] Whether these Matthean relationships, as well as those with other New Testament books, are based on oral or written tradition is a remarkably difficult question and remarkably different answers have been given. S.E. Johnson, for example, has argued that the *Didache* represents an expansion of the Gospel according to *Matthew,* especially 28:19-20: all nations are to be baptized in the Name of the Father, Son and Holy Spirit, and are to be taught to observe all the commandments given to the Apostles by the Lord. This kind of Baptism, he argues, is discussed in *Did.* 7; the "way of the teaching" is to be found, in catechetical form, in *Did.* 1-6; and the liturgical instructions based on Matthew 6 occur in *Did.* 8. To these materials the didachist has added liturgical models (chs. 9-10), advice on Church life (chs. 11-15) and an apocalypse based on *Matthew* 24.[37]

H. Köster, in a much more detailed study, has subjected the alleged quotations from, or allusions to, *Matthew* to individual analysis, with the conclusion that the didachist's primary source was the oral tradition.[38] He adds, however:

Did. 1,3ff. stehen zwar Logien, die auf Mt. und Luk. zurückgehen, aber nicht vom Kompilator selbst direkt aus schriftlichen Evangelien entnommen wurden, sondern innerhalb einer schon fertigen Logiensammlung auf ihn kamen. An einigen weiteren Stellen aber war die Wahrscheinlichkeit sehr gross, dass sie vom Kompilator der Did. nicht unbewusst innerhalb grösserer Komplexe übernommen, sondern von ihm bewusst aus eigener Kenntnis synoptischer Überlieferung in sein Werk eingefügt wurden (Did. 7,1; 8,2; 9,5; 15,3). In der unmittelbaren Nachbarschaft gerade solcher Stellen fanden sich auch die Hinweise auf das *euaggélion*, das zwar Did. 8,2 auch die mündliche Predigt bezeichnen könnte, aber in Did. 15,3.4 doch wohl ein schriftliches Evangelium meint. Dennoch stammen Did. 7,1; 8,2; 9,5; 15,3 nicht aus einem schriftlichen Evangelium sondern aus der freien Überlieferung.

Es ergibt sich also, dass der Kompilator der Did. wohl schon ein schriftliches Evangelium kannte, aber nicht selbst benutzte, sondern nur auf dasselbe verwies. Dass schriftliche Evangelien (Mt. und Luk.) zur Zeit der Did. schon für Herrenwortsammlungen benutzt wurden, beweist ihre Verwendung in Did. 1,3ff. Did. setzt also die Existenz der Synoptiker voraus, aber nicht ihre Geltung als massgebliche Quelle dessen, was der Herr gesagt und seiner Gemeinde zu tun befohlen hat. In dieser Beziehung steht die Did. nicht hinter den synoptischen Evangelien sonder neben ihnen.[39]

As to the Old Testament, the *Didache* quotes directly only from *Malachi* (1:11,14 in 14:3), from *Zachariah* (14:5 in 16:7), and apparently from *Sirach* (12:1; 7:22 in 1:6). According to R.M. Grant, these quotes from *Sirach* as well as a number of other allusions to it (*Sir.* 4:5[*Did.* 4:8], 4:36[4:5], 7:30[1:2], 7:31-32[13:3], 8:1[1:4]) point to the Jewish-Christian origin of its author.[40]

Those scholars who uphold a considerably later dating of the *Didache* and its dependence on the *Epistle of Barnabas* — F.E. Vokes and J. Muilenburg, to mention but two[41] — accept as quite obvious that the didachist worked with written New Testament texts, adapting and paraphrasing them to fit his work.

J.-P. Audet who upholds a 50-70 C.E. dating solves the relationship to Scripture by dividing the text at 11:3 into an earlier D I (excluding certain "interpolations") which drew on oral Gospel tradition, and D II (11:3 — 16:8) which was composed toward the year 70 C.E. after the publication of a pre-Matthean "Gospel" "apparenté à la tradition de *Mt.* sans être *Mt.* lui-même," which the compiler of the *Didache* then used.[42]

Besides the books of Scripture already mentioned, Bihlmeyer records word relationships or allusions(in most cases only a word or two) with the following books: *Exodus, Leviticus, Deuteronomy, Psalms, Proverbs, Wisdom, Isaiah, Jeremiah, John, Acts, Romans, 1 Corinthians, Ephesians, Colossians, 1 & 2 Thessalonians, 1 Timothy, Titus, Hebrews, 1 & 2 Peter, 1 & 2 John, Jude,* and the *Apocalypse.*[43] None of the New Testament resemblances just noted, however, are such that they could not be explained by a common religious language and the presence of a strong oral tradition.

II. Ministerial Groups

The *Didache* speaks of five ministerial groups. Let us turn immediately to the texts:

A) Apostles and Prophets — (11:3-12)

Now concerning the *apostles* and *prophets*. Act in accordance with the precept of the gospel. 4. Every *apostle* who comes to you should be received as the Lord. 5. But he should not remain more than one day, and if there is some necessity a second as well; but if he should remain for three, he is a false *prophet*. 6. And when the *apostle* departs, he should receive nothing but bread until he finds his next lodging. But if he requests money, he is a false *prophet*.

7. And you must neither put to the test nor pass judgement on any *prophet* who speaks forth in the spirit. For every (other) sin will be forgiven, but this sin will not be forgiven [see *Matt.* 12:31]. 8. And not everyone who speaks forth in the spirit is a *prophet,* but only if he has the kind of behavior which the Lord approves. From his behavior, then, will the false *prophet* and the true *prophet* be known. 9. And every *prophet* who, in the spirit, orders a table to be spread shall not eat therefrom; but if he does he is a false prophet. 10. And every *prophet* who teaches the truth, but does not do the things he teaches, is a false *prophet*. 11. And every *prophet* who has met the test — who is genuine — who acts with a view to symbolizing the mystery of the Church [literally: who acts with a view to a worldly mystery of the Church][44] but does not teach others to do what he is doing, he shall not be judged by you. For he has his judgement with God — for the *prophets* of old did similarly. 12. And whoever says in the spirit, "Give me money," or

anything else, do not listen to him. But if he says it should be given for others who are in need, let no one judge him.
(13-1 & 13:3-7)
1. And every true *prophet* who wishes to settle among you deserves his food. ... 3 Take, therefore, every first fruit — of the produce of the wine press and threshing floor, and of cattle and sheep — and give it to the *prophets*. For they are your high priests. 4. But if you have no *prophet*, give it to the poor. 5. If you make a batch of dough, take the "first fruit" and give it in accord with the commandment. 6. Similarly with a jug of wine or of oil, take the "first fruit" and give to the *prophets*. 7. And so with money, and clothing, and every possession — take whatever "first fit" seems appropriate to you and give it in accord with the commandment.
(10:7)
But permit the *prophets* to give thanks *(eucharisteîn)* as they see fit.

B) Teachers — (11:1-2)

1. Thus, whoever comes and teaches you all the aforesaid things, receive him. 2. And if the *teacher* himself turns aside and teaches another *Didache* which undermines the aforesaid, do not listen to him. But if his teaching fosters righteousness and knowledge of the Lord, receive him as the Lord.
(13:2)
Similarly, a true *teacher* is himself worthy, like the workman, of his food.

C) *Epískopoi* and *diákonoi* — (15:1-2)

Appoint for yourselves, therefore, *epískopoi* and *diákonoi* who are worthy of the Lord — men who are unassuming and not greedy, who are honest [cf. *1 Tim.* 3:2-13; *Tit.* 1:5-9] and have been proved, for they also minister *(leitourgoûsi)* to you the ministry *(leitourgían)* of the *prophets* and *teachers*. 2. Therefore, do not hold them in contempt, for they are honorable men among you, along with the *prophets* and *teachers*.

COMMENTARY

These are all the texts in the *Didache* where particular Christian ministers are named.[45] The first three of these, i.e. *apostles, prophets* and *teachers,* seem to have had in common the function of itinerant missionary. And among these it is quite clear that those called "apostles" were the most itinerant; indeed, if the prescriptions of 11:4-6 were carried out by the Christian communities, then these "apostles" were virtually forced to keep moving. From the texts themselves, this seems to be the only distinguishing characteristic between the "apostles" and the "prophets," for "no difference between their respective functions can be discerned."[46] In short, the "apostles" of the *Didache* appear to have been very mobile, prophetic teachers whose function it was to extend their witness throughout the whole Church.

The most striking point in the overall picture is the centrality of the true prophet. *Acts, 1 Corinthians* and *Ephesians* also record a very high regard for the Christian prophets, but not to the extent found in the *Didache*. This is especially true with regard to rendering them the "primitiae"(*Did.* 13:3-7).

According to the texts, the function of the *Didache* prophets is both charismatic(to speak "in the spirit"[11:7,8,9,12]) and liturgical (15:2). In the latter, their "giving of thanks" does not appear to be in any way limited by the models given in chs. 9 and 10 (cf. 10:7). Theirs is a ministry given by the Spirit not by the community, as is the case with *epískopoi* and *diákonoi* (15:1). The role of the community with regard to the prophet is rather, *via* several "ethical"[48] tests(11:7-12), to recognize him for what he is, be that a true or a false prophet. Having been proved genuine — i.e. having shown that he "has the kind of behavior which the Lord approves"(11:8), the prophet is not to be judged when speaking "in the spirit," for such an act would be the unforgivable sin (11:7, also recorded in *Mt.* 12:31).

It appears to be a desirable thing for a Christian community to have at least one true prophet settle among them if he so wishes (13:1 & 4), in which case he is worthy of his keep (13:1). The same can be said for a true teacher (13:2). With respect to the difficult question of the "primitiae", R.A. Kraft has remarked that:

> The "first fruit" section in 13:3-7 sounds like an adapted Jewish *halakic* tradition based on passages such as *Exod.* 22:29f.; *Num.* 18:12-30; *Deut.* 18:1-5 (cf. *Neh.* 10:35ff.; *Ezek.* 44:30). The ancient high priests are replaced by the prophets ... and provision for the needy is retained (13:4, cf. *Deut.* 26:12). ... The allusions to "the commandment"(13:5,7) are

obscure. Perhaps the Old Testament laws mentioned above are in view, or some saying attributed to Jesus (see *Matt.* 10:10b, or Irenaeus, *Adv. Haer.* 4:17:5—"[the Lord] counseled his disciples to offer first fruits to God..." !), although in the latter case we might expect reference to the "gospel"(see 8:2; 11:3; 15:3f.). The inclusion of personal possessions in 13:7 may be based on the "offering" extracted from the Eyptians by the Exodus Israelites (see *Exod.* 3:22; 12:35; cf. *Acts* 20:33). The allowance that, within the general obligation to give, the giver has some freedom to determine his exact contribution (13:7; cf. 6:2f.!) is similar to Justin's claim in *Apology* 67:6 (cf. *Acts* 5:4).[49]

The "teachers", like the "apostles" and "prophets," appear also to have been placed in their function by the Spirit, but the information in the text is so sparse that it is impossible to clarify this any further. Like the prophets, they minister to the community the *leitourgían;* unlike the prophets, who are tested on their conduct, the test for *didáskoloi* is a doctrinal one. If the teacher gives a different instruction than that found in the *Didache,* one that thereby undermines the *Didache's* instruction, he is not to be heard(11:2); only "if his teaching fosters righteousness and knowledge of the Lord" is he to be received "as the Lord"(11:2). There is no mention of teachers speaking "in the spirit," so perhaps we can presume as does Cayre that:

> ils instruisent, sans extases ni transports, à l'aide des seules connaissances rationelles acquises par l'étude. Ce sont des professeurs de science religieuse.[50]

It would seem that they, like the prophets, are beginning to settle into the Christian communities, but here again the information is not terribly clear (cf. 11:1; 13:2; 15:2). In short, we can perhaps best characterize the true teachers of the *Didache* as catechists particularly capable of imparting Christian teaching — as outlined in the *Didache* — and of inspiring Christian faith, and who also took some leading part in community worship or ritual.[51]

The *epískopoi* and *diákonoi,* mentioned but once (15:1-2), are to be "appointed" or "chosen"(the 2nd, plural imperative used is *cheirotonésate* [by a show of hands:][52]). "That these men also needed ordination by the proper authorities (cf. *1 Tim.* 4:14; 5:22; *2 Tim.* 1:6) the didachist does not say."[53] R. Knopf remarks that:

> Das Amt hängt also nicht am Charisma, sondern an der Wahl, und zwar der durch die ganze Gemeinde; die Wirkung der Amtsträger muss deshalb auf die Einzelgemeinde beschränkt sein, der von Kap. 14 ab ausschliesslich die gegebenen Vorschriften gelten. Das *oûn* führt auf enge Verknüpfung von 15:1 mit dem vorhergehenden: damit der sonntägliche Gottesdienst in Ordnung und Würde vor sich gehen kann, müssen Gemeindebeamte gewählt werden. Ihnen liegt die Vorbereitung der Feier ob, sie werden auch, allein oder mit den Propheten und Lehrern zusammen, die Leitung der Versammlung gehabt haben.[54]

While the relationship between ch. 14 and 15:1 *via* the connective *oûn* establishes the liturgical, communal aspect of the ministry of the *epískopoi* and *diákonoi,* we are at odds to say whether their ministry was then seen to be completely co-extensive with that of the *prophets* and *teachers,* as might be suggested by "for they also minister to you the ministry (*leitourgían*) of the prophets and teachers"(15:1). But, unfortunately, there is no way of learning the exact extension of the term *leitourgía* for it is a *hapax* in the *Didache,* as is also its verb *leitourgoûsi.* Nonetheless, even though the ministry of these *epískopoi* and *diákonoi* would arise out of the mutual agreement of the members of the community, this in no way precludes that those chosen might possess particular spiritual gifts. Just the opposite would be more then likely the case.

Thus the overall picture of the ministry in the *Didache* represents a period in which a group of men called "apostles" are continuing the type of intensified missionary work done by many of the earliest followers of Jesus (e.g. Paul to the Gentiles and the original Apostles to the Jews). It is a period when an ever-diminishing corps of itinerant "prophets" and "teachers" are beginning to settle in Christian communities and minister to them not only by way of ecstatic preaching and teaching but also by leading them in worship and ritual. Apparently to assure the continuation of ministerial service in the communities and/or the support of the existing forms, the *Didache* advocates the appointment of men proved honest and unselfish as *epískopoi* and *diákonoi.* Judging from 15:2, however, the author-editor of the *Didache* seems to realize that this step is not going to be terribly popular among the recipients, even though in their milieu false prophets are so common that tests of genuineness are in constant demand.

It is remarkable that a document such as the *Didache,* which evidences such strong Jewish and Jewish-Christian background, makes no mention whatever of *presbýteroi* — the institution (with Apostles) most identified with the early Jerusalem community and with Judeo-Christianity in general.[55] Nor can we speak of a *mono-epískopos* in the *Didache,* although B.H. Streeter's musing on the *Didache* prophets could well be correct, if it can be established that the *Didache* belongs to the late first century(or early second) mainstream of Church development. He writes:

> There follows, quite inevitably, this conclusion: in any church where one and only one, prophet had permanently settled on these terms, that prophet would have become, to all intents and purposes, a monarchical bishop. He would be the regular celebrant of the Eucharist; he would have control of the offerings from which clergy would be supported and the poor relieved; while in addition he would, on occasion, be able to speak as the mouthpiece of the Holy Ghost. ...[And the] analogy between him and the Jewish chief priest was one which had in it the seed of great future developments.
> Suppose, then, that in the Church of Antioch a time came when there was only one such resident prophet, and he a man of ambition and possessed of administrative ability — in a single generation the Church Order which the *Didache* implies would, *ipso facto,* and as it were automatically, harden into a threefold ministry of bishop, presbyters and deacons.[56]

A final point that should perhaps be mentioned in this section is that by J. Colson as to the presence of the "shaliach" function in *Did.* 11.[57] According to 11:2, the teacher whose "teaching fosters righteousness and knowledge of the Lord" is to be received "as *the Lord,"* and 11:4 states that: "Every apostle who comes to you should be received *as the Lord."* Colson claims:

> On retrouve dans ce texte[11:1-2] de la *Didaché,* la notion juive du *seliah* qu'on lit dans la *Mishna Berakoth,* V,5: "Le *seliah* de quelqu'un c'est comme si c'était lui-même." Cette notion était déjà appliquée par l'Évangile aux apôtres de Jésus: "qui vous reçoit me reçoit"(*Mt.* X,40. ...
> Et d'abord l'apôtre: Que tout apôtre 'itinérant' chez vous *(pâs dè apóstolos erchómenos pròs humâs)* soit reçu comme le Seigneur: *hōs kýrios* (XI,4). C'est a lui, très spécialement, que s'applique la notion du *seliah."*[58]

From here he goes on to cite the various examples from the New Testament where the term "apostle" is used in a sense broader than that of the Twelve.[59] Thus it is clear that he has already accepted the *Didache* as belonging to the mainstream of Christian development and the *Didache's* "apostles" as in some way continuous with the New Testament "apostles" taken in the wider sense. We might note in passing that these two points have not been conclusively established, neither by Prof. Colson nor by the best patristic thinking of the past hundred years. In fact, the most ardent defender of the "shaliach" function as the key to the early ministry, Dom Gregory Dix, calls the *Didache* an "abnormal"[60] "'Nazarene' apocryphon"[61] that "has no bearing on the evidence of the apostolic age."[62]

Nonetheless, if it can be established that the *Didache* is a mainstream document in the development of Christian history and that the ministry of those "apostles" is continuous with that broader circle mentioned in the New Testament, and if the disputed explanation of the "shaliach" function as the key to early Christian ministry can be established as correct, then the supposition of Prof. Colson is indeed possible. The *Didache* bears evidence of being a Judeo-Christian document,[63] and in such a milieu the concept of the "shaliach" would most probably have been known.[64] However, in final analysis, it might perhaps be better to interpret the texts of 11:2 & 4, in which Prof. Colson finds evidence of the "shaliach" function, rather in terms of a context which the *Didache* itself gives, namely 4:1-2, which states:

> My child, thou shalt remember, day and night, him who speaks the word of God to thee, and thou shalt honor him *as the Lord (hōs kýrion),* for where the Lord's nature is spoken of, there is he present. 2. And thou shalt seek daily the presence of the saints, that thou mayest find rest in their words.[65]

III. SACRAL-CULTIC TERMINOLOGY

Generally speaking, there are but four uses of sacral or sacral-cultic terminology in the *Didache:* (1) the three uses of *thusía* in ch. 14; (2) the statement in 13:3 that the "primitiae" are to be given to the prophets, "for they are your high priests" *(hoi archiereîs humôn);* (3) the remark in 15:1 concerning the *epískopoi* and *diákonoi* who are to be appointed: "for they also minister to you the ministry *(humîn gàr leitourgoûsi kaì autoì tèn* leitourgían) of the prophets and teachers;" and (4) the employment of the term "holy"(9:5; 4:2; 9:2, etc.).

A. *Thusía* in Ch. 14

Whatever interpretation one gives to the prayers (hymn?)[66] of chapters 9 and 10, it is clear that the Sunday service so scantily described in 14:1-3 was not completely different, but also not completely the same as the action in chs. 9 and 10. In ch. 14 it is a question of the Christian community coming together for a *fractio panis (klásate árton)* and a communal expression of thanksgiving *(eucharistésate)*. There is no mention of "the cup" as in 9:2, although we cannot conclude with any certainty that it was not included in the notion *klásate árton kaí eucharistésate*.[67] What we do find here, and not in chs. 9 and 10, however, is a confession of transgressions beforehand *(proexomologēsámenoi*[68] *tà paraptómata)* as well as the admonition that all who have a quarrel with their neighbor be reconciled before joining in. Each of these remarks concerning personal reconciliation (although in the 2nd plural) are immediately connected with the notion of *thusía:* "that your *sacrifice* may be pure/[i.e.] not defiled," and this, in turn, provides the occasion for introducing the prophecy of *Malachi* on the "pure sacrifice." The full text reads as follows:

> 14:1 - On the Lord's day (of the Lord) gather together and break bread and give thanks. But first confess your transgressions[69] so that your[70] *sacrifice* may be pure; 2. and let no one who has a quarrel with his friend join you until they are reconciled, that your *sacrifice* may not be defiled. 3. For this is that which was spoken by the Lord: "in every place and at all times offer to me a pure *sacrifice* [*Mal*.1:11]. For I am a great king, says the Lord, and my name is marvelous among the nations [*Mal.* 1:14b].[71]

Why the *Didache* uses the term *thusía* with respect to this particular eucharistic celebration in ch. 14, and only here, is indeed part (possibly the beginning) of the much wider problem of how one came to speak throughout Christianity of "the eucharistic sacrifice." A quite hypothetical answer to the immediate question here in the *Didache* has been suggested by P. Drews. It cannot be proved but it is reasonable enough to merit consideration. He writes:

Indessen nur von dieser Sonntagsabendmahlsfeier spricht der

Verfasser als von einer *thusía*. Warum? Weil davon bereits in der üblichen Liturgie die Rede war.[72]

From the text itself there are several points which stand out: A) the "sacrifice" can hardly be dissociated from the purified interior dispositions of the participants — thus the prayer of each one present plays an essential role in this "sacrifice."[73] B) the "sacrifice" here is identified with the "pure sacrifice" which Malachi prophesied would one day be offered — thus the fulfillment of an Old Testament prophecy (one which, as a matter of fact, implied a condemnation of the then current sacrificial practice[74]) also plays an essential role both in the understanding of and the nomenclature used for this action.[75] This prophecy of Malachi could well have been one of the texts used at the service. C) Also included in this "sacrifice" is the early Christian (what we might loosely call) ritual of the *fractio panis*. J. Colson was indeed correct in remarking that the total action concerned here:

> ne se réduit pas à une "action de grâces". Celle-ci accompagne une "fraction du pain".
> Dans ce texte de la *Didache,* encore qu'il y ait place pour une confession des péchés, la *thusía* semble donc *n'être pas purement spirituelle,* mais consister en un rite: fraction du pain avec "benediction" ou "eucharistie".[76]

thus the elements which make up this *fractio panis* (the bread [and wine][77] apparently)[78] also play a role in the "sacrifice." Indeed, on this particular point there is a danger, as Audet has remarked:

> de presser outre mesure cette qualification de *"sacrifice" (thusía),* avec le desir plus ou moins conscient d'incorporer la *Did.* au dossier de préoccupations théologiques en réalité bien postérieures.[79]

The other extreme, of course, is to deny the *fractio panis,* with the material elements involved, a place in the whole context which makes up the "sacrifice."

B. "YOUR HIGH PRIESTS"(13:3)

The passages in ch. 13 which call for the giving of the "primitiae" to the prophets on the grounds that they are the "high priests" of the community is unparalleled in Christian writing.[80] The text reads:

13:3 - Therefore thou shalt take the firstfruit of the produce of the winepress and of the threshing floor and of oxen and sheep, and shalt give them as the firstfruits to the prophets, *for they are your high priests.* 4. But if you have not a prophet, give it to the poor.

J.-P. Audet maintains — and not without good reason — that this passage as well as the three verses that follow it are a later interpolation.[81] Concerning the use of the term "high priests" *(archiereîs)* he writes:

Aussi bien le titre de "grand prêtre" qu'il donne aux prophètes pour justifier son instruction doit-il s'entendre en premier lieu dans ce contexte de redevances des prémices. Il n'implique pas que ce soit, sans plus, sa "conception" du prophète. De toutes manières, le grand prêtre n'enseignait pas. En revanche, nous pouvons considérer comme probable que l'interpolateur songe ici à la fonction liturgique des prophètes nouveaux (10:7; 15:1). Toutefois, nous ferons bien de ne pas l'enfermer pour autant de façon trop rigide dans les cadres de l'auteur de la *Did.* Il manifeste justement plus d'une tendance à s'en échapper.[82]

W. Telfer writes an interesting commentary on ch. 13:

The pastor, be he prophet or teacher, requires total support. That is, he has renounced all secular employment. Support may be given to him in the form of money, but he must not ask for money. The amenities of his life depend upon the generosity of the parishioners and their reverence for his office. Hence perhaps the emphasis on *arch*-iereîs. In the religion of the Spirit, the prophet is high priest. Dr. Armitage Robinson [*J.T.S.,* XXXV, 1934] saw here a subtle allusion to *John* xi 51, and the notion that the high priest of Israel was unconsciously a prophet. It seems safer to say that that passage and this belong to a common field of ideas. But there can be no doubt about the anti-Judaist flourish in the phrase '*your* high priests'. The destruction of the temple had rendered the Jewish law of First-fruits inoperative; whereas it had previously been operative for Syrian Jewry and constituted its particular dignity among extra-Palestinian communities.[83]

Obviously Prof. Telfer reads 13:1-2 (both the prophets and the teachers are worthy of their food) as in continuity with the rest of the chapter. He makes then the distinction at *arch*-iereîs, implying that the teachers are the *hiereîs*. But in this case, if we extend the Mosaic parallels, the teachers would have a right to the *primitiae* too just as did all the Levitical priests[84] How then are we to explain 13:4: "But if you have no prophet, give them[the *primitiae*] to the poor." And why is it that there is no mention whatsoever of the *primitiae* in relation to the teachers (nor to the *epískopoi* or *diákonoi* for that matter)? In short, the problem is that the text which confronts us does not seem to know of any other parallel with the Levitical priests of the Old Testament except the prophets. "Dann treten," writes E. Schweizer, "die Armen als 'Lückenbüsser' an die Stelle der Priester, die zum Emfang berechtigt sind nach dem Gesetz."[85] In fact we would expect the "Lückenbüsser" to be the teachers, or later the *epískopoi* and *diákonoi* for they are included as those who "minister to you the ministry of the prophets and teachers"(15:1), and in the Old Testament the *primitiae* were a reward to the Levites for their performance of the *leitourgía* (*Num.* 18:8ff.). In final analysis, it seems virtually impossible to solve this difficulty without positing an interpolation somewhere in ch. 13. If we accept the chapter as it stands, with the teachers and the other ministers left completely out of the picture, the message appears to be that the law of the *primitiae* is *foremost*, and must be kept — thus "to the prophets" — and this means giving them to the poor if there is no prophet in the community. Even if the teachers are reckoned among the poor, which is not unlikely,[86] the emphasis still seems to rest on fulfilling the law for the sake of the law rather than as a reward for service.

It is important to note that "Jesus" or "Jesus Christ" is never called *"the"* or *"a* high priest" in the *Didache,* nor is he spoken of as savior, nor is there any reference to his blood, suffering or death — as we have found, for example, in *Clement, Ignatius* and *Polycarp.* We get the impression in the *Didache* that the names of Jewish institutions (high priests, sacrifice, *primitiae*), as well as a sort of vestigal functioning of them in varying degrees, are being preserved *not* because they have been reflected upon and related to Jesus, but rather because they represent the recognized nomenclature and functions (past or present, depending on the dating of the document) of religion in that age (which, given a strong instinct for a certain continuity with Judaism, would be seen as the "types" for Christian institutions). But that upon which priesthood in Christianity came to be based, namely on a participation in the High Priesthood of Jesus Christ who offered on the Cross the sacrifice of his life, is quite absent.

C. *LEITOURGOÛSI TEN LEITOURGÍAN* (15:1)

This is the only appearance of the verb *leitourgéō* (and its noun derivitive) in the *Didache*. The text of 15:1 reads:

> Appoint for yourselves, therefore *(oûn)*, bishops and deacons who are worthy of the Lord — men who are unassuming and not greedy, who are honest and approved, for they also *minister* to you *the ministry* of the prophets and teachers.

We have already noted (p. 234) how the connective *oûn* here connects the appointment of *epískopoi* and *diákonoi* with the eucharistic celebration in ch. 14. The same can be said, it seems, for the ministry spoken of here. The phrase describing the ministry of all four groups mentioned is, as Schweizer has noted, "übrigens in einer für das AT typischen Wortverbindung *(leitourgeîn tèn leitourgían* 15,1; *Num.* 8,22; 16,9; 18,6f. vom Kult, an den zwei letzten Stellen im Plural).[87] We thus appear to have the vocabulary of Levitical priestly service applied here to that of prophets, teachers, *epískopoi* and *diákonoi,* and the tie-in with the use of *thusía* in ch. 14 is obvious. In short, the Old Testament sacral-cultic language is present, but whether this is simply meant to demonstrate a continuity between Christian ministers and their Old Testament "types" or whether the four groups mentioned here were actually considered to constitute a Christian priesthood is impossible to say in the light of the meager data given here. No one in ch. 15 is called a priest; only the prophets (in ch. 13) are called "high priests" and there in conjunction with the bestowal of the *primitiae.* And there is no further description of this "ministering the ministry" given in ch. 15. The most we can say is that whatever it involved (presumably in connection with ch. 14) was meant to be extended by the prescription of 15:1 to *epískopoi* and *diákonoi.*

D. THE CONCEPT OF THE "HOLY"

Obviously that which pertains to God and the "heavenly" will be considered in the *Didache* to be holy. Thus we read "Holy Father"(10:2), "Holy Name"(10:2),[88] "Holy Spirit" (7:1,3), "Hallowed be Thy Name"(8:2), and "the Lord shall come [at the end of the world] and all his *saints (hágioi)* with Him"(16:7). These texts fall, by and large, outside the pale of discussion. We turn rather to three uses of the term "holy" apparently more connected

with the earthly Church, namely those found in 9:5, 4:2 and 10:6.
The first of these reads as follows:

> But let none eat or drink of your Eucharist except those who
> have been baptized in the Lord's Name. For concerning this
> also did the Lord say: "Give not that which is holy *(tò hágion)*
> to the dogs." (9:5)

We have here, as R.A. Kraft has put it, "a rather technical use of
eucharistía,"[89] and there is little doubt that *tò hágion* refers to the cup and
the broken bread referred to in the earlier verses of ch. 9 of which here only
the baptized are to "eat" and "drink".[90] The last sentence of 9:5 is obviously
from *Matthew* 7:6 (or Matthean tradition), but it stands alone in the Gospel
without any real context that might help us here. On this verse, J. Betz has
commented:

> Die Didache bezeichnet ihre Eucharistie, worunter sie noch
> die ganze Agape versteht, als *tò hágion* (9,5)... Sie übernimmt
> damit eine alttestamentliche Forderung, die die Heiligkeit des
> Operfleisches einschärft (*Ex* 29,33; *Lv* 2,3; 22,10-16; *Num*
> 18,8-19).[91]

This point is indeed significant for it would seem to be another application
of Levitical sacral-cultic terminology to a Christian practice. G. Klein has
remarked that the statement at the end of 9:5 would seem to fit better in ch.
14.[92] Dom Gregory Dix states: "The 'blessed bread' of the agape is holy,
though not eucharistic."[93] In any case, we cannot tell whether it was the
didachist's intention simply to apply the words of the Lord to the elements
of the Agape and/or Eucharist spoken of here, or to inject a reference to the
Old Testament "Opferfleisch," or both. Whether we are dealing here with a
eucharistic celebration or an agape or a combination of both is a problem of
higher criticism that we will take up in the following section. One thing is
quite sure with respect to *tò hágion:* it was to have a widely accepted future,
for "in der späteren griechischen liturgischen Sprache ist *tò hágion* geradezu
die eucharistischen Speise."[94]

The next use of the concept "holy" that we should take up is an
application to persons. Ch. 4:1-2 reads:

> My child, day and night remember him who speaks the word
> of God to you, and honor him as the Lord. For where the

> Lord's nature is spoken of, there is he present. And seek out
> daily the company of *the saints (tôn hagíōn)* so that you might
> find refreshment in their words.

The question here is whether those who speak the word of God to the hearer
(presumably the prophets or the teacher-catechists) form a group of holy
ones — *the saints* — in whose words refreshment is to be found, and that
daily (possibly referring to a daily Christian gathering)? i.e. can we establish
from this text a separate "holy" group within the Church, or are 4:1 and 4:2
speaking of catechists and prophets and apostles in the first instance, and in
the second instance the conversation of *the saints,* meaning any Christian
who is without sin — in the sense of 10:6: "If any man be holy *(hagiós)*, let
him come! if any man be not, let him repent." The only answer we can give
is that the connection here is not strong enough to make those who speak
"the word of God" to the catechumens co-extensive with *the saints* in 4:2.
J.A. Kleist takes *the saints* to mean all Christians in the same sense as found
in *1 Peter* 2:9, i.e. in the wider sense — "a holy nation" — and 10:6 as
displaying the narrower sense, i.e. without personal sin. "In 10:6, the
context requires the wider sense (without excluding the narrower)."[95]

IV. THE ENIGMATIC PROBLEMS OF HIGHER CRITICISM

The possibility of arriving at a meaningful conclusion concerning the
origins of sacerdotal ministry with respect to the *Didache* depends to a large
extent on the possibility of situating this document in its authentic historical
context. But today, more than a century after its discovery, the *Didache* still
defies this possibility. Some of the other documents of the Apostolic
Fathers present great difficulties, it is true, but when it comes to the *Didache*
there is virtually no major problem of its higher criticism for which one can
claim the consensus of scholars, unless this be the earlier Jewish oral or
written patterns upon which the document is based. Thus it seems that
perhaps the best approach is simply to outline the major problems and give
a sampling of the opinions held by patristic scholars during the past hundred
years. This attempt can only hope to be representative for an exhaustive
explication would be voluminous.

A. The Dating of the *Didache*

As we have it, the *Didache* possesses virtually all of the ingredients necessary to render an accurate dating impossible:

a. it is an anonymous, quite impersonal church manual;
b. it is a short document (a little over 2000 words);
c. it shows clear signs of having gone through a development, or process of evolution (thus one will have to reckon with different levels of composition, blocks of traditional material, and possible interpolations);
d. there is hardly a single issue among the multiple problems of its higher criticism that even after more than a hundred years of research has won a consensus among scholars.

In short, anyone who attempts to date the *Didache* today has the whole burden of its literary history on their shoulders. It is inevitable, for with the *Didache* the one implies the other.

In a certain sense, though, the problem of dating the *Didache* is no problem at all, for (like any other ancient document) when the other problems of its criticism have been worked out and agreed upon, the dating will be self-evident. In other words, when the train-load of problems reaches the end of the line, the dating will simply *be there*. But a brief look at the wide variety of proposed dating — ranging from 50 C.E.[96] to the fourth century, and even later[97] — show clearly that the train has not yet reached the end of the line.

To arrive at even a provisional dating, a scholar is forced either explicitly or implicitly to take a position on a whole series of problems concerning intrinsic and extrinsic evidence. In a great many cases this evidence is so meager and ambiguous that calculated guesses are the only solution. And thus we find that a great portion of *Didache* scholarship centers on an evaluation of these calculated guesses. This is neither the time nor place to offer solutions to this whole series of problems, but we can at least pose some of the major ones that a person has to decide upon in one way or another before even a provisional dating becomes possible:

(1) With respect to literary relationships and the "Two Ways" material: Does the *Didache* depend upon *Barnabas*, or *vice versa*, or can one accept a "common source" theory?[98]

(2) If one accepts a "common source" theory, what would this source be and what, in turn, is its history?[99]

(3) Of the many mentionings of "the *Didache*" as well as the numerous parallel passages in ancient Christian writings, which are those that in fact know and refer to the *Didache* as we possess it in the Bryennios text?[100]

(4) Can the thesis of Vokes, and others, that our *Didache* arises from a "moderate Montanist" community be unequivocally rejected?[101]

(5) Have all the points which convinced a fairly significant group of English scholars (J. Armitage Robinson, R.H. Connolly, F.C. Burkitt, W. Telfer, etc.) that our *Didache* is an artificial construction, a well-meaning pious fraud, from the later second or third century been completely answered?[102]

(6) If the *Didache* is neither Montanist nor a pious fraud attempting to represent the late apostolic or sub-apostolic period, but rather an authentic document reflecting the actual development in the ancient Eastern Church, does it then belong to the *mainstream* of this development or is it to be regarded as quite *peripheral* to the whole unfolding of Christianity in the East?

These, then, are a few of the major issues that call for consideration before placing a date on the *Didache*. Nor do point of departure and method play a small part in the result one ultimately arrives at. J. Lebreton made the following observation back in 1940 and it is just as true today as it was then:

> La question de la date est beaucoup plus difficile à trancher; la position que l'on prend dépend en grande partie de la méthode que l'on suit dans la discussion du problème: si l'on commence par l'étude des relations littéraires qui peuvent faire déprendre tel ou tel chapitre de la *Didachè* de tel ou tel autre document, par exemple de l'épitre de *Barnabé*, on pourra être amené aux mêmes conclusions que Vokes [150-250 C.E.]; si au contraire on commence par l'étude d'ensemble du livre, et de la vie chrétienne qui y apparaît, on aura beaucoup de peine à reporter à la fin du second siècle cette description, dont le caractère archaïque est évident.[103]

Indeed, after reading through only a handful of attempts to date the *Didache*, one can already see the same patterns of argumentation recurring. After a while one needs only the starting point and method of an author in order to predict rather accurately the dating the author will arrive at.

Still it would be a hopeless task to try to categorize all the numerous attempts that have been made during the past hundred years. Perhaps the most we can say is that two central trends are quite evident: (A) those who accept the document as representing an authentic historical situation in the development of the Church in the East, whether that be a mainstream or a peripheral development. Here the primitive language, the undeveloped Christology and the ministerial forms taken as being in some way continuous with the Pauline forms with the same names receive the most emphasis. The dating here ranges from the early first half of the first century down into the first decade of the second. In this group we find: A. Adam (90-100), J.-P. Audet (50-70), J.V. Bartelet ("before or about 100 C.E."), K. Bihlmeyer (90-100), M. Goguel ("aux environs de l'an 100"), A.F.J. Klijn ("het begin van de tweede eeuw"), J.B. Lightfoot ("first or beginning of the second century"), A. Puech ("deuxieme moitie du premier siecle"), E. Schweizer (90-110), B.H. Streeter (90-100).[104] The second trend includes: (B) those who either deny that the *Didache* represents an authentic historical situation(maintaining rather that it is an artificial construction attempting to project an early "apostolic" situation) or who hold it to be the authentic document of a moderate Montanist community. Both these latter groups uphold the dependency of the *Didache* on *Barnabas* (and some of the authors accept Harnack's approx.131 C.E. dating of *Barnabas*). The span of dating here ranges from about 120 C.E. to on into the later third century. In this group we find: P. Bryennios (120-160), F.C. Burkitt (approx. 200), Dom G. Dix (175-200 or 230 C.E.), J. Muilenburg (131-early 3rd century), E. Peterson, J. Armitage Robinson, R.H. Connolly (all 2nd or 3rd c.), F.E. Vokes (150-250), and D. Völter (131-160).[105]

We can perhaps close this brief discussion on the dating of the *Didache* no better than by citing the best thought on this subject by three of the best-known *Didache* analysts: Kirsopp Lake, R.A. Kraft and Erik Peterson.

Lake writes:

> The chronology of this complex document is very obscure. The original "Two Ways" may be early first century or even earlier. The original "Teaching" is probably early second century, or possibly earlier, and the second recension of the "Teaching", represented by C [Bryennios' *Didache*], can scarcely be later than the second century, though it is possible that a few phrases in C may represent textual accretions.[106]

After a long and thoughtful discussion of this subject, R.A. Kraft concludes his essay with the following comment:

> All that can emerge is the twofold impression: the *Didache* contains a great deal of material which derives from very early (i.e. first-century and early second-century) forms of (Jewish) Christianity; but it would be difficult to argue convincingly that the *present form* of the *Didache* is earlier than mid-second century.[107]

The most critical of the three with respect to the textual problems connected with the dating of the *Didache* is E. Peterson, professor of ancient Christian literature at the Pontifical Archeological Institute in Rome. He writes:

> Unsere Didache-Ausgaben und Didache-Exegesen lassen kein Bild von der ganzen Unsicherheit der handschriftlichen Tradition erkennen. Noch immer erklärt man den Text so, als ob wir in der von Bryennios gefundenen Handschrift sozusagen das "authenticum" der Didache hatten. In Wirklichkeit scheint mir der Bryennios-Text eine späte Rezension der Didache darzustellen, die wohl auch von theologischen Tendenzen nicht freizusprechen ist. ...Es scheint mir sicher, dass der Verfasser mit Aszetenkreisen in Verbindung stand. Gewisse sprachliche Eigentümlichkeiten des Verfassers lassen sich doch wohl erkennen. ... Dass man die Didache in der Form des Br.-Textes an den Anfang der altkirchlichen Literatur stellt, scheint mir historisch nicht gerechtfertigt zu sein. Es ist wohl sicher, dass es eine ältere Form gegeben hat, aber diese auf Grund der Br.-Handschrift rekonstruieren zu wollen, scheint mir eine unlösbare Aufgabe zu sein. Wir können nur Aporien feststellen, aber nicht den ursprünglichen Text ermitteln. ... Es scheint mir gebotener zu sein, auf Grund des Br.-Textes die Schwierigkeiten und inneren Widersprüche dieser Textform herauszustellen, der man noch immer viel zu vertrauensvoll gegenübersteht.[108]

B. Place of Origin; Destination

Another of the major unsolved problems of the *Didache's* higher criticism is its place of origin (and, if the distinction is necessary, its destination). Scholars today admit three possible regions of origin: Egypt,

Syria or Palestine.[109] (Not what one could call a mammoth limiting of the problem!)

An Egyptian origin (i.e. Alexandria or its environs) has been upheld by: Bryennios, Zahn, Harnack, Bigg, Glover, Kraft, Richardson, Staniforth and Vokes.[110] The major arguments here are extrinsic to the text,[111] resting for the most part on the early widespread influence of *Didache* material in the Egyptian Church. C.C. Richardson summarizes them rather clearly:

> That the *Didache* comes from Alexandria is suggested by several factors. The "Two Ways" was in circulation there, for the *Letter of Barnabas* and the *Apostolic Church Order* come from that locality. It is possible, but not certain, that Clement of Alexandria knew our *Didache*.[112] The *Teaching's* liberal attitude toward the New Testament canon, apparently including *Barnabas* and *Hermas*, bespeaks Alexandria. Furthermore, up to the fourth century the *Teaching* was highly regarded in Egypt, itself hovering on the verge of the canon, and being mentioned by Athanasius as suitable for catechetical reading (*Festal Letter*, 39). Then again, Serapion of Thmuis (fourth century) has a quotation from the *Didache* in his Eucharistic prayer. In view of the conservative nature of these prayers, this is a weighty factor.[113]

Syria as the *Didache's* place of origin has been supported by: Audet, Barnard, Daniélou, Hamman, Klijn, Quasten, Schweizer, Streeter, Telfer, and Walker.[114] Several (by now classic) internal arguments have been given for Syria:

> a. Did. 9:4:"As this broken bread *(toûto klásma)* was *scattered upon the hills,* but was brought together and became one..." An Egyptian would hardly speak of grain being scattered on the barren hills of Egypt (where only the Nile valley is tilled), but this would be quite conceivable in Syria. A. Adam is one of several authors who has recorded a custom observed in this century by a scientific expedition in East Syria, "dass die syrisch-nestorianischen Gemeinden in dem Bergland östlich von Kirkuk noch um 1905 bei der Herstellung des Abendmahlbrotes eine eindrucksvolle Symbolik gekannt haben ...[d.h. dass] die nach der Durchführung der Nachlese auf den Feldern zurückgebliebenen Körner würden aufgesammelt und zur Bereitung des Abendmahlsbrotes benutzt."[115]

b. Did. 7:1-2:"Baptize... in running water, but if you do not
have running water, baptize with other water, and if you
cannot do it in cold water, use warm." On this W. Telfer
writes: "The passage on the types of water is peculiarly
appropriate to Syria where the lavish provision of public
and private baths made it necessary to give definite
injunction, if baptism by immersion in a river was to be
preferred. There was hardly anywhere but Syria where it
would be reasonable to expect that a private warm bath
could normally be obtained for the baptizing of the infirm,
and that baptism by aspersion should only be necessary in
emergencies[see 7:3]. With regard to this addiction of the
Syrians to the bath, passages from Lucian and Libanius
will come to mind, and also from Chrysostom, who
complains that even Christian landlords will build baths
for the workers on their estates, long before they think of
building them a chapel in which to worship.[116] The
Princeton expedition found a bath near Antioch with the
inscription on the wall: 'Through the bath Christ entered
into the world, and has opened to us the way to salvation.'[117]
The Syrian Jews carried out their ceremonial immersions
in baths."[118]

c. "The *undeveloped Christology,* resembling that of the early
chapters of *Acts,* suits Syria far better than Alexandria."
(B.H. Streeter)[119]

J.-P. Audet lists eleven reasons for thinking that the *Didache* proceeds
from the Church at Antioch. Several of these are intimately tied up with his
own particular thesis on the *Didache*; we list here those that are not:

(5) Le rite baptismal, offert à tous, sans restriction, et accompli
"au nom du Père et du Fils et du Saint Esprit"(7:1,3),
supposant une église de la tradition réprésentée par *Mt.*
28:19-20, tradition qu'on peut croire antiochienne;

(6) La double instruction sur le jeûne et la prière (8:1-3),
supposant une communauté chrétienne déjà différenciée et
consciente de soi, mais en même temps contiguë à un
judaïsme demeuré fermement en dehors de l'évangile;

(7) L'instruction sur l' "action de grâce"(9-10), supposant un
héritage palestinien riche et profond, et donc, dans une
certaine mesure, une église spécialement apparentée, selon
l'esprit, avec l'église-mère de Jerusalem;...

(9) Les instructions relatives aux apôtres, prophètes et

docteurs(11,13), supposant true communauté considérable
et en pleine expansion, dont l'autorité et les usages
s'imposent, autour d'elle, dans une large sphère
d'influence;

(10) L'institution ministérielle elle-même, dont la composition
rencontre parfaitement la scène de l'envoi d'Antioche,
telle qu'elle est décrite par Luc (*Act.* 13:1-3);

(11) L'instruction concernant l'élection des évêques et des
diacres (15:1-2), enfin, supposant l'initiative antérieure,
l'exemple et, de nouveau, l'autorité d'une grande église,
vivante et hardie, spirituellement située à la pointe du
progres de l'évangile et capable d'en promouvoir les
institutions.[120]

In his *Théologie du judéo-christianisme,* Daniélou gives some further
reasons for a Syrian origin of the *Didache*:

C'est d'ailleurs dans la liturgie syrienne qu'il sera conservé au
IVe siècle a côté de la *Didascalie* dans les *Constitutions
Apostoliques.* C'est en Syrie que les expressions araméennes
du texte: Hosa na, marana tha, amen se justifient le mieux. Et
c'est de là sans doute qu'elles ont été adoptée ailleurs. Les
contacts multipliés avec l'*Ascension d'Isaie* que nous avons
relevés confirment que la *Didache* appartient au même milieu.[121]

A third group of authors gives the opinion "Syria or Palestine,"
obviously conscious of a strong Palestinian influence in the *Didache* and
quite aware that we do not possess *definitive* evidence for Syria (in fact
many of the classic arguments for a Syrian origin apply equally well to
Palestine). In this group we find: Bardenhewer, Bihlmeyer, Ehrhard, Funk,
Knopf, Lightfoot and Smith.[122] A. Ehrhard expresses well the opinion of
this group when he writes:

Der Ort der Entstehung muss aus dem zweiten Teile der
Apostellehre erschlossen werden, da die Zwei Wege nur auf
den Orient überhaupt hinweisen. Der zweite Teil giebt aber
zwei Anhaltspunkte, die entschieden für Syrien-Palästina
sprechen: das erste eucharistische Gebet, worin von dem Brot,
das in Körnern zerstreut war auf den Hügeln, die Rede ist
(9,4), und das ganze Kap. 13, das eine Ackerbau und Viehzucht
treibende Christengemeinde voraussetzt; beides passt aber
nicht auf Ägypten. Wenn such das Abendmahlsgebet einen

anderen Ursprung haben sollte, so wäre es doch recht sonderbar, wenn in Ägypten die Erwähnung der Hugel beibehalten worden wäre. Für den syrischen Ursprung ist auch die Doxologie am Schluss des Vaterunsers (8,2) und in den eucharistischen Gebeten geltend gemacht worden(9,4; 10,5).[123]

Concerning a Palestinian origin for the Didache: Before 1900 there were at least four patristic scholars who held that the *Didache* was written at Jerusalem (i.e. Spence, Langen, Munchen and von Renesse).[124] In the '30's, Prof. F.C Burkitt voiced the opinion that both the *Epistle of James* and the *Didache* are writings that were composed by the later Gentile church at Jerusalem in language that simulated the old documents of the original Apostolic church there.[125] In 1935, H.G. Gibbins analyzing the liturgical sections of the *Didache* concluded that these sections point to Jerusalem between the years 30 and 70 C.E.[126] Erik Peterson, in 1944, maintained that chs. 9 and 10 of the Didache represent fragments of an ancient Christological hymn (built on Jewish prayer forms) which was once used by Judeo-Christians probably in Palestine.[127] But perhaps the most intriguing solution to the whole problem of the origin (and destination) of the *Didache* is that proposed by A. Adam at the Berliner Theologentag in 1956. The following is a summary of that conference;

Die Untersuchung des koptischen Fragments aus dem 5. Jhdt., das *Did.* 10, 3-12,2 umfasst (Texte und Übersetzung: ZNW 1925, 81-99), ergibt mir einiger Wahrscheinlichkeit, dass es sich in ihm nicht um eine Abschrift zu liturgischen Zwecken, sondern um eine Übersetzungsübung handelt. Die Vorlage aber war nicht griechisch, sondern syrisch; das zeigt sich in dem Anfang ("Kinder der Menschen" für *anthrópois),* der Übersetzung von *maràn 'athá* ("Der Herr ist gekommen") und der Fassung von 11,11("Jeder wahre Prophet, der erprobt worden ist, indem er eine weltliche *parádosis* in der Kirche lehrt und bezeugt, der soll bei euch nicht gerichtet werden, sondern sein Gericht ist bei Gott. In dieser Weise haben auch die Propheten der alten Zeiten gehandelt."). Diese vorauszusetzende syrische Vorlage ist gegenüber dem Bryenniostext teils erweitert, teils verkürzt.

Da einzelne ungewöhnliche Ausdruksweisen und Vorstellungen sich als im syrischen Sprachgebiet verwurzelt aufzeigen lassen, gewinnt die Zuweisung der *Didache* in den syrischen Raum an Wahrscheinlichkeit. Der Begriff *Christémporos* kommt in der Form "Arbeiter, die mit Christus Handel treiben" in den pseudoklementinischen Briefen *Ad virgines* mehrfach vor; das stellvertretende Fasten ist in der syrischen Didascalia vorgeschrieben, ebenso das Stationsfasten am Mittwoch und Freitag.

Die dunkle Stelle 11,11, deren koptischer Wortlaut die bisherige Auslegung auf asketisches Zusammenwohnen von Prophet und Jungfrau bestätigt, kann bei Heranziehung von Texten syrischer Herkunft in eine geschlossene historische Entwicklungslinie eingereiht werden. Vorstufe ist die Vorstellung vom himmlischen Geheimnis der Kirche *Eph.* 5, ebenso im weiteren Sinne die essenische Eheauffassung. Die Entfaltung findet sich in der Zeit nach der *Didache* im *Hirten des Hermas* und in Tatians *Oratio ad Graecos*. Ein scharfes Verbot ist in den pseudoklementinischen Briefen *Ad virgines* ausgesprochen, so dass danach die *Didache* nur noch in der Sekte der Messalianer als "Schrift" benutzt werden konnte. In dem messalianischen *Liber graduum* (um 300) ist sie so zitiert; *Did.* 2,7 ist als Herrenwort bezeichnet. ...

Die bisher aufgeführten Ergebnisse weisen auf eine Rezeption der *Didache* im ostsyrischen Raum. Fur die Zeit vor 150 aber kommt dabei nur die Adiabēnē in Betracht, die um 30 n. Chr. mit dem Übertritt des Königshauses zum Judentum bekehrt wurde. Die *Didache* ist als Kirchenbuch für die dort entstehenden christlichen Gemeinden aufzufassen; von den Kompilatoren sind einzelne Gewohnheiten und Zustände in diesen Gemeinden mit berücksichtigt worden, wahrend der Hauptinhalt in der Niederschrift festgefügter Traditionen besteht.

Diese Beobachtung rät dazu, zwischen Bestimmungsland und Abfassungsort zu unterscheiden. Die Adiabēnē mit ihrem Neujudentum, ist nach dem Bericht des Josephus zu Anfang sogar die Beschneidung ablehnte, ist als Bestimmungsland anzusehen. Als Abfassungsort kann nur ein Sitz alter und fester Tradition angenommen werden. Da Antiochien ausscheidet (die Ignatiusbriefe weisen keine Verbingung mit der Didache auf), kommen nur die Orte in Betracht, an die sich die Ausläufer der Urgemeinde bei ihrem Auszug aus Jerusalem um 68 n. Chr. zurückgezogen haben, also Galiläa oder genauer Pella. Ich möchte annehmen, dass von den Resten der Urgemeinde in Pella der entschlossene Versuch gemacht wurde, die Adiabēnē als das Land der nordisraelitischen 9 1/

2 Stämme zu missionieren; das Formularbuch für die junge Kirche Ostsyriens liegt uns in der *Didache* vor. — Die Frage nach dem ursprünglichen Text ist gesondert zu behandeln und bleibt offen.[128]

So ergibt sich als Antwort auf die Fragestellung des Themas: Es ist zu erwägen, ob nicht die *Didache* in ihrer Urgestalt zwischen 90 und 100 in Pella verfasst ist, mit der Bestimmung, den jungen ostsyrischen Gemeinden als Richtschnur für ihren Gemeindeaufbau zu dienen.[129]

Up to this point we have considered a sampling of the numerous and diverse hypotheses on the *Didache's* dating and place of origin that have been bequeathed to us by the scholarship of the past hundred years. Equally numerous and diverse are the opinions on the foremost internal problem to which we now turn our attention.

C. NATURE OF THE PRAYERS IN CHS. 9-10

The general question here — one of considerable importance for the whole Christian Church — is whether *Didache* 9 and 10 can be considered a chief link in the history of the Eucharist.

Patristic scholars readily admit that ch. 14 speaks of a Sunday eucharistic celebration. In that chapter we find the community directed to come together on the Lord's day to break bread and give thanks. This celebration is put into the context of the "pure sacrifice" prophesied by Malachi and those who participate are called upon to reconcile themselves with their neighbor and confess their transgressions. Neither ch. 9 nor ch. 10 makes mention of "sacrifice" nor of the reconciliation and confession mentioned in ch. 14. Ch. 9, however, speaks of *eucharistía* and contains prayers of thanksgiving to be said over the cup of wine and the broken bread; ch. 10 has more general prayers of thanksgiving, among other things for the blessing of "spiritual food and drink." In short, chs. 9 and 10 clearly contain a set of stylized thanksgiving prayers obviously intended for a particular purpose; they are Christian prayers, indeed, but based unmistakably on Jewish table prayers and blessings, as Klein, Middleton and Audet, among others, have shown.[130] The more particular question, therefore, is whether the prayers of chs. 9 and 10 were intended for use at a eucharistic celebration in *the strict sense of the term* (like that, for example in ch. 14, although allowing possibly for another setting).

Among those who say that it was indeed a question of the Eucharist "proprement dite" are: Batiffol, Creed, Daniélou, Decroos, Drews, Goguel, Hamman, Klijn, Knopf, Kraft, Quasten, de Riedmatten and de Watteville.[131] Those who say that the prayers of chs. 9 and 10 were not intended for a Eucharist in the strict sense of the term hold either (a) as Jungmann[132] that they are Christianized Jewish table prayers, i.e. graces for before and after meals, or (b) that they were intended for use at an agape (Dix, Connolly, Maurice-Denis & Boulet, and Vokes ["prayers for common meals or agapes"]),[133] or (c) that with 10:6 there is a transition to the Eucharist in the strict sense, the action of which is not described any further at this point (Adam, Bornkamm, Dibelius, Goppelt, Harnack, Jeremias, Prigent, Schurmann, and effectively Audet).[134] Those in this latter group give varying interpretations of what precedes 10:6, but in any case not a Eucharist in the strict sense.

There are still other interpretations which are quite difficult to fit into any one of the above groups. Betz sees *Did.* 9:1 - 10:3b as an agape and 10:3c - 10:6 as a genuine Eucharist.[135] Zahn calls ch. 9 an agape and ch. 10 a Eucharist.[136] Peterson maintains that chs. 9 and 10 are fragments of an ancient eucharistic hymn which originally was most likely used for the celebration of the *fractio panis* but which was later transformed into a table prayer for an agape.[137] And one could go on and on with the hypotheses.[138]

Those who hold that the prayers of chs. 9 and 10 represent a strict Eucharist generally consider them in the context of the foregoing prescriptions for Baptism and the catechesis prior to Baptism, i.e. as especially appropriate to a Eucharistic meal for the newly baptized. On this R.A. Kraft writes:

> This annual Baptism-Eucharist service seems to provide the most satisfactory setting for *Did. 9-10* — indeed for *Did. 1-10*. The climax of this service was the special Eucharistic meal that immediately followed the anointing and baptism of the catechumen, and from which all non-baptized persons were excluded (9:5; cf. Ethiopic *Ap. Trad.* 40). Such an approach to *Did. 9-10* does not solve all the problems — we should expect 10:8 [the anointing with oil, found only in the Coptic fragment and *Apost. Constit.*] to precede the meal, and 10:7 is best explained as a vestige from the older Love Feast setting — but there seldom is a tidy answer to the enigmas of evolved literature.[139]

That which J.-P. Audet in his book calls the "eucharistie majeure" (beginning at the end of ch. 10) he calls in another publication a "eucharistie pascale."[140]

Those who uphold a Eucharist "proprement dite" in chs. 9 and 10 usually base their position on one or more of the following four arguments:

(a) The explicit employment of the term *eucharistía* (9:1,5)[141]

(b) *Did.* 9:5: "But let no one eat or drink of your Eucharist except those who have been baptized in the Lord's Name. For concerning this the Lord has also said: *'Give not that which is holy to the dogs.'*"[142]

(c) *Did.* 10:2: "We give You thanks, 0 Holy Father, for Your Holy Name which You did make to tabernacle in our hearts..." Some authors see in this use of the "Name" of God one of the oldest forms of eucharistic epiclesis.[143]

(d) *Did.* 10:3: "But You have blessed us with *spiritual food and drink* and eternal life through Your Servant..."[144]

The largest group of those who do not regard the prayers of chs. 9 and 10 as strictly Eucharistic argue rather that this Eucharist in the strict sense follows the meal and its prayers, in the Pauline pattern, and is introduced by the formulae in 10:6. M. Dibelius and G. Bornkamm have written most on this; the former states:

> Der koptische Text verblet es, so scheint mir, die Sätze von 10,6 als Bruchstüke oder als Nachtrag zu nehmen. Der Wortlaut "es komme der Herr" und die Deutung von 10,6 als *prórrēsis* in einer kurzen Liturgie, die durch das zweimalige Amen nahegelegt ist, bestätigen die immer schon einmal erwogene These: die besondere *heilige Handlung,* worin sie auch bestanden haben mag,*finden nicht zwischen 9 und 10, sondern nach 10,6 statt.* Zwischen 9 und 10 liegt nur das eigentliche Mahl.
>
> Dafür gibt es noch einen mittelbaren Beweis. Die Bearbeitung der *Didache* in den Apostolischen Konstitutionen setzt die eigentliche Eucharistiefeier nach dem Dank für das durch Jesus "kundgetane" Leben an und hat diesen christologisch und sakramental, mit Erwähnung von *haîma* und *sôma* erweitert (*Const. apost.* VII,25). ...
>
> Es folgt ein christliches Gebet für die Kirche 10,5 und eine kurze Liturgie 10,6 die ganz dem kommenden Herrn zugewandt ist, aber damit auch dem Herrn, der sich jetzt der Gemeinde naht, in der eucharistischen Handlung. Sie wird nicht beschrieben, ist aber wohl das, was 14,1.2 *thusía* heisst.[145]

G. Bornkamm finds in chs. 9 and 10 the prayers for use at a Christian common meal or agape at the end of which, like the tradition reflected in *1 Corinthians*, the eucharistic Action in the strict sense was generally added:

> Wie im Urchristentum auch sonst feierte man das Herrenmahl im Rahmen einer gemeinsamen Mahlzeit, in deren Verlauf — jedenfalls in Korinth, aber natürlich nicht nur dort — der wohl unter Rezitation der Abendmahls-Paradosis begangene eigentliche Sakramentsaktus eingefügt war, offensichtlich als Ende der ganzen Feier. Dieselbe Anordnung des Ganzen ist auch in der *Didache* zu erkennen, wo auf die Tischgebete (Kap. 9) über Kelch und Brot und das abschliessende Dankgebet "nach der Sättigung" (Kap. 10 Formeln folgen, mit denen der eigentliche, nicht näher geschilderte heilige Akt unter Ausschluss der "Unheiligen" eingeleitet wird. Auch die Evangelien bestätigen das, wenn sie die Stiftung des Herrenmahles ausdrüklich in eine schon stattfindende Mahlzeit einfügen, aber zugleich als selbständigen Akt von ihr abheben *(kaì esthióntōn autôn labòn árton* usw. *Mark* 14,22; *Matth* 26,26). Die korinthische Feier zeigt also in der Tat, dass Agape und Eucharistie noch ungêtrennt sind...[146]

Bornkamm also reacts strongly to the suggestion of H. Lietzmann in *Messe und Herrenmahl* (p. 236ff) that 10:6 should be placed before 10:1:

> Lietzmann hat freilich ohne zureichenden Grund eine Umstellung von 10,6 vor 10,1 vorgenommen. Die Formeln beschliessen die voraufgehende Mahlzeit und leiten die von ihr abgehobene eigentliche eucharistische Handlung ein, die nicht mehr beschrieben wird. An dieselbe Stelle wie *Did* 10,6 gehören auch die Aufforderung, den Friedenskuss zu tauschen, das Anathema und das Maranatha samt dem Gnadenspruch von *1 Kor.* 16. Das Anathema hat dabei den Sinn, zu Beginn der Mahlfeier die Unwürdigen vom Genuss des Sakramentes auszuschliessen.[147]

Thus it is quite obvious that fairly solid arguments can be given both for and against the intention of a strict Eucharist in chs. 9 and 10. In any case, given the wide disagreement of scholars, we are not in a position to make definitive judgements on the early history of the Eucharist in the strict sense on the grounds of *Didache* 9 and 10.

With respect to our quest for the origins of sacerdotal ministry, we can only say that chs. 9 and 10 make no mention at all of who in particular might be expected to lead these specific prayers. They are, however, consistently in the plural (both here and in ch. 14). On this point M. Goguel has written a perceptive comment:

> Avec la *Didache* nous sommes dans une période de transition. La célébration de l'eucharistie est encore libre en principe, en ce sens que n'importe quel fidèle est théoriquement qualifié pour la présider, mais, en fait, l'habitude pourrait avoir été déjà en voie de s'introduire d'en resérver la présidence, à défaut d'inspirés, aux épiscopes et aux diacres.[148]

V. CONCLUSION

We have just considered three of the major problems of higher criticism in *Didache* study which still await a definitive solution. With them, and especially with the question of dating, go an enormous number of other equally unsolved problems. This presents us with a dilemma in trying to draw some conclusions from the Didache's ministry and sacral-cultic language with respect to the rise of a sacerdotal ministry within Christianity. If we cannot place the document in its historical setting, what value will our conclusions actually have? But, then, if the best patristic scholars of the past hundred years cannot come to a consensus on the *Didache's* historico-theological context, how can we in the course of a brief chapter ever hope to do so? The dilemma, at least, is eminently clear.

Let us begin with some of the conclusions that can be drawn from our study of the document's ministry and sacral-cultic language. After having done this, I would like to give briefly the direction of my own thinking on a possible historical context.

The *Didache* speaks of five ministerial groups. The *apostles, prophets* and *teachers* appear to be charismatics to one degree or another; the *epískopoi* and *diákonoi* are (or will be) two groups chosen by the community. Of the five groups, the *apostles* are undoubtedly the most itinerant, staying ideally only a few days at any one place. The *prophets* and *teachers,* who were apparently itinerant, too, are now beginning to settle into the Christian communities. Actually the text says so little about what these first three groups do that we have no sure grounds on which to distinguish the functions of *apostles* from those of *prophets,* nor those of the *prophets* from those of *teachers.* Functionally all we learn about the *epískopoi* and *diákonoi* is that they minister to the community the same ministry as the *prophets* and *teachers* (or at least will do so when they are chosen). This *leitourgía* appears (from the connective *oûn* between ch. 14 and 15:1) to be associated with the Sunday worship, although we find no mention of such terms as "presiding" or "leading." The closest we get to this is the not terribly clear statement in 10:7: "But permit the prophets to give thanks as much as they desire ."

The prophets, in fact, are the center of attraction among the ministerial groups. They are to receive the "first fruits" of virtually all edible goods which the members of the community possess. As for things like clothes, money and other possessions, here the members of the community may choose things out according to their own discretion "and give it according to the commandment." Only if there is no prophet in the community are the "first fruits" to be given *to the poor*. The reason for according the prophets the *primitiae* is stated quite simply: "For they are your high priests"(13:3). This is the only mention of "priest" in the *Didache,* and it is intimately tied up with the motivation behind the giving of "first fruits." Thus, with regard to ministerial function, we find only amorphous boundaries between the different groups; with respect to position, the prophet is exalted above any one or any group in the community; he is placed in parallel with the Jewish high priest. None of the other ministerial groups is paralleled in this way and none of the other groups are seen as worthy of receiving the *primitiae.* Moreover, once the prophet has been proved true, he may no longer be judged by the community lest they commit the unforgivable sin against the Spirit. Here we have, indeed, a great difficulty; the functions appear to be so much alike, and yet the prophet who settles in a community is accorded an unbelievably exalted "position"(although none of the traditional terms for "office" like *táxis, tágma,* or even their forerunner *tópos* are to be found in the *Didache).* In any case, one gets the idea that an enormous amount has been left unsaid in this matter of the prophet. But as the text stands, the prophet in his community appears to be ever so much more a monarch than any of the claims or accusations that have been made concerning the *epískopos* concept in the Ignatian Letters.

Nonetheless there seems to be an ever diminishing number of charismatic "inspirers" available to the Christian communities, and the source from which the *Didache* comes sees a clear value in introducing the *epískopoi-diákonoi* system in addition to the apostles, prophets and teachers. Apparently realizing that this step will not be so popular with the recipients, the *Didache* text adds: "Do not then despise them, for they are your honorable men together with the prophets and teachers"(15:2). It is interesting to note that nowhere in this document which practically seethes with Jewish Christian influences do we find mention of presbyters.

There is not an enormous amount of sacral-cultic language in the *Didache,* but what there is appears at genuinely key places. The Sunday eucharistic celebration is put into the context of the "pure sacrifice" prophesied by Malachi. Obviously the major point here is that this prophecy is being fulfilled by the Christians. And the sacrifice of personal prayer is obvious also from the requirements for personal preparation through reconciliation and confession of transgressions. But the *fractio panis* with the elements that it implies — bread and wine — are also included in that which is described as the fulfillment of the "pure sacrifice." The danger of seeing not the whole context of the celebration as a "pure sacrifice" which fulfills a major Old Testament prophecy, but only the bread and wine as the sacrifice is already inherent in the celebration. The application to the *eucharistía* of the term *tò hágion* where the former stands for the elements which the Christians "eat" and "drink" would only increase this danger. Moreover, the *epískopoi* and *diákonoi* are being introduced to fulfill a leitourgía. The word combination used here *(leitourgoûsi tèn leitourgían)* is a *hapax* in the *Didache,* so we can hardly make any major decisions concerning it. We do know, however, that the same combination is found several times in *Numbers* for the service of the Levites and we see also that this *leitourgía* in the *Didache* is connected with the Sunday eucharistic service. In short, add all of these sacral-cultic "type-" elements together — "your *thusía"*(14:1,2), *"tò hágion"*(9:5), *"leitourgoûsi tèn leitourgían"*(15:1), "your *archiereîs"*(13:3) — and you have the very combination of sacral-cultic terminology upon which a Christian priesthood might be based. From this point the only steps necessary would be for the charismatic or "inspired" members of the community to die out and the *epískopoi* and *diákonoi* become firmly implanted as those who exclusively "minister the ministry" and you virtually have a priesthood. It is interesting to note that this whole development (or being on the way to such a development) may have had little or nothing to do with the original intention for using the sacral-cultic terminology: the use of *thusía* is to show primarily the fulfillment of a prophecy; the use of *archiereîs* has to do with finding a recipient so that the "law" of the *primitiae* can be fulfilled; the *tò hágion* could well have been referring to an agape; the *leitourgoûsi tèn leitourgían* might simply have been Old Testament words given a new Christian meaning. But the publication and diffusion of this text with such a sacral-cultic schema would have opened in other communities at other places the possibility of far different interpretations.

In any case, the *Didache* gives us undoubtedly the clearest connections with the Old Testament sacral-cultic system of any of the Apostolic Fathers, much more so, for example, than Clement of Rome or Ignatius. All the *Didache's* "types" are at the right place to foster a development that could lead to a Christian priesthood along Levitical lines. The one aspect that is lacking — an aspect which played such a central part in the later development — is the connection of the "pure sacrifice" with the suffering and death of Jesus on the Cross.

I should now like to give the direction of my own thinking on the major problems of higher criticism that we have discussed in the foregoing section.

Considering the great Church manuals of the later third and fourth centuries which took over and expanded sections of or (in the case of the *Apostolic Constitutions*[VII:1-32]) all of the *Didache,* as well as the fragments we have of translations into Coptic, Arabic, Ethiopic Georgic, Syriac, etc., I would find it very difficult to admit that the *Didache* in its original form was a late artificial construction ("a pious fraud") or a Montanist piece of propaganda (no matter how "moderate"). It seems to me that we should rather accept the document as representing an authentic historical situation at some place in the early Eastern Church. At the same time, it seems to me that we do well to follow E. Peterson's mistrust of the Bryennios text as the "authenticum" of the *Didache*. I am inclined to think that the "authenticum" (at least the Christianized form of the Two Ways, but perhaps also the matter on Baptism, prayer, fasting, etc.) was most likely composed in Palestine and from there spread rapidly to Alexandria and Antioch. It seems to me that it was from this original *Didache* that our Bryennios original was compiled (a recension of the "authenticum" with sections adapted, for example, to forms of ministry in peripheral areas of the Church).

As to date and destination of this latter recension which we know through the Bryennios text, I would agree with A. Adam (cf. pp. 258-260), i.e. 90-100 C.E. with as destination the churches in east Syria (or possibly north Syria, as Telfer holds). Adam chooses Pella over Antioch as the place of origin for our *Didache* on the grounds that Ignatius' Letters contain no trace of *Didache* material. This seems to me the weakest part of his otherwise excellent argumentation. It is not necessary that the apparently hurried letters of Ignatius, not written at Antioch, should contain references to a document compiled, let us say, fifteen or twenty years before his journey to Rome and directed to the outlying areas of Syria. Not that I inject it as a weighty point here, but C.H. Turner and B.H. Streeter have already pointed out places in the Ignatian Letters which do not prove, but which seem to suggest that Ignatius was acquainted with the *Didache* (cf. Streeter, *op. cit.*, p. 279). The classic internal arguments combined with those of Audet, Daniélou and Ehrhard build a very strong case in the direction of Antioch as the place of origin, and which to my mind handily outweigh Adam's considerations for Pella (cf. pp. 256-258).

As to the nature of the prayers in chs. 9 and 10, I believe that Bornkamm is correct in saying that we have in these two chapters the case of a common meal and a Eucharist being celebrated together.

NOTES

[1]   B. Altaner, *Patrologie,* Herder, Freiburg, 1950, p. 38.

[2]   L.W. Barnard, "The Dead Sea Scrolls, Barnabas, the *Didache* and the Later History of the 'Two Ways,'" in *Studies in the Apostolic Fathers and their Background,* Blackwell, Oxford, 1966, p. 106.

[3]   See E. Jacquier, *La Doctrine des douze Apôtres et ses enseignements,* Lyon-Paris, 1891, p. 8: "C'est un codex en parchemin très bien conservé, écrit en belle cursive grecque, aux caractères très nets, avec les esprits, les accents et la ponctuation. Il contient 120 feuillets ou 240 pages de 0.19 centim. de hauteur sur 0.15 centim. de largeur."

[4]   The codex, which then carried the number 452, had been brought to Constantinople from Jerusalem in 1680 and was returned there in 1887 where it is now to be found in the Library of the Greek Patriarch of Jerusalem, catalogued as *Codex Hierosolymitanus,* 54.

[5]   P. Bryennios, *Didachè tôn dódeka apostólōn ek toû hierosolymítikoû cheirográphou nûn prôton ekdidoménē metà prolegoménōn kaì sēmeiōseōn, en hoîs kaì tês synópseōs tês palaías diathékēs tês hypò Iōánnou toû Chrysostómou sýgkrisis kaì méros anékdoton apò autoû cheirográphou hypò Philothéou Bryenniou, mētropolítou Nikomēdeías.* En Kōnstantinoupólei. Týpois S.I. Boutyra, 1883.

For a complete international bibliography of the editions, commentaries, translations and studies of Bryennios' text prior to 1900, cf. A. Ehrhard, *Die altchristliche Litteratur und ihre Erforschung von 1884-1900* [Strassburger Theologische Studien - Erster Supplementband], Herder, Freiburg, 1900, pp. 37-68. Most of the contributions after 1900 can be found in J.-P. Audet's *La Didache: Instructions des Apôtres,* Gabalda, Paris, 1958, pp. X-XVI.

[6]   Even the title of the *Didache* is disputed. On the problem one can consult J.-P. Audet, *op. cit.,* pp. 91-103, or W. Telfer, "The Didache and the Apostolic Synod of Antioch," *Journal of Theological Studies,* XL, 1939, p. 138.

[7]   Cf. J.A. Robinson, "The Didache," *Journ. of Theol. Studies,* 35, 1934, p. 224.

[8]   See J. Quasten, *Patrology,* Vol. 1, Spectrum, Utrecht, 1950, p. 30: "Nevertheless it would be rash to presume, as Duchesne suggested, that the title points to apostolic authorship. The text in no wise justifies this." Cf. also, B.H. Streeter, *The Primitive Church - Studied with Special Reference to the Origins of the Christian Ministry,* Macmillan, London, 1929, p. 38: "The precepts laid down in the *Didache* are conceived as being an amplification of, if not almost a commentary upon, the epistle (usually called the *Apostolic Decree)* sent out by that council [of the Apostles at Jerusalem] to the churches of Syria. In no way is it implied that the Twelve themselves

conducted a mission to the Gentiles..."

⁹ Cf. E. Jacquier, *op. cit.*, p. 8: "La Didachè contient en tout 2190 mots, dont 552 seulement sont differents. ... sur ces 552 mots, on en retrouve 504 dans le N.T., 479 dans la traduction des Septante, 497 dans le grec classique."

¹⁰ Cf. R.A. Kraft, *The Apostolic Fathers. Vol. III. The Didache and Barnabas,* Nelson, N.Y., 1965, p. 3: "We do not even catch a glimpse of the individual responsible for the publication of the manual. Its instructions are presented as timeless 'apostolic' teachings to successive generations in the community. Even the eschatological section in chapter 16 shares this flavor of impersonal timelessness."

¹¹ F. Cayré *(Patrologie et histoire de la théologie,* I, Desclée, Paris, 1945, p. 43) prefers to call it "une sorte de *Précis* des obligations morales, individuelles et sociales..." P. Verbraken *(The Beginnings of the Church,* Paulist, N.Y., 1968, p. 29) refers to the *Didache* as "a vade-mecum of the travelling preacher."

¹² Cf. B. Altaner, *op, cit.*, p. 38.

¹³ Which helps to explain why such a widely known document as the *Didache* dropped so definitively out of history only to await chance discovery more than 15 centuries later. Once taken up and enlarged upon in another document, the original *Didache* represented only a past stage in the Church's development. It then retained all the interest and value of last week's newspaper.

¹⁴ Cf. R.A. Kraft, *op. cit.*, p. 1.

¹⁵ See L.W. Barnard's discussion of this: *op. cit.*, p. 93ff.

¹⁶ G. Klein, *Der älteste christliche Katechismus und die jüdische Propaganda-Literatur,* Reimer, Berlin, 1909, pp. 214-230; see also: J.-P. Audet, *op. cit.*, pp. 372-433; J. de Watteville, *Le Sacrifice dans les textes euchar. des prem. siècles,* Neuchâtel, 1966, pp. 26-37; A. Hamman, *La Prière. II. Les trois prem. siècles,* Paris, 1963, pp. 15-31.

¹⁷ Cf. A. Benoît, *Le baptême au second siècle,* Presses univ. de France, Paris, 1953, pp. 12-21.

¹⁸ Cf. A. Puech, *Histoire de la littérature grecque chrétienne,* II, Paris, 1928, p. 18.

¹⁹ E. Jacquier, *op. cit.*, pp. 34-35.

²⁰ The author-editor, however, carefully unites Part I (the "Two Ways" catechism) with the teaching on baptism which opens Part II: "After first explaining all these points ... baptize..."(ch. 7:1).

²¹ This sketch follows, with some modifications, that presented by J.A. Kleist, S.J., in *The Didache, the Epistle of Barnabas ...* etc.(Ancient Christian Writers, 6), Newman, Westminster (Md.), 1948, pp. 3-4.

²² P. Batiffol, *L'Église naissante et le catholicisme,* Gabalda, Paris, 1922, pp. 125-126.

23   J. Lawson, *A Theological and Historical Introduction to the Apostolic Fathers*, Macmillan, N.Y., 1961, pp. 69-70.

24   *Ibid.*, p. 69.

25   B.H. Streeter, *op. cit.*, p. 149.

26   R.A. Kraft, *op. cit.*, p. 65.

27   Cf. G. Klein, *op. cit.*, pp. 213-214.

28   *Did.* 10:3 in the Coptic fragment and Georgian text also has "through Jesus your Servant/Child." The Bryennios text, however, reads "through your Servant/Child."

29   Cf. R.A. Kraft, *op. cit.*, p. 70: "By far the favorite Christological title in the *Didache* is *kýrios* — Lord. It is unambiguously applied to Jesus in the preserved subtitle of the *Didache* as well as in 8:2; 9:5(twice; 11:2b(second occurrence); 11:4; 12:1; 15:4; 16:1; 16:7f. The tradition also probably had Jesus in mind in such (ambiguous) passages as 4:1; 6:2; 10:5; 14:1,3(twice); and 15:1. Quite ambiguous are 4:12f.; 11:2(first occurrence); 11:8, although probably the final author-editor of the *Didache* also applied these to Jesus."

30   *Ibid.*, p. 70-71 [my italics]. With respect to "God" as Father and Creator and to "the Spirit," he remarks further(p. 71): References to "God" are frequent: he is the creator (1:2; see also 5:2i), the God of David (10:6), whose word has gone forth (4:1; cf. 6:1), who exercises judgement on his prophetic agents (11:11), who is God of slaves as well as of masters (4:10f). In 10:3 this creator God is called "Almighty Master." Nor is the concept of the divine "Father" lacking — but it occurs primarily in the liturgical portions of the *Didache* — in prayers (8:2; 9:2f.; 10:2; 10:8) and in the "trinitarian" formulas (7:1,3) and also in the almsgiving interpolation of 1:5 (the *Doctrina* parallel has "Lord"; *Hermas* has "God").

Apart from the "trinitarian" formulas of *Didache* 7, Holy Spirit as a divine agent (person?) is scarcely to be found (but see the Georgian translation in 11:7-8). Perhaps the majority of older translations are correct in reading 4:10b in this light — "he comes not to call preferentially, but (to call those) whom the (Holy) Spirit prepared."

We might note here that the relatively primitive Christology in the *Didache* has been used as an argument with respect to the place of origin. B.H. Streeter (*op. cit.*, p. 279), for example, writes: "The undeveloped Christology, resembling that of the early chapters of Acts, suits Syria far better than Alexandria."

31   Translation: J. Quasten, *op. cit.*, p. 35.

32   Cf. *Mark* 13; *Matt.* 24-25; *Luke* 21.

33   On this same point, F. Cayré (*op. cit.*, p. 50) notes: "Mais pas plus que dans les écrits apostoliques, cette Parousie n'y est expréssement annoncée comme proche ou imminente. C'est, au contraire, l'incertitude de l'heure qui est affirmée et donnée comme raison de se tenir sur ses gardes..."

34 R.A. Kraft, *op. cit.*, pp. 68-69.

35 *Ibid.*, p. 69.

36 *Die Apostolischen Väter*, 1. Teil, Mohr, Tübingen, 1956, pp. 150-151.

37 *In Munera Studiosa* W.H.P. Hatch, Harvard, Cambridge (Mass.), 1946, pp. 107-122.

38 *Synoptische Überlieferung bei den Apostolischen Väter* (TU 65), Berlin, 1957, p. 39; see also E. Flesseman-van Leer, *Tradition and Scripture in the Early Church*, Van Gorcum, Assen, 1954, p. 15.

39 H. Köster, *op. cit.*, p. 240.

40 *The Apostolic Fathers. I. An Introduction*, Nelson, N.Y., 1964, p. 75.

41 F.E. Vokes, *The Riddle of the Didache*, S.P.C.K., London, 1938, pp. 93-119; J. Muilenburg, *The Literary Relations of the Epistle of Barnabas and the Teaching of the Twelve Apostles*, Marburg, 1929, pp 91-97.

42 J.-P. Audet, *op. cit.*, pp. 166-186; 197-198. The quote from p. 197.

43 K. Bihlmeyer, *op. cit.*, pp. 150-151; see also R.A. Kraft, op. cit., pp. 186-188; for an in-depth account of these text likenesses, cf. *The New Testament in the Apostolic Fathers*, prepared by a Committee of the Oxford Society of Historical Theology, Clarendon, Oxford, 1905, pp. 31ff.

44 The sense here is unclear and disputed. A.F.J. Klijn *(De Apostolische vaders*, 2, Bosch & Keuning, Baarn, 1967, p. 119) has summarized the best present-day thinking on the point as follows: "De woorden *mystérion kosmikòn* moeten wel betekenen dat het geheimenis zich op aarde afspeelt. Man kan denken aan *Eph.* 5, 32 waar gesproken wordt over het geheimenis van *Gen.* 2, 24 dat betrekking heeft op Christus en de gemeente. Dat zou kunnen betekenen dat de profeten in overeenstemming met dat geheimenis een geestelijk huwelijk aangingen. Dit wordt dan niet van ieder gevraagt, vgl. A. Adam, *Erwägungen zur Herkunft der Didachè* in *Zeitschr. f. d. Kirchengesch.*, 6, 1957, pp. 1-47, sp. pp. 20-30. De vraag is echter wat hiermee de 'profeten van vroeger' te maken hebben. Daarom kan men ook denken aan symbolische handelingen die profeten in het Oude Testament verrichtten om hun woorden kracht bij te zetten, vgl. het juk van *Jeremia* 27, maar ook de gordel van Agabus in *Hand.* 21,10-14. Dan is echter de moeilijkheid dat de woorden 'en niet leert te doen war hij zelf doet' onduidelijk blijven. Daarom gaat het toch wel om een of andere buitengewone prestatie waarover de gemeente niet mag oordelen en die ze zelf niet behoeft te doen, vgl. A. Broek-Utne, *Eine schwierige Stelle in einer alten Gemeindeordnung (Did. 11/11)*, in: *Zeitschr. f.d. Kirchengesch.*, pp. 54, 1935, pp. 570-581.

45 Note that in the description of Baptism (ch. 7) the administrator is spoken of only as "the baptizer" *(ho baptízōn:* 7:4), nor is there any mention of who is to lead the community in the particular liturgical prayers recorded in chs. 9-10. On the former point,

cf. A. Benoît, *op. cit.*, p. 10; on the latter, J.A. Kleist, *op. cit.*, p. 159. We will return to these questions later.

46 B.H. Streeter, *op. cit.*, p. 147; also R.A. Kraft, *op. cit.*, p. 171: "Implicitly at least, the 'apostles' are identified with the 'prophets' through the unexpected use of 'false prophet'(not 'false apostle'; *2.Cor.* 11:13; cf. *Rev.* 2:2) in 11:5-6." Dom Gregory Dix ("The Ministry in the Early Church" in *The Apostolic Ministry*, ed. K.E. Kirk, London, 1946, pp. 240-241) takes great pains to warn that these terms "apostle," "prophet" and "teacher" in the *Didache* may in no wise be taken as the precise functional equivalents of the same terms in *I Cor.* 12:28. Daniélou (*op. cit.*, p. 406) disagrees with this. Harnack *(Lehre der zwölf Apostel* [TU, 2], Hinrichs, Leipzig, 1893, p. 38) states simply: "Die Reihenfolge: *apóstoloi, prophêtai, didáskoloi* ... entspricht überraschend genau der Reihenfolge *I Cor.* 12,28."

47 Cf. *I Cor.* 12:28f.; 14:1; *Acts* 11:27f.; 13.1; 21:10f.; *Eph.* 2:20; 4:11.

48 "Whereas *I John* 4:1ff. advocated a doctrinal test." Ref. R.A. Kraft, *op. cit.*, p. 170.

49 R.A. Kraft. *op. cit.*, p. 173

50 F. Cayré, *op. cit.*, p. 47.

51 Possibly, e.g., by baptizing the candidates they had prepared. Cf. A. Benoît, *op. cit.*, p. 10.

52 See W. Bauer, *Wörterbuch z. N.T.*, 5. aufl., Töpelmann, Berlin, 1963, col. 1742; also F.E. Vokes, *op. cit.*, pp. 150-151.

53 J.A. Kleist, *op. cit.*, p. 164.

54 R. Knopf, *Die Lehre der zwölf Apostel. Die zwei Clemensbriefe* (Handbuch zum NT - Ergänzungsband), J.C.B. Mohr(Paul Siebeck), Tübingen, 1920, p. 37.

55 Cf. E. Schweizer, *Gemeinde und Gemeindeordnung im Neuen Testament*, Zwingli, Zurich, 1959, p. 128.

56 B.H. Streeter, *op. cit.*, pp. 151-152.

57 J. Colson, *Ministre de Jésus-Christ ou le sacerdoce de l'Évangile*, Beauchesne, Paris, 1966, p. 258.

58 *Ibid.*, p. 258.

59 *Ibid.*, pp. 258-259.

60 Dix, *op.cit.* p. 246.

61 Dom Gregory Dix, *Jew and Greek: A Study in the Primitive* Church, Dacre, London, 1953, p. 63.

62 Dix, "Ministry...," p. 242.

63 Aside from those who maintain that the *Didache* is a Montanist document — of whom F.E. Vokes is the strongest proponent — there are few scholars to be found today who do not recognize the *Didache* as a whole, or at least in its major parts, to be Judeo-

Christian. Among the strongest proponents of this latter group one finds: J.-P. Audet, A. Benoît, J. Daniélou, A. Harnack, R. Knopf, R. Kraft, and many others.

64 Even if one were to admit that the "shaliach" function played a major role at the very beginning of Christian ministry, it is the transferability of this function thereafter that raises the most questions. It should be noted that in the OT the "shaliach" was one (usually a trusted servant) personally commissioned by the lord of the household and under oath to him to accomplish a specific, clearly limited task. "So," notes G. Dix *(op. cit.*, pp. 228-229), "Laban and Bethuel[the brother and the father of Rebekah], for instance, could act without hesitation upon the demand of Eliezer for Rebekah's hand in marriage for Isaac, since Abraham could not disavow the action of his *shaliach.[Gen.* 24]." For all the "shaliach" texts, see Strack-Billerbeck,III, p. 2ff, also *TWzNT* (ed. Kittel),p. 414ff.

65 Translation: K. Lake, *The Apostolic Fathers,*I (Loeb), Heinemann, London, 1912, p. 315.

66 Cf. E. Peterson, "Didachè Cap. 9 e 10," *Ephemerides Liturgicae,* 58, 1944, p. 3-13.

67 Cf. J. de Watteville, *Le Sacrifice dans les Textes eucharistiques des premiers siècles,* Neuchâtel, 1966, p. 35, n. 67.

68 See W. Bauer, *Wörterb. z. NT,* col 1398: "*Proex...éomai.* 1 Aor. *proexōmologēsámēn vorher seine Sünden bekennen* D 14,1 (näml. vor d. Herrenmahl; die Hs. hat *prosex...* (= indem ihr dabei euere Sünden bekennt)."

69 Cf. ch. 4:14:"In church(or in congregation: *en ekklēsía),* confess your transgressions, and do not go to prayer with an evil conscience. Here apparently prayer follows confession; in 14:1, "sacrifice." It is difficult not to see a connection.

70 The *Codex Hs* reads "our," but the Georgian transl. and the *Apost. Const,* have "your." This latter is favored by most editors; cf. Funk-Bihlmeyer, Audet, etc.

71 See A. Harnack, *op. cit.,* p. 35: "Maleach. 1,11.14:(LXX). Diese Stelle ist im 2. Jahrh. häufig angeführt worden und zwar mit Beziehung auf das Abendmahlsopfer; s. Just. *Dial* 28 fin;41;116 fin;117; Iren. IV,17,5; 18,1; Tertull. *adv. Iud.* 5; *adv. Marc.* III,22; Clem. *Strom.* V,14,136.

72 P. Drews, "Untersuchungen zur Didache," *Zeitschr.f.d.NT-lichen Wissensch.,* V, 1904, pp. 78-79.

73 Cf. A.F.J. Klijn, *op cit.,* p. 121; J.-P. Audet, *op. cit.,* pp. 462-463; P. Batiffol, *Études d'Histoire et de Théologie positive,* IIe serie, *Epilogue au Nouveau Testament, la Didachè et les épîtres ignaciennes,* Paris, 1905, pp. 121-122; F. Wieland, *Der vorirenäische Opferbegriff,* München, 1909, pp. 34-42; A. Lecerf, "Des moyens de la grâce," *Rev. Réformée,* 22, 1955, p. 85.

74 Cf. J. Blenkinsopp, *Celibacy, Ministry, Church,* B & O, London, 1968, p. 152.

75 Cf. E. Schweizer, *op. cit.*, p. 126; J. Lawson, *op. cit.*, p. 98; J. de Watteville, *op. cit.*, pp. 34-35. Lawson is especially good here on the strong instinct in the early Church to find OT "types" or anticipations to establish their continuity as the Church of the New Covenant with that of the Old.

76 J. Colson, *op. cit.*, p. 275.

77 Cf. J. de Watteville, *op. cit.*, p. 35, n. 67.

78 Although Kraft *(op. cit.*, p. 174) holds that "the passage is by no means unambiguous and a regular community meal could be in view."

79 J.-P. Audet, *op. cit.*, pp. 462-463.

80 "Unless Apostolic Constitutions, II, 25, supplies one" i.e. a parallel. Ref. F.E. Vokes, *op. cit.*, p. 170.

81 J.-P. Audet, *op. cit.*, pp. 105ff.

82 *Ibid.*, p. 458.

83 W. Telfer, "The Didache and the Apostolic Synod of Antioch," *J.T.S.*, XL, 1939, p. 268.

84 See *Exod.* 22:29ff; *Num.* 18:12-30; *Deut.* 18:1-5.

85 E. Schweizer, *op. cit.*, p. 126, n. 506.

86 A norm for giving part of the *primitiae* to the poor can be found in *Deut.* 26:12 where we find mention of "the resident alien, the orphan and the widow" who may share the *primitiae* with the Levites.

87 E. Schweizer, *op. cit.*, p. 129.

88 On "the Name" as a divine title in the *Did.*, cf. J. Ponthot, "La signification religieuse du 'nom' chez Clément de Rome et dans la Didachè," *Ephem. theol. Louv.*, 35, 1959, pp. 339-361; also, J. Daniélou, *op. cit.*, p. 208.

89 Kraft, *op. cit.*, p. 167.

90 The suggestion seems to be present here that the unbaptized had at one time been permitted to partake of the elements and that this was now being forbidden. The whole question of the unbaptized could, in fact, have had a great deal to do with the final and definitive distinction between Agapé and Eucharist.

91 J. Betz, *Die Eucharistie in der Zeit der griechischen Väter*, Band 1/1, Herder, Freiburg, 1955, p. 304.

92 G. Klein, *op. cit.*, pp. 222-223.

93 G. Dix, *The Shape of the Liturgy*, p. 93.

94 R. Knopf, *op. cit.*, p. 27.

95 J.A. Kleist, *op. cit.*, p. 156. Note also that the parallels in *Barnabas* (19:9-10) place the phrase "thou shalt remember the day of judgement night and day" between what in the *Didache* is 4:1 and 4:2.

96 The *terminus a quo* according to Audet *(op. cit.*, p. 199).

[97] See F.E. Vokes, op. cit., pp. 3-4: "C. Bigg believed it to be a fourth century apocryphal work. Coterill in the *Scottish Church Review* in 1884 thought it was written in the late Middle Ages. Sebatier thought it was written before the full effect of Paul's missionary work was felt. Harnack thought it gave a good picture of the Church about C.E. 140, Funk in C.E. 100. ... Burkitt thought it was an archeological reconstruction. In his *Primitive Church,* pp. 144-152, Canon Streeter says that in the Didache we can see a writer in some church with a well-developed presbyterian organization addressing a backward church whose prophets and teachers and bishops and deacons are still disputing for supremacy. ... C. Taylor thought it showed a Jewish synagogue just turning over to Christianity, the majority of its Jewish customs retained and merely tinged with the colour of the new creed. Here again there is no universal agreement on the solution of the problem to be given."

[98] In the past only a minority of scholars defended the originality of the *Didache,* but it is significant that among them were O. Bardenhewer, F.X. Funk and R.D. Hitchcock. That *Barnabas* was the Two Ways source for the *Didache* has been strongly supported by F.C. Burkitt, R.H. Connolly, J. Armitage Robinson, J. Muilenburg and F.E. Vokes. Among the advocates of a "common source" theory we can list: E. Hennecke, A. von Harnack(later view), K. Kohler, R. Knopf, B.H. Streeter, C. Taylor, J.M. Creed, E.J. Goodspeed, J.-P. Audet, L.W. Barnard, and R.A. Kraft. Needless to say, this latter group has grown considerably since the publishing of the Qumran *Manual of Discipline* which incorporates in its ch. 3:18ff. a primitive sort of Two Ways material — a point which helps but certainly does not solve the above problem.

[99] R.A. Kraft, who accepts the "common source" theory, makes the following qualifications (*op. cit.,* pp. 4-5,8-9): "There is no reason to think that the form of the Two Ways tradition shared by *Barnabas* and the *Didache* had direct and immediate ties with Semitic Judaism. Rather, it seems to have flourished in the Greek schools of Hellenistic Judaism for decades, if not centuries, before early Christian writers came to adopt it. Its ultimate origins are obscure and its family tree in terms of Greek and Semitic(and even Egyptian) developments cannot be reconstructed with any assurance. In its Jewish form(s), probably *Deuteronomy*]0:15-19 and *Psalm* 1 played a central role along with passages such as *Jeremiah* 21:8; *Proverbs* 2:13; 4:18f., and so forth. In any event, the theme is ancient and is by no means exclusively Jewish or Judeo-Christian in popularity (see, e.g., the "Choice of Heracles" in Xenophon, *Memorabilia* 2:1:21ff.). Thus it is impossible to say precisely how, when, or where the Two Ways theme took the form which became known to *Barnabas* and the *Didache*. The least that can be said is that it seems to have been a separate written tractate, in Greek, which came into early Christianity by way of Hellenistic Judaism and its practices (a "proselyte catechism"?)." (p. 8-9:) "The basic "common source" probably was not *directly* used by Pseudo-Barnabas or the

Didachist(almost certainly not by the latter) — it is "common" to *their traditions* but seems to lie at some distance in the shadowy background."

The most probable *direct* source of the Two Ways tradition in our *Didache* is in the opinion of E.J. Goodspeed *(Angl. Theol. Rev.,* 27, 1945, pp. 228-247) and L.W. Barnard *(op.cit.,* pp. 99-107), the original non-extant Greek text from which the Latin *Doctrina Apostolorum* was translated. This latter was first published by J. Schlecht in 1900 *(Doctrina XII apostolorum, una cum antiqua versione latina prioris partis de duabus viis,* Freiburg, 678 words, Did. 1-6:1), and comes from an 11th-century manuscript — the Freisinger Ms. or *Codex Frisingensis* 64 - which bore the title: *De Doctrina Apostolorum.* "According to Schiecht, the *de* of the latter MS [in contradistinction to the title of the *Codex Mellicensis: Doctrina Apostolorum,* discovered by von Gebhardt] signifies 'genommen aus', 'excepta ex' and indicates that the translated Two Ways Teaching formed only a portion of the complete Teaching." Ref. J. Muilenburg, *op. cit.,* p. 41. The von Gebhardt discovery was a 10th-century fragment of the Latin text *(Did.* 1:1-2:6), which had been printed in the *Thesaurus* of Bernhardt Pez, was found in the library of the monastery of Mölk, Austria. It was published by von Gebhardt in Harnack's 1886 ed. of the *Didache* (TU, 2, pp. 277ff.) and anew by F.X. Funk: *Doctrina duodecem apostolorum,* Tübingen, 1887, pp. LXII-LXVII and 102-104; also *ibid.,* "Zur alten lateinischen Übersetzung der Doctrina apostolorum," *Theol. Quartalschr.* LXVIII, 1886, pp. 650-655. The Freisinger Ms. discovered by Schlecht is now in the Munich library catalogued as *Codex Monacensis lat. 6264.*

Actually long before Goodspeed and Barnard voiced their opinions that the Greek original of the *Doctrina* was the *Didache's* Two Way source, E. Hennecke had already recorded his conviction that the finds of von Gebhardt and Schlecht give us the lost foundation text for our *Didache* in a Latin translation: "Die Grundschrift der Didache und ihre Recensionen," *Zeitschr. für NT-liche Wissensch.,* II, 1901, p. 69.

J.-P. Audet prints the Two Ways of the Bryennios *Didache,* of the Schlecht *Doctrina,* of *Barnabas* and of the common *Barnabas-Didache* passages in parallel columns, after which he states: "La conclusion s'impose: la *Doctrina* représente, à sa manière, le texte d'une source commune, que la *Did.* a absorbée en bloc (c'est un recueil), et que Barnabé a utilisé de sa facon habituelle. Il serait difficile d'aller contre cette evidence massive..." (op. cit., pp. 153-154). Nonetheless, a major difficulty remains, namely that the *Doctrina* leaves out *Did.* 1:3 - 2:1. Muilenburg *(op. cit.,* pp 40-47) and Völter *(Apos. Väter,* I, Leiden, 1904, p. 391) hold that this shows the dependence of the *Doctrina* on the Didache. H. Köster *(op. cit.,* p. 233), however, rejects such a thesis and upholds the original explanations given by Hennecke and Goodspeed.

[100] Manuals of Patrology often take an enormous amount for granted on this point. Detailed treatment on the mentionings of "the Didache" and the parallel passages

can be found in A. Ehrhard, *op. cit.*, pp. 47-58, F.E. Vokes, *op. cit.*, pp. 27-87, J. Muilenburg, *op. cit.*, pp. 32-47, and J.-P. Audet, *op. cit.*, pp. 211-219, and it is amazing to see how different their interpretations are of various texts. See also several special articles: Th. Zahn, "Justinus und die Lehre der zwölf Apostel," *Zeitschr. f.d. Kirchengesh.*, VIII, 1886, pp. 66-84; M.A. Smith, "Did Justin Know the Didache?" *Studia Patristica*, VII (TU, 92), Berlin, 1966, pp. 287-290; F.R. Hitchcock, "Did Clement of Alexandria Know the Didache?" *J.T.S.*, XXIV, 1923, pp. 397-401; J.E.L. Oulton, "Clement of Alexandria and the Didache," *J.T.S.*, XLI, 1940, pp. 177-179.

[101] Several articles against Vokes thesis are: J. Lebreton, Bulletin...," *Recherches de science religieuse*, XX, 1940, pp. 118-121(esp. 121); C.C. Richardson, *op. cit.*, p. 164; J.M. Creed, "The Didache," *J.T.S.*, XXXIX, 1938, p. 85ff.; but see J. Colson, *op. cit.*, p. 262 (Colson holds that the last levels of redaction were very probably done around 150 C.E., just before the Montanist crisis began.)

[102] Cf. J.A. Robinson, *Barnabas, Hermas and the Didache*, London, 1920; ibid.(posthum.) *J.T.S.* XXXV, 1934, pp. 113-146; 225-248; R.H. Connolly, "The Didache and Montanism," *Downside Rev.*, LV, 1937, pp. 339-347; *ibid.* "Barnabas and the Didache," *J.T.S.*, XXXVIII, 1937, pp. 165-167, and in same issue "Canon Streeter on the Didache," pp. 364-379; *ibid.*, "The Didache in Relation to the Epistle of Barnabas," *J.T.S.*, XXXIII, 1932, pp. 237-253; *ibid.*, "The Use of the Didache in the Didascalia," *J.T.S.*, XXIV, 1923, pp. 147-157; F.C. Burkitt, "Barnabas and the Didache," *J.T.S.*, XXXIII, 1932, pp. 25-27; W. Telfer, "The 'Didache' and the Apostolic Synod of Antioch," *J.T.S.*, XL, 1939, pp. 133-146; 258-271; *ibid.*, "The 'Plot' of the Didache," *J.T.S.*, XLV, 1946, pp. 141-151.

For a refutation of Armitage Robinson, see J. Lebreton, "Bulletin ...," *Rech. de sc. rel.*, XI, 1921, pp. 254-258; also along the lines of Lebreton, cf. J.M. Creed (see note 101); B.H. Streeter, "The Much-Belaboured Didache," *J.T.S.*, XXXVII, 1936, pp. 369-374.

[103] J. Lebreton, "Bulletin...," *Rech. de sc. rel.*, XX, 1940, p. 121.

[104] For all the major attempts at dating the *Didache* made prior to 1900, cf. A. Ehrhard, *op. cit.*, pp. 62-65; the references here in order of appearance are as follows: A. Adam, "Erwägungen zur Herkunft der Didache," *Zeitschr. f.d. Kirchengesch.*, 68, 1957, pp. 1 & 47; J.-P. Audet, *op. cit.*, pp. 187-206 (esp. p. 199); J.V. Bartelet, "The Didache Reconsidered," *J.T.S.*, XXII, 1921, pp. 239-249; K. Bihlmeyer, *op. cit.*, p. XIV; M. Goguel, *L'Église primitive*, Payot, Paris, 1947, p. 141; A.F.J. Klijn, *op. cit.*, p. 96; J.B. Lightfoot, *The Apostolic Fathers*, Baker, Grand Rapids (Mich.), 1967 [reprint of Macmillan ed. 1891, London], pp. 121-122; A. Puech, *op. cit.*, p. 19; E. Schweizer, *op. cit.*, p. 125; B.H. Streeter, *The Primitive Church*, p. 286.

We can note here five authors whose datings bridge both of the trends spoken of above: A. Hamman [100-150C.E.], *Naissance des lettres chrétiennes*, Ed. de Paris, Paris,

1957, p. 111; G.I. Konidaris [80-130 C.E.], *Istina*, X, 1964, p. 72; R. Knopf, *op. cit.*, p. 3: "Leider kann der weite Raum, etwa 90-150, schwer noch genauer abgegrenzt werden"; J. Quasten [100-150 C.E.], *op. cit.*, p. 37; C.C. Richardson [second century], *op. cit.*, p. 163.

[105] P. Bryennios(see Funk-Bihlmeyer, p. XIV); F.C. Burkitt, "Barnabas and the Didache," *J.T.S.*, XXXIII, 1932, pp. 25-27; Dom G. Dix, "Didache and Diatessaron," *J.T.S.*, XXXIV, 1933, pp. 242-250; J. Muilenburg, *op. cit.*, pp. 167-168; E. Peterson, "Über einige Probleme der Didache-Überlieferung," in *Frühkirche, Judentum und Gnosis*, Herder, Freiburg, 1959, pp. 181-182; J.A. Robinson [probably 3rd century], *Barnabas, Hermas and the Didache*, London, 1920, p. 82; R.H. Connolly, "The Did. in Relation...," *J.T.S.*, XXXIII, 1932, pp. 237-253; F.E. Vokes, *op. cit.*, p. 86; D. Völter, *op. cit.*, pp. 391ff.(cf. also Funk-Bihlmeyer, p. XIV).

[106] K. Lake, *op. cit.*, p. 307.

[107] R.A. Kraft, *op. cit.*, p. 76.

[108] E. Peterson, *op. cit.*, pp. 181-182.

[109] Although there have been those in the past who opted for *Asia Minor* (Hilgenfeld, P. Savi, J. Armitage Robinson), *Greece* (J. Wordsworth) and *Rome* (Massebieau). Cf. A. Ehrhard, *op. cit.*, p. 65-66; he also gives the authors prior to 1900 who held respectively for Egypt, Syria and Palestine.

[110] P. Bryennios, Th. Zahn, A. von Harnack (cf. C.C. Richardson, *op. cit.*, p. 163), C. Bigg, "Notes on the Didache," *J.T.S.*, VI, 1905, p. 414; R. Glover in *New Testament Studies*, 5, 1958/59, p. 27; R.A. Kraft, *op. cit.*, p. 77; C.C. Richardson, *op. cit., p.* 163; M. Staniforth, *Early Christian Writings: The Apostolic Fathers*, Penguin, Baltimore, 1968, p. 225; F.E. Vokes, *op. cit.*, p. 218. [111] Although E. Peterson finds some traces of Egyptian *liturgies* in the prayers of *Did.* 9-10; he maintains that the use of *klásma* in 9:4 is explicable against the background of Egyptian liturgical practice. Cf. "Über einige Probleme...," *op. cit.*, pp. 169ff. [112]See F.R. Hitchcock, *op. cit.*, pp. 397-401; J.E.L. Oulton, *op. cit.*, pp. 177-179; O. Stählin, "Zu dem Didachezitat bei Clemens Alexandrinus," *Zeitschr. f. NT-lichen Wissenschaft*, XIV, 1913, pp. 271ff.

[113] C.C. Richardson, *op. cit.*, p. 163. See also R.A. Kraft, *op. cit.*, p. 77.

[114] J.-P. Audet, *op. cit.*, pp. 208-210; L.W. Barnard, *op. cit.*, p. 99; J. Daniélou, *op. cit.*, p. 39; A. Hamman, *op. cit.*, p. 111; A.F.J. Klijn, *op. cit.*, p. 96; J. Quasten, *op. cit.*, p. 37; E. Schweizer, *op. cit.*, p. 125; B.H. Streeter, *op. cit.*, pp. 76, 140, 144, 279; W. Telfer, *op. cit.*, p. 144; J.H. Walker, "An Argument from the Chinese for the Antiochene Origin of the Didache," *Studia Patristica*, VII (TU, 93), Berlin, 1966, pp. 44-50.

[115] A. Adam, "Erwägungen zur Herkunft der Didache," *Zeitsch.f.d. Kirchengesch.*, 68, 1957, pp. 33-34.

[116] Cf. Lucian, *Hippas.* 4 sqq.; Libanus, *Or.* xi(Antiochicus) edn. Förster i 524;

Chrysostom, *Hom xviii in Acta* (Migne P.G. lx 146-147).

[117] E. Littman, *et al.*, Publications of the Princeton Archeological Expedition to Syria,1904, V and IX, iii n. 918, cited in V. Schultze *Antiocheia* (Bd.III of *Altchristliche Städte*), p. 145.

[118] W. Telfer, *op. cit.*, p. 144.

[119] *Op. cit.*, p. 279, and he adds: "Barnabas, the earliest document we have from Alexandria, already shows ... that tendency towards a high Christology which in later times was characteristic of Alexandrian as contrasted with Antiochene theology."

[120] J.-P. Audet, *op. cit.*, pp. 209-210.

[121] J. Daniélou, *op. cit.*, p. 39.

[122] O. Bardenhewer, *Patrologie*, Herder, Freiburg, 1894, p. 24; K. Bihlmeyer, *op. cit.*, p. XIV; A. Ehrhard, *op. cit.*, p. 66; F.X. Funk, *Patres Apostolici*, I, Laupp, Tübingen, 1901, pp. XIII-XIV; R. Knopf, *op. cit.*, p. 3; J.B. Lightfoot, *op. cit.*, p. 122; M.A. Smith, *op. cit.*, p. 287.

[123] A. Ehrhard, *op. cit.*, p. 66.

[124] *Ibid.*, p. 66.

[125] Cf. F.E. Vokes, *op. cit.*, p. 218; also F.C. Burkitt, "Barnabas and the Didache," *J.T.S.*, XXXIII, 1932, pp. 25-27.

[126] "The Problem of the Liturgical Sections of the Didache," *J.T.S.*, XXXVI, 1935, p. 368.

[127] Peterson, "Didachè Cap. 9 e 10," *Ephemerides Liturgicae*, 58, 1944, p. 13: "L'arcaismo del vocabolario è evidente. Cristo è il 'Nome di Dio e vite di David'. Si esclama: 'Osanna alla casa di David' e si aspetta il suo secondo arrivo *(Maràn athá)*, probabilmente in Palestina, sperando che i fedeli dalla sinagoga nel'regno: E purtroppo, i doni largiti da questo Cristo, sono formulati in termini greci: *zōé, gnôsis, athan, asía*. L'ambiente giudaico, in cui fu composto questo inno, aveva subito influenze greche. Il luogo di provenienza non è più da fissare, ma deve trattarsi di Giudeo-Cristiani in Palestina, per i quali l'origine davidica di Cristo era di somma importanza."

[128] A. Adam, "Erwägungen zur Herkunft der Didache," *Theologisch Literaturzeitung*, 81, 1996, pp. 353-356.

[129] A. Adam, *Zeitschrift f.d. Kirchengeschiche*, 68, 1957, p. 47.

[130] Cf. G. Klein, *op. cit.*, pp. 216-230; *ibid.*, "Die Gebete in der Didache," *Zeitsch. f.NT-lichen Wissensch.*, IX, 1908, pp. 132-146; R.D. Middleton, "The Eucharistic Prayers of the Didache," *J.T.S.*, XXXVI, 1935, pp. 258-267; J.-P. Audet, *op. cit.*, 377-410.

[131] Cf. P. Batiffol, *L'Eucharistie, la présence réelle et la transsubstantiation*, Paris, 1913, pp. 57-76; J.M. Creed, "The Didache," *J.T.S.*, XXXIX, 1938, p. 387; J. Daniélou, "Bulletin...," *Rech. de sc. rel.*, 47, 1959, pp. 63-124 (esp. p. 71); M. Decroos, "De Eucharistische Liturgie van Didache IX en X," *Bijdragen*, 28, 1967, pp. 376-398; P.

Drews, "Untersuchungen zur Didache," *Zeitschr. f. NT-lichen Wissensch.*, V, 1904, pp. 53-79; M. Goguel, *op. cit.*, pp. 362-368; A. Hamman, *La Prière*, II, Désclée, Tournai, 1963, pp. 15-31; A.F.J. Klijn, *op. cit.*, pp. 104-105; R. Knopf, *op. cit.*, p. 24; R.A. Kraft, *op. cit.*, p. 168; J. Quasten, *op. cit.*, p. 32; H. de Riedmatten, "La Didachè: solution du problème ou étape décisive?" *Angelicum*, XXXVI, 1959, p.426; J. de Watteville, *op.cit.* p. 24-37.

[132] J.A. Jungmann, *Missarum Sollemnia*, I, Paris, 1954, p. 36; *ibid.*, *La liturgie des premiers siècles*, Paris, 1962, p. 63.

[133] Cf. G. Dix, *The Shape...*, pp. 90-93; R.H. Connolly, "Agape and Eucharist in the Didache," *Downside Review*, LV, 1937, pp. 477-489; N. Maurice-Denis et R. Boulet, *Euchariste ou la messe dans ses variétés, son histoire et ses origines*, Paris, 1953, p. 402; F.E. Vokes, *op. cit.*, p. 207.

[134] Cf. A. Adam, *op. cit.*, p. 11; G. Bornkamm, *Das Ende des Gesetzes*, Kaiser, Munchen, 1952, p. 124; M. Dibelius, "Die Mahlgebete der Didache," *Zeitschr. f.d. NT-lichen Wissensch.*, 37, 1938, pp. 40-41; L. Goppelt, "Die apostolische und nachapostolische Zeit" in *Die Kirche in ihrer Geschichte*, herausg. Schmidt & Wolf, Göttingen, 1962, p. 31; A. von Harnack, *op. cit.*, pp. 28-36; J. Jeremias, *Die Abendmahlsworte Jesu*, Göttingen, 3rd ed., 1960, p. 111; P. Prigent, "Une thèse nouvelle sur la Didachè," *Rev. de théol. et de philo.*, X, 1960, p. 302; *ibid.*, *Apocalypse et Liturgie*, Neuchâtel, 1964, pp. 39-42; H. Schürmann, "Die Gestalt der urchristlichen Eucharistiefeier" *Münchener Theol. Zeitschr.*, 6, 1995, p. 119; J.-P. Audet, *op. cit.*, p. 398-424.

[135] J. Betz, *op. cit.*, p. 75.

[136] Th. Zahn, "Die Lehre der zwölf Apostel," in his *Forschungen*, III, pp. 293-297.

[137] E. Peterson, "Didachè Cap. 9 e 10," pp. 8-11[esp. 11].

[138] For a resumé of the principal hypotheses prior to 1930, cf. W. Goosens, *Les origines de l'Eucharistie*, Paris, 1931, pp. 141ff; "l'interprétation récente" can be found in J.-P. Audet, *op. cit.*, pp. 1-21.

[139] R.A. Kraft, *op. cit.*, p. 168.

[140] J.-P. Audet, "Esquisse historique du genre littéraire de la 'Bénédiction'juive et de l'Eucharistie' chrétienne," in *Revue biblique*, 65, 1958, p. 394, n. 1.

[141] Cf. e.g., J.M. Creed, "The Didache," *J.T.S.*, XXXIX, 1938, p. 386: "But this one word — taken in conjunction with the prominent position of the directions — is decisive. It is surely impossible that any Christian of any age could use the word *eucharistía* to denote a rite that was not the Eucharist."

[142] Cf. e.g., J. Daniélou, *op. cit.*, p. 71. "Je reste partisan du caractère eucharistique au sens fort des bénédictions. La formule de 9,5:..., me paraît décisive en ce sens." See also H. de Riedmatten, *op. cit.*, p. 426.

[143] Cf., e.g., E. Peterson, *op. cit.*, p. 13: "A causa del 'Nome' di Dio è stato creato

tutto, anche cibo e bevanda, e pronunciando il 'Nome' di Dio sopra il nutrimento abbiamo ricevuto una *'pneumatikè trophé'*, con altre parole: Il 'Nome' di Dio, pronunciato sopra il cibo ha una funzione santificatrice. In questo punto io vorrei cercare l'origine dell'epiclesi nelle liturgie orientali." See also J. Daniélou, *Théologie...,* p. 208; J. Ponthot, *op. cit.,* pp. 339-361.

[144] Cf., e.g. P. Drews, *op. cit.,* p. 77: "In c. 10:3 werden die genossenen gesegneten Elemente *pneumatikè trophé kaì potós* genannt. (Vgl. auch 9,5:*tò hágion)* Dass kann nur vom Abendmahl gemeint sein. Eine Deutung auf die 'Erkenntnis, den Glauben und das ewige Leben' ist eine unerträgliche Verflüchtigung der ganz konkreten Vorstellung. Dieser Punkt ist durchschlagend: in c. 9 u. 10 denkt der Verfasser unbedingt an das Herrnmahl."

[145] M. Dibelius, *op. cit.,* pp. 40 & 41.

[146] G. Bornkamm, *op. cit.,* p. 120.

[147] *Ibid.,* p. 124, in n. 5 he adds: "Eine genaue Parallele zu der aus *1. Kor* 16,22 und *Did* 10,6 zu erkennenden Einladungs- und Ausschlussformel bietet die von Lucian *Alex.* 38 erwähnte Ausschlussformel*(prórrēsis)* und -handlung *(exélasis)* vor der Mysterienfeier, die, wie Lucian ausdrücklich bemerkt, aus Athen (d.h. Eleusis) stammt (Hinweis von J. Leipoldt). Die Formel lautet: *ei tis átheos è Christianòs è Episkoúreios hékei katáskopos tôn orgiōn, pheugétō, hoi dè pisteúontes tô theô teleísthōsan túchē tê agathê.* Bei der Austreibung lässt Lucian den heidnischen Liturgen rufen: *éxō Christianoús* und die Menge mit *éxō Epikoureíous* respondieren. — Näheres siehe in meinem Artikel *mystérion* in *Th. W.* IV S. 811 Anm 17; F.J. Dölger, *Antike und Christentum* (1932)S. 132f.; J. Leipoldt, *RAC* I 260f.s.v. Alexander von Abonuteichos."

[148] M. Goguel, *op. cit.,* p. 368.

CONCLUSIONS

Chapter I was an attempt to place the rise of Christian ministerial priesthood into its broader context, namely as part of the more fundamental human and religious problem of the sacred and the profane. Priesthood, whether it emerges from an ancient pagan culture or from the Levitical family of Israel or from early Christianity, is one answer to the problem of the sacred and the profane. That answer is that there are persons, places and things that are or ought to be set apart from ordinary life because they possess in themselves or have been given a certain sacredness. Either expressed or implied is that persons, places or things which do not possess this sacredness belong to the domain of the profane.

One crucial thing that Christianity did, however, was to end the distinction on which late Judaism rested between the sacred and the profane. This is symbolized in the Gospels by the rending of the Temple veil from top to bottom at Jesus' death (Robinson). Jesus in his life, death and resurrection surmounts this distinction, indeed abolishes the ancient frontier between the sacred and the profane; henceforth there is but one sacred reality, His body, at the same time temple, sacrifice and priest (Congar).

Yet relatively early in Christianity's history a long and complicated development took place, a process of sacralization or sacerdotalization as some have called it, which re-introduced the Levitical answer to the problem of the sacred and the profane, recouping, as it were, the sacerdotal connotations that the first centuries had set aside. Church ministers returned progressively to the Levitical idea of the priest and began seeing their ministry as mediatory and sacrificial action. Christian "priests" were becoming the ones in charge of local sanctuaries, men "separated", members of a clergy, invested with particular powers over sacred things (Wackenheim).

This process has its earliest beginnings in some of the documents that would be part of the New Testament. A few, very few, sacrificial and sacerdotal elements that would later provide some support for the existence of a Christian ministerial priesthood are put in place by: (a) St. Paul in *1 Corinthians*, *e.g.* 5:7 "Christ our Passover has been sacrificed..." or 11: 27 "anyone who eats the bread or drinks the cup of the Lord unworthily will be behaving unworthily toward the body and blood of the Lord..." or *Romans* 15:16 "He [God] has appointed me a *leitourgós* (cultic minister, priest, servant) of Jesus Christ, and I am to carry out my priestly (sacred) duty by bringing the Good News from God to the gentiles, and so make them acceptable as an offering... " (b) by the author of the *Epistle to the Hebrews* who repeatedly calls Jesus the great "High Priest" and that "according to the order of Melchizedek" and (c) *1 Peter* and the *Apocalypse* which speak of the faithful as a "priestly community" and a "kingdom and priests to our God" (*1 Peter* 2:5, 9; *Rev.* 5:10). There is no document in the New Testament, however, that mentions both Jesus Christ as "High Priest" **and** the whole body of the faithful as a "priestly community." But these documents do come together and form a unity nonetheless when they are accepted into the New Testament canon. If these admittedly few, indeed sparse and minimal sacrificial and sacerdotal elements had never been put in place in the authoritative Scriptures of the Christians there would certainly have been little to no chance of a Christian ministerial priesthood ever developing.

On the other end of the development, we noted that patristic scholarship, past and present, has established that it was only in the third century, after the widespread emergence of the single bishop/leader, that the term "High Priest" is first applied unequivocally to the *epískopos*, especially in the writings of Cyprian of Carthage in the second quarter of the third century. Later, during the sporadic persecutions of the second half of the third century, when Cyprian and other bishops send out their presbyters to preside over the Eucharist in outlying areas, the term "priest" begins to be applied to the presbyters, but in a reserved sense, i.e. priests "of the second order" or "of the second rank." Finally, with the massive growth of the Church in the fourth century and the increased need for local pastoral leaders, the qualification was gradually dropped and by the end of the fourth century presbyters, along with the bishops, were simply called "priests." Thus a development takes place in early Christianity after the destruction of the Jerusalem Temple and roughly between the completion of the New Testament canon and approximately the year 400 C.E. whereby Christianity, which does not have a ministerial priesthood at the outset, begins to recognize its *epískopoi* and *presbýteroi* as Christian "priests" (*hiereîs, sacerdotes*).

Given the above pre-notes, the question still remains, and it is the major focus of this study: *How did the Old Testament and pagan nomenclature for the priestly class find its way into the Church, and along with it the sacral-cultic conception of priesthood and of Christianity?* Obviously the Jewish roots of Christianity and the history of Levitical priesthood within Israel as well as the sacral-cultic tenor of the whole Mediterranean world in the first century of our era play a role. Obviously the destructive end of the Temple cult in Jerusalem influenced the development. But to have something you have to name it, and priesthood has its own sacrificial/sacerdotal nomenclature. The task we have set out here is to search for that sacral-cultic nomenclature in the first set of authentic, non-canonical Christian documents after the New Testament, some of which are actually contemporaneous with the canonical documents ready mentioned. That set of documents is the *Apostolic Fathers* and we have chosen here to investigate the primary documents in that collection, namely *1 Clement,* the *Letters of Ignatius of Antioch,* the *Letter(s) of Polycarp to the Philippians,* the *Epistle of Barnabas,* the *Shepherd of Hermas* and the *Didache.*

1. Clement of Rome's letter from the Church at Rome to the Church at Corinth, i.e. *1 Clement,* presents a positive picture of the old Levitical order, and we saw several indications in the text that suggest that he would prefer to see the priesthood of Jesus Christ more in the line of 'the order of Aaron' than in 'the order of Melchizedek' as found in the *Epistle to the Hebrews.* But to maintain as some have that in chapters 40-44 Clement represents the pastoral service of the Church as a new 'priesthood' not only simplifies, but actually misconstrues Clement's thought. A careful consideration of the four admonitory analogies in chapters 37-44 in their full context, taking into account Clement's use of *ho despótes* and the (possible) anachronism with regard to the Temple cult, shows that it is the **orderliness** in religious life and practice under the Old Covenant that the Corinthian Christians are being called upon to imitate and re-establish in their community.

Nonetheless sacral-cultic terminology abounds in *1 Clement,* and his use in chapter 44 of *prosenegkóntas tà dôra* ('who have offered the gifts [offerings, sacrifices]') and of the term used in the Letter for the ministry of the Temple priests, namely *leitourgía* four times for the work of the Christian overseers shows that Clement and those to whom he most closely relates know that at least part of the broader work of the Christian overseers can be described, however metaphorically, in priestly terminology. While the use of this imagery or typology would not have been terribly unusual or shocking in a Judeo-Christian milieu of the first century, still in later years, as the Letter became widely known and even read publicly, its clear admiration for the orderly service of the Jerusalem priesthood could have suggested a more permanent structure to a Christianity already buffeted by persecution from without and division from within.

Several recent authors add additional dimensions to our discussion of *1 Clement*. James Jeffers sees in *1 Clement* an internalization of the ideals of the Roman ruling class, particularly the ideal of the 'father of the family', who exerts ultimate power over his household where "order and harmony must reign if dire consequences are to be avoided." He notes that Clement equates leaders with officeholders whereas Hermas, his contemporary, sees charismatic and prophetic authority as the validation of leadership. Jeffers holds that Clement's apparently smaller and wealthier community could overlook the past persecutions and the present non-acceptance of Christianity by the Roman elite because it believed the government was basically benevolent. Thus they readily embraced the hierarchical structure of Roman society and its strong ideal of the *paterfamilias*.

It would therefore be no surprise that the Clementine community, one among many as it apparently was, when finally gaining authority over Roman Christianity, would opt for an orderly, hierarchical *church* structure with a single *paterfamilias* in charge, although this was not as yet the case. It is understandable that this structural model, rather than the charismatic one of Hermas (and we might add that of St. Paul), would have to triumph before any type of institutionalized Christian priesthood could be possible.

Gerbert Brunner sees Clement as dealing with the new and demanding situation at Corinth, where for the first time a community of Christians had displaced their *presbyteroi-episkopoi*, by reinterpreting the tradition that he has received, namely that the apostles 'appointed' successors to lead the communities they left behind, into a tradition that the apostles thereby gave an 'order' of office, i.e. that they "added the stipulation [codicil, continuance]" that other approved persons should succeed to that office, and consequently that it would be no small sin to remove such persons from that office. I would add that this position would be even more strongly reinforced if Clement is indeed making a play on the word *tópos*, meaning certainly 'place' but very probably in the letter also 'office' (40:5 and 44:5). Nonetheless, for Brunner it was this move, this reinterpretation of the tradition received, caused as it was by historical necessity, that paved the way for future structural and ministerial developments. For him, it is *the* first-century preamble to the *Apostolic Constitutions* and all the other church orders of later centuries. Should that be the case, certainly an apostolically given order of office would be an additional element to lend strong support to a Christian priesthood. But then, in all honesty, we would also have to be open to the possibility that the *presbyter-epískopoi* were given an apostolically willed office, a pastoral office, which was not a priesthood nor ever intended as such.

In recent times a number of patristic scholars have challenged the almost sacrosanct 95-96 C.E. dating of *1 Clement* primarily on the grounds that the key piece of internal evidence, namely the "sudden and repeated misfortunes that have befallen us" in the opening lines do not refer to a persecution of Christians under Domitian, as both Lightfoot and Harnack had posited. These arguments, especially the cumulative ones presented by Thomas J. Herron, may well earn a consensus of the international patristic community, but we are not presently at that point. If such a consensus does develop, especially should the Letter be redated to 69 or 70 C.E., then clearly a number of internal problems in the Letter would be solved immediately: Clement's speaking throughout of the Temple in the present tense (the Temple would still be functioning), his apparent obliviousness to the friction between Christians and Jews after the fall of the Temple (it would not have occurred), the short development time with the traditional dating between the *presbyteroi-episkopoi* of Clement's Letter and the monoepiscopacy in those of Ignatius (the time would be extended to about 40 years), etc. My hope is that we will hear more about this in the coming years.

2. The Letters of Ignatius clearly present an advanced ministerial structure for the early years of the second century: a single bishop surrounded by his presbyters and deacons. The argumentation of Jean Colson for a "condition sacerdotale" in these leaders, however, I believe is insufficiently founded. From the texts which Colson employs one might possibly arrive at a sort of "condition sacerdotale" in the *epískopos* and the whole (*Eph* 5:2) who celebrate the Eucharist together, although even here we would be reasoning on the metaphorical application of Old Testament sacral-cultic terminology, and rather exclusively on Ignatius' use of *thusiastérion* (*Tr* 7:2; *Mg* 7:2; *Eph* 5:2; *Phld* 4). I do believe, however, that Professor Colson could have shown and *implied* "caractère sacrificiel" with respect to the Eucharist had he taken as his point of departure Ignatius' understanding of his own martyrdom in his *Letter to the Romans* (especially 2:2; 4:1-2; 6:3; 7:3). While this would not have shown *per se* a "condition sacerdotale" in the Christian ministers named in the Letters, it would have shown that at least implied is one of the elements that would need to be in place for a Christian priesthood to develop, indeed a *sine qua non*, namely that the major Christian ritual, the celebration of the Eucharist, be perceived as a sacrificial action united in some faith-filled way with the sacrificial death of Jesus on the Cross.

Although the imagery in the Ignatian letters is often sacral-cultic, we cannot show from these writings the presence of a separate priestly class within the Christian communities known to Ignatius. The clergy/laity-type categories that would express this are lacking and the categories he does use are so inclusive, e.g. *hoi kat' ándra*, "the individual members" of the Church, which expresses otherness without connoting separateness, that even the suggestion of a priestly class would be completely out of keeping not only with his all-embracing theology of unity but also with his own mystical vision of the Church and its leadership.

Over the past twenty-five years the Ignatian letters appear to have survived three critical challenges to their authenticity, i.e. those launched by R. Weijenbourg, J. Rius-Camps and R. Joly. Surprisingly all three challenges have been met with a certain amount of restrained scepticism from the international scholarly community, while readily admitting occasional fine points and poignant insights. In the ensuing years excellent translation/commentaries have been published by William Schoedel and Henning Paulsen, the latter of whom also authored a book of studies on Ignatius. Over the past decade, Christine Trevett of the University of Wales, Cardiff, has probably been the most prolific writer on Ignatius and her 1992 book, *A Study of Ignatius of Antioch in Syria and Asia*, is a truly impressive piece of scholarship.

3. Polycarp's Letter(s) to the Philippians, a veritable mosaic of quotes from the New Testament and other early Christian documents, advises the Philippians to deal compassionately with the embezzling presbyter Valens and his wife. Included with this letter, I would argue, is another cover letter to a collection of Ignatian letters written probably at an earlier date. Perhaps the only genuinely creative insight is found in ch. 8 where he speaks of Christ Jesus as "the pledge (*arrabôni*) of our righteousness."

Polycarp never once uses the term *epískopos* in either the singular or plural, while Ignatius who writes to him apparently knows of the existence of a mono-episcopal hierarchy at Ephesus, Magnesia, Tralles, Philadelphia and also there in Smyrna with Polycarp as *the* bishop. Polycarp mentions rather presbyters and deacons in terms of local ministers as well as prophets and apostles. Widows are also spoken of (ch. 4) and appear to have had a special office of prayer. Polycarp says nothing about the ministerial structures in Smyrna and from his remarks it appears that the church at Philippi has an exclusively presbyterial church organization with deacons.

There are but two instances of sacral-cultic terminology: (1) Jesus Christ is called "eternal High Priest" once and (2) the widows are called "an altar of God" (*thusiastérion theoû*) in a clearly metaphorical sense (4:3). There is no mention of communal worship. Polycarp's calling Jesus Christ "eternal High Priest" coupled with his strong emphasis on the Crucifixion as the salvific moment in history (8:1) and his Ignatian-type admonition "to be subject to the presbyters and deacons as to God and Christ" (5:3) are all elements that would be supportive of a ministerial priesthood if it existed there, but there is no evidence in his writing that would substantiate this.

4. The Epistle of (Pseudo-) Barnabas, an epistle/homily probably designed to be read at a Paschal feast, can be dated roughly between 70 and 135 C.E. Robert Kraft calls it "evolved literature" and Pierre Prigent sees a need to speak of "éditions successives." The document spotlights the Church's tenuous relationship with Judaism, which apparently had reached acute proportions in a community which the author/editor knows. The text tells us more than the other Apostolic Fathers about the life of Jesus, but even this is quite limited. There is no explicit statement about the Eucharist in the Epistle, but some scholars find an indirect reference to it in the much repeated theme of the "land flowing with milk and honey" (milk and honey, according to Hippolytus, were given to the newly baptized as part of their first Eucharist). Actually in reading through the Epistle one gets the impression that Pseudo-Barnabas knows but one sacrament — Baptism, and that in the narrowest of relationships with the Cross.

The most difficult problem is trying to find some hint of Church organization or Christian ministry in the Epistle. There is no explicit mention of *epískopoi, presbýteroi* or *diákonoi*. In fact, the only explicit ministerial function the author seems to know is his own, that of "teacher." There is, however, an allusion to the 12 Apostles in ch. 8: 1-4: "boys who sprinkle the people one by one (with ashes of a burnt heifer), that they may be sanctified by the remission of their sins." They are "those who brought us the good tidings of the forgiveness of sins and the sanctification of the heart — those whom He empowered to preach the Gospel. They were twelve in number to represent the Tribes of Israel...." It is upon this allusion to the Apostles that Professor Colson bases his argument for the presence of a sacerdotal function in the Epistle. For him, the Apostles "apparaissent comme *substitués au sacerdoce lévitique* mais *dans une perspective spiritualisée.*" This argument, however, is weak to the point of being untenable since in the sources Pseudo-Barnabas is citing here, namely *Numbers* 19 and the *Mischna Parah*, the parallel is not between the "boys" and the (Levitical) "priest" (*Num.* 19:4) but between the "boys" and "a person in the state of (ritual) purity (*Num.* 19:19), a state to which every good Israelite constantly aspired.

Although Pseudo-Barnabas says "we also observe with gladness the eighth day in which Jesus rose from the dead..." (15:9), there is no further precision as to what this entailed.

In the first main section we do find a radically anti-cultic stand along with the author's call for a spiritualization of the Mosaic notion of sacrifice along the lines of *Psalm* 51 (see, also *1 Clement* 18:16-17). The concept of sacrifice itself, though, is not rejected. Indeed Jesus is seen throughout as *the* Paschal sacrifice (cf., e.g. 5:1-2; 7:3; 8:2). Perhaps it was the practice of a spiritualized, internalized form of sacrifice among Christians that would in a later era call for external expression in the Christian ritual. Thus while there are some implicit suggestions that a Christian ministry is operative in the community to which Pseudo-Barnabas writes (some persons must have led the community, called them together, baptized them, etc.), a curtain of silence lies over any further precision in the matter and *a fortiori* over any sacerdotal dimension that could or could not have been present.

5. The Shepherd of Hermas, the longest of the Apostolic Fathers — about 39,000 words — was composed at Rome during the first half of the second century. It recounts five Visions, twelve Mandates (Commandments) and ten Similitudes (Parables) in a simple and direct style. In the Church of the later second century, this text was one of the most widely read of the popular writings, and widely accepted as inspired. In the third century, however, the *Shepherd* met a rapid decline in popularity.

A number of recent scholarly works on the *Shepherd* (e.g. those of Osiek, Jeffers, Maier and Leutzsch), take a socio-cultural approach and see much more in the document than the traditionally accepted purpose of introducing a second forgiveness after Baptism. They see the *Shepherd* primarily as a document challenging the social attitudes of Christians everywhere toward wealth and poverty, especially toward the use and abuse of riches and their responsibility toward the poor.

The *Shepherd* contains a broad spectrum of ministerial nomenclature: *apóstoloi, didáskaloi, prophétai, epískopoi, presbýteroi, poímenes, diákonoi* and various other more general terms for leadership. No other Apostolic Father nor any single book of the New Testament contains such a wide variety of ministerial terms. Yet nowhere is there any mention of how individuals or groups are installed in their function/office and very little is given whereby we might distinguish one group from another. Surprisingly, as Perveden has noted, Hermas does not seem to have any fixed concept of ministry. Brox, in writing about church order in his recent, massive commentary on the *Shepherd*, observes that the document simply shows no great interest in this theme.

There is no mention of Eucharist, nor of a common meal, nor of "the breaking of the bread," nor of an "agape," not even the vaguest suggestion of a table or altar ritual. The several uses of the terms *thusía* and *thusiastérion* refer either to personal fasting or private prayers of thanksgiving or an "altar" in the heavens representing the presence of God. There is nothing that might connect these terms to a communal Christian cultic act.

The only rite clearly mentioned is Baptism, and that by immersion — "when we went down into the water" (*Mand.* IV, 3,1, also *Vis.* III, 7,3), but there is no mention of the one or ones who administered this rite. Professor Colson has attempted to find in *Sim.* IX, 16, 5 a progress in the "prise de conscience" of a sacerdotal function based on the purifying function of the deceased "apostles and teachers" who preach the Gospel to and baptize the righteous dead of pre-Christian times. His attempt is praiseworthy since this is the only place in the *Shepherd* where any group of ministers is clearly connected with an apparent "sacramental" rite. But it is not a strong argument. The soteriology of the *Shepherd* is eons removed from any suggestion of priestly activity of Jesus Christ. Moreover, the totally indefinable type of "baptism" this might have been simply leaves this argumentation too tenuous upon which to base any solid conclusion, let alone a sacerdotal function in the living Church.

In short, the elements upon which a Christian priesthood could be built are absent in this lengthy Roman document called the *Shepherd of Hermas*. The incorporation of God's people in the death and resurrection of Christ and a consciously argued theology of atonement have no place in the author's thinking. Salvation in the *Shepherd*, rather than being a once-and-for-all action, is taken to be an ongoing process dating from Creation based on the work of the holy angels, of the Holy Spirit and of the Law. This approach is all the more unusual when one considers that the *Shepherd* presents us with the richest vocabulary of ministerial functions in the Apostolic Fathers.

6. The Didache is a small (2190 words), anonymous, impersonal community manual on morals, ritual and church order. Since its discovery by Bryennios in 1873 and its publication in 1883 down to the present day, the *Didache* or the *Teaching of the Twelve Apostles* has defied any clear solution to the problems of its dating, origin, destination and authorship.

The document speaks of five ministerial groups. The apostles, prophets and teachers appear to be charismatics to one degree or another; the *epískopoi* and *diákonoi* are (or will be) two groups chosen by the community. The apostles are undoubtedly the most itinerant; the prophets and teachers have been so, but are now beginning to settle into the Christian communities. There are no grounds in the text to distinguish the functions of apostles from those of prophets nor the functions of prophets from those of teachers. All we learn about the function of the *epískopoi* and *diákonoi* is that they minister to the community the same ministry (*leitourgían*) as prophets and teachers (or at least will do so when they are chosen). This ministry appears (from the connective *oûn* between ch. 14 and 15) to be associated with the Sunday worship, although we find no mention of such terms as "presiding" or "leading." The closest we get to this is the statement in 10:7: "But permit the prophets to give thanks (eucharistize?) as much as they desire." Prophets are clearly the center of attraction: they are to receive the "first fruits" of virtually all products in the community as well as money, clothes and possessions, as the community sees fit. The reason for this is stated simply: "For they are your high priests" (13:3). This is the only mention of "priest" in the *Didache*, and it is intimately tied up with the motivation behind giving of the "first fruits." No other ministerial group is seen as worthy to receive the *primitiae*; in fact, if there is no prophet in the community, they are to give the "first fruits" to the poor (13:4). Once the prophet has been proven to be true, he may no longer be judged by the community and is accorded an unbelievably high "position," although none of the traditional terms for "office" like *táxis*, *tágma*, or even their forerunner *tópos* are to be found. Actually the prophet in the didachist's community appears to be ever so much more of a monarch than any such claims for the *epískopos* in the Ignatian letters.

The prophet in the *Didache* is clearly the closest person to being a Christian "priest" that we find in the Apostolic Fathers. With an apparently diminishing number of prophets, the *Didache* sees a clear value in introducing *epískopoi* and *diákonoi,* realizing nonetheless that this step will not be so popular with the recipients: "Do not despise them, for they are your honorable men together with the prophets and teachers" (15:2). Nowhere in the document is there mention of presbyters.

The little sacral-cultic language that appears in the *Didache* appears at genuinely key places. In ch. 14, the Sunday eucharistic celebration is put into the context of the "pure sacrifice" prophesied by Malachi (*Mal.*1:11&14) which the Christians are fulfilling: "In every place and time offer me a pure sacrifice..." (14:3). It is clear from the requirements for personal preparation through reconciliation and confession of transgressions that the sacrifice here involves personal offering of one's worship and prayer. But the mention of the *fractio panis* with the elements that this implies — bread and wine — are also included in what is described as the fulfillment of the "pure sacrifice": "On the Lord's day of the Lord, come together, break bread and give thanks (hold Eucharist?), after confessing your transgressions so that your sacrifice (*thusía*) may be pure" (14:1). The danger of focusing this "pure sacrifice" completely on the elements and not on the whole personal and communal context of the celebration is already inherent in the situation. Moreover, the application in ch. 9 of the term "holy" (*tò hágion*) to the eucharistic elements would only increase this tendency: "But let none eat or drink of your Eucharist except those who have been baptized in the Lord's Name. For concerning this also did the Lord say, "Give not that which is holy to the dogs" (14:5). Paul had stated something similar in *1 Corinthians* 11: 27-29.

In ch. 15 *epískopoi* and *diákonoi* are being introduced to fulfill a *leitourgía,* apparently that mentioned in ch. 14. The combination of words used here for their function: to "minister the ministry (*leitourgoûsi tèn leitourgían*) of the prophets and teachers" (15:2). is a *hapax* in the *Didache,* so we are hardly able to draw conclusions from it. We do know, however, that the same combination is found in *Numbers* (8:22; 16:9; 18:6ff.) for the service of the Levites and in the *Didache* it does appear to be connected with the Sunday eucharistic service through the connector *oûn* (therefore) at the beginning of ch. 15.

In short, there are four sets of sacral-cultic terms in the *Didache:* [1] "your sacrifice (*thusía*)" in 14:1,2; [2] "that which is holy (*tò hágion*)" in

9:5; [3] "minister the ministry (*leitourgoûsi tèn leitourgían*) in 15:1; and [4] "your high priests (*archhiereîs*) in 13:3 which together comprise the elements upon which a Christian priesthood might be based. When the prophetic/charismatic leaders of the community die out and the *epískopoi* and *diákonoi* become institutionally implanted as those who exclusively "minister the ministry," you would have at least an implicit Christian "priesthood." There is, however, one essential sacerdotal element missing in the *Didache*: the connection of the "pure sacrifice" of the eucharistic celebration with the suffering and death of Jesus on the Cross. Consequently it is no surprise that we find here no mention of Jesus Christ as "priest" or "High Priest", nor a theology of atonement whereby Jesus' death atones for our personal sinfulness. Therefore, despite the fact that the *Didache* gives us the clearest connections with the Levitical sacerdotal system of any of the Apostolic Fathers, the soteriological foundation upon which a priesthood within Christianity came to be based is lacking in the *Didache*.

I believe that the *Didache* is one of the documents that played a significant role in the development of Christian priesthood (all the *Didache's* "types" are at the right place to foster such a development), but at the same time I think we need to be open to the possibility that a sacerdotal development (or the beginning of such a development) may have had little or nothing to do with the original intention behind the *Didache's* use of this sacral-cultic terminology: the use of *thusía* could have been primarily to show the fulfillment of a prophecy; the use of *archiereîs* could deal primarily with finding a recipient so the "law" of the *primitiae* could be fulfilled; the *tò hágion* could well have been referring to an agape; and the *leitourgousi tèn leitourgían* might simply have been Old Testament terms given a new Christian meaning. Nonetheless the publication and diffusion of such a text with these sacral-cultic terms in place would have opened to other communities at other places the possibility of a very different interpretation.

In summary, it would be naive to think that Christian priesthood simply popped up in the third century when we can first document that Christians began to call the local bishop their "high priest" and then intensified in the fourth century when we can document that presbyters, after a fairly long period of being called "priests of the second order" (*sacerdotes secundi ordinis*), came simply to be called "priests". Our study here, limited as it is, has shown that Christian ministerial priesthood is rather the result of a gradual development over about 300 years, a slow and cumulative development, much like pieces of snow that begin to roll down a mountain side, combining and gathering mass and momentum as they go. The development was clearly influenced both by concrete historical situations and by the analogous application of sacral-cultic language to the Christian situation or to Christian leaders. Among the concrete historical situations that influenced this development would certainly be, among others, the destruction of the Jerusalem Temple and end of the Levitical cult, the emergence in Christian communities around the Mediterranean of a single overseer/bishop (*monepískopos*), the dying out of earlier generations of Jewish Christians who had clearly broken with and put aside the whole sacerdotal system of Israel, and the gradual finalization of the New Testament canon.

Among the analogous applications of sacral-cultic, particularly sacerdotal language to the Christian situation or to Christian leaders, we mentioned the scant New Testament references in *Romans, 1 Corinthians, 1 Peter*, the *Epistle to the Hebrews* and the *Apocalypse*, without which the whole later development would probably never have occurred.

The next group of authentic Christian documents, the *Apostolic Fathers* investigated here, while also not witnessing to a Christian priesthood, do show more sacral-cultic analogies that place the Levitical system in parallel with Christianity and Christian leaders than does the New Testament. These instances, however, are usually isolated and in most cases clearly metaphorical. But while metaphors are indeed great conveyers of attitudes and insights, there still appears to be great hesitation in the first and second centuries to go beyond metaphor. Only *1 Clement* and the *Letter of Polycarp* speak explicitly of Jesus as High Priest (Ignatius does so implicitly), and only the *Didache* calls a particular group of ministers "your high priests," namely the Christian prophets. Understandably absent is any consistent and universally agreed upon theology of Christian ministry. Who has time for theological reflection when you are dodging imperial troops or dealing with messy divisions within your own community? Missing, too, in most cases is an operative theology of atonement that sees Jesus as sacrificing himself for the sins of the world that is in some way connected with the community's celebration of Eucharist where the gifts of bread and wine offered are recognized in faith to be the Body and Blood of the Lord, as in *1 Corinthians* 11. In short, a Christian ministerial priesthood will be in demand when the potential priest has a concrete sacrifice to offer up. Some of the elements for this are indeed present in the *Apostolic Fathers* by means of Old Testament typology and metaphor but not yet sufficiently organized or accepted for us to confirm the reality of a Christian ministerial priesthood. That reality is yet to develop, but its elements are clearly rooted in these first few centuries.

Thus rather than think of Christian ministerial priesthood as a phenomenon dominically or apostolically given, since priesthood for Jesus and his immediate followers was not an issue (they already had and recognized a Levitical priesthood), it would be much more accurate to consider Christian ministerial priesthood as part of the development of that Spirit-inspired sacrament which is the Church, the *ursakrament* as Rahner would say, processing its way through the centuries, evangelizing and adapting itself to every culture, and in the post-Temple period adapting its vision of ministry to a more culturally acceptable form in the already highly sacral-cultic Roman Empire with its many religions and many priesthoods. Some Christian communions believe this development of priesthood within Christianity took place under the guidance of the Holy Spirit; some hold it happened despite the Holy Spirit. One thing is historically certain: *it developed,* and that means it can continue to develop and to adapt to the ever-changing spiritual, communal and cultural needs of the faithful, those called "the priestly people of God."

Moreover, using the Gamaliel principle, we can still say today that if this development of Christian priesthood in the early centuries had not in some way been from God, then it surely would have perished centuries ago.

CHAPTER BIBLIOGRAPHIES

BIBLIOGRAPHY: CLEMENT OF ROME

Baljon, J. M. S. *Grieksch-Theologisch Woordenboek*. Utrecht: 1899.

Bardy, G. "Expressions stoiciennes dans la I Clémentis." *Recherches de science religieuse;* 1922; 13: 73-85.

Beahrens, W. A. *Origines Werke* (Die Griechischen Christlichen Schriftsteller, 29). Leipzig: 1920.

Beyschlag, Karlmann. *Clemens Romanus und der Frühkatholizismus.* Tübingen: J. C. B. Mohr (Paul Siebeck); 1966.

_____. "I Clements 40-44 und das Kirchenrecht." *Reformatio und Confessio; Festschrift W Mauer;* F Kantzenbach; 1965; 9-22.

Bissoli, Giovanni C. "Rapporto fra chiesa e stato nella Prima Lettera di Clemente." *Studium Biblicum Franciscanum;* E Testa; A Niccacci, et al; 1979; 29: 145-174.

Blum, G. G. "Eucharistie, Amt und Opfer in der Alten Kirche." *Oecumenica-1966,* Gerd Mohn; 1966; 19-27.

Boismard, M. E. "Clément de Rome et l'Évangile de Jean." *Revue biblique;* 1948; 55: 376-387.

Botte, Dom B. *Hippolyte de Rome: La Tradition Apostolique.* Paris: 1946.

Boulenger, F. *Grégoire de Nazianze: Discours Funèbres* (Texte grec., trad. franc., introd. et index). Paris: 1908.

328

Bowe, Barbara Ellen. *A Church in Crisis: Ecclesiology and Paraenesis in Clement of Rome*. Minneapolis: Fortress Press (Harvard Dissertations in Religion); 1988. 158 pages.

Brent, Allen. "History and Eschatological Mysticism in Ignatius of Antioch." *Ephemerides Theologicae Lovaniensis;* 1989; 65(4): 309-329.

Brunner, Gebert. *Die theologische Mitte des Ersten Klemensbriefs*. Frankfurt: Josef Knecht Verlag; 1972.

Bumpus, Harold Bertram. *The Christological Awareness of Clement of Rome and Its Sources*. Cambridge, Mass.: University Press of Cambridge; 1972. 196 pages.

Campenhausen, H.F. von. *Kirchliches Amt und geistliche Vollmacht in den ersten drei Jahrhunderten*. Tübingen: J. C. B. Mohr (Paul Siebeck); 1953.

Colson, J. *Les Fonctions ecclésiales aux deux premiers siècles*. Paris: 1956.

_____. *Ministre de Jésus-Christ ou le sacerdoce de l'Évangile*. Paris: Beauchesne; 1966.

_____. *Clément de Rome*. Paris: Les Éditions Ouvrières; 1960.

Crouzel, Henri. "Les origines de l'Épiscopat: fin du Ier siècle, début du IIe." *L'Évêque dans l'histoire;* H Crouzel; J Durliat, et al; 1984; 13-20.

Daniélou, Jean. *The Theology of Jewish-Christianity*. London: Darton, Longman & Todd; 1964.

de Gebhardt & Harnack. *Patrum Apostolicum Opera: Epistulae Clementis Romani*, fasc. I, part I, ed. II. Leipzig: 1876.

de la Potterie, Ignace "L'origine et le sens primitif du mot 'laic'." *Nouvelle Revue Théologique;* 1958; 90.

de Watteville, J. *Le Sacrifice dans les textes eucharistiques des premiers siècles*. Neuchâtel: Delachaux & Niestle; 1966.

Dictionnaire de la Bible, Supplement II. Paris: 1934.

Dix, Dom Gregory. "The Ministry in the Early Church - A.D. 90-410." *The Apostolic Ministry*, ed. K. E. Kirk. London. Hodder & Stoughton; 1946; 183-303.

DuCange, D. *Glossarium ad Scriptores Mediae et Infimae Graecitatis.* Lyon: 1688.

Dünsing, Hugo. "Die dem Klemens von Rom Zugeschriebenen Briefe über die Jungfräulichkeit." *Zeitschrift für Kirchengeschichte;* 1950-1951; 63(2): 166-188.

Ellis, P. *The Men and Message of the Old Testament.* Collegeville: Liturgical Press; 1963.

Faivre, Alexandre. "Clerc/Laic: Histoire d'une frontière." *Revue des sciences religieuses*; Juil 1983; 57:195-220.

_____. "Le "système normatif" dans la lettre de Clément de Rome aux Corinthiens." *Revue des science religieuses;* April 1980; 54: 129-152.

Fisher, Edmund Warner. *Soteriology in First Clement.* Ann Arbor, Michigan: University Microfilms International; 1974. Claremont Graduate School, Ph.D. Religion.

Foster, Lewis. *Clement of Rome and his Literary Sources.* Thesis (Ph. D.) — Harvard University; 1958. 297 pages.

Fuellenbach, John. *Ecclesiastical Office and the Primacy of Rome: An Evaluation of Recent Theological Discussion of First Clement.* Washington, D.C.: Catholic University of America Press; 1980. 278 pages.

_____. *An Evaluation of the Recent Theological Discussion of First Clement: The Question of the Primacy of Rome.* Thesis (S.T.D.) - Catholic University of America. Studies in Sacred Theology; 1977. 533 pages.

Funk, F. X. *Didascalia et Constitutiones Apostolorum,* Vol. I. Paderborn: 1905.

_____. *Patres Apostolici,* Vol. I. Tübingen: Laupp; 1901.

330

Giet, Stanislas. "Le témoignage de Clément de Rome sur la venue à Rome de Saint Pierre." *Recherches de science religieuse;* 1955; 29: 123-136.

_____."Le témoignage de Clément de Rome, I: sur la venue à Rome de saint Pierre." *Revue des sciences religieuses;* 1955; 29: 123-136.

_____."Le témoignage de Clément de Rome, II: la cause des persécutions romaines." *Revue des sciences religieuses;* 1955; 29: 333-345.

Grant, Robert M. "The Apostolic Fathers' First Thousand Years." (Repr. fr 31:421-429, 1962.) *Church History;* 1988; 57: 20-28.

Grelot, Pierre. *Le Ministère de la nouvelle Alliance.* Paris: du Cerf; 1967.

_____. "Pierre et Paul fondateurs de la "primauté" romaine." *Istina;* July-September 1982; 27: 228-268.

Hagner, Donald Alfred. "The Sayings of Jesus in the Apostolic Fathers and Justin Martyr." *Gospel Perspectives: The Jesus Tradition Outside the Gospels,* ed by D. Wenham. Sheffield (Engl): JSOT Press; 1985; 233-268.

_____. *The Use of the Old and New Testaments in Clement of Rome.* Leiden, Brill; 1973. 395 pages.

Hall, A. "I Clement as a Document of Transition." *Miscellanea Patristica:* A C Vega by T Alonso, et al; 1968; 264-274.

Harnack, A. *Das Schreiben der römischen Kirche an die korinthische aus der Zeit Domitians.* Leipzig: J. C. Hinrichs; 1929.

Hatch & Redpath. *A Concordance to the Septuagint,* Vol. 1. Oxford: 1897.

Heikel, I. A. *Eusebius Werke* (Die griechischen christlichen Schriftsteller, 7). Berlin; 1956.

Henne, Philippe. *La christologie chez Clément de Rome et dans le Pasteur d'Hermas.* Freibourg, Suisse: Éditions universitaires; 1992. 371 pages.

_____. "Le sceptre de la majeste en Clém. 16,2. *Studia Patristica,* ed by E Livingstone; 1989; 21: 101-105.

Herron, Thomas J. "The Most Probable Date of the First Epistle of Clement to the Corinthians." *Studia Patristica;* ed by E Livingstone; 1988; 21: 106-121.

Jaubert, A. "Les sources de la conception militaire de l'Église en 1 Clément 37." *Vigiliae Christianae;* 1964; 18: 77-84.

Jeffers, James Stanley. *Conflict at Rome: Social Order and Hierarchy in Early Christianity.* Minneapolis: Fortress Press; 1991. 215 pages.

_____. *Social Foundations of Early Christianity at Rome: The Congregations Behind I Clement and The Shepherd of Hermas.* Thesis (Ph.D. History) — University of California, Irvine; 1988. 344 leaves.

Jellicoe, Sidney. "The psalter-text of St Clement of Rome." *Wort, Lied, und Gottesspruch: Septuaginta;* ed by J Schreiner; 1972; 59-66.

Johanny, Raymond (ed). *L'Eucharistie des premiers chrétiens.* Éditions Beauchesne; 1976. 216 pages.

Jones, Frederick Stanley. *Pseudo-Clementine 'Recognitions' 1.27-71 Early Jewish Christian Perspectives On The Nature And History Of Christianity (Clement Of Rome).* Thesis (Ph.D.) - Vanderbilt University; 1989. 229 pages.

Jourjon, Maurice. "Remarques sur le vocabulaire sacerdotale dans la Ia Clémentis." *Epektasis: Mélanges patristiques offerts au Card. Jean Daniélou.* Paris: Beauchesne; 1972; 109-110.

_____. "Textes eucharistiques des Pères antenicëens." *L'Eucharistie: le sens des sacrements;* ed by R Didier; 1971; 94-118.

Kilmartin, E. *The Eucharist in the Primitive Church.* Englewood Cliffs (N.J.): 1965.

Kleist, J. A. *The Epistles of St. Clement of Rome and St. Ignatius of Antioch* (Ancient Christian Writers, 1). Westminster, Md.: Newman; 1946.

Klijn, A. F. J. *Apostolische Vaders, 1.* Baarn: Bosch & Keuning; 1966.

Knoch, Otto. "Die Ausführungen des 1. Clemensbriefes über die kirchliche Verfassung im Spiegel der neueren Deutungen seit R. Sohm und A. Harnack." *Theologische Quartalschrift;* 1961; 141: 385-407.

————. "Petrus and Paulus in den Schriften der Apostolischen Väter." *Kontinuität und Einheit; für Franz Mussner;* ed by P Mueller; 1981; 240-260.

Knopf, R. "Clemens und die Korinther." *Handbuch zu den neutestamentlichen Apokryphen,* Tübingen; 1904; 173-190.

————. "Die zwei Clemensbriefe." *Handbuch zum Neuen Testament, Ergänzungsband: Die Apostolischen Väter,* Tübingen; 1920; 41-150.

Konidaris, G. "Warum die Urkirche von Antiochia den 'proestota presbyteron' der Ortsgemeinde als 'ho Episkopos' bezeichnete." *Münchener Theol. Zeitschr.;* 1961; 12: 281-283.

Kroymann, A. *Opera Tertulliani* (Corpus scriptorum ecclesiasticorum latinorum, 47). Wien: 1906.

Küng, H. *Die Kirche.* Freiburg: Herder; 1967.

Lake, K. *The Apostolic Fathers,* I (Loeb Classical Library). London: Heinemann; 1912.

Lampe, G. W. H. *A Patristic Greek Lexicon.* Oxford: beginning 1961.

Lampe, Peter. *Die stadtrömischen Christen in den ersten beiden Jahrhunderten.* Tübingen: J.C.B. Mohr (Paul Siebeck); 1987.

Lecuyer, J. *Le Sacerdoce dans le Mystère du Christ.* Paris: 1957.

Lemarchand, L. "La composition de l'épître de saint Clément aux Corinthiens." *Revue des sciences religieuses.;* 1938; 18: 448-457.

Lightfoot, J. B. *The Apostolic Fathers.* Grand Rapids, Mich.: Baker; 1967. (photoprint from the Macmillan ed., London, 1891).

Livingstone, Elizabeth A., (ed.). *Studia Patristica,* 21. Leuven: Peeters; 1989. 455 pages.

Maier, Harry O. *The Social Setting of the Ministry as Reflected in the Writings of Hermas, Clement and Ignatius.* Waterloo (Ont.): Published for the Canadian Corporation for Studies in Religion/Corporation Canadienne des Sciences Religieuses by Wilfrid Laurier University Press; 1991.

Mees, Michael. "Die Hohepriester-Theologie des Hebräerbriefes im Vergleich mit dem Ersten Clemensbrief." *Biblische Zeitschrift;* 1978; 22(1): 115-124.

Meinhold, P. "Geschehen und Deutung im Ersten Clemensbrief." *Zeitschr. für die Kirchengeschichte;* 1939; 58: 82-129.

Merill, E. T. "On Clement of Rome." *American Journal of Theology;* 1918; 22: 426-442.

Metzger, Marcel. "La théologie des Constitutions Apostoliques par Clément." *Revue des sciences religieuses;* 1983; 57: 29-49 (January); 112-122 (Ap); 169-194 Jl; 273-294 (Oct).

Migne, J. P. *Patrologiae cursus completus, series graeca,* Vol. I. Paris: 1857.

Mullins, Michael. *Called To Be Saints: Christian Living in First-Century Rome.* Dublin: Veritas; 1991. 471 pages.

Murray, Robert. "Christianity's 'Yes' to Priesthood." *The Christian Priesthood,* ed by N. Lash & J. Rhymer. London: Darton, Longman & Todd; 1970; 17-43.

Neumann, J. "Der theologische Grund fuer das kirchliche Vorsteheramt nach dem Zeugnis der Apostolischen Väter." *Münchener Theol. Zeitschr.;* 1963; 14.

Noll, R. R. "The Search for a Christian Ministerial Priesthood in I Clement." *Studia Patristica;* ed by E Livingstone; 1975; 13(2): 250-254.

Norris, Frederick W. "Ignatius, Polycarp, and I Clement: Walter Bauer reconsidered." *Vigiliae Christianae;* 1976; 30(1): 23-44.

Panthot, Joseph. "La signification religieuse du "Nom" chez Clément de Rome et dans la Didachè." *Ephemerides Theologicae Lovaniensis;* 1959; 35: 339-361.

Peterson, E. "Das Praescriptum des 1 Clemens." *Pro Regno Pro Sanctuario...* G. van der Leeuw, Nijkerk (Holland); 1950; 351-357.

Praetorius, W. "Die Bedeutung der beiden Klemensbriefe für die älteste Geschichte der kirchlichen Praxis." *Zeitschr. für die*

Kirchengeschichte; 1912; 33: 347-363, 501-528.

Quasten, J. *Patrology,* Vol. I. Utrecht: Spectrum; 1950.

Roberts, Donaldson and Crombie. *The Writings of the Apostolic Fathers* (Ante-Nicene Christian Library, 1). Edinburgh: T. & T. Clark; 1873.

Robinson, John A.T. *Redating the New Testament.* London: SCM Press, Ltd.;1976; 313-335.

Rogers, Barry Michael. *The Hermeneutics of Clement of Rome.* Thesis (M.A.) - Wheaton College; 1979. 107 pages.

Rordorf, Willy. *The Eucharist of the Early Christians.* New York: Pueblo Publ. Co.; 1978.

Schweizer, E. "Glaube und Werke bei Klemens Romanus." *Theologische Quartalschrift;* 1903; 85: 417-437, 547-575.

Smith. M. "The Report about Peter in 1 Clement V. 4." *New Testament Studies;* 1960-1961; 7: 86-88.

Smulders, P. J. "Colson: Ministre de Jésus-Christ ou le sacerdoce de l'Évangile" (review). *Bijdragen;* 1967; 28(2): 217.

Sophocles, E. A. *Greek Lexicon of the Roman and Byzantine Periods, From B.C. 146 to A.D. 1100.* New York: 1887.

Strathmann. 'Leitourgeo' in *Theol. Wörterbuch zum Neuen Testament* (ed. G. Kittel), Band 4. Stuttgart: 1942; 235-236.

Suiceri, J. C. *Thesaurus Ecclesiasticus e Patribus Graecis.* Amsterdam: 1682.

Tarelli, C. C. "Clement of Rome and the Fourth Gospel." *The Journal of Theological Studies;* 1947; 48: 208-209.

Torrance, T. F. *The Doctrine of Grace in the Apostolic Fathers.* Edinburgh: 1948.

van Cauwelaert, F. R. "L'Intervention de l'Église de Rome à Corinthe vers l'an 96." *Revue d'histoire ecclésiastique;* 1935; 31: 267-306.

van Unnik, W. C. "1 Clement 34 and the Sanctus." *Vigiliae Christianae;* 1951; 5: 204-248.

_____. "Is 1 Clement 20 Purely Stoic?" *Vigiliae Christianae;* 1950; 4: 181-189.

_____. "Le nombre des élus dans la première épître de Clément." *Revue histoire et de philisophie religieuses;* 1962; 42: 237-246.

Vogt, Hermann J. "Zum Bischofsamt in der frühen Kirche." *Theologische Quartalschrift;* 1982; 162(3): 221-236.

von Rad, G. *Old Testament Theology,* Vol I (transl. D. Stalker). London: Oliver & Boyd; 1962.

Werner, Eric. "Post-biblical Hebraisms in the Prima Clementis." *Harry Austryn Wolfson Jubilee Volume;* by L W Schwarz, et al; 1965; 2: 793-818.

Wickert, U. "Eine Fehlübersetzung zu 1 Clem. 19.2." *Zeitschr. für die NT-lichen Wiss.;* 1958; 49: 270-275.

Wilhelm-Hooijbergh, Ann E. "A Different View of Clemens Romanus." *Heythrop Journal;* 1975; 16: 266-288.

_____. "Is Clemens Romanus Imitating the Seditious Corinthians?" *Studia Patristica;* ed by E Livingstone; 1985; 16(2): 206-208.

_____. "Rome or Alexandria: Which was Clemens Romanus' Birthplace?" *Studia Patristica;* ed by E Livingstone; 1982; 17(2): 756-759.

Wong, D. W. F. "Natural and Divine Order in I Clement." *Vigiliae Christianae;* 1977; 31(2): 81-87.

Wrede, W. *Untersuchungen zum Ersten Klemensbriefe.* Göttingen: 1891.

Ziegler, A. W. *Neue Studien zum ersten Klemensbrief.* München: 1958.

Zizioulas, John D. "Episkope et episkopos dans l'église primitive: bref inventaire de la documentation." *Irenikon: Revue des Moines de Chevetogne;* 1983; 56(4): 484-502.

336

Bibliography: Ignatius of Antioch

Bardsley, H. J. "The Testimony of Ignatius and Polycarp to the Writings of St. John." *The Journal of Theological Studies;* 1913; 14: 207-220, 489-499.

Barnard, L. W. "The Background of St. Ignatius of Antioch." *Vigiliae Christianae;* 1963; 17: 193-206. (Also published in his *Studies in the Apostolic Fathers and their Background.* Oxford: Blackwell; 1966; 19-30).

Barrett, Charles K. "Jews and Judaizers in the Epistles of Ignatius." *Jews, Greeks and Christians;* ed by R Hamerton-Kelly; 1976; 220-244.

Bartsch, H. W. *Gnostiches Gut und Gemeindetradition bei Ignatius von Antiochien.* Gütersloh: C. Bertelsmann; 1940.

Battifol, P. *L'Eucharistie dans N. T., Didachè et Épîtres ignaciennes* (Études d'histoire et de théologie positive, 2ème série). Paris: 1909.

Bauer, Walter. *Die Briefe des Ignatius von Antiochia und der Polykarpbrief.* Tübingen: J. C. B. Mohr (Paul Siebeck); 1920. (*Handbuch zum Neuen Testament,* ed. H. Lietzmann, Ergänzungs-Band, *Die Apostolischen Väter,* Vol. 2).

_____. *Orthodoxy and Heresy in Earliest Christianity.* Philadelphia: Fortress Press; 1971.

Bauer, W. and Paulsen, H. *Die Briefe des Ignatius von Antiochia und der Brief des Polykarp von Smyrna.* Tübingen: J. C. B. Mohr (Paul Siebeck); 1985.

Bayes, Jonathan. "Divine apatheia in Ignatius of Antioch." *Studia Patristica;* ed by E Livingstone; 1989; 21: 27-31.

Bergamelli, Ferdinando. "L'unione a Cristo in Ignazio di Antiochia." *Cristologia e catechesi patristica;* ed by S Felici; 1980; 1: 73-109.

_____. "'La verginita di Maria' nelle lettere di Ignazio di Antiochia." *Studia Patristica;* ed by E Livingstone; 1989; 21: 32-41.

Bieder, W. "Das Abendmahl im christlichen Lebenzusammenhang bei

Ignatius von Antiochien." *Evang. Theol.;* 1956; 16: 75-97.

_____. "Zur Deutung des kirchlichen Schweigens bei Ignatius von Antiochien." *Evang. Theol. Zeitschrift;* 1956; 16: 28-43.

Bommes, Karin. "Weizen Gottes: Untersuchungen zur Theologie des Martyriums bei Ignatius von Antiochien." Koln: P. Hanstein. *Theophaneia, Beitrage zur Religions - und Kirchengeschichte des Altertums;* 1976; 27. 284 pages. (Originally presented as the author's thesis, Ratisbon, 1974.).

Bouchier, E. S. *A Short History of Antioch.* Oxford: Blackwell; 1921.

Brent, Allen. "History and Eschatological Mysticism in Ignatius of Antioch." *Ephemerides Theologicae Lovaniensis*; 1989; 65(4): 309-329.

Brown, M. P. *The Authentic Writings of Ignatius: A Study of Linguistic Criteria.* Durham, N. C.: Duke University Press; 1963.

Bruston, H. *Ignace d'Antioche, ses épîtres, sa vie, sa théologie.* Paris: 1897.

Bultmann, R. "Ignatius und Paulus." *Studia Paulina.* Haarlem: J. de Zwaan; 1951; 37-51.

Burghardt, W. J. "Did Saint Ignatius of Antioch Know the Fourth Gospel?" *Theological Studies;* 1940; I: 1-26, 140-156.

Camelot, Th. *Ignace d'Antioche: Lettres* (Source chrétiennes, 10). Paris: Éditions du Cerf; 1944.

Campenhausen, H. F. von,. *Die Idee des Martyriums in der alten Kirche.* Göttingen: Vandenhoeck & Ruprecht; 1963.

_____. *Kirchliches Amt und geistliche Vollmacht in den ersten drei Jahrhunderten* (Beiträge zur historischen Theologie, 14). Tübingen: J. C. B. Mohr (Paul Siebeck); 1953.

Chadwick, H. "The Silence of Bishops in Ignatius." *Harvard Theological Review;* 1950; 43: 169-172.

Colson, Jean. "Agape chez Saint Ignace d'Antioche." *Studia Patristica,* III. Berlin: Akademie Verlag; 1961; 78: 341-353.

338

_____. *Les fonctions ecclésiales aux deux premiers siècles.* Paris: Désclée; 1956.

_____. *L'Évêque dans les communautés primitives* (Unam Sanctam, 21). Paris: Éditions du Cerf; 1951.

_____. *Ministre de Jésus-Christ ou le sacerdoce de l'Évangile.* Paris: Beauchesne; 1966.

Corwin, V. *St. Ignatius and Christianity in Antioch.* New Haven: Yale University Press; 1966.

Crehan, J. H. "A New Fragment of Ignatius' Ad Polycarpum." *Studia Patristica,* I. Berlin: Akademie Verlag; 1957; 23-32.

Crouzel, Henri. "Les origines de l'Épiscopat: fin du Ier siècle, début du IIe." *L'Évêque dans l'histoire;* H Crouzel; J Durliat, et al; 1984; 13-20.

Cureton, W. *The Ancient Syriac Version of the Epistles of St. Ignatius to St. Polycarp, the Ephesians and the Romans.* London: Rivington; 1845.

Daley, Brian E. "The Ministry of Disciples: Historical Reflections on the Role of Religious Priests." *Theological Studies;* December 1987; 48: 605-629.

Daniélou, J. *Théologie du judéo-christianisme.* Paris: 1958.

Dassmann, Ernst. "Hausgemeinde und Bischofsamt." *Vivarium: Festschrift T. Klauser* ed by E Dassmann & K Thraede; Münster: Aschendorf; 1984; 82-97.

_____. "Zur Entstehung des Monepiskopats." *Jahrbuch für Antike und Christentum;* by G Stählin, *et al;* 1975; 17: 74-90.

Davies, Stevan L. "Predicament of Ignatius of Antioch." *Vigiliae Christianae: A Review of Early Christian Life and Language;* 1976; 30(3): 175-180.

de Genouillac, H. *L'Église chrétienne au temps de saint Ignace d'Antioche* (Bibliothèque de théologie historique). Paris: 1907.

Dehandschutter, Boudewijn A. G. M. "Polycarp's Epistle to the Philippians: An Early Example of "Reception"." *The New Testament in Early Christianity;* ed by J Sevrin; 1989; 275-291.

Delafosse, H. *Lettres d'Ignace d'Antioche* (Les Textes du Christianisme, Vol. 2). Paris: Rieder; 1927.

_____. "Nouvel examen des lettres d'Ignace d'Antioche." *Revue d'histoire et de littérature religieuses;* 1922; 8: 303-337, 477-533.

Dietze, P. "Die Briefe des Ignatius und das Johannesevangelium." *Theol. Studien und Kritiken;* 1905; 78: 563-603.

Donahue, Paul J. "Jewish Christianity in the Letters of Ignatius of Antioch." *Vigiliae Christianae: A Review of Early Christian Life and Language;* 1978; 32(2): 81-93.

Downey, G. *A History of Antioch in Syria.* Cambridge, Mass.: Harvard University Press; 1960.

Duff, Paul Brooks. *The Theology of Ignatius of Antioch: An Inquiry Concerning the Possibility of Applying Bultmann's Hermeneutic Method to Non-canonical Literature.* Oxford, Ohio: Miami University. Thesis (M.A.) Miami University, Department of Religion.; 1979. 84 pages.

Dupuy, Bernard. "Aux origines de l'épiscopat: le corpus des Lettres d'Ignace d'Antioche et le ministère d'unité." *Istina;* July-September 1982; 27: 269-277.

Essig, Klaus Gunther. "Mutmassungen über den Anlass des Martyriums von Ignatius von Antiochien." *Vigiliae Christianae: A Review of Early Christian Life and Language;* June 1986; 40(2): 105-117.

Estrade, M. *Les cartes de sant Ignasi d' Antioquia. Traduccio, introducions i notes,* (Coleccion Blanquerna, 24). Barcelona: Edicions 62; 1966.

Facchini, D. "S. Ignazio martire, vita, lettere, atti di martirio." *Bessarione;* 1916; 19: 310-324.

_____. "S. Ignazio martire, vita, lettere, atti di martirio." *Bessarione;* 1916; 20: 52-66.

Fincke, E. "Das Amt der Einheit." *Das Amt der Einheit.* Stuttgart: Schwabenverlag (W. Stählin, ed.); 1964; 140-146.

Funk, F. X. *Patres Apostolici,* Vol. I. Tübingen: H. Laupp; 1901.

Gaston, Lloyd. "Judaism of the Uncircumcised in Ignatius and Related Writers." *Anti-Judaism in Early Christianity;* ed by S Wilson; 1986; 2: 33-44.

Gibbard, S. M. "The Eucharist in the Ignatian Epistles." *Studia Patristica,* VIII, Akademie Verlag, Berlin; 1966; 93: 214-218.

Goltz, E. von der,. *Ignatius von Antiochien als Christ und Theologe* (Texte und Untersuchungen, Band 12, Heft 3). Leipzig: Hinrichs; 1894.

Grant, Robert M. *The Apostolic Fathers: An Introduction.* New York: Nelson & Sons; 1964.

_____. *The Apostolic Fathers,* Vol IV, *Ignatius of Antioch.* Camden, N. J.: Nelson & Sons; 1966.

_____. *Gnosticism and Early Christianity,* 2nd ed. New York: Columbia University Press; 1966.

_____. "Hermeneutics and Tradition in Ignatius of Antioch." *Ermeneutica e tradizione,* Rome. E. Castelli, ed.; 1963; 183-201. (same article slightly revised: "Scripture and Tradition in St. Ignatius of Antioch," in *Catholic Biblical Quarterly,* 25, 1963, pp 322-335).

_____. "The Odes of Solomon and the Church of Antioch." *Journal of Biblical Literature;* 1944; 63: 363-377.

_____. "'Holy Law' in Paul and Ignatius." *The Living Text;* ed by D Groh and R Jewett; 1985; 65-71.

_____. "Jewish Christianity at Antioch in the Second Century." *Judéo-Christianisme;* by B Gerhardsson, et al; 1972; 97-108.

Halleux, Andre de. "'L'Église catholique' dans la lettre ignacienne aux Smyrniotes." *Ephemerides Theologicae Lovaniensis;* 1982; 58(1): 5-24.

Hammond Bammel, C. P. "Ignatian Problems." *The Journal of Theological Studies;* April 1982; 33: 62-97.

Hann, Robert R. "Judaism and Jewish Christianity in Antioch: Charisma and Conflict in the First Century." *The Journal of Religious History* (Australia); December 1987; 14: 341-360.

_____. "Post-apostolic Christianity as a Revitalization Movement: Accounting for Innovation in Early Patristic Traditions." *Journal of Religious Studies;* 1988; 14(1-2): 60-75.

Hannah, Jack. "Ignatian Long Recension: Relationship to Pastorals in Households Rules." *Proceedings: Eastern Great Lakes & Midwest Biblical Soc.;* ed by P Sigal; 1984; 4: 153-165.

_____. "The Long Recension of the Ignatian Epsitles by the Redactors of Paul and John." *Proceedings: Eastern Great Lakes Biblical Society;* ed by P Sigal; 1983; 3: 108-121.

Hanson, A. T. "The Theology of Suffering in the Pastoral Epistles and Ignatius of Antioch." *Studia Patristica;* ed by E Livingstone; 1982; 17(2): 694-696.

Harnack, A. *Die Zeit des Ignatius.* Leipzig: Hinrichs; 1878.

Hoffman, Daniel. "The Authority of Scripture and Apostolic Doctrine in Ignatius of Antioch." *Journal of the Evangelical Theological Society;* March 1985; 28: 71-79.

Ignatius, Saint Bp of Antioch. "Epistle to the Ephesians." *Sourozh: A Journal of Orthodox Life and Thought;* November 1982; 10: 45-52.

Jay, Eric G. "From Presbyter-bishops to Bishops and Presbyters: Christian Ministry in the Second Century; A Survey." *The Second Century: A Journal of Early Christian Studies;* Fall 1981; 1(3): 125-162.

Johnson, Sherman E. "Parallels Between the Letters of Ignatius and the Johannine Epistles." *Perspectives on Language and Text;* ed by E Conrad and E Newing; 1987; 327-338.

Joly, Robert. "Le dossier d'Ignace d'Antioche: réflexions liminaires." *Mélanges Armand Abel;* ed by A Destrée; 1978; 3: 116-125.

_____. *Le dossier d'Ignace d'Antioche.* Bruxelles: Éditions de l'Université de Bruxelles, Université libre de Bruxelles, Faculté de philosophie et lettres; 1979. 144 pages.

Kannengiesser, Charles. "Bulletin de théologie patristique: Ignace d'Antioche et Irénée de Lyon." *Recherches de science religieuse;* Oct-Dec 1979; 67: 599-623.

342

Katzenmayer, H. "Die Stellung des Bischofs nach den Briefen des Ignatius von Antiochia." *Internationale kirchliche Zeitschrift;* 1951; 41: 104-107.

Kleist, J. A. *The Epistles of St. Clement of Rome and St. Ignatius of Antioch* (Ancient Christian Writers, Vol. I). Westminster, Md.: Newman; 1946.

Klijn, A. F. J. *Apostolische vaders, 1, Ignatius en Polycarpus.* Baarn: Bosch & Keuning N. V.; 1966.

Köster, H. "Geschichte und Kultus im Johannesevangelium und bei Ignatius von Antiochien." *Zeitschrift für Theologie und Kirche;* 1957; 54: 56-69.

Lake, K. *The Apostolic Fathers,* vol. I (Loeb). London: Heinemann; 1912.

Lebreton, J. "La théologie de la Trinité d'après Saint Ignace d'Antioche." *Recherches de science religieuse;* 1925; 15: 97-126, 393-419.

Lightfoot, J. B. *The Apostolic Fathers* Part II: *S. Ignatius. S. Polycarp.* London: Macmillan; 1885, 2nd ed. 1889.

Lindemann, Andreas. "Paul in the Writings of the Apostolic Fathers." *Paul and the Legacies of Paul;* ed by W Babcock; 1990; 25-45.

Livingstone, Elizabeth A. (ed.). *Studia Patristica,* Vol 16, Pt 2. Berlin: Akademie Verlag; 1985. 614 pages.

Lucchesi, Enzo. "Le recueil copte des lettres d'Ignace d'Antioche." *Vigiliae Christianae: A Review of Early Christian Life and Language;* 1988; 42(4): 313-317.

Lusk, David C. "What is the Historic Episcopate: An Inquiry Based on the Letters of Ignatius of Antioch." *Scottish Journal of Theology;* 1950; 3: 255-277.

Maier, Harry O. "The Charismatic Authority of Ignatius of Antioch: A Sociological Analysis." *Studies in Religion-Sciences religieuses;* 1989; 18(2): 185-199.

_____. *The Social Setting of the Ministry as reflected in the Writings of Hermas, Clement, and Ignatius.* Waterloo, Ont., Canada: Published for the Canadian Corp for Studies in Religion-Corporation Canadienne des Sciences Religieuses by Wilfrid Laurier University Press; 1991;

Malina, Bruce J. "The Social World Implied in the Letters of the Christian Bishop-martyr (Named Ignatius of Antioch)." *Society of Biblical Literature Seminar Papers;* 1978; 14: 71-119.

Mauer, C. *Ignatius von Antiochien und des Johannesevangelium* (Abhandlungen zur Theologie des Alten und Neuen Testaments, ed W. Eichrodt und O. Cullmann). Zürich: Zwingli Verlag; 1949.

McArthur, A. A. "The Office of the Bishop in the Ignatian Epistles and in the Didascalia Apostolorum Compared." *Studia Patristica,* IV, Akademie Verlag, Berlin; 1961; 79: 298-304.

Meinhold, Peter. "Christologie und Jungfrauengeburt bei Ignatius von Antiochien." *Studia mediaevalia et mariologica;* by P Capkun-Delic, et al; 1971; 465-476.

_____. "Die Anschauung des Ignatius von Antiochien von der Kirche." *Wegzeichen: Festgabe zu H M Biedermann,* ed by E C Suttner. Würzburg: Augustinus Verlag; 1971; 1-13.

_____. "Die geschichtstheologischen Konzeptionen des Ignatius von Antiochien." *Kyriakon: Johannes Quasten;* ed by P Granfield; 1970; 1: 182-191.

Moffatt, J. "An Approch to Ignatius." *Harvard Theological Review;* 1936; 29: 1-38.

_____. "Ignatius of Antioch: A Study in Personal Religion." *Journal of Religion;* 1930; 10: 169-186.

Molland, E. "The Heretics Combatted by Ignatius." *Journal of Ecclesiastical History;* 1954; 5: 1-6.

Mullins, Terence Y. "Word Study: The Use of Hypotassein in Ignatius." *The Second Century: A Journal of Early Christian Studies;* Spring 1982; 2(1): 35-39.

Munier, Charles. "À propos d'Ignace d'Antioche." *Revue des sciences religieuses;* January 1980; 54: 55-73.

_____. "À propos d'Ignace d'Antioche: observations sur la liste épiscopale d'Antioche." *Revue des sciences religieuses;* April 1981; 55: 126-130.

Musurillo, H. "Ignatius of Antioch: Gnostic or Essene? A Note on Recent Work." *Theological Studies;* 1961; 22: 103-110.

Nirschl, J. *Die Theologie des hl. Ignatius des Apostelschülers und Bischofs von Antiochien aus seinen Briefen dargestellt.* Mainz: Kirchheim; 1880.

Norris, Frederick W. "Ignatius, Polycarp, and I Clement: Walter Bauer reconsidered." *Vigiliae Christianae: A Review of Early Christian Life and Language;* 1976; 30(1): 23-44.

Nouskas, Constantine Dem. *Ignatius of Antioch, Theological Perspective in Relation to Social Ethics.* Thessaloneiki; 1976.

Pannenberg, Wolfhart. "Revelation in Early Christianity." *Christian Authority;* ed by G Evans; 1988; 76-85.

Patrick, Mary Webber. *Ethos in Epistles: Rhetorical Analyses of Ignatius' Epistles.* Lutheran School of Theology, Th.D.; 1992. 447 pages.

Paulsen, Henning. *Die Briefe des Ignatius von Antiochia und der Brief des Polykarp von Smyrna.* Neubearbeitete Aufl. der Auslegung - von Walter Bauer. Tübingen: J.C.B. Mohr (Paul Siebeck); 1985. 126 seiten.

_____. "Ignatius von Antiochien." *Alte Kirche;* ed by M Greschat; 1984; 1: 38-50.

_____. *Studien zur Theologie des Ignatius von Antiochien.* Göttingen: Vandenhoeck & Ruprecht; 1978.

Pelland, Gilles. "Le dossier des lettres d'Ignace d'Antioche: à propos d'un livre récent." *Science et Esprit;* October-December 1980; 32: 261-297.

Perler, O. "Das vierte Makkabäerbuch, Ignatius von Antiochien, und die ältesten Märtyrerberichte." *Revista di archeologia cristiana;* 1949; 25: 47-72.

_____. "Eucharistie et Unité de l'Église d'après S. Ignace d'Antioche

(35ème Congr. Euchar. Internat.)." *Sesiones de Estudio* II, Barcelona; 1954; 424-429.

Pizzolato, L. F. "La visione della Chiesa in Ignazio d'Antiochia." *RSLR;* 1967; 3: 371-385.

Preiss, T. "La mystique de l'imitation du Christ et de l'unité chez Ignace d'Antioche." *Revue d'histoire et de philosophie religieuses;* 1938; 18: 197-241.

Prigent, Pierre. "Heresie asiate et l'église confessante: de l'apocalypse à Ignace." *Vigiliae Christianae: A Review of Early Christian Life and Language;* 1977; 31(1): 1-22.

Rackl, M. *Die Christologie des heiligen Ignatius von Antiochien* (Freiburger Theol. Studien, XIV). Freiburg: 1914.

Rathke, Heinrich. *Ignatius von Antiochien und die Paulusbriefe* (Texte und Untersuchungen, 99). Berlin: Akademie Verlag; 1967.

_____."Einstehen für Gemeinschaft in Christus: im Gespräch mit Ignatius von Antiochen über Sammlung und Einung in der Kirche." *Theologische Versuche;* ed by J Rogge; 1979; X: 83-106.

Rebell, Walter. "Das Leidensverständnis bei Paulus und Ignatius von Antiochien." *New Testament Studies: An International Journal;* July 1986; 32(3): 457-465.

Reicke, Bo. "Evangelium und Sakrament im len Jahrhundert." *Evangile et sacrement;* ed by G Gassmann; 1970; 82-93.

Richardson, Cyril. C. *The Christianity of Ignatius of Antioch.* New York: Columbia University Press; 1935.

_____. "The Church in Ignatius of Antioch." *Journal of Religion;* 1937; 17: 428-458.

_____. (ed.). *Early Christian Fathers,* Vol. I. Philadelphia: Westminster Press; 1953; 74-120.

Riesenfeld, H. "Reflections on the Style and the Theology of St. Ignatius of Antioch." *Studia Patristica,* IV, Akademie Verlag, Berlin; 1961; 79: 312-322.

Rius-Camps, Josep. *The Four Authentic Letters of Ignatius, the Martyr*. Rome: Pontificium Institutum Orientalium Studiorum; 1980.

_____. "Arcaismos en la teologia de Ignacio de Antioquia." *Studia Patristica;* ed by E Livingstone; 1989; 21: 175-184.

_____. "Ignacio de Antioquia, testigo ocular de la muerte y resurreccion de Jesus?" *Biblica;* 1989; 70(4): 449-473.

Robillard, Edmond. "Christologie d'Ignace d'Antioche." *Le Christ hier, aujourd' hui et demain;* ed by R Laflamme; 1976; 479-487.

Roddy, Nicolae. "The Campaign for Catholicity in the Letters of Saint Ignatius of Antioch." *Coptic Church Review: A Quarterly of Contemporary Patristic Studies;* Summer 1991; 12: 49-57.

Romanides, J. S. "The Ecclesiology of St Ignatius of Antioch." *Greek Orthodox Theological Review;* 1961-62; 7: 53-77.

Rozemond, K. "L'Église chez S. Ignace d'Antioche." *Verbum Caro;* 1955; 9: 157-166.

Ryan, Patrick J. "The Ministry of Unity." *Faith and Culture: Challenges to Ministry;* ed by N Brown; 1989; 131-136.

Saddington, D. B. "St Ignatius, Leopards, and the Roman Army." *The Journal of Theological Studies;* October 1987; 38: 411-412.

Saliba, Issa A. A. "The Bishop of Antioch and the Heretics: A Study of a Primitive Christology." *The Evangelical Quarterly;* April-June 1982; 54: 65-76.

Sauser, Ekkart. "Tritt der Bischof an die Stelle Christi: zur Frage nach der Stellung des Bischofs in der Theologie des hl Ignatios von Antiocheia." *Festschrift Franz Loidl;* ed by V Flieder; 1970; 1: 325-339.

Schilling, F. A. *The Mysticism of Ignatius of Antioch*. Philadelphia: University of Pennsylvania Press; 1932.

Schindler, Judy. "The Rise of One-bishop-rule in the Early Church: A Study in the Writings of Ignatius and Cyprian." *Baptist Reformation Review;* 1981; 10(2): 3-9.

Schlatter, Fredric W. "The Restoration of Peace in Ignatius' Antioch." *The Journal of Theological Studies;* October 1984; 35: 465-469.

Schlier, H. *Religionsgeschlichtliche Untersuchungen zu den Ignatiusbriefen.* Giessen: A. Toepelmann; 1929.

Schoedel, William R. "Ignatius and the Archives." *The Harvard Theological Review;* January-April 1978; 71: 97-106.

_____. *Ignatius of Antioch: A Commentary on the Letters of Ignatius of Antioch;* edited by Helmut Köster. Philadelphia: Fortress Press; 1985.

_____. "Polycarp's Witness to Ignatius of Antioch." *Vigiliae Christianae: A Review of Early Christian Life and Language;* 1987; 41(1): 1-10.

_____. "Theological Norms and Social Perspectives in Ignatius of Antioch." *Jewish and Christian Self-Definition;* ed by E Sanders; 1980; 30-56.

Schöllgen, Georg. "Monepiskopat und monarchischer Episkopat: eine Bemerkung zur Terminologie." *Zeitschrift für die Neutestamentliche Wissenschaft und die Kunde der Älteren Kirche;* 1986; 77(1-2): 146-151.

Sieben, Hermann J. "Die Ignatianen als Briefe: einige formkritische Bemerkungen." *Vigiliae Christianae: A Review of Early Christian Life and Language;* 1978; 32(1): 1-18.

Speigl, Jakob. "Ignatius in Philadelphia: Ereignisse und Anliegen in den Ignatiusbriefen." *Vigiliae Christinae: A Review of Early Christian Life and Language;* 1987; 41(4): 360-376.

Staats, Reinhart. "Die Katholische Kirche des Ignatius von Antiochien und das Problem ihrer Normativität im zweiten Jahrhundert; Pt 1." *Zeitschrift für die Neutestamentliche Wissenschaft und die Kunde der Älteren Kirche;* 1986; 77(1-2, 3-4): 126-145, 242-254.

_____. "Die martyrologische Begründung des Romprimats bei Ignatius von Antiochien." *Zeitschrift für Theologie und Kirche;* 1976; 73(4): 461-470.

Stander, Hendrik F. "Ignatius." *Hervormde Teologiese Studien;* 1989; (1): 98-106.

Stockmeier, Peter. "Zum Begriff der katholike ekklesia bei Ignatios von Antiochien." *OrtsKirche WeltKirche:* Julius Doepfner; ed by H Fleckenstein; 1973; 63-74.

Stoops, Robert F., Jr. "If I Suffer: Epistolary Authority in Ignatius of Antioch." *The Harvard Theological Review;* April 1987; 80: 161-178.

Story, Cullen I. K. "The Christology of Ignatius of Antioch." *The Evangelical Quarterly;* July 1984; 56: 173-182.

_____. "The Text of Ignatius' Letter to the Trallians 12:3." *Vigiliae Christianae: A Review of Early Christian Life and Language;* 1979; 33(4): 319-323.

Strand, K. A. "The Rise of the Monarchical Epsicopate." *Andrews University Seminary Quarterly* (Berrien Springs, Mich.); 1966; 4: 65-88.

Sweeney, Michael Leroy. *From God's Household to the Heavenly Chorus: A Comparison of the Church in the Pastoral Epistles with the Church in the Letters of Ignatius of Antioch.* Thesis (Ph.D.) - Union Theological Seminary in Virginia; 1989. 178 pages.

Tanner, R. G. "Martyrdom in Saint Ignatius of Antioch and the Stoic View of Suicide." *Studia Patristica;* ed by E Livingstone; 1985; 16(2): 201-205.

_____. "Pneyma in Saint Ignatius." *Studia Patristica;* ed by E Livingstone; 1975; 12(1): 265-270.

Tenny, M. C. "The Influence of Antioch on Apostolic Christianity." *Bibliotheca sacra;* 1950; 107: 298-316.

Thurian, M. "L'organisation du ministère dans l'Église primitive selon saint Ignace d'Antioche." *Verbum Caro;* 1967; 81: 26-38.

Tinsley, E. J. "The Imitatio Christi in the Mysticism of St. Ignatius of Antioch." *Studia Patristica,* II. Berlin; Akademie Verlag, 1957; 553-560.

Trevett, Christine. "Anomaly and Consistency: Josep Rius-Camps on Ignatius and Matthew." *Vigiliae Christianae: A Review of Early Christian Life and Language;* 1984; 38(2): 165-171.

_____. "Apocalypse, Ignatius, Montanism: Seeking the Seeds." *Vigiliae Christianae: A Review of Early Christian Life and Language;* 1989; 43(4): 313-338.

_____. "Approaching Matthew from the Second Century: The Under-used Ignatian Correspondence." *Journal for the Study of the New Testament;* 1984; 20: 59-67.

_____. "Ignatius and the Monstrous Regiment of Women." *Studia Patristica;* ed by E Livingstone; 1989; 21: 202-214.

_____. "The Much-maligned Ignatius." *The Expository Times;* July 1982; 93: 299-302.

_____. "The Other Letters to the Churches of Asia: Apocalypse and Ignatius of Antioch." *Journal for the Study of the New Testament;* October 1989; 37: 117-135.

_____. "Prophecy and Anti-Episcopal Activity: A Third Error Combatted by Ignatius?" *The Journal of Ecclesiastical History;* January 1983; 34: 1-18.

_____. *A Study of Ignatius of Antioch in Syria and Asia.* Lewiston: E Mellen; 1992. 248 pages.

van Haarlem, A. "De kerk in de brieven van Ignatius van Antiochia." *Nederlandsch Theologisch Tijdschrift;* 1964; 19: 112-134.

Vial, J. L. *Ignatius von Antiochien,* übertr. von E. Klien. Stuttgart: Schwabenverlag; 1962.

Visser, J. "Episcopacy Today: An Old Catholic View." *Bishops But What Kind;* ed by P Moore; 1982; 41-50.

Völter, D. *Die ignatianischen Briefe.* Tübingen: Heckenhauer; 1892.

_____. *Polycarp und Ignatius.* Leiden: Brill; 1910.

Walaskay, Paul W. "Ignatius of Antioch: The Synthesis of Astral Mysticism, Rational Theology, and Christian Witness." *Religion in Life;* Autumn 1979; 48: 309-322.

Ware, Kallistos. "Patterns of Episcopacy in the Early Church and Today: An

Orthodox View." *Bishops But What Kind;* ed by P Moore; 1982; 1-21.

Wehr, Lothar. *Arznei der Unsterblichkeit: die Eucharistie bei Ignatius von Antiochien und im Johannesevangelium.* Munster: Aschendorff: Neutestamentliche Abhandlungen, 18; 1987. 399 pages.

Weijenborg, O. F. M., Reinoud. *Les Lettres D'Ignace D'Antioche.* Leiden: E. J. Brill; 1969.

Weiss, Hans-Friedrich. "Ut omnes unum sint: zur Frage der Einheit der Kirche im Johannesevangelium und in den Briefen des Ignatius." *Theologische Versuche;* ed by J Rogge; 1979; X: 67-81.

_____. *Earliest Christianity,* vol II. New York: Harper Torchbooks; 1959.

Wiles, Maurice F. "Ignatius and the Church." *Studia Patristica;* ed by E Livingstone; 1982; 17(2): 750-755.

Winling, Raymond. "Datation des Lettres d'Ignace d'Antioche: Notes de lecture, recherche thématique." *Revue des science religieuses;* July 1980; 54: 259-265.

Zabel, Sheryl B. *Apostleship: An Investigation of the Gospel According to Matthew, The Didache, and Ignatius of Antioch.* [Rochester, NY: St. Bernard's Institute] Thesis (M.A.) - St. Bernard's Institute; 1985. 121 pages.

Zahn, T. *Ignatii et Polycarpi, Epistulae, Martyria, Fragmenta, Patrum Apostolicorum Opera,* Fasc. II, ed. O. de Gebhardt, A. von Harnack, T. Zahn. Leipzig: Hinrichs Verlag; 1876.

_____. *Ignatius von Antiochien.* Gotha: Perthe Verlag; 1873.

Zanarut, Sergio. "Les concepts de vie et de mort chez Ignace d'Antioche." *Vigiliae Christianae: A Review of Early Christian Life and Language;* 1979; 33(4): 324-341.

Zanetti, Paolo S. "Una nota ignaziana: antipsychon." *Forma futuri;* by A Maddalena, et al; 1975; 963-979.

BIBLIOGRAPHY: POLYCARP'S LETTER(S)

Barnard, L. W. "The Problem of St. Polycarp's Epistle to the Philippians." *Studies in the Apostolic Fathers and their Background.* Oxford: Blackwell; 1966; pp 31-39.

Bauer, Walter. *Die Apostolischen Väter* (Handbuch zum N.T.-Ergänzungsband). Tübingen: 1923.

_____ and Paulsen, H. *Die Briefe des Ignatius von Antiochia und der Brief des Polykarp von Smyrna.* Tübingen: J.C.B. Mohr (Paul Siebeck); 1985.

Bihlmeyer, K. *Die Apostolischen Väter, 1er Teil.* Tübingen: J. C. B. Mohr (Paul Siebeck); 1956; XXXVIII - XLIV, 114-120.

Camelot, O.P., P.-Th., *Lettres: Ignace d'Antioche, Polycarpe de Smyrne; Martyre de Polycarpe* (SC, 10). Paris: Éditions du Cerf; 1951 (2e edit. revue et augmentée).

Cardoux, C. J. "Polycarp's Two Epistles to the Philippians, by P. N. Harrison." *The Journal of Theological Studies;* 1937; 38: 267-270.

Dehandschutter, Boudewijn. "Le Martyre de Polycarpe et le développement de la conception du martyre au deuxième siècle." *Studia Patristica;* ed by E Livingstone; 1982; 17(2): 659-668.

_____. "Polycarp's Epistle to the Philippians: An Early Example of 'Reception'." *The New Testament in Early Christianity,* ed by J.M. Sevrin. Leuven: Leuven University Press; 1989; 275-291.

Fischer, J. A. *Die Apostolischen Väter* (Schriften des Urchristentums, 1). Darmstadt: Wissenschaftliche Buchgesellschaft; 1966; 229-265.

Goodspeed, E. J. *A History of Early Christian Literature.* University of Chicago Press; 1942.

Grant, R. M. *The Apostolic Fathers,* Vol. I. An Introduction. New York: Nelson & Sons; 1964.

Harrison, P. N. *Polycarp's Two Epistles to the Philippians.* Cambridge University Press; 1936.

Kleist, J. A. *The Didache, The Epistle of Barnabas, The Epistles and the Martyrdom of St. Polycarp, The Fragments of Papias, The Epistles of Diognetus* (Ancient Christian Writers, Vol. VI). Westminster, Md.: Newman; 1961; 69-82.

Klijn, A. F. J. *Apostolische Vaders*, 1, Ignatius en Polycarpus. Baarn: Bosch & Keuning; 1966.

Köster, H. *Synoptische Überlieferungen bei den Apostolischen Vätern* (TU, 65). Berlin: Akademie Verlag; 1957.

Koetting, Bernhard. "Darf ein Bischof in der Verfolgung die Flucht ergreifen?" *Vivarium: Festschrift T. Klauser* ed by E Dassmann and K Thraede. Munster: Aschendorf; 1984; 220-228.

Lake, K. *The Apostolic Fathers*, I (Loeb Classical Library). London: W. Heinemann; 1912; 280-301.

_____. "Polycarp's Two Epistles to the Philippians, by P. N. Harrison." *Journal of Biblical Literature;* 1937; LVI: 72-75.

Lightfoot, J. B. *The Apostolic Fathers*, Part II: *S. Ignatius, S. Polycarp*, Vol. I & Vol. II, Section II. London: Macmillan; 1885.

Puech, A. *Histoire de la littérature grecque chrétienne*, tome II. Paris: Soc. d'édit. "les belles lettres;" 1928; 62-70.

Puech, H. C. "P. N. Harrison, Polycarp's Two Epistles to the Philippians." *Revue de l'histoire des religions;* 1939; 119: 96-102.

Richardson, Cyril C. *Early Christian Fathers* (Library of Christian Classics, Vol I). Philadelphia: Westminster Press; 1953; 121-137.

Schoedel, William R. *The Apostolic Fathers*. Vol V. *Polycarp, Martyrdom of Polycarp, Fragments of Papias*. Camden, N. J.: Nelson & Sons; 1967.

_____. "Polycarp's Witness to Ignatius of Antioch." *Vigiliae Christianae: A Review of Early Christian Life and Language;* 1987; 41(1): 1-10.

Weiss, J. *Earliest Christianity* (orig. *Das Urchristentum*), Vol II. New York: Harper; 1959.

BIBLIOGRAPHY: BARNABAS

Andry, C. F. "Barnabas Epist. Ver. DCCCL." *Journal of Biblical Literature;* 1951; 70: 233-238.

Arnold, G. *Quaestiones de compositione et fontibus Barnabae epistolae.* Köningsberg: 1886.

Audet, Jean-Paul. "L'hypothèse des Testimonia. Remarques autour d'un livre récent." *Revue biblique;* 1963; 70: 381-405.

_____. "Affinités littéraires et doctrinales du Manuel de Discipline." *Revue biblique;* January 1953; 59: 41-82.

Barcellona, Francesco Scorza. *Epistola di Barnaba.* Torino: Societa Editrice Internazionale; 1975.

Bardy, G. *La Théologie de l'Église de saint Clément de Rome à saint Irénée.* Paris: 1945.

Barnard, Leslie William. "Barnabas 1:8." *The Expository Times;* 1958; 69: 239.

_____. *Studies in the Apostolic Fathers and their Background.* Oxford: B. Blackwell; 1966.

_____. "Epistle of Barnabas and the Tannaitic Catechism." *Anglican Theological Review;* 1959; 41: 177-190.

_____. "Problem of the Epistle of Barnabas." *Church Quarterly Review;* April-June 1958; 159: 211-230.

Bauckham, Richard J. "Sabbath and Sunday in the Post-apostolic Church." *From Sabbath to Lord's Day;* ed by D Carson; 1982; 252-298.

Baumstark, A. "Der Barnabasbrief bei den Syrern." *Oriens Christianus,* Neu Serie; 1912; 2: 235-240.

Beatrice, Pier F. "Une citation de l'Évangile de Matthieu dans l'Épître de Barnabé." *The New Testament in Early Christianity;* ed by J Sevrin; 1989; 231-245.

Braun, Francois M. "La Lettre de Barnabé et l'Évangile de Saint Jean." *New*

Testament Studies: An International Journal; 1957-1958; 4: 119-124.

Braunsberger, O. *Der Apostel Barnabas; sein Leben und der ihm beigelegte Brief wissenschaftlich gewürdigt.* Mainz: 1876.

Brock, Sebastian P. "The Two Ways and The Palestinian Targum." *A Tribute to Geza Vermes;* ed by P Davies and R White; 1990; 139-152.

Burkitt, F. C. "Barnabas and the Didache." *The Journal of Theological Studies;* 1932; 33: 25-27.

Cadbury, H. J. "The Epistle of Barnabas and the Didache." *Jewish Quarterly Review;* 1936; 26: 403-406.

Chandler, Karen K. "The Rite of the Red Heifer in the Epistle of Barnabas and Mishnah Parah." *Approaches to Ancient Judaism;* ed. by W Green; 1985; 5: 99-114.

Connolly, R. H. "Barnabas and the Didache." *The Journal of Theological Studies;* 1937; 38: 165-167.

_____. "The Didache in Relation to the Epistle of Barnabas." *The Journal of Theological Studies;* 1932; 33: 237-253.

Cunningham, W. and Rendall, G. H. *A Dissertation on the Epistle of Barnabas, including a discussion of its date and authorship.* London: 1877.

Dahl, N. A. "La terre où coulet le lait et le miel selon Barnabé 6, 8-19." *Aux sources de la tradition chrétienne, Mélanges M. Goguel,* Neuchâtel-Paris; 1950; 62-70.

Daniélou, J. "Un Testimonium sur la vigne dans Barnabé XII,I." *Recherches de science religieuse;* 1962; 50: 389-399.

Duchesne, L. "Saint Barnabé." *Mélanges de Rossi,* Paris; 1892; 41-71.

Ferguson, Everett. "Was Barnabas a Chiliast? An Example of Hellenistic Number Symbolism in Barnabas and Clement of Alexandria." *Greeks, Romans, and Christians;* ed by D Balch, *et al;* 1990; 157-167.

Fitzmyer, J. A. "IV Q. Testimonia and the N. T." *Theological Studies;* 1957; 18: 513-537.

Flesseman-van Leer, E. "Het Oude Testament bij de Apostolische Vaders en Apologeten." *Nederlandsch Theologisch Tijdschrift;* 1954-5; 9: 230-244.

Funk, F. X. "Der Banabasbrief, eine Schrift vom Ende des ersten Jahrhunderts." *Theologische Quartalschrift;* 1884; 66.

_____. "Die Zeit des Banabasbriefes." *Kirchengeschichtliche Abhandlungen und Untersuchungen,* t. 11, Paderborn; 1899; 77-108.

Hauser, Ph. *Der Barnabasbrief neu untersucht und erklärt* (Forschungen zur christl. u. Dogmengesch., Bd. 11, Heft 2). Paderborn: 1912.

Heer, J. M. *Die Versio Latina des Barnabasbriefes und ihr Verhältnis zur altlateinischen Bibel.* Freiburg: Herder; 1908.

Hefele, C. J. *Das Sendschreiben des Apostels Barnabas.* Tübingen: 1840.

Herbigny, M. d'. "La date de l'épître de Barnabé." *Recherches de science religieuse;* 1910; 1: 417-443, 540-566.

_____. "Nouvelles études sur l'épître de Barnabé." *Recherches de science religieuse;* 1913; 4: 402-408.

Hermans, Albert. "Le pseudo-Barnabé: est-il millénariste?" *Ephemerides Theologicae Lovaniensis;* 1959; 35: 849-876.

Heydecke, K. "Dissertatio qua Barnabae epistola interpolata demonstratur." *Jenäer Literaturzeitung;* 1875; 491. (also in *Brunsvigae,* 1874, and *Theol. Literaturzeitung,* 1895, col 396).

Hilgenfeld, A. *Barnabae epistola integ.graece, primum edita, vetus interpretatio latina, commentarius criticus et adnotationes additi.* Lipsiae: 1866.

Holzmann, H. J. "Barnabas und Johannes." *Zeitschrift für Wiss. Theol.;* 1871; 366ff.

Hommes, N. J. *Het Testimoniaboek, Studien over O. T. Citaten in het N. T. en bij de Patres, met critische beschouwingen over de theorieen van J. Rendel Harris en D. Plooy.* Amsterdam: 1935.

Hvalvik, Reidar. "Barnabas 9:7-9 and the Author's Supposed Use of

Gematria." *New Testament Studies: An International Journal;* 1987; 33(2): 276-282.

Jaubert, Annie. "Echo du livre de la Sagesse en Barnabé 7, 9." *Judéo-Christianisme;* by B Gerhardsson, *et al;* 1972; 193-198.

Johnson, Allen E. "Interpretative Hierarchies in Barnabas 1-17." *Studia Patristica;* ed by E Livingstone; 1982; 17(2): 702-706.

Kayser, A. "L'épître de Barnabé." *Revue de théologie;* 1851; 2: 202ff.

_____. *Über den sog. Barnabasbrief.* Paderborn: 1866.

Kister, Menahem. "Barnabas 12:1; 4:3 and 4Q Second Ezekiel." *Revue biblique;* January 1990; 97: 63-67.

Kraft, Robert A. "Barnabas' Isaiah Text and the 'Testimony Book Hypothesis'." *Journal of Biblical Literature;* 1960; 79: 336-350.

_____. *Barnabas and the Didache. New Translation and Commentary.* New York: Nelson; 1965.

_____. *The Epistle of Barnabas. Its Quotations and His Sources.* Harvard: 1961. (Harvard dissertation).

_____. "An Unnoticed Papyrus Fragment of Barnabas." *Vigiliae Christinae;* 1967; 21: 150-163.

Ladeuze, P. "L'épître de Barnabé." *Revue d'hist. eccl;* 1900; 1: 31-40, 212-225.

Liagre Boehl, Franz M. de. "Christentum, Judentum und Altes testament in ihrem gegenseitigen Verhältnis nach dem Brief des Barnabas." *Schrift en uitleg;* by D Attema, *et al;* 1970; 95-111.

Loman, E. "De apocalypse van Barnabas." *Theol. Tijdschrift;* 1884; 461ff.

MacLennon, Robert. "Four Christian Writers on Jews and Judaism in the Second Century." *From Ancient Israel to Modern Judaism;* ed by J Neusner, et al; 1989; 1: 187-202.

Massaux, Edouard. "L'influence littéraire de l'évangile de Saint Matthieu sur la Didachè." *Ephemerides Theologicae Lovaniensis;* 1949; 25: 5-41.

Meinhold, P. "Geschichte und Exegese im Barnabasbrief." *Zeitschrift für Kirchengeschichte;* 1940; 255-303.

Mueller, J. G. *Erklärung des (ps.)-Barnabasbriefes. Ein Anhang zu de Wette's exegetisches Handbuch zum N. T.* Leipzig: 1889.

Muilenburg, J. *The Literary Relations of the Epistle of Barnabas and the Teaching of the Twelve Apostles.* Marburg: 1929. (Dissertation).

O'Hagan, A. "Early Christian Exegesis Exemplified from the Epistle of Barnabas." *Australian Biblical Review;* 1963; 39-40.

Pearson, Birger A. "Christians and Jews in First-century Alexandria." *Christians Among Jews & Gentiles;* G Nicklesburg & G MacRae, eds; 1986; 206-216.

Philonenko, Marc. "Une tradition esséniènne dans l'évangile de Barnabas." *Mélanges d'histoire des religions;* by A Bareau, et al; 1974; 191-195.

Prigent, Pierre. *L'épître de Barnabé I-XVI et ses sources* (Études bibliques; les testimonia dans le christianisme primitif). Paris: Gabalda; 1961.

_____. *Épître de Barnabé.* Paris: Éditions du Cerf; 1971. (Texte grec établi et présenté par Robert A. Kraft.)

Richardson, Peter; Shukster, Martin B. "Barnabas, Nerva, and the Yavnean Rabbis." *The Journal of Theological Studies;* April 1983; 34: 31-55.

Riggenbach, C. J. *Der sog. Brief des Barnabas.* Basel: 1873.

Robinson, J. A. *Barnabas, Hermas and the Didache.* London: 1920.

Schenkel, K. "Über den Brief des Barnabas." *Theol. Studien und Kritiken;* 1837; 3: 652-686.

Schille, Gottfried. "Zur urchristlichen Tauflehre: stilistische Beobachtungen am Barnabasbrief." *Zeitschrift für die Neutestamentliche Wissenschaft und die Kunde der Älteren Kirche;* 1958; 49(1-2): 31-52.

Schlaeger, G. "Die Komposition des Barnabasbriefes." *Nieuw Theologisch Tijdschrift;* 1921; 10: 264-273.

Shea, W. H. "The Sabbath in the Epistle of Barnabas." *Andrews University Seminary Studies;* 1966; 4: 149-175.

Shukster, Martin B.; Richardson, Peter. "Temple and Bet Ha-midrash in the Epistle of Barnabas." *Anti-Judaism in Early Christianity;* ed by S Wilson; 1986; 2: 17-31.

Simon, Marcel. "L'Épîitre de Barnabé et le Temple." *Les Juifs au regard de l'histoire;* ed by G Dahan; 1985; 31-36.

Soffritti, O. *La lettera di Barnaba.* Alba: Edizioni paoline; 1974. 132 pages.

Strecker, G. "Christentum und Judentum in den ersten beiden Jahrhunderten." *Ev. Theol.;* 1956; 16: 458-477.

Timm, Stefan. "Der Heilige Mose bei den Christen in Ägypten: eine Skizze zur Nachgeschichte alttestamentlicher Texte." *Religion im Erbe Ägyptens;* ed by M Goerg; 1988; 197-220.

Tischendorf, C. *Nov. Test. Sinaiticum s. N. T. cum epistula Barnabae et fragmentis Pastoris ex Cod. Sin. descripsit.* Lipsiae: 1863.

Veldhuizen, A. van. *De Brief van Barnabas.* Groningen: 1901.

Vesco, Jean Luc. "La lecture du Psautier selon l'Épître de Barnabé." *Revue biblique;* January 1986; 93(1): 5-37.

Völter, D. "Der Barnabasbrief, neu untersucht." *Jahrb. für prot. Theol.;* 1888; 14: 106ff.

Vokes, F. E. *The Riddle of the Didache: Fact or Fiction, Heresy or Catholicism?* London: 1938.

Volkmar, G. "Über Clemens von Rom ... mit bes. Beziehung auf den Barnabasbrief." *Tübingen Theol. Jahrbuch;* 1856; 350ff.

Vossius, Is. *Barnabae epistula; accessit universi translatio vetus; editit et notas addidit.* Amsteldami: 1646.

Weiss, J. *Der Barnabasbriefe kritisch untersucht.* Berlin: 1888. (also in *Theol. Literaturzeitung,* 1889, pp. 595-599).

Weizsaecker, K. *Zur Kritik des Barnabasbriefes aus dem Codex Sinaiticus.* Tübingen: 1863.

Wengst, Klaus. *Tradition und Theologie des Barnabasbriefes.* Berlin: De Gruyter; 1971. Habilitationsschrift - Bonn.

Wenschkewitz, H. *Die Spiritualisierung der Kultusbegriffe Tempel, Priester und Opfer im N. T.* Leipzig: 1932.

Wieseler, K. "Der Brief des Barnabas." *Jahrb. f. deutsche Theol.;* 1870; IV: 603ff.

Williams, A. L. "The Date of the Epistle of Barnabas." *The Journal of Theological Studies;* 1933; 34: 337-346.

Williamson, Clark M. "Adversus Judaeos' Tradition in Christian Theology." *Encounter* (Indianapolis); Summer 1978; 39: 273-296.

Wills, Lawrence. "The Form of the Sermon in Hellenistic Judaism and early Christianity." *The Harvard Theological Review;* July-October 1984; 77(3-4): 277-299.

Windisch, H. *Der Barnabasbrief.* Handbuch z. N. T.-Ergänzungsband: *Die Apostolische Väter,* III. Tübingen: 1920.

Wohleb, L. "Zur Versio latina des Barnabasbriefes." *Berliner Philol. Wochenschrift;* 1913; 33: 1020-1024. (*idem.,* in 1914, vol 34, pp 573-575).

Bibliography: The Shepherd of Hermas

Abramowski, Luise. "Die Entstehung der dreigliedrigen Taufformel - ein Versuch; Mit einem Exkurs: Jesus der Naziräer." *Zeitschrift für Theologie und Kirche*; 1984; 81(4): 417-446.

Adam, K. "Die Lehre von dem hl. Geiste bei Hermas und Tertullian." *Theol. Quartalsch.*; 1906; 88: 36-61.

Alfonsi, L. "La vite e l'olmo." *Vigiliae Christianae*; 1967; 21: 81-86.

Arnera, Georges. "Du rocher d'Esaie aux douze montagnes d'Hermas." *Études theologiques et religieuses*; 1984; 59(2): 215-220.

Audet, J.-P. "Affinites littéraires et doctrinales du Manuel de Discipline." *Revue biblique*; 1953; LX: 41-82.

Aune, D. E. "Hermas Mandate 11:2; Christian False Prophets Who Say What People Wish To Hear." *Journal of Biblical Literature;* March 1978; 97: 103-104.

Balmas, Enea. "L'adattamento valdese del Pastore di Erma." *Bollettino della Societa di Studi Valdesi*; December 1980; 148: 3-17.

Barberet, F. "La formule 'zen to theo' dans le Pasteur d'Hermas." *Recherches de science religieuse;* 1958; XLVI: 379-407.

Bardy, G. *La conversion au christianisme durant les premiers siècles* (Théologie, 15). Paris: 1949.

_____. "Les écoles romaines au second siècle." *Revue d'histoire ecclésiastique*; 1932; XXVIII: 501-532.

_____. "Le Pasteur d'Hermas et les livres hermétiques." *Revue biblique*; 1911; 8: 391-407.

_____. *La théologie de l'Église de saint Clément de Rome à saint Irénée* (Unam Sanctum, 13). Paris: Éditions du Cerf; 1945.

Barnard, L. W. "Hermas, the Church and Judaism." *Studies in the Apostolic Fathers and their Background.* Oxford: Blackwell; 1966: 151-163.

_____. "The Shepherd of Hermas in Recent Study." *Heythrop Journal*; 1968; 9: 29-36.

Barnes, A. S. *Christianity at Rome in the Apostolic Age*. London: 1938.

Batiffol, P. "L'Église naissante. Hermas et le problème moral au second siècle." *Revue biblique;* 1901; 10: 337-351.

Bausone, Carla. "Aspetti dell'ecclesiologia del Pastore di Hermas." *Studia Patristica;* ed by F Cross; 1972; 11(2): 101-106.

Benoît, A. *Le baptême chrétien au second siècle* (Études d'histoire et de philosophie religieuses de l'Université de Strasbourg, 43). Paris: Presses universitaires de France; 1953; 115-137.

Bergh, G. v. d. *De Apostolische Vaders III. De Herder van Hermas* (Oud-christelijke geschriften in Ned. vert., 22). Leiden: 1916.

Beylot, Robert. "Hermas: le Pasteur: quelques variantes inédites de la version éthiopienne." *Mélanges Antione Guillaumont;* ed by R Coquin; 1988: 155-162.

Bonner, C. *A Papyrus Codex of the Shepherd of Hermas* (University of Michigan Studies, Hum. Ser. Vol. XXII). Norwood: 1934.

Brox, Norbert. *Der Hirt des Hermas*. Göttingen: Vandenhoeck & Ruprecht; 1991. 589 seiten [Kommentar zu den Apostolischen Väter, Siebenter Band.]

_____. "Die reichen und die armen Christen: eine Parabel aus der altrömischen Kirche." *Biotope der Hoffnung;* ed by N Klien (2nd ed); 1988: 224-229.

_____. "Die unverschämten Fragen des Hermas." *Anfänge der Theologie;* N Brox, A Felber, W Gombocz, *et al;* 1987; 175-188.

_____. "Die weggeworfenen Steine im Pastor Hermae Vis III, 7, 5." *Zeitschrift für die Neutestamentliche Wissenschaft und die Kunde der Älteren Kirche;* 1989; 80 (1-2): 130-133.

Campenhausen, H. F. von. *Kirchliches Amt und geistliche Vollmacht in den ersten drei Jahrhunderten* (Beitraege zur historischen Theologie, 14). Tübingen: J. C. B. Mohr (Paul Siebeck); 1953.

362

Chadwick, H. "The New Edition of Hermas." *Journal of Theological Studies*; 1957; 8: 274-280.

Clark, Kenneth W. "The Sins of Hermas." *Early Christian Origins*. Chicago; 1961; 102-119.

_____. "Sins of Hermas." *Early Christian Origins: Studies for H R Willoughby*; A Wikgren; 1961; 102-119.

Coleborne, W. "The Shepherd of Hermas: A Case for Multiple Authorship and Some Implications." *Studia Patristica*; ed by F Cross; 1970; 10(1): 65-70.

Colson, J. *Ministre de Jésus-Christ ou le sacerdoce de l'Évangile* (Théologie historique, 4). Paris: Beauchesne; 1966; 313-328.

Crouzel, Henri. "Les origines de l'Épiscopat: fin du Ier siècle, début du IIe." *L'Évêque dans l'histoire*; H Crouzel, J Durliat, *et al*; 1984; 13-20.

d'Ales, A. "La discipline pénitentielle d'après le Pasteur d'Hermas." *Recherches des science religieuse*; 1911; XII: 105-139, 240-265.

_____. *L'édit de Calliste*. Paris: 1914; 52-113.

Daniélou, J. *Théologie du judéo-christianisme*. Tournai: Désclée; 1958.

_____. "Trinité et angélologie dans le théologie judéo-chrétienne." *Recherches de science religieuse;* 1957; 45: 5-41.

Davison, James Edwin. *Spiritual Gifts in the Roman Church: I Clement, Hermas, and Justin Martyr*. Thesis (Ph.D.) - University of Iowa. (On microfilm) Ann Arbor, MI: University Microfilms International; 1981. 201 pages.

Deemter, R. van. *Der Hirt des Hermas: Apocalypse oder Allegorie?* Delft; 1929.

Dibelius, M. *Der Hirt des Hermas* in *Die apostolischen Väter* (Handb. z. N.T.-Ergänzungsband). Tübingen: J. C. B. Mohr (Paul Siebeck); 1923.

Dorsch, S. J., E. "Zur Hierarchie des 'Hirten'." *Zeitsch. f. kath. Theol.*; 1904; 28: 250-294.

Edmundson, G. "The Date of the Shepherd of Hermas." *Expositor*; 1922;. 161ff.

Eynde, D. van den. *Les Normes de l'Enseignement chrétien dans la littérature patristique des trois premiers siècles.* Paris: Gabala; 1933.

Ferguson, Everett. "Canon Muratori: Date and Provenance." *Studia Patristica*; ed by E Livingstone; 1982; 17(2): 677-683.

Franses, D. *De Apostolische Vaders.* Hilversum: Brand; 1941; 164-272.

Funk, F. X. "Die Einheit des Hirten des Hermas." *Theol. Quartalsch.*; 1899; 321-360.

_____. *Patres Apostolici, I.* Tübingen: Laupp; 1901.

Gebhardt, O. de, & Harnack, A. *Hermae Pastor (Patrum Apostolicorum Opera,* Fasc. III). Lipsiae: 1877.

Giet, S. "De trois expressions: Auprès de la tour, la place inférieure et les premiers murs, dans le Pasteur d'Hermas." *Studia Patristica*; VIII (TU, 93). Berlin: Akademie Verlag; 1966; 24-29.

_____. *Hermas et les Pasteurs.* Paris: Presses universitaires de France; 1963.

_____. "L'Apocalypse d'Hermas et la Pénitence." *Studia Patristica*; III (TU, 78). Berlin: Akademie Verlag; 1961; 214-218.

_____. "Pénitence ou repentence dans le Pasteur d'Hermas." *Rev. de droit can.*; 1967; XVII: 15-30.

_____. "Les trois auteurs du Pasteur d'Hermas." *Studia Patristica*, VIII (TU, 93). Berlin: Akademie Verlag; 1966; 10-23.

_____. "Un courant judéo-chrétien à Rome au milieu du IIe siècle?" *Aspects du judéo-christianisme, Colloque de Strasbourg.* Paris; 1965; 95-112.

Goguel, M. "Le problème de l'Église dans le christianisme primitif." *Rev. d'hist. et de phil. rel.*; 1938; 18: 293-320.

Gollar, Walker Lyddane. *The Shepherd of Hermas and The Gospel of Truth*

364

of Valentinus: Two Early Christian Perspectives on Salvation. Dayton, Ohio: Thesis (M.A. in Religious Studies) — University of Dayton; 1983. 82 pages.

Goodspeed, Edgar J. "Lexical notes on ... Hermas." *Journal of Biblical Literature;* 1953; xii.

_____. "Some Greek Notes." *Journal of Biblical Literature*; 1954; 73(2): 84-92.

Grant, R. M. *The Apostolic Fathers. Vol. I. An Introduction.* New York: Nelson; 1963.

Greenslade, S. L. "The Unit of Pastoral Care in the Early Church." *Studies in Church History*, II; London; 1965; 102-118.

Grobel, K. "Shepherd of Hermas, Parable II." *Vanderbilt Studies in Humanities*, I; 1951; 50-51.

Haas, C. *De geest bewaren: achtergrond en functie van de pneumatologie in de paraenese van de Pastor van Hermas.* 's-Gravenhage: Boekencentrum; 1985. 361 pages. (Summary in English.)

Hahn, Ferdinand. "Prophetie und Lebenswandel: Bemerkungen zu Paulus und zu zwei Texten der Apostolischen Väter." *Neues Testament und Ethik*; ed by H Merklien. Freiburg: Herder; 1989; 527-537.

Hamman, A. "La signification de 'sphragis' dans le Pasteur d'Hermas." *Studia Patristica*, IV (TU, 79). Berlin: Akademie Verlag; 1961; 286-290.

Hanson, Anthony T. "Hodayoth vi and viii and Hermas Sim, VIII." *Studia Patristica*; ed by F Cross; 1970; 10(1): 105-108.

Haufe, Guenter. "Taufe und Heiliger Geist im Urchristentum." *Theologische Literaturzeitung;* August 1976; 101: 561-566.

Hellholm, David. *Das Visionbuch des Hermas als Apokalypse: Formgeschichtliche und texttheoretische Studien zu einer literarischen Gattung - Vol. I: Methodologische Vorüberlegungen und makrostrukturelle Textanalyse.* Lund: CWK Gleerup; 1980. [Coniectanea Biblica - New Testament Series 13:1.]

Henne, Philippe. "La polysémie allégorique dans le Pasteur d'Hermas." *Ephemerides Theologicae Lovaniensis*; 1989; 65(1): 131-135.

_____. "A propos de la christologie du Pasteur d'Hermas: la cohérence interne des niveaux d'explication dans la Cinquième Similitude." *Revue des sciences philosophiques et théologiques;* October 1988; 72: 569-578.

_____. "La véritable christologie de la Cinquième Similitude de Pasteur d'Hermas." *Revue des sciences philosophiques et théologiques;* April 1990; 74: 182-204.

Hilgenfeld, A. *Hermae Pastor*; veterem latinam interpretationem e codicibus. Lipsiae: R. Riesland; 1873.

Hilhorst, A. *Sémitismes et latinismes dans le Pasteur d'Hermas*. Nijmegen: Dekker & Van de Vegt; 1976.

Hinson, E. Glenn. "Evidence of Essene Influence in Roman Christianity: An Inquiry." *Studia Patristica*; ed by E Livingstone; 1982; 17(2): 697-701.

Hoerman, K. "Das Reden im Geiste nach der Didache und dem Pastor Hermae." *Mystische Theologie*, III; 1957; 135-161.

Hoh, J. "Die Busse im Pastor Hermae." *Theol. Quartalsch.* 1930; 111: 253-288.

Jardine, William. *The Shepherd of Hermas: The Gentle Apocalypse*. Redwood City, CA: Proteus Publishing; 1992. 159 pages.

Jay, Eric G. "From Presbyter-bishops to Bishops and Presbyters: Christian Ministry in the Second Century; A Survey." *The Second Century: A Journal of Early Christian Studies*; Fall 1981; 1(3): 125-162.

Jeffers, James S. *Conflict at Rome: Social Order and Hierarchy in Early Christianity*. Minneapolis: Fortress Press; 1991. 215 pages.

_____. "The Influence of the Roman Family and Social Structures on Early Christianity in Rome." *Proceedings: Society of Biblical Literature*; ed by D Lull; 1988; 370-384.

_____. "Pluralism in Early Roman Christianity." *Fides et Historia;* Winter-Spring 1990; 22: 4-17.

_____. "*Social Foundations of Early Christianity At Rome: The Congregations Behind I Clement and The Shepherd Of Hermas.*" University of California, Irvine. Ph. D.; 1988. 355 pages.

Joly, R. "La doctrine pénitentielle du Pasteur d'Hermas et l'exégèse récente." *Revue de l'histoire des religions;* CXLVII; 1955; 32-49.

_____. "Hermas et le Pasteur." *Vigiliae Christianae;*1967; 21: 201-218.

_____. *Hermas; Le Pasteur* (Sources chrétiennes, 53 bis). Paris: Éditions du Cerf; 1968.

_____."Judaisme, christianisme et hellénisme dans le Pasteur d'Hermas." *La nouvelle Clio;* 1953; 5: 394-406.

_____. "Philologie et Psychanalyse, C. G. Jung et le Pasteur d'Hermas." *L'Antiquité classique*; 1953; 422-428.

_____. "La doctrine pénitentielle de pasteur d'Hermas et l'exégèse récente." *Revue de l'histoire des religions*; January-March 1955; 147: 32-49.

Kirkland, Alistair. "The Literary History of the Shepherd of Hermas - Visions I to IV." *The Second Century*; 1990; 87-102.

Koch, H. "Die Bussfrist des Pastor Hermae." *Festgabe Harnack*. Tübingen; 1921; 173-182.

Lake, K. *The Apostolic Fathers,* II (Loeb Class. Lib., 25), 9th ed. London: Heinemann; 1965.

_____. "The Shepherd of Hermas and Christian Life in Rome in the Second Century." *Harvard Theological Review*; 1911; 4: 25-47.

_____."The Shepherd of Hermas." *Harvard Theological Review;* 1925; 279-280.

Lampe, Peter. *Die stadtrömischen Christen in den ersten beiden Jahrhunderten: Untersuchungen zur Sozialgeschichte.* Tübingen: J.C.B. Mohr (Paul Siebeck); 1987.

Lantschoot, Arnold van. "Un second témoin Éthiopien du "Pasteur" d'Hermas." *Byzantion*; 1962; 32: 93-95.

Lawson, J. *A Theological and Historical Introduction to the Apostolic Fathers.* New York: Macmillan; 1961; 219-267.

Lebreton, J. &. Zeiller, J. "Le développement des institutions ecclésiastiques à la fin du IIe siècle et au début du IIIe siècle." *Revue des sciences religieuses*; 1934; 24: 24-164.

_____. *Histoire de l'Église. Vol. 1. L'Église Primitive.* Paris: Blond & Gay; 1946; 347-357.

Leutzsch, Martin. *Die Wahrnehmung sozialer Wirklichkeit im "Hirten des Hermas.* Göttingen: Vandenhoeck & Ruprecht [Forschungen zur Religion und Literatur des Alten und Neuen Testaments]; 1989. 286 seiten.

Lightfoot, J. B. *The Apostolic Fathers* (English transl.). Grand Rapids: Baker; 1967; 159-243. (Reprint of 1891 Macmillan edition, London.)

Lipsius, D. "Der Hirt des Hermas und der Montanismus in Rom." *Zeitsch. f. Wiss. Theol.*; 1865; 8: 266-308. (Also in 1866, Vol. 9, pp.183-218.).

Lluis-Font, P. "Sources de la doctrine d'Hermas sur les deux esprits." *Revue d'ascétique et de mystique;* 1963; 39: 83-89.

Lucchesi, Enzo. "Le Pasteur d'Hermas en Copte: perspective nouvelle." *Vigiliae Christianae: A Review of Early Christian Life and Language*; 1989; 43(4): 393-396.

Luschnat, Otto. "Die Jungfrauenszene in der Arkadienvision des Hermas." *Theologia Viatorum;* ed by M Rektor; 1975; 12: 53-70.

Macmillan, K. D. "The Shepherd of Hermas, Apocalypse or Allegory?" *Princeton Theological Studies*; 1911; IX: 61-94.

Maier, Harry O. *The Social Setting of the Ministry as Reflected in the Writings of Hermas, Clement and Ignatius.* Waterloo (Ontario): Wilfrid Laurier University Press; 1991. [Published for the Canadian Corporation for Studies in Religion/ Corporation Canadienne des Sciences Religieuses.]

Marique, J. M. -F. *The Shepherd of Hermas.* Translated by..., in L. Schopp (ed. dir.), *The Fathers of the Church.* New York: 1948; 223-352.

McGuckin, John A. "The Vine and the Elm Tree: The Patristic Interpretation of Jesus' Teachings on Wealth." *The Church and Wealth*; ed by W Shiels and D Wood; 1987; 1-14.

Michaels, J. R. "The 'Level Ground' in the Shepherd of Hermas." *Zeitsch. f. NT-lichen Wissensch.*; 1968; 59: 245-250.

Miller, Patricia Cox. ""All The Words Were Frightful": Salvation by Dreams in the Shepherd of Hermas." *Vigiliae Christianae: A Review of Early Christian Life and Language;* 1988; 42(4): 327-338.

Morgan-Wynne, John E. "The "Delicacy" of the Spirit in the Shepherd of Hermas and in the Tertullian." *Studia patristica;* ed by E Livingstone; 1989; 21: 154-157.

Moyo, Ambrose. *Angels and Christology in the Shepherd of Hermas*. Thesis (Ph.D.) - Harvard; 1978. 214 pages.

Musurillo, S. J., Herbert A. *The Fathers of the Primitive Church*. New York: Mentor-Omega; 1966; 88-101.

_____. "The Need for a New Edition of Hermas." *Theological Studies;* 1951; XII: 382-387.

Nijendijk, Lambartus Wilhelmus. *Die Christologie des Hirten des Hermas: exegetisch, religions - und dogmengeschichtlich untersucht = De Christologie van de Herder van Hermas: een exegetische, godsdienst - en dogmen-historische studie.* Rijksuniversiteit te Utrecht - Thesis (Th.D.); 1986. 239 pages.

O'Hagan, A. P. "The Great Tribulation to Come in the Pastor of Hermas." *Studia Patristica*, IV (TU, 79). Berlin: Akademie Verlag; 1961; 305-311.

Opitz, H. *Ursprünge frühkatholischer Pneumatologie. Ein Beitrag zur Entstehung der Lehre vom Heiligen Geist in der römischen Gemeinde unter Zugrundlegung des I Clemensbriefes und des Hirten des Hermas* (Theologische Arbeiten, XV). Berlin: 1960.

Osiek, Carolyn A. "The Genre and Function of the Shepherd of Hermas." *Semeia: An Experimental Journal for Biblical Criticism;* 1986; 36: 113-121.

_____. "Rich and Poor in the Shepherd of Hermas." *The Harvard Theological Review;* July-October 1978; 71: 322-323.

_____. *"Rich and Poor in the Shepherd of Hermas: An Exegetical-Social Investigation."* Catholic Biblical Quarterly: Monograph Series. Washington, D.C.; 1983. 184 pp. (Originally presented as the author's doctoral thesis - Harvard Divinity School.).

_____. "The Second Century Through the Eyes of Hermas: Continuity and Change." *Biblical Theology Bulletin;* Fall 1990; 20: 116-122.

_____. "Wealth and Poverty in the Shepherd of Hermas." *Studia Patristica;* ed by E Livingstone; 1982; 17(2): 725-730.

Pernveden, L. *The Concept of the Church in the Shepherd of Hermas.* Lund: C. Gleerup; 1966.

Peterson, Erik. "Beitraege zur Interpretation der Visionen im Pastor Hermae." *Frühkirche, Judentum und Gnosis* (Studien und Untersuchungen). Freiburg: Herder; 1959; 254-270.

_____. "Die Begegnung mit dem Ungeheuer: Hermas, Vision 4." *Vigiliae Christianae;* 1954; 8(1-2): 52-71.

Porter, Stanley E. "Is Dipsuchos (James 1:8; 4:8) a "Christian" Word?" *Biblica;* 1990; 71(4): 469-498.

Puech, A. *Histoire de la littérature grecque chrétienne,* II. Paris: 1928; 71-95.

Rahner, K. "Die Busslehre im Hirten des Hermas." *Zeitsch. f. kath. Theol.;* 1955; 77: 385-431.

Reiling, J. *Hermas and Christian Prophecy: A Study of the Eleventh Mandate.* Leiden: E. J. Brill; 1973. [Supplement to *Novum Testamentum,* No. 37.]

Roberts, A. Donaldson, J., and Crombie, F. *The Writings of the Apostolic Fathers* (Ante- Nicene Library). Edinburgh: T. & T. Clark; 1873; 319-435.

Robillard, Edmond. "Aux sources de la prière: l'Esprit-Saint dans l'homme nouveau." *Revue des sciences religieuses;* April 1976; 50: 157-168.

Robinson, J. Armitage. *Barnabas, Hermas and the Didache*. London: 1920.

Robinson, John A.T. *Redating the New Testament*. London: SCM Press; 1976.

Sahlin, Harald. "Wie wurde ursprünglich die Benennung "Der Menschensohn" verstanden?" *Studia Theologica: Scandinavian Journal of Theology*; 1983; 37(2): 147-179.

Savignac, de. "Quelques problèmes de l'ouvrage dit 'Le Pasteur d'Hermas.'" *Études théol. rel.*; 1960; 35: 59-170.

Schlaeger, G. "Der Hirt des hermas eine ursprünglich jüdische Schrift." *Nederlandsch Theol. Tijdsch.*; 1927; 16: 327-342.

Schmid, W. "Eine frühchristliche Arkadienvorstellung." *Convivium: Festgabe f. Konrat Ziegler*. Stuttgart; 1954; 121-130.

Schwartz, J. "Survivances littéraires païennes dans le Pasteur d'Hermas." *Revue biblique*; 1965; 72: 240-247.

Schweizer, E. *Gemeinde und Gemeindeordnung in Neuen Testament*. Zürich: Zwingli Verlag; 1959; 141-145.

Seitz, Oscar J.F.. "Afterthoughts on the term Dipsychos." *New Testament Studies;* 1957-1958; 327-334.

_____. "Relationship of the Shepherd of Hermas to the Epistle of James." *Journal of Biblical Literature*; 1944; 63: 131-140.

_____. "Two Spirits in Man. An Essay in Biblical Exegesis." *New Testament Studies*; 1959-1960; 92-95.

_____. "Afterthoughts on the Term Dipsychos." *New Testament Studies;* 1957-1958; 4: 327-334.

Sgherri, Giuseppe. "Textkritische Bemerkungen zu Hermas 51, 5." *Vigiliae Christianae: A Review of Early Christian Life and Language*; 1977; 31(2): 88-93.

Smith, Martha Montague. *Feminine Images in the Shepherd of Hermas*. Thesis (Ph.D.) - Duke University; 1979. 229 pages.

Snyder, G. F. *The Apostolic Fathers. Vol. VI. Hermas*. Camden, N. J.: Nelson; 1968.

Stahl, A. *Patristische Untersuchungen, III, Der Hirt des Hermas*. Leipzig: 1901.

Strock, A. Wallace. *The Shepherd of Hermas: A Study of his Anthropology as seen in the Tension between Dipsychia and Hamartia* [romanized form]. Thesis (Ph.D.) - Emory University; 1984. 289 pages.

Tugwell, O.P., Simon. *The Apostolic Fathers*. Harrisburg, PA: Morehouse Publishing; 1989. 148 pages.

Turner, Ch. "Is Hermas also among the Prophets?" *Journal of Theological Studies;* 1913; 404-407.

_____. "The Shepherd of Hermas and the Problem of its Test." *Journal of Theological Studies;* 1920; XXI: 193-209.

von Ström, A. "Der Hirt des Hermas, Wirklichkeit oder Allegorie?" *Arbeiten und Mitteilungen aus dem NT-lichen Seminar zu Uppsala;* 1936.

Weinel, H. *Der Hirt des Hermas* - Handb. z. den NT-lichen Apokryphen. (ed. E. Hennecke). Tübingen: 1904; 290-323.

White, John Carroll. *The Interaction Of Language And World In The "Shepherd Of Hermas*. Thesis (Ph.D.) - Temple University; 1973.

Whittaker, M. *Die apostolischen Väter I. Der Hirt des Hermas* (GCS, 48). Berlin: Akademie Verlag; 1956.

Wilson, John Christian. *Toward a Reassessment of the Milieu of the Shepherd of Hermas: Its Date and Its Pneumatology*. Thesis (Ph.D.) - Duke University; 1977. 302 pages.

Wilson, W. J. "The Career of the Prophet Hermas." *Harvard Theological Review*; 1927; 20: 21-62.

Bibliography: The Didache

Adam, A. "Ein vergessener Aspekt des frühchristlichen Herrnmahles. Ein Beitrag zur Geschichte des Abendmahlverständnisses der Alten Kirche." *Theologische Literaturzeitung;* 1963; 88: 9-20.

_____. "Erwägungen zur Herkunft der Didache." *Zeitschr. für die Kirchengeschichte;* 1957; 68: 1-47. (summary of the same in *Theol. Literaturzeitung,* 1956, vol. 81, pp 353-356).

Altaner, Berthold. *Patrologie.* Freiburg: Herder; 1950; 37-40.

_____. "Zum Problem der lateinischen Doctrina Apostolorum." *Vigiliae Christianae;* 1952; 6(3): 160 ff.

Arnold, A. *Der Ursprung des christlichen Abendmahles.* Freiburg: Herder; 1937.

Audet, J.-P. *La Didachè, Instructions des Apôtres.* Paris: Lecoffre; 1958.

Bardy, G. "Didachè ou Doctrine des Apôtres." *Catholicisme;* 1952; III: 747-749.

Barnard, L. W. "The Dead Sea Scrolls, Barnabas, the Didache and the Later History of the 'Two Ways.'" *Studies in the Apostolic Fathers and Their Background.* Oxford: Blackwell; 1966; 87-107.

Bartelet, J. V. "The Didache Reconsidered." *The Journal of Theological Studies;* 1921; XXII: 239-249.

Benoît, A. *Le baptême chrétien au second siècle.* Paris: Presses universitaires de France; 1953; 5-33.

Betz, J. *Die Eucharistie in der Zeit der griechischen Väter,* Vol. I. Freiburg: Herder; 1955.

Bigg, C. "Notes on the Didache." *The Journal of Theological Studies;* 1904; V: 579-589. (*ibid.,* 1905, VI, 411-415).

Bihlmeyer, K. *Die Apostolischen Väter,* Erster Teil. Tübingen: J. C. B. Mohr (Paul Siebeck); 1956; XII-XX, LII, 1-9.

Blum, G. G. "Eucharistie, Amt und Opfer in der Alten Kirche." *Oecumenica-1966*, Gerd Mohn; 1966;

Broek-Utne, A. "Eine schwierige Stelle in eine alten Gemeindeordnung (Did. 11,11)." *Zeitschr. für die Kirchengeschichte;* 1935; LIV: 576-581.

Burkitt, F. C. "Barnabas and the Didache." *The Journal of Theological Studies;* 1932; XXXIII: 25-27.

Cadbury, H. J. "The Epistle of Barnabas and the Didache." *Jewish Quarterly Review;* 1936; XXVI: 403-405.

Campenhausen, H. F. von. *Kirchliches Amt und geistliche Vollmacht in den ersten drei Jahrhunderten.* Tübingen: J. C. B. Mohr (Paul Siebeck); 1953.

Castania, Kenneth Robert, Jr. *The Teaching of the Twelve Apostles: A New Translation.* Lexington, Ky.: Thesis (M.Div.) — Lexington Theological Seminary; 1989. 31 pages.

Cerfaux, Lucien. "La multiplication des pains dans la liturgie de la Didachè: Did 9:4." *Biblica;* 1959; 40(3): 943-948.

_____. "La situation du chrétien dans le monde d'après le Nouveau Testament et la multiplication des pains dans la liturgie de la Didachè." *Recueil Lucien Cerfaux;* by L Cerfaux; 1962; 3: 201-223.

Colson, Jean. *L'évêque dans les communautés primitives* (Unam Sanctam, 21). Paris: 1951; 125-131.

_____. *Ministre de Jésus-Christ ou le sacerdoce de l'Évangile.* Paris: Beauchesne; 1966; 257-279.

Connolly, R. H. "Agape and Eucharist in the Didache." *Downside Review;* 1937; LV: 477-489.

_____. "Barnabas and the Didache." *The Journal of Theological Studies;* 1937; XXXVIII: 165-167.

_____. "Canon Streeter on the Didache." *The Journal of Theological Studies;* 1937; XXXVIII: 364-379.

_____. "The Didache in Relation to the Epistle of Barnabas." *The Journal of Theological Studies;* 1932; XXXIII: 237-253.

374

_____. "The Didache and Montanism." *Downside Review;* 1937; LV: 339-347.

_____. "New Fragments of the Didache." *The Journal of Theological Studies;* 1924; XXV: 151-153.

_____. "The Use of the Didache in the Didascalia." *The Journal of Theological Studies;* 1923; XXIV: 147-157.

Court, John M. "The Didache and St Matthew's Gospel." *Scottish Journal of Theology;* 1981; 34(2): 109-120.

Creed, J. M. "The Didache." *The Journal of Theological Studies;* 1938; XXXIX: 370-387.

Cullmann, O. *La foi et le culte de l'Église.* Neuchâtel: Delachaux et Niestle; 1963.

Daniélou, J. *Théologie du judéo-christianisme.* Tournai: Désclée; 1958.

Danker, Frederick W. "Bridging St Paul and the Apostolic Fathers: A Study in Reciprocity." *Currents in Theology and Mission;* February 1988; 15: 84-94.

de Watteville, J. *Le Sacrifice dans les textes eucharistiques des premiers siècles.* Neuchâtel: Delachaux & Niestle; 1966; 23-37.

Decroos, M. "De Eucharistische Liturgie van Didache IX en X." *Bijdragen;* 1967; 28: 376-398.

Dibelius, M. "Die Mahl-Gebete der Didache." *Zeitschr. für die NT-liche Wissenschaft;* 1938; 37: 32-41.

Didach'e - Didache ton Dodeka Apostolon: The Unknown Teaching of the Twelve Apostles - edited by Brent S. Walters. San Jose, California: Ante-Nicene Archive; 1991. 224 pages.

Dix, Dom Gregory. "Didache and Diatessaron." *The Journal of Theological Studies;* 1933; XXXIV: 242-250.

_____. *The Shape of the Liturgy.* London: Dacre; 1945.

Dollar, G. W. "The Lord's Supper in the Second Century." *Bibliotheca sacra;* 1960; 117: 144-154.

Draper, Jonathan A. "The Jesus Tradition in the Didache." *The Jesus Tradition Outside the Gospels;* ed by D Wenham; 1984; 269-287.

_____. "Lactantius and the Jesus Tradition in the Didache." *The Journal of Theological Studies;* April 1989; 40: 112-116.

Drews, P. "Untersuchungen zur Didache." *Zeitschr. für die NT-liche Wissenschaft;* 1904; V: 53-79.

Dugmore, C. W. "The Study of the Origins of the Eucharist." *Studies in Church History,* II, London; 1965; 1-18.

Funk, F. X. "Didache und Barnabasbrief." *Theol. Quartalschr.;* 1905; LXXXVII: 161-179.

_____. "L'agape." *Revue d'hist. eccl.;* 1903; IV: 5-23.

_____. *Patres Apostolici,* Vol. I. Tübingen: H. Laupp; 1901; VI-XX, 2-37.

_____. "Zur Didache. Die Frage nach der Grundschrift und ihre Rezensionen." *Theol. Quartalschr.;* 1902; LXXXIV: 73-88.

Genderen, J. van. "Het avondmaal in de oude kerk en in de kerk van het oosten." *Bij brood en beker;* W Spijker; W Balke; K Exalto, *et al;* 1980; 67-89.

Gero, Stephen. "So-called Ointment Prayer in the Coptic Version of the Didache: A Re-evaluation." *The Harvard Theological Review;* January-April 1977; 70: 67-84.

Gibbins, H. G. "The Problem of the Liturgical Section of the Didache." *The Journal of Theological Studies;* 1935; XXXVI: 373-386.

Giet, Stanislas. "L'énigme de la Didachè." *Studia Patristica;* ed by F Cross; 1970; 10(1): 84-94.

_____. *L'énigme de la Didachè.* Paris: Les Éditions Ophrys; 1970.

_____. "Coutume, évolution, droit canon: À propos de deux passages de la Didachè." *En hommage à Gabriel Le Bras;* by M Nedoncelle, *et al;* 1966; 118-132.

Giordano, Oronzo. "L'escatologia nella Didache." *Oikoumen; studi paleocristiani;* by J Courcelle, *et al;* 1964; 121-139.

Glover, Richard. "Didache's Quotations and the Synoptic Gospels." *New Testament Studies: An International Journal;* October 1958; 5: 12-29.

Goodspeed, E. J. "The Didache, Barnabas and the Doctrina." *Anglican Theological Review;* 1945; XXVII: 228-247.

Gordon, Thomas N. *The Contribution of the Didache to Ecclesiology.* Thesis (Th.M.) — Dallas Theological Seminary; 1970. 55 pages.

Grant, R. M. *The Apostolic Fathers.* Vol. I. *An Introduction.* New York: Nelson & Sons; 1964.

Greiff, A. *Das älteste Pascharituale der Kirche. Did. i - x, und das Johannesevangelium.* Paderborn: 1929.

Hahn, Ferdinand. "Prophetie und Lebenswandel: Bemerkungen zu Paulus und zu zwei Texten der Apostolischen Väter." *Neues Testament und Ethik;* ed by H Merklien; 1989; 527-537.

Halleux, Andre de. "Les ministères dans la Didachè." *Irenikon: Revue des Moines de Chevetogne;* 1980; 53(1): 5-29.

Hamman, A. *Prières eucharistiques des premiers siècles.* Paris: Désclée; 1957.

Harnack, A. *Texte und Untersuchungen zur Geschichte der altchristlichen Literatur,* Band II, Heft 1 & 2: *Lehre der zwölf Apostel.* Leipzig: Hinrichs; 1893.

Herzog, William R. "The Origins of Ministry in the New Testament." *American Baptist Quarterly;* June 1984; 3(2): 117-148.

Hitchcock, F. R. M. "Did Clement of Alexandria Know the Didache." *The Journal of Theological Studies;* 1923; XXIV: 397-401.

Jefford, Clayton N. *An Analysis of the Sayings of Jesus in the Teaching of the Twelve Apostles: The Role of the Matthean Community.* Thesis (Ph.D.) - Claremont Graduate School; 1988. 267 pages.

_____. "Presbyters in the Community of the Didache." *Studia Patristica;* ed by E Livingstone; 1989; 21: 122-128.

_____. *The Sayings of Jesus in the Teaching of the Twelve Apostles.* Leiden; New York: E.J. Brill. Supplements to *Vigiliae Christianae;* 1989.

Kilmartin, Edward J. "The Eucharistic Prayer: Content and Function of Some Early Eucharistic Prayers." *Word in the World;* ed by R. Clifford; 1973; 117-134.

Klein, G. "Die Gebete in der Didache." *Zeitschrift für die Neutestamentliche Wissenschaft;* 1908; IX: 132-146.

Kleist, J. A. *The Didache, The Epistle of Barnabas, The Epistles and Martyrdom of St. Polycarp, etc.* (Ancient Christian Writers, 6). Westminster, Md.: Newman; 1948; 3-25.

Klijn, A. F. J. *Apostoliche Vaders, 2, I en II Clemens, Onderwijs van de Twaalf Apostelen.* Baarn: Bosch & Keuning; 1967; 91-123.

Kloppenborg, John S. "Didache 16:6-8 and Special Matthaean Tradition." *Zeitschrift für die Neutestamentliche Wissenschaft und die Kunde der Älteren Kirche;* 1979; 70(1-2): 54-67.

Knopf, R. *Die Lehre der zwölf Apostel. Die zwei Clemensbriefe in Handbuch zum NT-Ergänzungsband: Die Apostolischen Väter.* Tübingen: 1920; 1-40.

Konidaris, G. I. "De la prétendue divergence des formes dans le régime du christianisme primitif. Ministres et ministères du temps des Apôtres à la mort de S. Polycarpe." *Istina;* 1964; X: 59-92.

Kraft, R. A. *The Apostolic Fathers,* Vol. III. *The Didache and Barnabas.* New York: Nelson & Sons; 1965.

L'Eplattenier, Charles. "Présentation de la "Didache"." *Foi et Vie;* October 1982; 81(48-54):

Lake, K. *The Apostolic Fathers,* Vol. I (Loeb Classical Library). London: Heinemann; 1912; 305-333.

Lanoir, Corinne. "Un exemple d'enseignement sans Passion: la Didachè." *Foi et Vie;* October 1982; 81: 55-61.

Lietzmann, H. *Die Didache* (Kleine Texte, Nr. 6). Bonn: 1912. (mit kritischem Apparat).

Lightfoot, J. B. *The Apostolic Fathers.* Grand Rapids, Mich.: Baker; 1967; 119-129 (photoprint of Macmillan ed., London, 1891).

Lohmeyer, E. "Das Abendmahl in der Urgemeinde." *Journal of Biblical Literature;* 1937; 56: 217-252.

Loisy, A. "La Didachè et les lettres des Pères apostoliques." *Revue d'hist. et de lit. rel.;* 1921; N.S. VII: 433-442.

Magne, Jean. "Klasma, sperma, poimnion: le voeu pour le rassemblement de Didachè IX, 4." *Mélanges d'historie des religions;* by A Bareau, et al; 1974; 197-208.

Massaux, Edouard. "L'influence littéraire de l'évangile de Saint Matthieu sur la Didachè." *Ephemerides Theologicae Lovaniensis;* 1949; 25: 5-41.

Mazza, Enrico. "L'Eucaristia di 1 Corinzi 10:16-17 in rapporto a Didache 9-10." *Ephemerides Liturgicae;* May-June 1986; 100: 193-223.

Middleton, R. D. "The Eucharistic Prayers of the Didache." *The Journal of Theological Studies;* 1935; XXXVI: 259-267.

Milavec, Aaron A. "The Pastoral Genius of the Didache: An Analytical Translation and Commentary." *Religious Writings and Religious Systems;* ed by J Neusner; 1989; 2: 89-125.

Moule, Charles F. D. "A Note on the Didache IX, 4." *The Journal of Theological Studies;* 1955; N.S. VI: 240-243.

_____. "Note on Didache 9:4." *The Journal of Theological Studies;* October 1955; 6: 240-243.

Muilenburg, J. *The Literary Relations of the Epistle of Barnabas and the Teaching of the Twelve Apostles.* Marburg Dissertation: 1929.

Musurillo, H. A. *The Fathers of the Primitive Church.* New York: Mentor-Omega (New American Library); 1966; 57-62.

Nauck, W. "Probleme des frühchristlichen Amtsverständnisses." *Zeitschr.*

für die NT-liche Wissenschaft; 1957; 48: 200-220. (summarized in *Theol. Literaturz.*, nr. 5-6, 1956).

Nautin, Pierre. "La composition de la 'Didachè' et son titre." *Revue de l'histoire des religions;* April-June 1959; 155: 191-214.

_____. "Notes critiques sur la Didachè." *Vigiliae Christianae: A Review of Early Christian Life and Language;* 1959; 13:118-120.

Niederwimmer, Kurt. *Die Didache.* Göttingen: Vandenhoeck & Ruprecht; 1989. 329 pages.

Oulton, J. E. L. "Clement of Alexandria and the Didache." *The Journal of Theological Studies;* 1940; XLI: 177-179.

Peterson, E. "Didachè cap. 9 e 10." *Ephemerides Liturgicae* (Rome); 1944; 58: 3-13.

_____. "La leitourgia des prophètes et des didascales à Antioche." *Revue des sciences religieuses;* 1949; 36: 577-579.

Pillinger, Renate. "Die Taufe nach der Didache: Philologisch-archaeologische untersuchung der Kapitel 7, 9, 10 und 14." *Wiener Studien;* ed by R Hanslik, et al; 1975; 88: 152-160.

Ponthot, J. "La signification religieuse du 'nom' chez Clément de Rome et dans la Didachè." *Ephemerides Theologicae Louvanienses;* 1959; 35: 339-361.

Prigent, P. "Une thèse nouvelle sur la Didachè." *Revue de théol. et de philos.;* 1960; 10: 298-304.

Puech, A. *Histoire de la littérature grecque chrétienne,* tome II. Paris: Soc. d'édit. "les belles lettres;" 1928; 10-21.

Quasten, J. *Patrology,* Vol. I. Utrecht: Spectrum; 1950; 29-39.

Richardson, C. C. *Early Christian Fathers* (Library of Christian Classics, 1). Philadelphia: Westminster; 1953; 161-179.

Riggs, John W. "From Gracious Table to Sacramental Elements: The Tradition-history of Didache 9 and 10." *The Second Century: A Journal of Early Christian Studies;* Summer 1984; 4(2): 83-101.

Robinson, J. A. *Barnabas, Hermas and the Didache*. London: 1920. (chapters 1-3 reprinted in *The Journal of Theological Studies*, 1934, XXXV, 113-146; 225-248).

Robinson, John A.T. *Redating the New Testament*. London: SCM Press; 1976.

Rordorf, Willy. "Le baptême selon la Didachè." *Mélanges liturgiques offerts à A B Botte;* by J von Allmen, et al; 1972; 499-509.

_____. "La didachè." *L'eucharistie des premiers chrétiens;* W Rordorf, et al; 1976; 7-28.

_____. "The Didache." *The Eucharist of the Early Christians;* by W Rordorf, et al; 1978; 1-23.

_____ & Tuilier, A. *La Doctrine des douze apôtres (Didachè)*. (Sources chrétiennes, No. 248) Paris: Éditions du Cerf; 1978.

_____. "Les prières eucharistiques de la Didachè." *Eucharisties d'orient et d'Occident;* by H Cazelles, et al; 1970; 1: 65-82.

_____. "Le problème de la transmission textuelle de Didachè 1, 3b-2, 1." *Überlieferungsgeschichtliche Untersuchungen;* ed. by F Paschke; 1981; 499-513.

_____. "La remission des pêchés selon la Didachè." *Liturgie et remission des pêchés;* ed by A Pistoia; 1975; 225-238.

_____. "Un chapitre d'éthique judéo-chrétienne: Les deux voies." *Judéo-Christianisme: Recherches offertes au Card. Jean Daniélou*. Paris: Recherches de science religieuse; 1972: 109-128.

_____. "Une nouvelle édition de la Didachè (problèmes exégètiques, historiques et théologiques)." *Studia Patristica;* ed by E Livingstone; 1984; 15(1): 26-30.

Savelich, Stephen P. "The Prophets in the Church of the Second Century: A Study Based on an Examination of the Didache and The Shepherd of Hermas." Paper presented to the Northwest Regional Meeting of the Evangelical Theological Society; March 18, 1989. 24 pages.

Saxer, Victor. "La tradizione nei testi canonico-liturgici: Didache, Traditio apostolica, Didascalia, Constitutiones apostolorum." *La tradizione;*

W Rordorf, *et al;* 1990; 251-263.

Schermann, Th. "Die Gebete in Didache c. 9 und 10." *Festschrift-Knöpfler,* München; 1907; 225-239.

Schöllgen, Georg. *Didache: Zwölf-Apostel-Lehre.* Freiburg: Herder; 1991. (Also included in this work: Geerlings, Wilhelm. *Traditio Apostolica: Apostolische Überlieferung.*)

_____. "Die Didache: ein frühes Zeugnis für Landegemeinden?" *Zeitschrift für die Neutestamentliche Wissenschaft und die Kunde der Älteren Kirche;* 1985; 76(1-2): 140-143.

_____. "Die Didache als Kirchenordnung: Zur Frage des Abfassungszweckes und seinen Konsequenzen für die Interpretation." *Jahrbuch f Antike u Christentum;* E Dassmann; *et al;* 1986; 5-26.

_____. "Wandernde oder sesshafte Lehrer in der Didache?" *Biblische Notizen: Beitrage zur exegetischen Diskussion;* 1990; 52: 19-26.

Schürmann, H. "Die Gestalt der urchristlichen Eucharistiefeier." *Münchener Theol. Zeitschr.;* 1955; 6: 107-131.

Schweizer, E. *Gemeinde und Gemeindeordnung im Neuen Testament.* Zürich: Zwingli Verlag; 1959; 125-131.

Seelinger, Hans R. "Erwägungen zu Hintergrund und Zweck des apokalyptischen Schlusskapitels der Didache." *Studia Patristica;* ed. by E Livingstone; 1989; 21: 185-192.

Smith, M. A. "Did Justin Know the Didache?" *Studia Patristica,* VII (TU, 92). Berlin: Akademie Verlag; 1966; 287-290.

Staniforth, M. *Early Christian Writings. The Apostolic Fathers.* Baltimore: Penguin; 1968; 225-237.

Stempel, Hermann A. "Der Lehrer in der "Lehre der Zwölf Apostel"." *Vigiliae Christianae: A Review of Early Christian Life and Language;* 1980; 34(3): 209-217.

Streeter, B. H. "The Much-belaboured Didache." *The Journal of Theological Studies;* 1936; XXXVII: 369-374.

Stuiber, Alfred. "Die drei semeia von Didache XVI." *Jahrbuch f Antike und Christentum;* T Klauser, *et al;* 1981; 24: 42-44.

Taylor, C. *The Teaching of the Twelve Apostles with Illustrations from the Talmud.* Cambridge: 1886.

Telfer, W. "The Didache and the Apostolic Synod of Antioch." *The Journal of Theological Studies;* 1939; XL: 133-146, 258-271.

_____. "The 'Plot' of the Didache." *The Journal of Theological Studies;* 1944; XLV: 141-151.

Tsirpanlis, Constantine N. "The Structure of the Church in the Liturgical Tradition of the First Three Centuries." *The Patristic and Byzantine Review;* 1982; 1(1): 44-62.

Tuckett, Christopher M. "Synoptic Tradition in the Didache." *The New Testament in Early Christianity;* ed. by J Sevrin; 1989; 197-230.

Tugwell, O.P., Simon. *The Apostolic Fathers.* Harrisburg, PA: Morehouse Publishing; 1989.

Tuilier, André. "Une nouvelle édition de la Didachè (problèmes de méthode et de critique textuelle)." *Studia Patristica;* ed. by E Livingstone; 1984; 15(1): 31-36.

Vokes, F. E. "The Didache and the Canon of the New Testament." *Studia Evangelica,* III (TU), Akademie Verlag, Berlin; 1964; 427-436.

_____. "Montanism and the Ministry." *Studia Patristica,* IX (TU, 94), Akademie Verlag, Berlin; 1966; 306-315.

_____. *The Riddle of the Didache.* London: S.P.C.K.; 1938.

Walker, John H. "An Argument from the Chinese for the Antiochene Origin of the Didache." *Studia Patristica,* VIII (TU, 93); Berlin; Akademie Verlag; 1966; 44-50.

_____. "A Pre-Marcan Dating for the Didache: Further Thoughts of a Liturgist." *Studia Biblica;* ed. by E Livingstone; 1978; III: 403-430.

Weiss, J. *Earliest Christianity,* Vol. II. New York: Harper; 1959. (transl. F. C. Grant).

Zahn, Th. "Justinus und die Lehre der zwölf Apostel." *Zeitschr. für die Kirchengeschichte;* 1886; VIII: 66-84.

GENERAL BIBLIOGRAPHY

CHRISTIAN PRIESTHOOD AND THE HISTORY OF MINISTRY

Amalorpavadass, D.S.(ed.) *Ministries in the Church in India.* New Delhi: C.B.C.I. Centre; 1976.

Audet, Jean-Paul. *Structures of Christian Priesthood.* London and Melbourne: Sheed and Ward; 1967.

Baum, Gregory. "Ministry in the Church." *Women and Orders;* ed by R Heyer; 1974; 57-66.

Bausch, William J. *MINISTRY: Traditions, Tensions, Transitions.* Mystic, Connecticut: Twenty-Third Publications; 1982.

Becker, Karl J. "Der Unterschied von Bischof und Priester im Weihedekret des Konzils von Trient und dem Kirchenkonstitution des II Vatikanischen Konzils." *Zum Problem Unfehlbarkeit;* ed by K Rahner; 1971; 289-327.

Becker, Klaus M. "Das Sacerdotium Episcopi nach der Lehre des Zweiten Vatikanischen Konzils." *Episcopale Munus;* ed by P Delhaye and L Elders; 1982; 63-82.

Bernier, Paul. *Ministry in the Church: A Historical and Pastoral Approach.* Mystic, CT.: Twenty-Third Publications; 1992.

Blaisdell, Charles R. "Beyond the "profession" of Ministry: The Priest, The Teacher, and The Christ." *Encounter* (Indianapolis); Winter 1986; 47(1): 41-60.

Bouesse, Humbert. "Èpiscopat et sacerdoce, pt 2: l'opinion de Saint Thomas."

Revue des sciences religieuses; 1954; 28: 368-391.

Bower, Richard A. "Parish Priesthood: Expectations and Reality." *Anglican Theological Review;* 1984; 66(9): 6-17.

Bradley, Robert I. ""Minister" or "Priest": The Historical Perspective." *Catholic Ministries in Our Time;* ed by G Kelly; 1981; 58-83.

Brown, Raymond E. *Priest and Bishop: Biblical Reflections.* New York: Paulist Press; 1970.

_____. *The Community of the Beloved Disciple.* New York: Paulist Press; 1979.

Burghardt, Walter J. "Church Structure: A Theologian Reflects on History." *Proceedings: Canon Law Society of America: 33rd Convention;* by R Kennedy, *et al;* 1971; 11-22.

Burtchaell, James Tunstead. *From Synagogue to Church: Public services and offices in the earliest Christian communities.* Cambridge: Cambridge University Press; 1992. 375 pages.

Campenhausen, H.F. von. *Ecclesiastical Authority and Spiritual Power in the Church of the First Three Centuries.* Stanford CA: Stanford University Press; 1969.

Campiche, Roland J.; Bovay, Claude. "Prêtres, pasteurs, rabbins: changement de rôle; bibliographie thématique." *Archives de sciences des religions;* July-September 1979; 24: 133-183.

Carey, G.; Hind, John. "Ministry, Ministries, and The Ministry." *Stepping Stones;* ed by C Baxter; 1987; 42-67.

Catechisme de L'Église Catholique. Paris: Mame\Plon-Libraire Éditrice Vaticane; 1992.

Clark, Charles Gordon. "A Rumour of Priests." *Theology;* January 1989; 92: 20-25.

Colson, Jean. *Ministre de Jésus-Christ ou le sacerdoce de l'Évangile.* Paris: Beauchesne et ses fils; 1966.

Congar, Yves M. J. "Ministry in the Early Church and Subsequent Historical

Evolution." *Asian Colloquium on Ministries in the Church;* ed P Archutegui; 1977; 348-354.

_____. "Note sur une valeur des termes ordinare, ordinatio." *Revue des sciences religieuses;* January-July 1984; 58(1-3): 7-14.

Cooke, Bernard. *Ministry to Word and Sacraments: History and Theology.* Philadelphia: Fortress Press; 1976.

Coppens, Joseph. *Le sacerdoce chrétien: ses origines et son développement.* Leiden: E.J. Brill; 1970.

Crehan, Joseph H. "Priesthood, Kingship, and Prophecy." *Theological Studies;* June 1981; 42: 216-231.

Cunningham, Agnes. "Elements for a Theology of Priesthood in the Teaching of the Fathers of the Church." *Priests: Identity and Ministry;* ed by R Wister; 1990; 30-53.

Delorme, Jean. "Sacrifice, sacerdoce, consécration: typologie et analyse sémantique du discours." *Recherches de science religieuse;* July-September 1975; 63: 343-366.

Denzler, Georg ed). *Priester für heute: Antworten auf das Schreiben Papst Johannes Pauls II an Priester: mit Dokumentation das Papstschreibens vom 8/79.* München: Kösel Verlag; 1980.

Descamps, Albert L. *Priester, geloof en contestatie.* Patmos-Verlag; 1970;

Dianich, Severino. "The Ordained Ministry in Rites and Actions." *The Right of the Community to a Priest;* ed by E Schillebeeckx; 1980; 59-65.

Dix, Dom Gregory. *The Shape of the Liturgy.* London: Dacre Press; 1945.

Dixon, John W. "What The Priesthood Is All About." *The Christian Century;* March 12, 1975; 92: 244-245.

Donovan, Daniel. *What Are They Saying About The Ministerial Priesthood?* New York and Mahwah, N. J.: Paulist Press; 1992.

Dupuy, Bernard D. "Theologie der kirchlichen Ämter." *MYSTERIUM SALUTIS:* Band IV, 2. Einsiedeln: Benzinger Verlag; 1973; 488-523.

Eastwood, Cyril. *The Royal Priesthood of the Faithful*. London: The Epworth Press; 1963.

Ehrhardt, Arnold. *The Apostolic Ministry*. Edinburg: *Scottish Journal of Theology Occasional Papers*, No 7, Oliver and Boyd Ltd.; 1958.

Eisenkopf, Paul. "Das Verhältnis von Gemeinde und Amt nach der Konvergenzerklärung von Lima." *Mitverantwortung aller in der Kirche;* F Courth & A Weiser, eds; 1985; 265-275.

Elliott, John Hall. *The Elect and the Holy: An Exegetical Examination of I Peter 2:4-10 and the Phrase "Basileion hierateuma"*. Leiden: E.J. Brill; 1966.

Empie, Paul C. and Murphy, T. Austin. (eds.) *Eucharist and Ministry (Lutherans and Catholics in Dialogue, IV.)* Washington, D.C.: USCC; 1970.

Esquerda Bifet, Juan. "Bibliografia postconciliar sobre el sacerdocio." *Los presbiteros;* by N Lopez Martinez, *et al;* 1975; 587-664.

_____. "Boletin bibliografico de teologia sobre el sacerdocio (1972 y parte de 1973)." *Escritos sobre el caracter sacerdotal;* by J Ibanez, *et al;* 1974; 287-356.

Feuillet, Andre. *The Priesthood of Christ and His Ministers;* transl. M. J. O'Connell. Garden City, N. Y.: Doubleday & Co., Inc.; 1975.

Fink, Peter E. "The Sacrament of Orders: Some Liturgical Reflections." *Worship;* November 1982; 56: 482-502.

Fiorenza, F. S., and Galvin, J. P. (eds.). *SYSTEMATIC THEOLOGY: Roman Catholic Perspectives*, Volume II. Minneapolis: Fortress Press; 1991.

Flores, Patrick F. "The Priesthood and The Sacrament of Reconciliation." *Penance and Reconciliation;* John Paul II, Pope; E Szoka; *et al;* 1984; 25-28.

Forrester, David. "The Parish and the Priesthood." *The Church Now - Catholic Church in Britain & Ireland;* ed by J Cumming; 1980; 82.

Fransen, Piet. "The Priest Today." *Rethinking The Priesthood;* ed by F Joannes; 1970; 1-27.

Fuller. Reginald H. "Scripture, Tradition and Priesthood." *Scripture, Tradition and Reason;* R Bauckham & B Drewery, eds; 1988; 101-114.

Galot, J. *Theology of the Priesthood.* San Francisco: Ignatius Press; 1985.

Gardiner, Anne Marie, ed. "Women and Catholic Priesthood." *Proceedings of the Detroit Ordination Conference.* New York: Paulist Press; 1976.

Geaney, Dennis J. "What Must I Be to Minister?" *Ministering in a Servant Church;* ed by F Eigo; 1978; 151-174.

Greeley, Andrew M. "Going Whose Way? The Role of Priests Today." *Worship;* 1959; 33(6): 354-358.

_____. "Priesthood." *Tomorrow's Church;* ed by E Herr; 1982; 92-106.

Greeley, Dolores L. "John Chrysostom, On The Priesthood: A Model For Service." *Studia Patristica;* ed by E Livingstone; 1989; 22: 121-128.

Greenwood, Robin P. "Presiding: A Parish Priest's Work." *Theology;* November 1984; 87: 412-419.

Grindel, John A. "Old Testament and Christian Priesthood." *Communio: International Catholic Review;* Spring 1976; 3: 16-38.

Groome, Thomas H. "From Chauvinism and Clericalism to Priesthood: The Long March." *Women and Religion;* ed by R Coll; 1982; 111-126.

Hardon, John A. "What is the Catholic Priesthood?" *Catholic Ministries in Our Time;* ed by G Kelly; 1981; 84-93.

Harnack, Adolf. *Entstehung und Entwickelung der Kirchenverfassung und des Kirchenrechts in den zwei ersten Jahrhunderten.* Darmstadt: Wissenschaftliche Buchgesellschaft; 1980.

Harris, Maria. "Education for Priesthood." *Education For Peace and Justice;* ed by P O'Hare; 1983; 14-25.

Hebblethwaite, Peter. "From Priesthood to Ministry." *The Experience of Ordination;* ed by K Wilson; 1979; 61-73.

Herzog, William R. "The Origins of Ministry in the New Testament." *American Baptist Quarterly*; 1984; III(2): 117-148.

Hind, John. "Varieties of Priesthood." *Working for the Kingdom;* ed by J Fuller and P Vaughan; 1986; 88-93.

Hotchkin, John F. "The Christian Priesthood: Episcopate, Presbyterate and People in the Light of Vatican II." *Eucharist and Ministry;* ed by P Empie; 1979; 189-208.

Jacobs, Thomas. "Ministry in Vatican II and Post-Conciliar Development." *Asian Colloquium on Ministries in the Church;* ed P Achutegui; 1977; 355-398.

James, E.O. *The Nature and Function of Priesthood.* London: Thames & Hudson; 1955.

Jay, Eric G. "From Presbyter-Bishops to Bishops and Presbyters: Christian Ministry in the Second Century: A Survey." *The Second Century*; Fall, 1981; 1(3): 125-162.

Kavanagh, Aidan. "Christian Ministry and Ministries." *Anglican Theological Review;* 1984; 66(9): 36-48.

Kessel, R. van. "Theologie und Amtsführung seit dem Zweiten Vatikanischen Konzil." *Bilanz der niederlaendischen Kirche;* ed by J Lescrauwaet; 1976; 146-215.

Kilmartin, Edward J. *Church, Eucharist and Priesthood.* New York: Paulist Press; 1981.

_____. "Authenticity of Christian Ministry: A Reply." *Communio: International Catholic Review;* Summer 1977; 4: 185-188.

_____. "The Eucharistic Prayer: Content and Function of Some Early Eucharistic Prayers." In *Word in the World. Essays in Honor of Frederick L. Moriarity, S.J.* Edited by R.J. Clifford and G.W. McRae. Cambridge MA: Weston College Press; 1973.

King, John A. "Ordination of Women to the Priesthood; Some Current Roman Catholic Attitudes." *Theology;* March 1975; 78: 142-147.

Kirk, Kenneth E.(dir.) *The Apostolic Ministry: Essays on the History and the Doctrine of Episcopacy.* London: Hodder & Stoughton, Ltd.; 1962.

Kokkinakis, Athenagoras Bp. "Priesthood as a Sacrament." *The Greek Orthodox Theological Review;* Winter 1957; 3: 168-181.

Konidaris, Gerasimos I.(Orth.). "De la prétendue divergence des formes dans le régime du Christianisme primitif." *Istina;* 1964; 10: 59-92.

Küng, Hans. *Why Priests?* Garden City: Doubleday; 1972.

L'Huillier, Paul. "La différence de pouvoir d'après la katastase entre prêtre et évêque." *Les sacrements d'initiation et ministères;* by P. Smulders, et al; 1974; 219-243.

Lash, N. and J. Rhymer (eds.). *The Christian Priesthood, 9th Downside Symposium.* London: Darton, Longman & Todd; 1970.

Lawler, Michael G. *A Theology of Ministry.* Kansas City, MO.: Sheed and Ward; 1990.

LeBlanc, Paul J. "A Survey of Recent Writings on Ministry and Orders." *Worship;* 1975; 49: 35ff.

Legrand, Herve-Marie. "The Presidency of the Eucharist According to the Ancient Tradition." *Worship;* 1979; 53(5): 413-438.

Lightfoot, J.B. *The Christian Ministry.* Wilton CT: Morehouse-Barlow Co., Inc.; 1983.

Löser, Werner. "Das Amt in der Kirche nach der dogmatischen Konstitution "Lumen Gentium" des II Vatikanischen Konzils." *Die eine heilige christliche;* ed by M Roensch and J Schoene; 1981; 100-116.

Magnani, S. J., Giovanni. "Does the So-called Theology of the Laity Possess a Theological Status?" *VATICAN II: Assessment and Perspectives,* Volume One. New York: Paulist Press; 1988.

Martos, Joseph. *Doors to the Sacred: A Historical Introduction to Sacraments in the Catholic Church.* Liguori MO: Triumph Books; 1991.

McBrien, Richard. *MINISTRY: A Theological, Pastoral Handbook.* San Francisco: Harper & Row; 1987.

McCormick, Richard A. and Dyer, George J. *Future Forms of Ministry.* A project of the CTSA sponsored by the NFPC in conjunction with *Chicago Studies;* 1971.

McDonald, Durstand R. (ed). "Theology of Priesthood: A Consultation." *Anglican Theological Review;* 1984; 66(9): 1-121.

Mettayer, Arthur. "Jusqu'à quel point les motifs du sacrement de l'ordre excluent-ils les femmes?" *Studies in Religion-Sciences Religieuses;* 1981; 10(4): 387-398.

Mitchell, Nathan. *Mission and Ministry: History and Theology in the Sacrament of Order.* Wilmington: Michael Glazier; 1982.

Moberly, R. C. *Ministerial Priesthood.* London: SPCK; 1969.

Mohler, James A. *The Origin and Evolution of the Priesthood.* New York: Alba House; 1970.

Moingt, Joseph. "Authority and Ministry; tr by M A Fahey." *Journal of Ecumenical Studies;* Spring 1982; 19: 202-225.

Mollat, Guillaume. "Quelques documents relatifs à l'usurpation des fonctions sacerdotales par des diacres au 14e siècle." *Revue des sciences religieuses;* 1956; 361-363.

Montefiore, Hugh W. "The Theology of Priesthood." *Yes to Women Priests;* ed by H Montefiore; 1978; 1-14.

Moore, Peter, ed. *BISHOPS But What Kind?* London: SPCK; 1982.

_____. *Man, Woman, and Priesthood.* London: SPCK; 1978.

Moran, Rev William. *The Government of the Church in the First Century.* New York: Benzinger Brothers; 1913.

Neumann, Bernhard. "Die Rolle des Priesters in der mitverantwortlichen Gemeinde: Zum Priesterbild der Gememeinsamen Synode." *Mitverantwortung aller in der Kirche;* F Courth & A Weiser, eds; 1985; 276-295.

Norris, Richard A. "The Beginnings of Christian Priesthood." *Anglican Theological Review;* 1984; 66(9): 18-32.

Nouwen, Henri J. *Creative Ministry: Beyond professionalism in teaching, preaching, counseling, organizing, and celebrating.* Garden City, New York: Doubleday & Co., Inc.; 1971.

O'Meara, O. P., Thomas F. *Theology of Ministry.* New York: Paulist Press; 1983.

Osborne, O. F. M., Kenan B. *Priesthood: A History of the Ordained Ministry in the Roman Catholic Church.* New York: Paulist Press; 1988.

Passi, Dave. "From Pagan to Christian Priesthood." *The Gospel is Not Western;* ed by G Trompf; 1987; 45-48.

Patsavos, Lewis J. "Image of the Priest According to the Three Hierarchs." *Greek Orthodox Theological Review;* Spring 1976; 21: 55-70.

Paul VI, Pope. "Priest and People." *Worship;* 1955; 29(4): 197-200.

Porter, H. Boone. "Ministerial Priesthood and Diaconate in Holy Scripture." *Worship;* July 1977; 51: 326-331.

Portier, William L. "Ministry From Above, Ministry From Below: An Examination of the Ecclesial Basis of Ministry According to Edward Schillebeeckx." *Communio: International Catholic Review;* Summer 1985; 12: 173-191.

Power, David N. *Ministers of Christ and His Church: A Theology of Priesthood.* London: Geoffrey Chapman; 1969.

_____. "Order" *Systematic Theology: Roman Catholic Perspectives. Vol. II.* F.S. Fiorenza and J.P. Galvin, editors. Minneapolis: Fortress Press; 1991: 291-304.

Rademacher, William J. *LAY MINISTRY: A Theological, Spiritual and Pastoral Handbook.* New York: Crossroad; 1991.

Ramos, Felipe F. *Sacerdocio ministerial y laical.* Ediciones Aldecoa (Series: Teologia del Sacerdocio 2); 1970;

Rausch, S. J.; Thomas, P. *Priesthood Today: An Appriasal.* New York and Mahwah, N. J.: Paulist Press; 1992.

Rordorf, Willy, *et al. The Eucharist of the Early Christians*. New York: Pueblo Publishing Company; 1978.

Rosato, Philip J. "Priesthood of the Baptized and Priesthood of the Ordained: Complementary Approaches to their Interrelation." *Gregorianum;* 1987; 68(1-2): 215-266.

Sabourin, Leopold. "Questions on Christian Priesthood." *Religious Studies Bulletin;* January 1982; 2(1): 1-15.

The Sacrament of Holy Orders: Some Papers and Discussions concerning Holy Orders at a session of the Centre de Pastorale Liturgique. Collegeville, MN: The Liturgical Press; 1962.

Sauras, Emilio. "El sacerdocio ministerial en la doctrina de Santo Tomas." *San Tommaso e l'odierna problematica;* by A Piolanti, *et al;* 1974; 329-343.

Schillebeeckx, Edward. *The Church With A Human Face: A New and Expanded Theology of Ministry.* New York: Crossroad; 1985.

_____. *MINISTRY: Leadership in the Community of Jesus Christ.* New York: Crossroad; 1981.

_____. "Offices in the Church of the Poor." *La iglesia popular;* ed by L Boff and V Elizondo; 1984; 98-107.

_____ and Metz, Johann-Baptist (eds.) *The Right of the Community to a Priest. (Concilium, No. 133.) New York: Seabury Press; 1980.*

Schelkle, Karl Herman. *Discipleship and Priesthood: A Biblical Interpretation.* New York: Herder & Herder; 1965.

Schmitz, Heribert. "Die Weisungen des Vaticanum II zur Altersversorgung der Presbyter." *Ius et salus animarum;* ed by U Mosiek; 1972; 139-158.

Schrör, H. & Muller, G.(eds.) *Vom Amt des Laiens in Kirche und Theologie: Festschrift für Gerhard Krause zum 70ten Geburtstag.* Series: Theologische Bibliotek Toepelmann, 39: Walter de Gruyter; 1982; 431 pages.

Schweizer, Eduard. *Church Order in the New Testament.* London: SCM Press; 1963.

Sedgwick, Timothy F. "On Theology, Ministry, and Holy Orders." *Anglican Theological Review;* April 1987; 69: 157-170.

Seguy, Jean. "Le clergé dans une perspective sociologique ou que faisons-nous de nos classiques?" *Prêtres, pasteurs et rabbins;* J Seguy; J Sutter; *et al;* 1982; 13-58.

Shelp, Earl E., and Sunderland, Ronald R. (eds.). *The Pastor as Priest.* Pilgrim Press; 1987.

Sofield, S.T., Loughlan, and Juliano, S.H.C.J., Carroll. *Collaborative Ministry: Skills and* Guidelines. Notre Dame, IN: Ave Maria Press; 1987.

Sousa, Alves de. *El carisma permanente del sacerdocio ministerial.* Ediciones Aldecoa (Series: Teologia del Sacerdocio 5); 1973;

Stuhlmueller, Carroll, ed. *Women and Priesthood: Future Directions: A Call to Dialogue from the Faculty of the Catholic Theological Union at Chicago.* Collegeville, MN: Liturgical Press; 1978.

Synod of Bishops (2nd General Assembly). *The Ministerial Priesthood.* Washington, D. C.: Publications Office - USCC; 1972.

Thannikot, Anthony. "Ministerial Priesthood and Its Forms in History." *Ministries in the Church in India;* ed by D S Amalorpavadass; 1976; 307-324.

Thome, Josef. "Der Amtspriester in der Kirche der Zukunft." *Die Zukunft der Glaubensunterweisung;* ed by F Pöggeler; 1971; 67-83.

Tillard, J. M. R. "Ministère ordonné et sacerdoce du Christ." *Irenikon: Revue des Moines de Chevetogne;* 1976; 49(2): 147-166.

Torrance, T. F. *Royal Priesthood.* Edinburg: *Scottish Journal of Theology* Occasional Papers No 3, Oliver and Boyd Ltd.; 1963.

Van Beneden, Pierre. "Ordo. Über den Ursprung einer kirchlichen Terminologie." *Vigiliae Christianae;* 1969; 23: 161-176.

Vanhoye, Albert. *Old Testament Priests and the New Priest: According to the New Testament.* Petersham MA: St. Bede's Publications; 1986. 333 pages.

Van Iersel, B. & Murphy, R. (eds.) *Office and Ministry in the Church (Concilium, No. 80.)* New York: Herder & Herder; 1972.

Vogt, Hermann Josef. "Zum Bischofsamt in der frühen Kirche." *Theologische Zeitschrift*; 1982: 221-236.

Waldenfels, Hans. "The Right to a Priest?" *The Right of the Community to a Priest;* ed by E Schillebeeckx; 1980; 66-74.

Walsh, John and DiGiacomo, James. *So You Want To Do Ministry?* Kansas City, MO.: Sheed and Ward; 1986.

Webster, John B. "Ministry and Priesthood." *The Study of Anglicanism;* ed by S Sykes and J Booty; 1988; 285-296.

Whitehead, James D., and Whitehead, Evelyn Eaton. *METHOD IN MINISTRY: Theological Reflection and Christian Ministry.* New York: The Seabury Press; 1981.

Wister, Robert J. (ed.). *PRIESTS: Identity and Ministry.* Michael Glazier; 1990.

Wright, John H. "Church and Priesthood: A Perspective on Ordained Ministry." *Communio: International Catholic Review;* Fall 1977; 4: 261-274.

Wuerl, Donald. "On the Priesthood." *The Pastoral Vision of John Paul II;* ed by J Bland; 1982; 49-65.

Zizioulas, John D. "Episkopè et Epískopos dans l'Église primitive: Bref inventaire de la documentation." *Irenikon*; 1983; 56: 484-501.

INDEX